A TRAILS BOOKS GUIDE

PADDLING SOUTHERN WISCONSIN

82 GREAT TRIPS BY CANOE AND KAYAK

MIKE SVOB

Trails Books
Black Earth, Wisconsin

D1065738

Library of Congress Catalog Card Number: 2001086830
ISBN: 0-915024-92-6

Editor: Stan Stoga
Production: Carol Lynn Benoit
Photos: Mike Svob
Maps: Mapping Specialists
Cover photo: Michael Shedlock

Printed in the United States of America

06 05 04 03 02 01 6 5 4 3 2 1

Trails Books, a division of Trails Media Group, Inc.
P.O. Box 317 • Black Earth, WI 53515
(800) 236-8088 • e-mail: info@wistrails.com
www.trailsbooks.com

CONTENTS

APPENDIXES

ACKNOWLEDGMENTS

The heart of a canoeing guidebook is the hundreds of hours spent in a canoe or kayak (good weather and bad!), dictating notes into a tape recorder for later transformation into maps and trip descriptions. But a book like this could never come to fruition without the assistance of many people, whose help assumes a great variety of forms. First of all, I'm grateful to my wife, Donna, who accompanied me on a number of trips, served as a sounding board and proofreader, and put up with my frequent absences. Thanks, also, to the members of the Rock River Canoe Association, Rock Dodgers Canoe Club, Mad City Paddlers, and Sierra Club River Touring Section for their company on many trips and their willingness to share experiences and information with me. I am indebted to the paddlers who accompanied me on many of the trips in this book, especially Pat Wilson, Gail Coss, Bob Kane, Pat Scullin, Karen Jackson, Dave Schmidtke, Jim Hart, Herb Reynolds, Arvid Cummings, Mark McGroarty, Mary Brusewitz, Pat Waack, and Mike Bonnie. From Stephanie Lindloff of the River Alliance of Wisconsin I have frequently gotten updates on the status of dam removals. Thanks also to those who have helped proofread trip descriptions, such as John and Marilyn Ziegler.

An immense amount of homework goes into a book of this kind (reading source materials, poring over maps, surfing the Internet, conversing with DNR officials, "picking the brains" of anyone who might be a potential source of information, etc.). Some people stand out as particularly valuable resources. I am indeed fortunate to have made contact with the following individuals, whose input is reflected in the book: Baraboo (Joe Van Berkel, Ken Peterson, Dennis Plantenberg, Jon Hillmer, Jim Brockman, Ed Schultz, Scott Heading, Mike Schultz, Dick Schara); Bark (Pat Scullin, Herb Reynolds); Black (Pat Wilson, Lisa and Robby McDonald); Chippewa (Jim and Pat Rolbiecki); Crawfish (Roger Kramz); Crystal (Don Schmidt); Des Plaines (Jim Hart); Eau Claire (Mike Torud); Fox (Paul Harvey); Galena (Tony Wiegel); Grant (Dick Donaldson); Illinois Fox (John Angel, Gail Coss, Jim DeCleene); Kickapoo (Tony Kelbel, Susan McCurdy); La Crosse (Mike Ulrich, Lloyd Larson); Lemonweir (Harlie Myhre, Guy Rodgers, Barbara Baker); Little Wolf (Mark McGroarty, Gail Coss); Manitowoc (John Roberts, Terry Paulow); Mecan (Paul Harvey); Milwaukee (Gary Pruitt, Jim McGinnity, Rich Krause, Matt Coffaro, Jill Goodrich); Oconomowoc (Art Boettcher); Pecatonica (Tony Wiegel); Red Cedar (Larry Theberge); Rock (Dave Schmidtke); Sheboygan (Al Thill); Sugar (Karen Jackson, Dave Schmidtke); Tomorrow (Arvid Cummings); Trempealeau (Gary Holen); Waupaca (Arvid Cummings); and Wisconsin (Mark Johnson, Phyllis Wyco, Larry White, Cindy Shifflet, Chuck Judd, Julie Romeo, Lee Bilkey).

I've been very lucky, too, to have worked with the encouraging, competent, and affable staff of Trails Media Group, especially Stan Stoga, Anita Matcha, Patty Mayers, and Laura Kearney. Don Larson of Mapping Specialists has also been a joy to work with in this and other guidebook projects.

Finally, a big thank you to the many DNR officials, local and area chambers of commerce, city offices, recreation departments, city and county park personnel, and other agencies and organizations for their assistance. It is comforting to know that so many people are actively involved in the preservation of beautiful and wild places in Wisconsin.

Let Us Hear From You!

We welcome your suggestions and comments on this book. If there are other rivers, streams, or sections that you would like to see included in the next edition, please let us know. If you find any errors in the text or maps, we would appreciate hearing about them so that we can make corrections. Send the information, along with your name and address, to:

PADDLING SOUTHERN WISCONSIN
Trails Media Group
P.O. Box 317
1131 Mills Street
Black Earth, WI 53515
e-mail: info@wistrails.com

INTRODUCTION

More populated and developed than the northern part of the state, southern Wisconsin nevertheless offers canoeists and kayakers a tremendous range of excellent paddling opportunities. Many southern Wisconsin waterways offer a sense of remoteness that rivals the wild isolation of the North Woods, combined with picturesque scenery, historic sites, and bountiful wildlife. Wisconsin is a beautiful state, and many of its most attractive places are located in the southern portion: the magnificent unglaciated Driftless Area that occupies the southwestern corner, the lovely rolling countryside of the Kettle Moraine in the southeast, the rugged quartzite hills of the Baraboo Range, the startling buttes and mesas left behind by the last glacier, and many others. Most can be seen by motorists, bicyclists, and hikers, but the best perspective of all is enjoyed by paddlers.

There is little of the whitewater that is so common in northern Wisconsin, but the region abounds in delightfully intimate "little rivers," often located conveniently close to large population centers. Several rivers are in a class of their own, especially the remarkably unspoiled Lower Wisconsin and the popular Kickapoo. Many other, seldom-paddled streams—the Little Wolf, Eau Claire, and Plover, for instance—will be a pleasant surprise to boaters experiencing them for the first time. Paddlers who are interested in unique geological structures, beautiful rock formations, exhilarating riffles and rapids, riverside camping, circuitous streambeds, charming old bridges, and multitudes of other river characteristics have numerous locales to choose from in southern Wisconsin.

Hopefully the descriptions in this book will provide beginning canoeists and kayakers with lots of ideas about places to go. At the same time, seasoned paddlers will find new rivers and sections to try. The ultimate goal is to introduce as many people as possible to the rivers of southern Wisconsin, in the hope that they will join the effort to protect and preserve them.

WHICH RIVERS ARE INCLUDED

This guidebook presents 32 rivers in southern Wisconsin (i.e., the area south of Highway 29), typically recommending 1, 2, or 3 of the best and most accessible sections. A total of 82 sections are mapped and described in detail. No waterway is covered in its entirety, but most trip descriptions include supplemental vignettes (labeled "Other Trips") that briefly point to other paddleable stretches. Adventurous paddlers who are willing to do their homework and take proper precautions will find that there are many other opportunities for pleasant and safe paddling.

With a couple of exceptions, only stretches that usually have enough water to paddle for a significant portion of the paddling season are included. (Please remember, however, that this factor is highly dependent upon the amount and frequency of precipitation in a given season.) Scenic value is another criterion for deter-

mining which sections to include: many of the prettiest places in Wisconsin are to be seen along the rivers described here. For an occasional change of pace, there is something to be said for city paddling—such as the unique downtown vistas of the Milwaukee River—but in this book the emphasis is on quiet, natural places.

Safety, too, is an important consideration; thus, only two trips require portages of dams. Such portages are not only time-consuming and sometimes difficult, but often dangerous as well. Wide, currentless, and often-windy lakes are not included—only moving water. A few trips necessarily involve take-outs at the end of narrow flowages, but all of these impoundments are small and attractive.

Because most canoeists regard big logjams with annoyance and dread, I have described only sections where paddlers can have a reasonable expectation of encountering no major blockages. This sometimes means eliminating otherwise pleasant sections where total obstructions are common and irksome (e.g., the Baraboo from Reedsburg to Rock Springs, and the Kickapoo from La Farge to Viola). Bear in mind that a wind storm can quickly drop one or more trees across a usually unobstructed stretch. Routine maneuvering around limbs and trees can be a lot of fun, of course, especially for experienced boaters; the trip descriptions in this book indicate stretches where some limb dodging is usually necessary.

Convenient and safe accesses are another criterion for inclusion. These range from concrete boat ramps with adjacent parking lots, to bare spots on the riverbank. While some accesses are much easier than others, none of the put-ins and take-outs in this book are hazardous if you exercise reasonable precautions. Always be careful at accesses, especially when steep, slippery banks and nearby dams are involved.

The Mississippi River constitutes the western border of southern Wisconsin and occasionally is canoed. However, its width, volume, current, windiness, and barge traffic make it unattractive and dangerous for most paddlers. Therefore, it is not among the rivers described in this book. One day trip includes a brief stint on the Mississippi (Wisconsin River 12).

The rivers of southern Wisconsin are almost exclusively quietwater, but there are many streams with exciting riffles and Class I rapids, and two good whitewater rivers (the Black and Little Wolf). A couple of whitewater rivers in the northern part of the region (the Embarras and Big Eau Pleine) are not included because they are runnable only a few days a year.

In addition to the 32 rivers described here, there are many creeks that are canoeable, at least part of the year. Typically, these are small, winding, intimate, often-obstructed, and sometimes riffly, and have enough water for paddling only in the spring or after sustained rainfall. The list of such frequently paddled streams includes Neenah, Wingra, Hall's, Turtle, Dell, Badfish, and Cedar

Creeks, together with a number of small rivers (such as the Pine, Yellow, Montello, and Root).

Finally, I would like to be able to say that I've excluded all streams that have some degree of pollution. Indeed, most of the rivers in this book are clean (and often clear), but a few have shown the effects of agricultural and urban runoff or industrial pollution. Like the lower Fox between Lake Winnebago and Green Bay, the lower Sheboygan (downstream from Sheboygan Falls) has PCB contamination.

INTENDED AUDIENCE

The wide variety of canoeing and kayaking opportunities in southern Wisconsin means that there are plenty of places for paddlers of all interests and skill levels. Consequently, this book is intended for beginner, experienced/intermediate, and advanced/expert paddlers alike. Trip descriptions of individual sections provide an indication of which skill level is appropriate. In addition, a chart in Appendix 1 provides a convenient listing of sections by skill level. Most of all, *Paddling Southern Wisconsin* is meant for everyone who loves nature, scenic beauty, peacefulness, and the company of like-minded people.

WHAT'S IN THE BOOK

Each day trip is described in two parts: (1) a detailed narrative, and (2) a map that shows roads, put-ins and take-outs, mileage, and other significant information. After a general summary, each description covers camping opportunities, shuttle routes, canoe rentals and shuttle services (when available), average gradient, water levels, and accesses. Then the paddler is led systematically down the river or stream. There is a suggested length for each trip, but in most cases it is easy to make the trip shorter or longer by using alternate accesses (which are indicated in the narrative and on the map). No attempt is made to estimate paddling time because this is dependent on such variables as skill level, weather conditions, speed of current, type of boat, etc. Generally, 2 to 3 miles an hour is a good rule of thumb for making a rough estimate of time on the river.

Recreational kayaks have become quite popular in recent years.

Maps

The maps in this guidebook are designed to provide all the essential information that boaters need to get to the designated stretch and paddle down it safely and enjoyably. Maps are kept as simple and uncluttered as possible. All roads are not included—only those relevant to paddlers (for running shuttles and other purposes). Because of the small scale of the maps, all river bends and islands cannot be shown. Cities and villages are shaded, while tiny communities are indicated only with labels. Eight important components and their symbols are indicated in the key to each map: accesses, mile markers, railroads, rapids, cities or villages, campgrounds, public land, and nearby bicycle routes.

Mile markers provide a convenient means of estimating trip length and determining how long you can expect to be on the water. Calculating mileage for a river or stream is not an exact science; we have done our best to be as accurate as possible. Incidentally, local people are often excellent sources of information on nearby streams, but you generally cannot count on them to provide an accurate estimate of river-miles on a stretch. They are usually on the high side. Canoe rental firms are fairly dependable in this respect, however.

Unlike northern Wisconsin, the southern part of the state has little whitewater. There are lots of exhilarating riffles and Class I rapids, however, and even a few Class IIs. These are mentioned in the trip narratives, but only the significant rapids (i.e., Class II or higher) are marked on the maps with hash marks. For the criteria used to classify the difficulty of rapids, see the later section "Paddling Safely."

Paddlers can determine where they are at any given time by observing such features as creek mouths, bridges, bends, prominent islands, etc., and comparing these with the map. A compass is helpful, too.

If additional maps are desired, the following are recommended.

The most useful single resource is the *Wisconsin Atlas and Gazetteer* (published by the DeLorme Mapping Company and available in bookstores), which provides 81 quadrangular maps of the state. DeLorme is especially helpful in locating back roads, state parks, campgrounds, etc. Serious paddlers always have a well-worn DeLorme tucked away somewhere in their vehicles.

For detailed information on elevations, contours, wetlands, etc., consult the topographical maps available from the U.S. Geological Survey in various scales. Overall, the 7.5-minute maps are most detailed and useful. To obtain free indexes and catalogs and to order maps, contact USGS Information Services, Box 25286, Denver, CO 80225.

The Wisconsin Department of Transportation publishes a detailed highway map of each of the state's counties, in a half-inch-per-mile scale. These inexpensive maps show all state and county roads but no city streets, and are thus more useful for the less-populated parts of the state. To order copies, contact the Wisconsin Department of Transportation, Maps and Publications Sales, 3617 Pierstorff Street, P.O. Box 7713, Madison, WI 53707-7713.

Many rivers pass through city, county, and state

parks, state wildlife areas, state forests, and other public property. Altogether, public land represents about 19 percent of the total area of Wisconsin. Maps designating these areas are available upon request from the appropriate agency (e.g., the Wisconsin Department of Natural Resources).

Another useful tool for visualizing many of the streams of Wisconsin is the fascinating Microsoft Terra-Server Web site (http://terraserver.microsoft.com), which displays aerial photographs and satellite images of much of the planet. Included in the database are sizable areas in southern Wisconsin. There are excellent images of many of the rivers that are described in this book.

For streams that pass through urban areas (e.g., the Pecatonica through Darlington and the La Crosse through Sparta), city maps are helpful. These are available at local and area chambers of commerce, visitor centers, and gas stations.

To determine land ownership along any stream in southern Wisconsin, consult the land atlas and plat book for the appropriate county. These may be found at most county courthouses and libraries, or may be ordered from Rockford Map Publishers, P.O. Box 6126, Rockford, IL 61125. Plat books are particularly valuable when you are trying to determine whether shoreline land is privately or publicly owned, and when you want to identify landowners for the purpose of seeking permission to gain access to a stream.

Biking Trails

Because canoeists often combine paddling and bicycling trips, biking trails that are located near recommended stretches are shown on the maps. These trails are often used by hikers as well. Wisconsin is a national leader in the development of off-road trails, including trails that parallel or cross the Baraboo, Chippewa, Crawfish, La Crosse, Pecatonica, Plover, Red Cedar, Rock, and Sheboygan Rivers. A number of excellent books describe such trails, and contain a great deal of information relating to the rivers and streams in *Paddling Southern Wisconsin:*

Wisconsin Biking Guide. Madison, WI: Wisconsin Department of Tourism, 2000.
Biking Wisconsin's State Park Trails. Madison, WI: Wisconsin Department of Natural Resources, n.d.
Phil Van Valkenberg. *Best Wisconsin Bike Trips.* Madison, WI: Trails Books, 1995.
Cliff and Shirley Christl. *Bicycling Wisconsin.* Wauwatosa, WI: Milwaukee Map Service, 1996.
Shawn Richardson. *Biking Wisconsin's Rail-Trails.* Adventure Publications, 1998.
Jane E. Hall and Scott D. Hall. *30 Bicycle Tours in Wisconsin.* Backcountry Publications, 1994.

Camping

Both public and private campgrounds that are located on or near a given stretch of water are mentioned

in the narrative and shown on the map. Wisconsin has an excellent system of well-maintained state parks with attractive and inexpensive campgrounds. Many rivers included in this book—including the Black, Eau Claire, Kickapoo, Mecan, Plover, Sugar, Trempealeau, and Wisconsin—lend themselves to multiday canoe-camping trips because of conveniently located riverside campgrounds. Moreover, it is common practice to camp out on the beaches, sandbars, and islands of the Black, Chippewa, and Wisconsin (provided that the campsites are not on private property).

Canoe Rental and Shuttle Service

Whenever there is a known provider of canoe rentals and shuttle service, that information is included. Some outfitters provide shuttles only for customers who rent canoes, but others will shuttle canoeists' boats and vehicles for a fee. Incidentally, these service providers are often an excellent source of water level information.

Shuttle Routes

The easiest and most obvious shuttle route from the put-in to the take-out is described for each trip, together with the driving distance. In a few instances this is not the shortest possible way to go; feel free to change the recommended route if you like. Of course, the recommended route also will have to be altered if you modify the trip by using different accesses.

Beginning boaters often ask about the best way to shuttle people, boats, gear, and vehicles between the put-in and take-out. At times, shuttling can get quite complicated, but usually it's a rather simple process. Paddlers generally meet at the put-in at a designated time, drop off their boats and gear (along with at least one person to look after the equipment), then drive to the take-out to

Southern Wisconsin has several great canoe-camping rivers.

leave most of the cars. Crowding into as few vehicles as possible, the entourage heads back to the put-in, where they park the shuttle vehicle(s), climb into the boats, and paddle off. At the end of the canoe trip, most of the paddlers load up their vehicles and head for home, but someone must drive the shuttle driver(s) back to the put-in to retrieve the vehicle(s) left there. There are many variations. For example, the above process is occasionally reversed to save time at the beginning of the trip. Or if one or more boaters in a group wish to paddle only part of a trip, their car(s) can be dropped off at an intermediate access point so that they can take out there. Finally, boaters with only one vehicle can double their exercise by using a bike shuttle. Drop your boat and gear off at the put-in; drive to the take-out and drop off your car; bicycle back to the put-in and secure the bike; paddle down the stream, then load up your boat and gear; drive back to the put-in and pick up your bike.

Gradient

Riffles and rapids are most common on rivers and streams with relatively high gradient (i.e., the rate of descent, expressed in feet per mile). As a general rule, a gradient of 5 to 9.9 feet per mile indicates the likelihood of riffles and rapids, while gradient of 10 feet or more is a predictor of demanding whitewater. Gradient is an insignificant factor on most southern Wisconsin waterways, but four stretches included in this book have a drop of 10 feet or more (Black 2, Little Wolf 1, Manitowoc 2, and Waupaca 1), and nine more sections are in the 5 to 9.9 range: Black 1, Crystal, Galena, Grant 2, La Crosse 1, Milwaukee 2, Platte 1, Sheboygan 1, and Waupaca 2.

Unique, little rental canoes on the Crystal River.

Water Levels

Water level is one of the most important pieces of information that you need to have before going paddling. Ideally, the water will be flowing at a safe, pleasant level. But if it's too low, you can be in for a miserable time, dragging your boat through shallows. If it's too high, your life can be in peril. EVERY RIVER AND STREAM IN THIS BOOK IS DANGEROUS WHEN HIGH, ESPECIALLY IN THE SPRING. Stay home or do something else when the water is high; risking your life isn't worth it. If you drive to the put-in for a day of

paddling and discover that the water is high, turn around and go home.

The best source of current and historical water level information is the United States Geological Survey Web site that presents "real-time water data." At this Internet location you can obtain recent readings (i.e., within the last 24 hours) from 149 active gauges located on rivers, creeks, lakes, and other waterways throughout Wisconsin. This data may be accessed at http://wi.water.usgs.gov. The site also provides rainfall data for the previous 48 hours and a detailed explanation of the USGS gauging system. Paddlers are urged to become familiar with the USGS data; by clicking on various options, you can obtain a wealth of information that will enhance the enjoyment and safety of your trips. Whenever an active gauge is located on or near a given section, this book indicates the station number of the gauge in the trip description.

The significance of the data is not immediately clear. The current reading for each station is presented in terms of (1) a water level number (e.g., "Stage: feet above datum") that is based on an arbitrary gauge, and (2) streamflow expressed in cubic feet per second (cfs). By themselves, these figures do not tell you whether the stream is low, medium, or high, unless you have paddled it many times before and can make a correlation. Fortunately, you can obtain graphed historical data from USGS for the previous week, month, or other period of time, thus giving you a good idea of how high and low a given stream gets and what the current gauge reading means. Note that the gauging stations are not always advantageously located for judging how canoeable a given section is, so you may have to make a water level estimate on the basis of a gauge located some distance away. Paddlers also should be aware that not all of the gauges that they see on rivers and streams are currently active. Disappointingly, gauges are periodically removed from the active list due to lack of funding.

For several sections in this book there is no active USGS gauge, but you can obtain water level and recent precipitation data on the National Weather Service's Interactive Weather Information Network (IWIN) site: http://iwin.nws.noaa.gov/iwin/wi/hydro.html. Unlike the USGS Web site, IWIN does not display historical or graphical data, but does present four columns for each gauge: flood stage, bankful stage, this morning's stage, and the 24-hour change. To use the site, you must scroll through a great deal of data.

In addition, paddlers seeking general information on water levels (high, medium, or low) often telephone canoe rental businesses, campgrounds, forest preserve districts, and state, county, and city parks that are located on or near a given stream. You will find that some sources of water level information are more reliable than others, for a variety of reasons. The methods of judging water conditions as a criterion for canoeability are somewhat inconsistent, varying from place to place and person to person. Gauge readings are arbitrary and localized, and terms such as low and high tend to be subjective and to have different meanings for paddlers of different skill levels. Nevertheless, when you have been informed by a local source that a river is low, medium, or high, you are wise to take heed. ULTIMATELY, YOU ARE RESPONSIBLE FOR DECIDING WHETHER OR NOT TO PADDLE. For some telltale indicators of high water, see the section "Paddling Safely" later in this introduction.

In general, canoeing conditions are best through June. Typically, water levels start to go down in July, and by August you can usually expect some scraping of your boat on many rivers. Even in the ordinary dry months of late summer and fall, however, heavy rainfall can quickly restore low rivers to paddleability (or to dangerously high levels).

Accesses

Put-ins and take-outs range from designated boat landings to grassy banks near bridges. Always check out the put-in and take-out carefully before beginning a trip. When in doubt about being able to spot an inconspicuous take-out, it's a good idea to hang a bright bandanna or piece of surveyor's tape from a branch at the landing. Most of the accesses in this book are public landings, or private ones that are commonly used by the public with permission. Whenever in doubt, be sure to ask permission from landowners.

Trip Descriptions

After these preliminaries, the trip description itself provides a verbal road map of the river section, conveying a lot of information that is not on the map. Except for a few rivers that are usually paddled in the springtime, the descriptions are based on normal summer flows, that is, neither low nor high. Places where it is appropriate to scout and, perhaps, portage are pointed out, together with historical sites (such as old mills), pleasant lunch spots, nature preserves, alternate accesses, scenic highlights, etc.

Other Trips

Usually, when the river upstream or downstream from the described section is not included elsewhere in the book, a brief paragraph summarizes other paddleable stretches, if there are any.

Good Reading

When an outstanding publication is available to provide further information on a given river or stream, that fact is often noted. In addition, a short list of highly recommended reading is provided in Appendix 2, together with a list of paddling-related Internet sites in Appendix 3.

Low-clearance bridges can be lethal when the water is high.

Fishing Opportunities

Drawing upon a variety of sources—mainly Wisconsin DNR publications, observations of what fishermen are catching, and conversations with anglers and DNR fisheries personnel—Appendix 7 lists the game fish that are found in the rivers included in this book. Not all of the stretches included here are great producers of fish, of course, but some are quite popular with fishermen.

The best single source of information is the DNR's Surface Water Resources series (one booklet for each county in the state), but the following are also recommended:

Steve Born, Jeff Mayers, Andy Morton, and Bill Sonzogni. *Exploring Wisconsin Trout Streams: The Angler's Guide.* Madison, WI: University of Wisconsin Press, 1997.

Jim Humphrey and Bill Shogren. *Wisconsin and Minnesota Trout Streams.* Backcountry Publications, 1995.

Dan Small. *Fish Wisconsin.* Krause Publications, 1993.

Another good source of fishing information is the Wisconsin DNR Web site www.dnr.state.wi.us.

Historical Background

Most of the rivers in this book are deeply steeped in historical significance. Some of that history is briefly recounted in the trip descriptions and in occasional sidebars.

RIVER READING AND MANEUVERS

Most of the rivers described in this guidebook are normally placid and suitable for beginning or intermediate paddlers, but all of the trips involve situations that require at least a modicum of ability to "read" the water and to maneuver a boat. Moreover, even the peaceful stretches occasionally present obstructions and other hazards for the unwary paddler. Thus, for both enjoyment and safety, all paddlers should master the basic principles of river dynamics and boat handling. Moving-water technique is much more complex than lake paddling.

In addition to knowing about equipment (boats, paddles, life jackets, boat flotation for whitewater, throw-ropes, etc.), canoeists and kayakers should learn the fundamentals of river dynamics and boat handling. These include current differentials, downstream and upstream Vs and waves, and the effects of obstacles, such as eddies, trees and limbs, "holes," horizon lines, ledges and falls, and "rock gardens."

In order to maneuver a boat in moving water, boaters need to become familiar with six basic paddling strokes: forward and back, draw and pry, sweep and brace. These allow paddlers to move forward efficiently, to stop movement downstream or even go backward, to turn, to move the boat sideways, to avoid obstacles, and to prevent the boat from capsizing. By combining these strokes with the ability to read the water, paddlers can execute such river moves as sideslips, eddy turns, peel-outs, and ferries, all of which are essential if you wish to paddle whitewater.

Confidence and skill in river reading and maneuvering are essential for safe paddling. An added bonus, however, is the spirit of playfulness that such skill makes possible. It is fun to "run" a river, certainly, but it is pure joy to be able to slow things down and play on the river in a leisurely fashion.

Since this is a guidebook, not a manual on canoeing and kayaking, detailed information on river reading and maneuvering must be found elsewhere. Of course, the best source of such information is a paddling class or clinic. Fortunately, many such opportunities are available in Wisconsin; for a listing, see Appendix 4. Other excellent sources are the instructional books and videos that introduce the basics of paddlesports; for a selection, see Appendix 5. Still another way for novice paddlers to learn about the basics is to accompany safety-oriented, experienced boaters on non-threatening trips. Watch, ask questions, follow the example of accomplished boaters, and don't be reluctant to walk your boat around situations that don't feel right. For a list of paddling clubs and organizations in and near southern Wisconsin, see Appendix 6.

Fishermen on the lower Milwaukee.

PADDLING SAFELY

Canoeists and kayakers paddle for many reasons, including relaxation, communion with nature, excitement, fellowship, and self-development. But whatever their intent, all paddlers should have one overriding consideration at all times: safety for themselves and their companions. Knowledge, skill, and good judgment are essential to having a good, safe time on the water, unmarred by damaged equipment, injuries, or perhaps worse. To that end, the following potential hazards warrant special emphasis. All are encountered somewhere on the trips described in this book, and all demand extra care.

1. High Water

During the spring and after downpours, all of the rivers in this book can become dangerously high, a situation that causes fast current, huge waves, powerful eddies, and sometimes big holes. High water requires skillful boat control and quick decisions, takes away slow, shallow recovery areas, and increases the odds that you will encounter fallen trees and floating debris. Add the likelihood of cold water, and you have a high-hazard situation. No one has any business being on the water when it is in flood. In general, inexperienced and unskilled boaters should limit themselves to low-to-medium water levels. If in doubt, don't go.

Telltale signs that a river is dangerously high are water flowing through the trees or shrubs; fast, turbulent, muddy, sometimes "boiling" current; water close to the bottom of bridges; and floating debris.

2. Cold

Usually, after springtime thaw, most Wisconsin rivers and creeks flow forcefully, and boaters enthusiastically take their equipment out of winter storage. Unfortunately, the early weeks of the paddling season are prime times for hypothermia, a potential killer. Water temperature below 60 degrees is dangerous; immersion can quickly take away your strength and even your will. Wear a wet suit or dry suit and layered synthetic fabric whenever the air or water temperature is low. Unless you are skilled, properly clothed and equipped, and accompanied by other skilled paddlers, you should not venture out under such conditions.

3. Strainers

Fallen trees and limbs are potentially lethal on all of the rivers and creeks of Wisconsin and should always be avoided. Small, winding rivers like the Lemonweir and Baraboo, and the upper reaches of larger rivers like the Pecatonica and Milwaukee are prone to such "strainers"—so-called because water rushes through them, trapping boats and boaters. Be especially watchful for strainers on the outside of bends, in constrictions, and under bridges. Trees often fall into the water as a result of bank erosion or storms, sometimes in unexpected

Late-winter and early-spring paddling can be fun, but guard against hypothermia.

from the obstruction, is the worst thing you can do.) Maintaining the downstream lean, you can often work your boat off the obstruction by "scrunching" it forward or backward a few inches at a time, then continuing on downstream. Sometimes if the situation allows, you can step out onto an obstruction, free the boat, and climb back in. Fellow paddlers can be of assistance, too. Broaching is especially dangerous when bridge piers and old pilings are involved; stay clear of such obstacles, and keep your boat parallel to the current.

5. Capsizing

All boaters "dump" sooner or later. For properly equipped paddlers on a warm day in calm, unobstructed water, it's no big deal. But coming out of your boat when the water is swift, cold, obstructed, or turbulent is a different matter. If you capsize in quiet-water situations, stay with your boat if possible (upstream from it), and work your way toward the shore or a shallow spot, staying clear of any brush and other obstructions. Fellow boaters can help. In a capsize situation, the first concern should always be the safety of the paddlers involved; retrieving equipment is a secondary consideration. It's always a good idea to take along extra clothing in a drybag just in case. ALWAYS WEAR A PFD OR LIFE JACKET. Most canoe and kayak fatalities involve people who aren't wearing one!

In whitewater, try to stay upstream from your boat (so it won't crush you against a rock), lie flat on your back with your feet pointed downstream, and back-paddle to slow yourself down as you head toward shore. Do not try to stand up until you're in very shallow, slow water; otherwise, you're in danger of trapping your foot in a crevice, a not-uncommon cause of drowning. In the hands of someone who knows how to use it, a throw-rope can be used to advantage in rescuing capsized boaters.

Reentering the river after portaging around a hazardous strainer.

and awkward places. If you're lucky, a passage of open water allows you to paddle by (often through a very narrow opening). If the blockage is complete, however, don't take any chances; pull over to the shoreline well upstream and portage around the obstruction. Occasionally, such portages are unpleasant and difficult, especially when the banks are steep or muddy. Always take strainers seriously: they are the most common hazard you will encounter. Incidentally, the terms strainer, snag, and deadfall mean essentially the same thing.

A related hazard that is occasionally encountered is cattle wire strung over the water from bank to bank. Usually you can squeeze under it somewhere, but sometimes it must be raised with a paddle or portaged. Obviously, you can quickly get in trouble if the water is fast and you don't see the wire in time. Fortunately, this hazard is rare in Wisconsin. During the preparation of this book, wire was encountered on only one section, Platte River 1.

4. Broaching

In general, you must keep your boat parallel to the current, particularly in rapids or in other situations where there are obstacles in the water. Otherwise, you are at risk of pinning the boat sideways on an obstruction (a "broach"). The force of moving water is awesome, and can quickly "wrap" your craft, with you in it! Potentially catastrophic though a broach is, you can usually avert disaster by staying calm and aggressively leaning the boat toward the obstruction so the onrushing water won't flip the boat and fill it. (Remember: leaning upstream, away

6. Dams

Because of the danger posed by dams, together with the monotonous paddling upstream from them, this book includes only two trips requiring dam portages. Dams are dangerous in many ways and should be given a wide berth, particularly so-called low-head dams (low, uniform structures that may appear innocuous but are often fatal because of the recirculating current downstream, which can pull you into danger and keep you there). Dams in Wisconsin occasionally claim the lives of canoeists who are swept over them (e.g., at Gays Mills on the Kickapoo in 2000). If you put in below a dam, be sure to launch your boat as far downstream as possible to assure that you don't get pulled into the turbulence. If you choose to paddle on an impoundment, take out as far upstream from the dam as possible. Take-outs that oblige you to land within a few feet of the lip of a dangerous dam (e.g., at Johnsonville on the Sheboygan) aren't worth the risk for most paddlers. Inexperienced boaters often underestimate the life-threatening danger of dams. The best practice is to go nowhere near them, whenever possible.

Canoeists and kayakers who are paddling downstream from hydroelectric dams (e.g., on the Wisconsin River below Prairie du Sac or the Black River below Black River Falls) must always be aware of the potential for rising water levels due to dam releases, especially during and after heavy rainfall.

A killer low–head dam on the Milwaukee River at Waubeka.

7. Holes

When swift water flows over a dam, rock, or ledge, it sometimes creates a downstream depression into which the surrounding water rushes turbulently, creating a "hole" (also known as a "hydraulic" or "reversal"). The recirculating current in particularly strong holes, which are called "keepers" or "stoppers," holds onto a boat and traps swimmers. Small, weak holes can easily be run (and even played in by skilled boaters), but large, "sticky" ones should be carefully avoided, by portaging if necessary. In addition to the deadly hydraulics found just downstream from many Wisconsin dams, holes develop at various locations on the whitewater sections of the Black River when the water is high.

8. Drop-offs and Rising Water

Paddlers on the Lower Wisconsin, Black, and Chippewa Rivers must be aware of a unique danger posed by these wide, sandy waterways. Big, beautiful sandbars are irresistible for lunch stops, rest breaks, wading, camping, and just messing around in general. What must be remembered, however, is that there are often sudden drop-offs on the downstream side of sandbars. You can be carelessly wading one moment, and in deep water the next, usually being carried along by the current. If you're ever caught in this situation, it's usually best to swim downstream or laterally to the next shallow spot rather than fight the current to get back to the sandbar.

Another caution for campers on the same three rivers is to anticipate the possibility of the water rising during the night. A nocturnal rainstorm upstream or a dam release can raise water levels enough to be a problem for low-lying campsites. Thus, it's always a good idea to set up camp a few feet higher than the water.

9. Rapids

This book includes only one true whitewater river, the Black upstream from Black River Falls. Especially in high water, the Black can be quite dangerous because of big waves, swift current, and difficult rapids. Exciting but somewhat less intimidating rapids are found on the Little Wolf, Manitowoc, and Eau Claire.

Much more common than rapids are riffles—fast, wavy, relatively unobstructed water that is usually safe and easy to run. Experienced paddlers will enjoy the many riffly sections on the Grant, Platte, Crystal, Galena, Waupaca, and Red Cedar. As noted earlier, the gradient of a stream is usually a helpful predictor of riffles and rapids.

Standing waves (or "haystacks") are often formed when water rushes through a constriction, over submerged rocks or shallows, or into slower water, sometimes accompanied by a drop. Waves can mark the deepest, most unobstructed channel for paddlers to follow, but in high-water conditions they can be large enough to "stall out" a canoe and swamp it. Often they can be skirted along one side or the other to avoid the biggest ones. Big waves are often found on Black 1 and 2.

For seasoned whitewater paddlers, rapids are beautiful and exhilarating—a wonderful complement to the much more plentiful quietwater that is the norm in southern Wisconsin. Remember, however, that rapids pose dangers, especially for the inexperienced and unskilled. Even veteran paddlers sometimes run into trouble when they fail to scout, attempt rapids that exceed their skill level, paddle when the water is too high, or simply "have a bad day."

Turbulent water is infinitely varied, ranging in difficulty from easy, relatively unobstructed riffles and waves to extremely violent water that threatens the lives of all boaters, including experts. In order to provide a consistent method of comparing rapids worldwide, the International Scale of River Difficulty was devised to categorize rapids, using six classes from "easy" to "extreme." The following is a brief adaptation of this scale, and is the rating system used in this book. Please note that whenever the water is high and/or cold, rapids are usually considered at least one class higher.

Class I: Fast water with some waves and obstructions but easily negotiated; requiring little maneuvering and involving slight risk; suitable for paddlers with some moving-water experience. Class I rapids are one step up from riffles. Most rapids in southern Wisconsin are Class Is.

Class II: Fast water with awkwardly located rocks, ledges, sizable waves, and other river features requiring considerable river-reading ability and maneuvering skills; broaching a possibility; suitable for trained and experienced (intermediate) whitewater paddlers. At normal water levels, Class IIs are found on Black 1 and 2, Little Wolf 1, and Manitowoc 2.

Class III: Very difficult rapids with large, often irregular waves, "pushy" current, big drops of 3 feet or more, difficult-to-determine routes, holes, and other features requiring complex maneuvers and precise boat control; often involving negative consequences in case of a dump, including difficult rescue; suitable only for advanced whitewater paddlers. At higher water levels, parts of Black 1 and 2 are IIIs.

Class IV: Intense, powerful, turbulent, sometimes unpredictable and dangerous rapids involving large, often unavoidable holes and big waves; necessitating fast, "must-do" maneuvers under pressure; consequences of capsize often nasty; rescue quite difficult; suitable only for highly skilled paddlers with a great deal of demanding whitewater experience.

Always be alert to potential hazards, even on seemingly calm stretches, such as this part of the Plover.

Class V: Long, obstructed, violent, and extremely dangerous rapids, with such features as big drops, constricted routes, undercut shorelines and rocks, broaching situations, and "keeper" holes; grave danger to life and limb; little chance of rescue; suitable only for teams of experts under optimal conditions of weather, water level, etc.

Class VI: Super difficult, unpredictable, and dangerous; all of the above criteria carried to an extreme; injury or death likely; suitable only for suicidal fools.

There are no Class IVs, Vs, or VIs on the river sections described in this book.

An Important Reminder

Whenever in doubt about what lies ahead, especially when you suspect a hazard of some kind, do not hesitate to get out and scout. (Incidentally, be careful when scouting. Slippery rocks and other shoreline hazards can be just as injurious as dangers on the water.) If scouting reveals something that you're not sure you can handle, portage. Never let false pride, peer pressure, or daredevilry push you into situations that exceed your skill and experience level. Always wear a suitable PFD, and don't paddle alone.

THE QUESTION OF PUBLIC ACCESS

Unlike many, more restrictive states—such as neighboring Illinois—Wisconsin has clearly established the right of canoeists and kayakers to paddle on most streams in the state. According to the DNR:

> Navigability determines whether a waterway is public or private. Navigable lakes and streams are public waterways. A waterway is navigable if it has a bed and banks, and it is possible to float a canoe or other small craft at some time of the year—even if only during spring floods. Because they are public, you may use navigable waters for fishing, boating, swimming, or other recreational activities, provided public access is available, or you have permission of the landowner to cross their property to reach the waterway. Once on a navigable waterway, as long as you keep your feet wet, you may walk along the bed of the stream, fish, swim, or boat in any navigable lake or stream.

In 1999 the "keep your feet wet" requirement was modified by a law that now allows anglers, swimmers, and boaters to stand in the streambed or on the exposed banks up to the ordinary high watermark, defined as "the point on the shore where the water is present often enough to leave a distinct mark." Often difficult to recognize, the mark is typically "the lip right at the bank of the river and normally does not extend into the woods along the bank where boaters might walk in order to scout or portage a drop." The DNR sensibly suggests:

> It remains good policy to seek landowner permission before pursuing any activities on private

Don't forget sunscreen.

lands. Cooperation and mutual respect will be the key to preventing conflicts. The Department recommends that users limit their activities to the water to the greatest extent possible, and use the exposed shore area only to portage around obstructions, such as fallen trees, or water that is too shallow for floating or too deep for wading. Do so in the least intrusive manner possible. (Michael Lutz, DNR Legal Services)

Paddlers in Wisconsin must always remember that, while they have the right to paddle on all navigable streams, the law does not guarantee public access to such streams and does not allow walking along the bank above the high watermark on private property. Most of the shoreline along the rivers in this book is privately owned. Please respect the rights of property owners whenever you're looking for a put-in or take-out, a lunch stop, a campsite, or a scout/portage trail. If in doubt about a given location, don't step foot on it, or ask permission to do so. Occasionally you will be presented with ambiguous situations and must use your common sense and good judgment.

WHAT TO BRING ON A CANOE TRIP

As an aid to beginning paddlers, here's a basic checklist of things to bring along on canoeing and kayaking trips. All the items listed are not necessary on every trip, of course, and you may wish to bring other things not listed here. It's a good idea to develop and use a checklist of your own. Even experienced paddlers forget important items occasionally (to their chagrin and embarrassment).

A good PFD.

An extra paddle (just in case).

Clothing appropriate for the weather, including rain gear and an adequate hat and shoes. Dress warmly; you can always shed a layer of clothing, if necessary.

A bailer and a sponge to keep your boat dry.

A plastic water bottle with plenty of drinking water.

A waterproof bag or box for extra clothing, lunch, wallet, camera, and everything else you want to keep dry.

Car keys (in a secure place).

Basic first aid materials.

Sunscreen.

Insect repellent.

Short lengths of cord for tying gear to thwarts.

For whitewater: an air bag tied into the boat to keep your boat afloat in case of a capsize, and a paddling helmet to protect your head from rocks.

For overnight canoe trips: basic camping equipment and supplies.

PADDLING RESPONSIBLY

Along with the enjoyment of paddling the waterways of southern Wisconsin come certain responsibilities for all of us:

1. Be considerate of other paddlers when you're on the water. If you're with a group, keep other members of the group in sight at all times, and don't go off on your own. On most trips, the first boat and last boat ("lead" and "sweep") are paddled by experienced boaters; always stay behind the lead boat and in front of the last boat. Follow the instructions of designated trip leaders when you go on trips sponsored by canoe clubs.

2. Help preserve the environment by leaving no litter, especially when you stop for lunch. When you find trash left by others, it's always a good idea to remove some (or all) of it into a bag for disposal later in an appropriate place. Build fires only where you know it's permissible to do so (e.g., in riverside parks that provide fire rings).

3. All of the waterways of southern Wisconsin have at least some private property on their shoreline. Always put yourself in the place of the landowner and respect his or her rights. Ask permission before stepping foot on private land, and express your gratitude. Please keep the noise level down, and stay away from cattle. Giving cattle a wide berth is a matter of common courtesy toward the owner, of course, but it's also a prudent way to avoid being trampled.

The Chippewa River State Trail—one of Wisconsin's many "Rails-to-Trails" projects.

4. For obvious reasons, it's not a good idea to take alcohol on canoe trips.

5. If you plan to fish, be sure to obtain a Wisconsin license and abide by the regulations. See the annually published DNR booklets *Wisconsin Trout Fishing Regulations and Guide* and *Guide to Wisconsin Hook and Line Fishing Regulations*.

6. Because radios and other noise generators detract from the get-away-from-it-all benefit of paddling, they are generally considered taboo on canoe trips.

7. If your dog is well behaved and under control, it's okay to bring it along. Otherwise, for everyone's sake (including the dog's), leave it home.

8. Be responsible for your own safety and well-being. This includes paddling only on streams that match your skill level, being properly equipped, staying with your group, knowing how to swim, wearing your PFD and weather-appropriate clothing, following your trip leader's instructions, kneeling in rough water (to stabilize your boat by lowering the center of gravity), knowing where you are on the river (by taking along a map and using it), installing extra flotation in your boat if you're going to paddle whitewater, mastering the essentials of boat control, turning your bow into the wake created by powerboats, staying away from strainers and other obstructions. Failing to follow basic principles of safe paddling not only puts you in harm's way but also may put fellow boaters in the position of endangering themselves to rescue you. Poison ivy is another factor to be aware of when paddling in southern Wisconsin: stay clear of it during put ins, take outs, lunch stops, and portages. In the final analysis, YOU ARE RESPONSIBLE FOR YOUR OWN ACT-IONS AND DECISIONS.

9. Don't allow yourself to be goaded into paddling situations that exceed your ability or confidence level. Canoeing and kayaking skills develop—in steady increments—with experience.

10. Canoeing club members should contribute to the group by volunteering to lead a trip, write the newsletter, keep track of memberships, or other activities according to their interests and abilities.

11. When parking vehicles at the put-in or take-out, don't block access for motorists, farmers, property owners, and other boaters. Keep your parked vehicles away from driveways, lanes to farm fields, and accesses to motorboat ramps, and don't park along shoulders with part of your vehicle on the road.

12. "Weekend warriors" who careen down the river, boozed-up and obnoxious, miss the whole point of canoeing and blemish the image of paddlesport. They are strongly encouraged to find a different outlet for their boorishness.

The historic Cedarburg bridge—the only original covered bridge still remaining in Wisconsin.

BARABOO RIVER 1
Union Center to Wonewoc (5.5 Miles)

Castles in Wisconsin

A striking feature of this part of Wisconsin is the presence of picturesque rock "castles" that suddenly rise from the landscape. Third Castle (Baraboo River 1) is a striking example that can be viewed from the river or from the "400" State Trail. More dramatic examples can be found by driving north a few miles to the small community of Camp Douglas; just north of town is the fascinating spire of Castle Rock. More stone towers are to be seen alongside Interstate 90/94 as you head west toward Tomah, and in Mill Bluff State Park, also near Camp Douglas. Farther to the northeast, another Castle Rock is found along the Wisconsin River; Castle Rock Lake is named after it (see Wisconsin River 1).

These beautiful structures go back 12,000 years, when a blockage of glacial melt in the Baraboo Range formed a huge 825-square-mile impoundment known as Glacial Lake Wisconsin, stretching north all the way to the Stevens Point area. Here and there sandstone bluffs formed islands in this vast lake, which later subsided and left behind the eroded stone formations that reminded early settlers of castle walls in Europe. To geologists they're known as outliers. Large ones are called mesas, smaller ones buttes, and slender ones pinnacles.

Originating near Elroy, not far from the headwaters of the popular Kickapoo River, the Baraboo twists 120 miles to the southeast before joining the Wisconsin a few miles downstream from Portage. Along the way it passes through a mostly low-canopied, wooded setting that feels remote and wild but which often necessitates maneuvering or portaging around fallen trees. In several locations the Baraboo flows past impressive rock formations, especially where it cuts through the ancient Baraboo Range near Rock Springs (the Upper Narrows gorge) and east of the city of Baraboo (the Lower Narrows).

Through most of its course the river has a modest gradient, but at the city of Baraboo it drops 45 feet in only 4 miles. As a result, early settlers constructed several dams there in the 1800s to provide power for industry, and another upstream at La Valle. Having outlived their usefulness, most of the aged dams have been removed in recent years, and the river soon will be free-flowing once again.

Located close to the river's source, the first recommended section passes through forested corridor and grassy lowland, never far from wooded bluffs. The streambed is only 20–40 feet wide, and paddlers are likely to encounter some limbs and trees in the water. At one point the river flows beneath a towering bankside cliff called Third Castle. Paralleling the entire section is the "400" State Trail, which pulls alongside the banks several times and twice crosses the river. Developed on the abandoned Chicago-Northwestern railroad grade, the 22-mile trail runs close to the Baraboo from Reedsburg to Elroy and connects with the well-known Elroy-Sparta Trail.

The unique name of the river comes from the Baribeau brothers, who established an early mill near the mouth.

Camping is available on the north side of Wonewoc at Legion Park, at Chapparal Campground and Resort off Highway 33 between Wonewoc and La Valle (608-464-3200), and in Elroy at the downtown Elroy Commons.

Canoe rental and shuttle service are available at Chapparal Campground and Resort (888-283-0755). Canoe rental without shuttle is available in Baraboo at Riverside Rentals (608-356-6045 or 800-924-6225).

The **shuttle route** (3.8 miles) goes east on Highway 33 to Wonewoc, then west on County FF.

Gradient is 2.7 feet per mile.

For **water levels,** check the downstream gauge at Baraboo (#05405000) on the USGS Web site. See "Water Levels" in the introduction.

Put in from the grassy banks just downstream from the Highway 33 bridge at Union Center. After the put-in, the narrow Baraboo quickly passes under a small bridge used by the Hillsboro Snowmobile Trail. From here to Schaller Road the river bends back and forth through grassy lowlands, with thin tree cover. Patches of wetlands lie here and there in the floodplain. After Schaller Road, the river passes under two "400" State Trail bridges, approaches Highway 33, then flows past old abutments at the end of Bottom Road.

Downstream, after a couple of sharp turns, Third Castle—a sheer, 150-foot sandstone cliff topped with pine and hemlock trees—suddenly looms on the right. Picnic tables on the steep left bank make this a good stopping point. First and Second Castles are located nearby but can't be seen from the river.

In the approach to Wonewoc, the "400" State Trail twice runs alongside the left bank again. After winding past the west edge of town, the river passes in quick succession under two vehicular bridges, County FF and Washington Street/Gehri Road. **Take out** on the river-left bank between the two bridges, alongside a publically owned field where there's room to park a few cars.

Other trips. (1) Chapparal Campground and Resort is located near the river a few miles downstream; boaters who are renting canoes from Chapparal may take out at the landing on Gardner Creek. (2) Another very pleasant day trip begins 2 miles east of La Valle just downstream from the Lake Redstone dam (on Big Creek) and ends at Reedsburg. For canoe rental and shuttle service, contact the Baraboo River Bike Shop in Reedsburg (608-524-0798). (3) In the beautiful stretch from Reedsburg to North Freedom, paddlers must contend with many obstructions.

Tree-topped cliffs along the upper Baraboo.

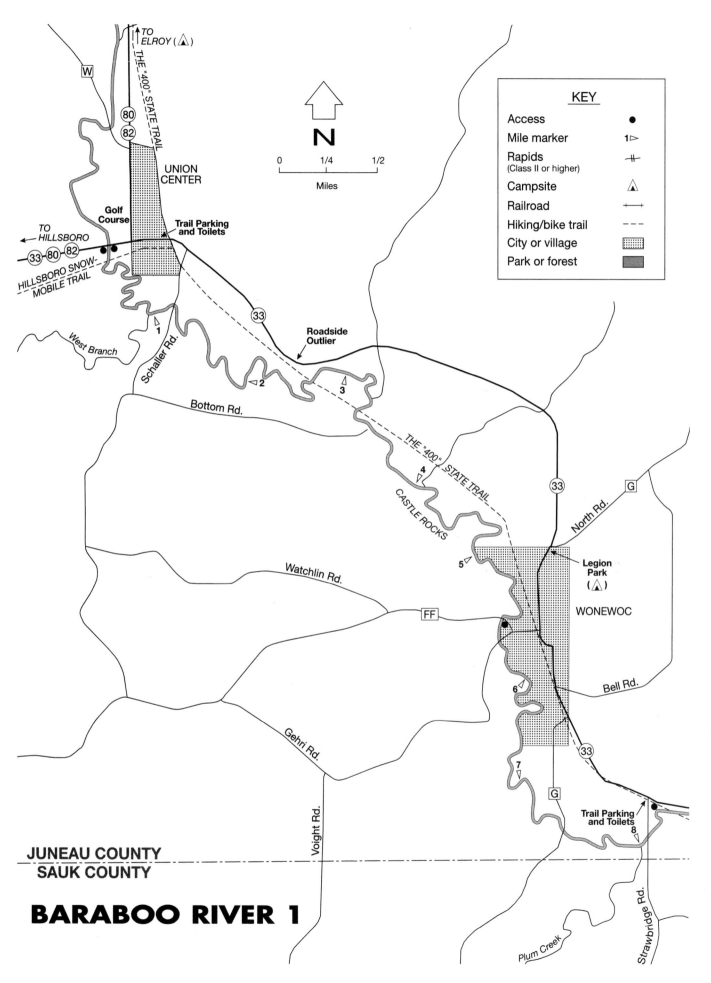

KEY

Access	●
Mile marker	1▷
Rapids (Class II or higher)	–⫴–
Campsite	△
Railroad	+—+—+
Hiking/bike trail	– – –
City or village	▦
Park or forest	▨

N

0   1/4   1/2
Miles

TO ELROY (△)

THE "400" STATE TRAIL

UNION CENTER

W

80
82

Golf Course

TO HILLSBORO

33 80 82

HILLSBORO SNOW-MOBILE TRAIL

Trail Parking and Toilets

West Branch

Schaller Rd.

1

33

Roadside Outlier

Bottom Rd.

2

3

4

CASTLE ROCKS

THE "400" STATE TRAIL

Watchlin Rd.

33

North Rd.

G

Legion Park (△)

5

FF

WONEWOC

6

Bell Rd.

Gehri Rd.

7

33

G

Trail Parking and Toilets

8

Voight Rd.

JUNEAU COUNTY
SAUK COUNTY

Plum Creek

Strawbridge Rd.

BARABOO RIVER 1

BARABOO RIVER 2
North Freedom to Baraboo (10.7 Miles)

Except for a few sharp turns early in the trip, this frequently paddled section of the Baraboo consists of big, gentle bends in a mixed environment of woods, cropland, and pastures. Current is usually good, blockages are seldom encountered, and gradient is gentle until the end. Wooded hills are usually some distance away, but at one point the river runs alongside attractive rock formations. Accesses are convenient, including an intermediate one that can be used to shorten the trip to a more leisurely 6.5 miles.

Camping is available at Devil's Lake State Park 3 miles south of Baraboo (608-356-8301), Baraboo Hills Campground 3 miles northwest of Baraboo (608-356-8505 or 800-226-7242), Del Boo Campground 6 miles northwest of Baraboo (608-356-5898), Double K-D Ranch Camping Resort 2.5 miles southeast of Baraboo (608-356-4622), the Green Valley Campground 3.5 miles south of Baraboo (608-355-0090), the Red Oak Campground 6 miles north of Baraboo (608-356-7304), and Wheeler's Campground 2 miles south of Baraboo (608-356-4877).

The Linen Mill Dam: the last dam on the Baraboo River.

For **canoe rental** and **water levels**, see Baraboo River 1. For general information on water levels (high, medium, low), call Riverside Rentals in Baraboo (608-356-6045 or 800-924-6225).

The **shuttle route** (7.2 miles) for the full 10-mile trip goes north a short distance on South Linn Street; east, then north on County PF; east on Highway 136, which becomes Highway 33 at West Baraboo; and south on Willow Street to Haskins Park. For the shorter 6.5-mile trip, the shuttle (5 miles) goes east on South Linn Street; east, then north on County PF; east on Highway 136; south on Hatchery Road; and west a short distance on Rocky Hill Road.

The **gradient** of most of the section is 3.7 feet per mile, but it steepens to 10 feet per mile in the city of Baraboo.

Put in at the river-left boat ramp in the North Freedom Village Park, which has water, toilets, picnic facilities, and parking. To get to the park, go south 0.2 mile on Linn Street, off County PF (Walnut Street in North Freedom). The park is about 125 yards downstream from the County PF bridge. After an initial straight stretch, there are several sharp turns. The surroundings are rather open, with a thin tree line and steep, grassy banks.

After Seeley Creek enters on the right in a left bend, the woods become more dense and the river widens to 45 feet. Several hundred yards downstream from the creek there's a modest rock outcropping in the wooded bluff on

the right; cedars and other coniferous trees attractively cover the bluff. Downstream, another lovely rock formation is partially undercut, continuing for 100 yards, and again topped with coniferous trees.

Then, after a metal railroad bridge, the river arcs right alongside pastureland toward Kohlmeyer Road. After a straightaway, the river is deflected sharply to the right by a high wooded bluff where you can briefly see traffic on Highway 136. The Kohlmeyer Road bridge appears soon; a slight drop on both sides of the center pier creates small waves.

The river is open on both sides for a while after Kohlmeyer Road, and curves left into another sizable straightaway. Several long bends follow, mostly through pastureland. Eventually, after a long left bend, woods begin again on both sides and railroad tracks run atop a high bank on the right. An arched stone bridge crosses a creek mouth on the right. This pretty part of the river, with thin tree line on the left and wooded embankment on the right, arcs gently to the Hatchery Road bridge. There's a good place to take out on the grassy bank 50 yards upstream-right from the bridge, at a small wayside off Rocky Hill Road. The wayside has a toilet and a turnoff where several cars can be parked.

Another 3 miles—partly wooded, partly open, 45-50 feet wide, and quiet—takes you to the city of Baraboo. After a couple of very long, gentle bends following Hatchery Road, the river comes alongside Highway 136 on the left, then closely parallels the railroad again before passing under Highway 12. Rocky riffles and low-level rapids begin near the bridge.

The next place to **take out** is at Haskins Park, located on river-left upstream from the next bridge (Shaw Street); the grassy bank is adjacent to a parking lot, toilet, and picnic facilities. If you wish to paddle another half mile of riffles and rapids, you can follow the big loop around to Ochsner Park, and **take out** on the river-left grassy bank upstream from the metal-truss pedestrian bridge. Once the Linen Mill Dam on the eastern edge of Baraboo has been removed (scheduled for 2002), you'll be able to continue through the rest of the Baraboo Rapids and take out at the Highway 113 boat landing (downstream-right).

Other trips. Several miles downstream from Baraboo, Luebke Landing (on river-right, alongside County W) is a splendid access. Between Highway 113 and this landing there's a large logjam, but downstream from Luebke (or County X, upstream-right) the river is generally clear. From Luebke Landing (or County X), the river flows past the impressive bluffs of the Lower Narrows, then past steep banks to a difficult access at the second Highway 33 bridge (downstream-left, alongside a wayside). From here the Baraboo flows through floodplain forest to the Wisconsin River (see the map for Wisconsin River 4).

BARABOO RIVER 2

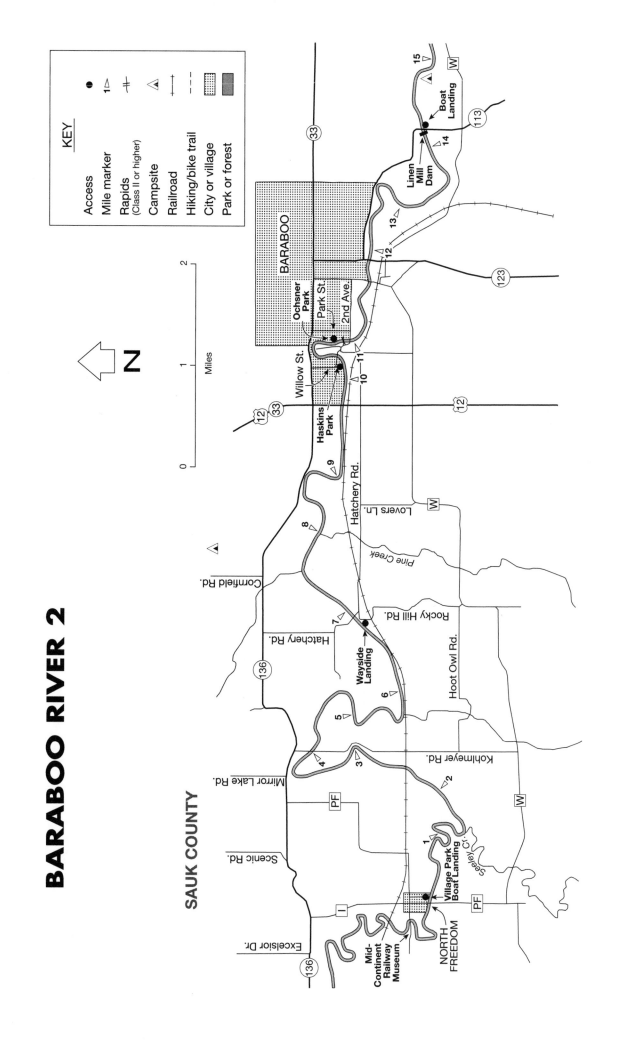

KEY

Access
Mile marker
Rapids (Class II or higher)
Campsite
Railroad
Hiking/bike trail
City or village
Park or forest

N

Miles
0   1   2

SAUK COUNTY

BARABOO

Ochsner Park
Park St
2nd Ave.
Willow St.
Haskins Park

Linen Mill Dam
Boat Landing

Wayside Landing

Mid-Continent Railway Museum
NORTH FREEDOM
Village Park Boat Landing

Excelsior Dr.
Scenic Rd.
Mirror Lake Rd.
Cornfield Rd.
Hatchery Rd.
Hatchery Rd.
Lovers Ln.
Pine Creek
Rocky Hill Rd.
Hoot Owl Rd.
Kohlmeyer Rd.
Seeley Ct.

136
33
12
33
12
12
123
113
136
W
W
W
PF
PF
PF
I

1
2
3
4
5
6
7
8
9
10
11
12
13
14
15

BARK RIVER 1
Prince's Point to County N (6.7 Miles)

The Big Puddle

Just a few miles downstream from the mouth of the Bark, the Rock River suddenly widens to form Wisconsin's second-largest natural lake. According to the famous surveyor and historian Increase Lapham, who described the area in detail in his book on prehistorical villages and mounds in Wisconsin (*Antiquities of Wisconsin,* 1852), the name *Koshkonong* is from a Native American word meaning "the lake we live on." Archeological evidence shows that people of different cultures have lived in the vicinity for almost 12,000 years, including several Ho Chunk villages in the 1700s and 1800s.

Today the 10,500-acre lake is a big attraction for fishermen, water-skiers, and jet ski enthusiasts. Nine miles long and 4.5 miles wide, Koshkonong is very shallow—no more than 7 feet—and generates dangerous waves when the wind is up. Downstream several miles the Indianford Dam on the Rock helps maintain a constant water level on the lake, which otherwise would revert to shallow marshland. Originally built in 1850, the dam was rebuilt in 1917 and periodically repaired since then. Numerous public boat landings, marinas, resorts, campgrounds, restaurants, and bars are found near the lake.

Originating at Bark Lake near Menomonee Falls, the Bark River twists for many miles toward the southwest, passing through farmland, marshes, hardwood forests, lakes, and a couple of small communities before joining the Rock River at Fort Atkinson. The most popular canoeing stretch on the river is the final westward leg from Prince's Point to Fort Atkinson, paddleable in one long trip or more sensibly in two leisurely day-trips.

The Bark has no remarkable scenic highlights, but is pleasantly isolated, with few signs of development. It passes through countryside that is flat or gently rolling, with thousands of acres of nearby wetlands. After Prince's Point the river flows placidly through woodlands, lowland marshes, and a few open areas. Usually suitable for beginners, it nevertheless requires occasional maneuvering around fallen trees and limbs. The colorful history of the area adds a nice touch for spending a day or two on the river.

Camping is available nearby at the Kettle Moraine State Forest Southern Unit a few miles north of Eagle (262-594-6200), Pilgrim's Campground 3 miles northwest of Fort Atkinson (920-563-8122 or 800-742-1697), Bark River Campground 2 miles southwest of Rome (262-593-2421), and Yogi Bear's Jellystone Park 4 miles south of Fort Atkinson (920-568-4100). Several additional campgrounds are located at the southwest end of Lake Koshkonong near Newville and Edgerton.

Canoe rentals are available in Madison at Rutabaga (608-223-9300) and Carl's Paddlin' (608-284-0300), and in Milwaukee at the Laacke and Joys downtown store (414-271-7878).

The **shuttle route** (5.5 miles) goes north a short distance on County D, west on Lower Hebron Road, and south a short distance on County N to the take-out bridge.

Gradient is negligible (less than a foot per mile).

For **water levels,** check the Rome gauge (#05426250) at the USGS Web site. See "Water Levels" in the introduction.

Put in at the Prince's Point Wildlife Area near the County D bridge, upstream-left, where an access road leads to a parking lot and gravel landing. If you have the time, you'll find it enjoyable to paddle upstream for a while, heading east for a little side trip on the Scuppernong River—a narrow, quiet, and intimate stream that joins the Bark a short distance from County D.

West of the put-in, the Bark is only about 40 feet wide and overhung with trees. Sometimes limbs in the water must be dodged. Then the river widens somewhat in a lowland environment where maples, willows, and marsh grass are plentiful.

After winding through a long and attractive marshy area, sometimes widening to as much as 100 feet, the river passes through a long, straight east-west stretch that has a channelized appearance. Then woods close in again on both sides, and curves resume. In a right bend a small metal bridge crosses a creek that enters on the left. Twice you can see farm buildings off in the distance, and at one point several radio towers are passed. Otherwise, the environs feel quite remote.

Eventually a big right bend carries the river alongside County N. **Take out** at the concrete boat landing on the left, upstream from the bridge. Burnt Village County Park, a popular spot for bank fishermen, is located here. A Ho Chunk (Winnebago) village dating back to the 1700s once stood at this location and was burned during a tribal conflict in the 1800s. During the Black Hawk War of 1832, U.S. troops who camped here named the site Burnt Village.

Other trips. The section of the river from Rome to Prince's Point is occasionally paddled, but access is a problem here, and a couple of old dams (one partially removed, at Hebron) must be dealt with. Farther upstream, in the Dousman area, the river is also good for paddling. A popular 6-mile trip starts at Lower Nemahbin Lake (put in at the DNR access on the lake at the end of Sugar Island Road, off Sawyer Road) and wends through marshes and woods to the Highway 18 wayside or to Main Street in Dousman.

A peaceful day on the Bark.

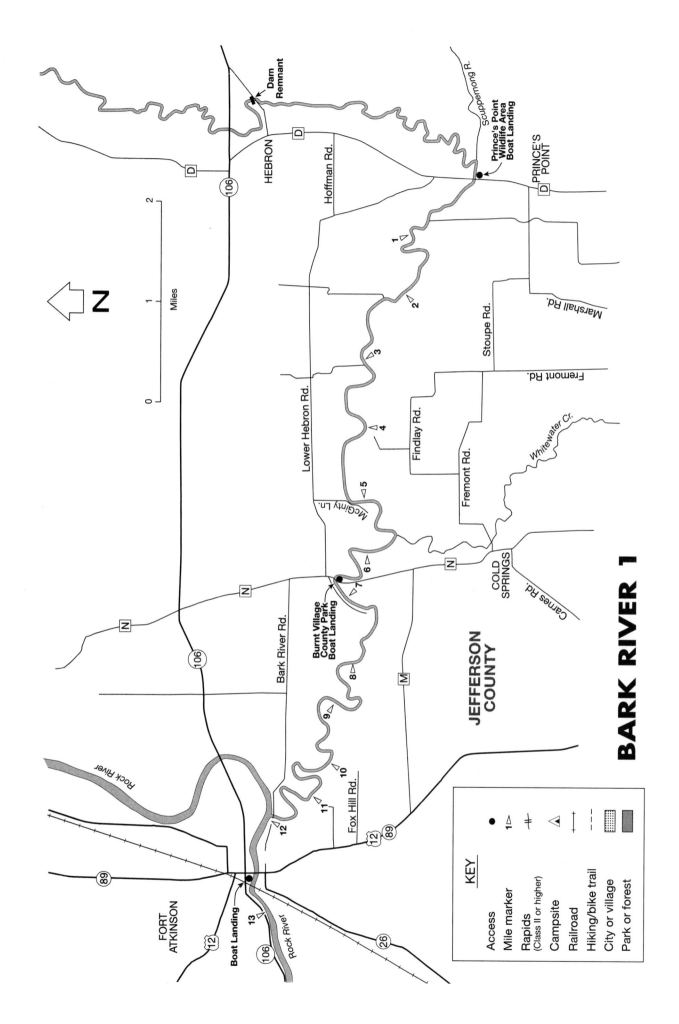

BARK RIVER 1

JEFFERSON COUNTY

KEY

- ● Access
- 1▷ Mile marker
- ╪ Rapids (Class II or higher)
- ◁ Campsite
- ┼ Railroad
- --- Hiking/bike trail
- ▦ City or village
- ▬ Park or forest

BARK RIVER 2
County N to Fort Atkinson (6 Miles)

Another pleasant day trip, this stretch of the Bark is as isolated as the previous section. There are a few open areas during the first half of the trip, but after that the surroundings are wild and the river passes through dense lowland forest, with sizable sloughs here and there. Accesses are first-rate, and obstructions are uncommon. The trip ends in the urban environs of Fort Atkinson.

For **camping, canoe rentals,** and **water levels,** see Bark River 1.

The **shuttle route** (3.8 miles) goes a short distance north on County N, then west on Bark River Road (which becomes Milwaukee Avenue in Fort Atkinson), north on South Main Street (Highway 12) across the Rock River, and finally west on Water Street to the boat landing.

A gentle flatwater section, this stretch has a minimal **gradient** of less than 1 foot per mile.

Put in upstream-left from the County N bridge at Burnt Village County Park. A gravel road parallels the river in the park, leading to a sizable parking area and a concrete boat ramp.

The trip begins with a very long left bend, where the streambed is 45 feet wide. Trees—especially maple and willow—line both banks, with occasional clearings. Periodically the river widens, and sloughs are frequent in bends. Increasingly, floodplain hardwood forest grows dense beyond the low banks. There are a few glimpses of farm fields, but no dwellings near the river. Marsh grass and lily pads sometimes appear along the edge, especially in sloughs.

For a considerable distance the river narrows and the environs become quite wild. Eventually, in the approach to Bark River Road, the river widens and turns right. At this point there's a very large island with a low metal bridge over the beginning of the narrow left channel. The main (right) channel heads toward Bark River Road, where bank fishermen are often seen along the low, river-right shoreline. This is a good alternate take-out, but there's little room for parking alongside the road. The right channel now loops left around the island, and you can soon see the other channel, with numerous metal pipes driven into the bottom at its mouth.

Coming back to the right, you begin passing houses on the outskirts of Fort Atkinson—the only buildings of the trip. After passing under the Milwaukee Avenue bridge, the Bark flows into the Rock River. Houses and docks line both sides of the 300-foot-wide Rock, but the setting is not unattractive. **Take out** a few hundred yards downstream from the Main Street bridge, at the public boat landing on river-right, upstream from a metal railroad bridge.

Other trips. For additional exposure to the Rock River, see the trip descriptions and maps for Rock River 1, 2, and 3, the Crawfish, and the Yahara elsewhere in this book.

Wisconsin's Mound Builders

Well worth a visit is a 5-acre Jefferson County park just south of Fort Atkinson, where 11 ancient effigy mounds are well-preserved and accessible. An estimated 1,400 years old, the mounds are in the shape of a bird, muskrat, lizard, turtle, heron, woodcock, fish, hawk, and several eagles. The park is located on the east side of Lake Koshkonong, on Koshkonong Mounds Road at Vinne Ha Ha Road.

Increase Lapham—an early surveyor, first president of the Wisconsin State Historical Society, and founder of the U.S. Weather Service—painstakingly located and sketched hundreds of Wisconsin mounds in the 1850s, including many in the Lake Koshkonong area. Archeologists estimate that as many as 15,000 mounds were built in Wisconsin over a 3,000-year period; modern development has destroyed almost half of these. Unlike the earlier conical mounds that were built to house the dead, and the later "platform mounds" found at Aztalan and elsewhere, the effigy mounds were unique to southern Wisconsin, and small areas in northern Illinois, eastern Iowa, and southeastern Minnesota.

While you're in the area, be sure to check out the "panther intaglio" effigy alongside Highway 106 on the western edge of Fort Atkinson. The only one of its kind, this 900-year-old effigy was scooped out of the earth instead of being built up.

Another location in southern Wisconsin where you can inspect ancient effigy mounds is Wyalusing State Park at the confluence of the Wisconsin and Mississippi Rivers (see Wisconsin River 12). To learn more about these fascinating structures, take a short drive across the Mississippi to Effigy Mounds National Monument, near Marquette, Iowa (west of Prairie du Chien), which has an excellent interpretive program.

Other well-preserved mounds in southern Wisconsin are found at Nelson Dewey, Perrot, Lake Kegonsa, Governor Nelson, and Devil's Lake State Parks. For more on Wisconsin's mounds, see the sidebar for Black River 5.

The remnant of the old dam on the Bark at Hebron.

BARK RIVER 2

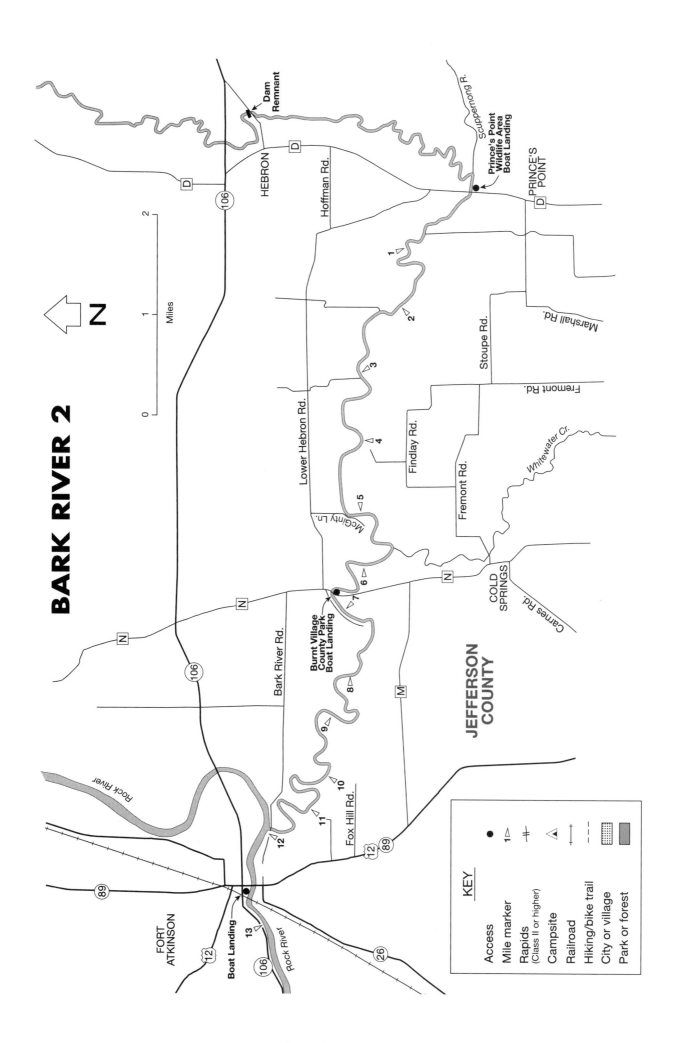

Dam Remnant

HEBRON

Prince's Point Wildlife Area Boat Landing

Scuppernong R.

PRINCE'S POINT

Hoffman Rd.

Marshall Rd.

Stoupe Rd.

Fremont Rd.

Findlay Rd.

Fremont Rd.

Whitewater Cr.

Lower Hebron Rd.

McGinty Ln.

COLD SPRINGS

Carnes Rd.

JEFFERSON COUNTY

Bark River Rd.

Burnt Village County Park Boat Landing

Fox Hill Rd.

Rock River

FORT ATKINSON

Boat Landing

Rock River

N

Miles

0   1   2

KEY

- ● Access
- 1 △ Mile marker
- ╫ Rapids (Class II or higher)
- ◁ Campsite
- ┼ Railroad
- --- Hiking/bike trail
- ▦ City or village
- ▨ Park or forest

BLACK RIVER 1
Neillsville to Lake Arbutus (12.5 Miles)

Eighteen miles north of Neillsville, where the Popple River joins the Black River, the previously placid Black becomes a whitewater river. Except for the impoundment of Lake Arbutus, the next 38 river-miles are relatively high in gradient and filled with boulders. Loaded with riffles and Class I-II rapids, this part of the river offers excellent springtime paddling for experienced whitewater boaters, but is unpaddleable when the water is low. Most of the surroundings are undeveloped, and rugged rock formations frequently add to the beauty of the wooded setting. Except during periods of higher water, when the river is quite dangerous, the water is clear and has a dark cast from iron, tannins, and other organic matter—thus the name Black.

For the upper part of the whitewater section, there are good accesses at the Popple River wayside north of Greenwood (alongside Highway 73) and at Greenwood County Park (just north of town), together with a couple of undeveloped accesses at county roads. However, the most popular run begins at Neillsville and continues all the way to Lake Arbutus. Beautiful and challenging, this stretch includes two mini-gorges, densely wooded shoreline, and few houses. Often there are low, grassy banks where you can easily stop to relax or scout. There are no big drops, but lots of high-gradient boulder beds. An excellent intermediate landing makes shorter runs possible.

Public **camping** is plentiful near Lake Arbutus: Russell County Park Campground on the west side (715-333-7948), West Arbutus County Campground nearby (715-284-8475), East Arbutus County Campground on the other side of the lake (715-284-0224), Sherwood County Park just north of the lake (715-743-5140), and East Fork State Campground east of the lake (715-284-4103). Camping is also available to the north at Greenwood County Park.

The **shuttle route** (approximately 13 miles) goes east a short distance on Hill Road, south on Grand Avenue through Neillsville, south on Highway 73, south and west on Highway 95, and south on Riviera Avenue.

The **gradient** is a riffle-and-rapid-filled six feet per mile.

For **water levels,** check the gauges at Neillsville (#05381000) and Black River Falls (#053813595) on the USGS Web site; the Neillsville gauge currently shows only stage levels. See "Water Levels" in the introduction.

Put in on river-right alongside Hill Road on the north edge of Neillsville, 0.3 mile west of the Grand Avenue bridge. A path leads from the road to the bank, either upstream or downstream from a small rapid, with plenty of room to park beside the road. The river is rather wide here, with a continuous shoreline of pines and deciduous trees—a typical setting for the whole trip. Class I boulder beds occur downstream in the left bend that approaches River Avenue, then in the right bend leading to the County B bridge. Note the lovely rock outcroppings on the left below the bridge. Mild rapids continue to the high, modern bridge at Highway 10.

After a relatively brief stretch of calm water, a long series of steep boulder gardens called the Lower Neillsville Rapids lead to a big right bend alongside Highway 73. Here, just upstream from the mouth of Cunningham Creek, the river narrows to 45 feet and speeds through a small, rocky gorge—a solid Class II under normal conditions. This part of the river gets quite pushy in high water and is filled with sharp, angular rocks that can be hard on boats and bodies.

Swinging away from the highway, the river flattens, with riffles and easy rapids here and there. Then, in a long left bend alongside Opelt Avenue, a public boat landing appears on the right, just downstream from a creek mouth. Downstream 1.3 miles is the next bridge, followed by a huge wooded island. Several big bends and a couple of straightaways—mostly flatwater—now lead to the Highway 95 bridge, which is preceded by the remains of an old dam on the left. A few yards downstream-left from the bridge is a fisherman's access that makes a good alternate take-out.

Another Class II stretch begins at Highway 95. Red Granite Rapids commences at the bridge, then quickly intensifies as the river narrows, steepens, and passes for several hundred yards through another beautiful little gorge. Ledges, boulders, and swift water make this an exciting place; huge waves form when the water is high. Before running the river, you can easily scout Red Granite Rapids from the old abutments accessed from Resewood Avenue or Riviera Avenue.

After the gorge the river gradually widens, gradient subsides, and homes and cabins begin to appear as the river slows for Lake Arbutus. **Take out** half a mile after Red Granite Rapids, at the river-right landing off Riviera Road, immediately downstream from a creek mouth.

Other trips. (1) In addition to the 21 river-miles north of Neillsville, springtime paddlers often canoe and kayak the East Fork of the Black. A 12-mile westward trip from Pray Road (2 miles north of the tiny community of Pray) to the East Fork State Campground is mostly quietwater paddling, but there are numerous riffles and Class I rapids. Putting in a few miles farther upstream at Steponik Road adds a couple of Class II-III rapids (for skilled whitewater paddlers only). (2) For a placid 12.4-mile section of the Black River north of Highway 29, see my *Paddling Northern Wisconsin*, p.18.

BLACK RIVER 1

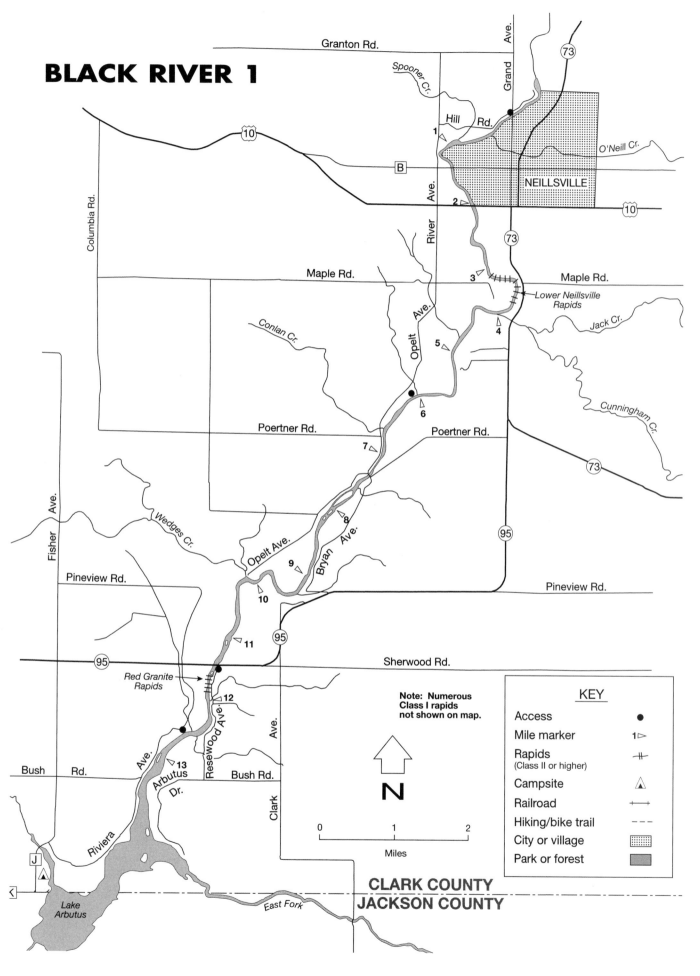

Granton Rd.

Spooner Cr.

Grand Ave.

73

Hill Rd.

1

B

River Ave.

O'Neill Cr.

NEILLSVILLE

10

10

2

73

Maple Rd.

3

Maple Rd.

Lower Neillsville Rapids

Jack Cr.

Opelt Ave.

4

5

Conlan Cr.

Cunningham Cr.

6

Poertner Rd.

Poertner Rd.

7

73

95

Wedges Cr.

Opelt Ave.

8

Bryan Ave.

Fisher Ave.

Pineview Rd.

9

10

Pineview Rd.

11

95

95

Sherwood Rd.

Red Granite Rapids

12

Resewood Ave.

Bush Rd.

13

Arbutus Dr.

Clark Ave.

Bush Rd.

Note: Numerous Class I rapids not shown on map.

N

0   1   2
Miles

J

Riviera Ave.

Lake Arbutus

East Fork

KEY

Access	●
Mile marker	1▷
Rapids (Class II or higher)	╫
Campsite	△
Railroad	┼┼┼
Hiking/bike trail	---
City or village	▦
Park or forest	▬

CLARK COUNTY
JACKSON COUNTY

BLACK RIVER 2
Hatfield to Hall's Creek Landing (7.2 Miles)

The steep, rocky channel of the Black below the Lake Arbutus Dam.

A popular whitewater run in the spring and after plentiful rainfall in the summer, this short stretch has several excellent play spots. When the water level is medium to high (i.e., at least 1,000 cfs) the stretch is pushy, with big waves and sticky holes—a great place for skilled paddlers to play for hours, and a good training ground for intermediate paddlers who want a taste of challenging, higher-volume whitewater. Play boaters generally shorten the trip by taking out at the powerhouse, just downstream from the best rapid of the stretch. Paddlers who aren't completely preoccupied with the whitewater will be pleased with the beautiful setting, especially the rugged igneous and metamorphic rock formations and huge boulders found alongside and in the water.

Since 1997 water has been released for whitewater paddlers from the Lake Arbutus Dam by the Hatfield Hydro Partnership on the third Saturday of April, May, June, July, and August. Hopefully this practice will continue beyond the 5-year trial period that was agreed to as part of the dam relicensure process in the mid-1990s. A recorded phone message provides information on the release schedule and the anticipated volume of release in cubic feet per second. During most of the year the volume is too low for pleasant paddling in this section. Early-spring paddlers must be aware of both the Class II-III rapids and the risk of hypothermia.

For **camping,** see Black River 1.

The **shuttle route** (6.3 miles) goes west on Clay School Road, north on County K, west on County E, and east on Hall's Creek Landing Road. The shuttle (4.1 miles) for a shorter trip goes west on Clay School Road, north on County K, west on County E, and south on Powerhouse Road to the powerhouse.

Gradient for the full 7.2-mile section is a brisk 10.4 feet per mile, but most of the gradient (17.7 feet per mile) is in the 3.1-mile stretch before the powerhouse.

For **water levels** on dam-release days, call for the recorded message at 888-HYDROWI. Also check the gauges upstream at Neillsville (#05381000) and downstream at Black River Falls (#053813595) on the USGS Web site. See "Water Levels" in the introduction.

Put in along the rocky, river-left shoreline a couple hundred yards downstream from the dam. A long path leads to the river through the woods from Clay School Road (where the road turns east); when you reach a steep embankment at the end of the trail, carry or drag your boat(s) a little farther upstream and put in between two wavy constrictions. This put-in is excellent for play boaters because the constrictions are good for surfing and pop-ups. The short stretch upstream to the dam is a beautiful gorge with a series of awesome Class IV–V drops and holes. A much easier put-in is the sandy bank at the County K bridge, upstream-left; all that you miss by starting here are a couple of play spots.

Just downstream from the County K bridge is a big, rocky island. The left channel tends to be shallow, but the right channel forms big waves and is another good place to surf. In the long flatwater stretch that follows, the shoreline is densely wooded with both deciduous and coniferous trees, and stone formations continue to be gorgeous.

After a right turn, another Class II rapid begins at a small rocky island, dropping and rushing for several hundred yards through big boulders. There's a short, placid stretch of 100 yards before Stairstep Rapids begins in a left curve, continuing in a right bend for a couple hundred yards. The best rapid of the day, it can be a Class III in higher water conditions. Most of the flow is to the left of a big rocky outcrop in the river; to the right is a series of complex, difficult drops (thus, stairstep). There are huge boulders in the water, and—as usual—an impressive rocky shoreline.

Immediately after Stairstep, the river becomes peaceful again and quickly turns left to the powerhouse, where there's a shorter Class II rapid. Paddlers who wish to take out here can do so immediately downstream-right from the powerhouse and carry their boats over the steep riprap to the nearby parking area. Be careful of turbulence when water is being discharged.

The remaining stretch from the powerhouse to Hall's Creek is a transition area between the rock-strewn, steep gradient of the upper Black and the sandy, peaceful quietwater of the lower Black. A couple of rapids remain, but not as intense. Approximately a mile after the powerhouse, an 18-inch ledge is found in the left channel of an island. The scenery continues to be good all the way to Hall's Creek, where an excellent gravel landing is located just downstream-right from the mouth, near a sizeable asphalt parking lot. Hall's Creek Landing is a very comfortable and convenient **take-out.**

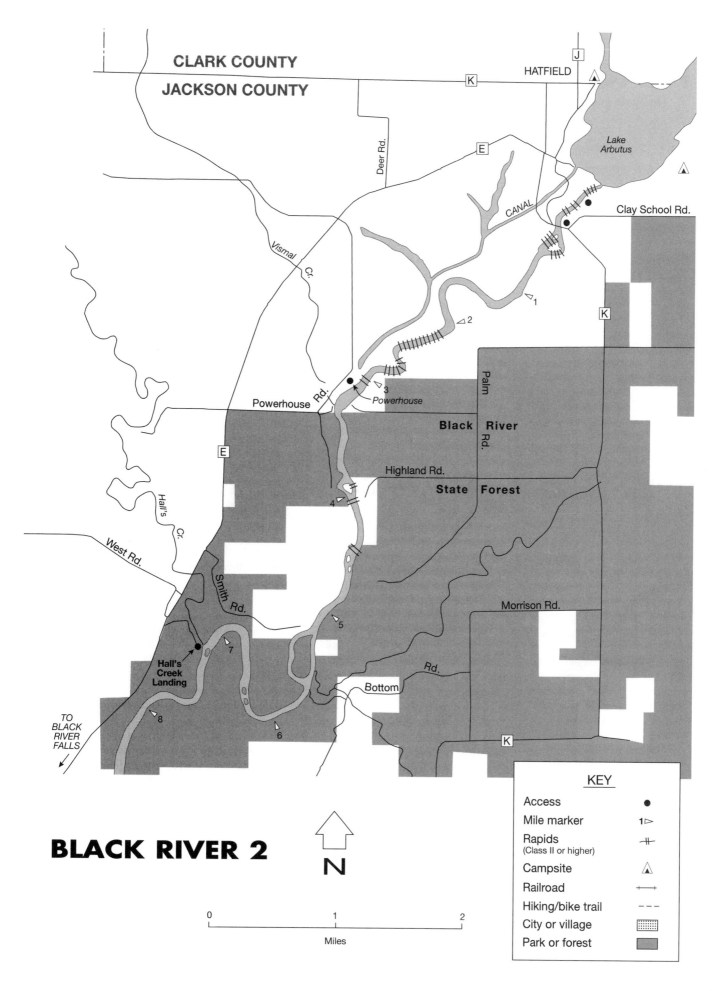

CLARK COUNTY

JACKSON COUNTY

HATFIELD

K

J

Lake
Arbutus

E

CANAL

Clay School Rd.

Vismal
Cr.

Deer Rd.

⊲ 1

⊲ 2

K

Powerhouse
Rd.

⊲ 3
Powerhouse

Black River

Palm
Rd.

E

Hall's
Cr.

Highland Rd.

State Forest

West Rd.

4

Morrison Rd.

Smith
Rd.

⊲ 5

Hall's
Creek
Landing

⊲ 7

Rd.

TO
BLACK
RIVER
FALLS

⊲ 8

⊲ 6

Bottom

K

BLACK RIVER 2

N

KEY

Access	●
Mile marker	1▷
Rapids (Class II or higher)	╫
Campsite	◬
Railroad	┼─┼
Hiking/bike trail	– – –
City or village	▦
Park or forest	▬

0   1   2

Miles

BLACK RIVER 3
Hall's Creek Landing to Black River Falls (6.2 Miles)

Where Did Wisconsin Get Its Names?

As any paddler knows, many of Wisconsin's streams, lakes, and cities derive their names from Native American words and phrases. Indeed, the trips described in this book provide many examples. But there are many other name sources as well. (a) Quite early, for instance, the French left their linguistic imprint across the state with such now-familiar names as Baraboo, Eau Claire, La Crosse, Montello, Portage, Prairie du Sac, Racine, and the Dells. (b) As settlers came to Wisconsin from Europe or the eastern United States, they often brought with them the names of their home communities, such as Albany (N.Y.), Berlin (Germany), New Lisbon (Ohio), and Wyalusing (Pa.). (c) Many Wisconsin places still bear the name of an early settler who built the first mill, established a ferry, or otherwise put a community on the map. A few familiar examples are Gays Mills, Hustisford, Janesville, Stevens Point, Mauston, Thiensville, and Neillsville.

Other sources of names include (d) words suggesting physical characteristics of a place (Rock River, Big Bend, Black River), (e) military or historical figures (Fort Atkinson, Madison, Dodgeville, Allouez), and many other less common origins.

If you want to delve into this interesting subject, two books are recommended: Robert Gard and L. G. Sorden's *Romance of Wisconsin Place Names*, and Virgil J. Vogel's *Indian Names on Wisconsin's Map* (see the bibliography in Appendix 2).

By the time the Black River reaches Hall's Creek, its turbulence has subsided. Having widened because of the added volume of one tributary after another, it is now relatively flat all the way to its junction with the Mississippi, with no more boulder-beds or rapids. The last remaining drop on the river—feared by lumbermen during the logging era—now lies harmlessly under the dam at Black River Falls.

This stretch has a character all its own. Suitable for beginners, it starts in a wild setting and ends in a semideveloped area, but is wooded all the way. The scenery is outstanding: beautiful rock formations, often topped with coniferous trees, are like those found in the wilds of Canada. Current is slack, and there are few of the sandbars that are associated with the lower river. Accesses are excellent.

In addition to the Hatfield-area campgrounds listed in Black River 1, **camping** is available at the Castle Mound State Campground 1.5 miles southeast of Black River Falls (715-284-4103), Wazee Lake Recreation Area 6 miles east of Black River Falls (715-284-3171), Pigeon Creek State Campground 11 miles southeast of Black River Falls (715-284-4103), Lost Falls Resort and Campground 8 miles south of Black River Falls (800-329-3911 or 715-284-7133), Jamboree Campground 4 miles north of Black River Falls (888-345-CAMP or 715-284-7138), and Parkland Village Campground near Black River Falls (715-284-9700).

The **shuttle route** (6.6 miles) goes west on Hall's Creek Landing Road, south on County E, south on Highway 12/27, east on Highway 54 across the bridge, and north on Roosevelt Street to the public landing.

Gradient is negligible (less than a foot per mile).

For **water levels,** check the Black River Falls gauge (#053813595) on the USGS Web site. See "Water Levels" in the introduction.

Put in at the gravel landing at the end of Hall's Creek Landing Road, off County E. An asphalt parking lot is located nearby. Heavily wooded and 150 feet wide, the river flows over a sand-and-rock bottom and bends right alongside high bluffs. Just before a left turn, impressive cliffs appear; gigantic chunks of rock have fallen to the river-left shoreline. As the long left bend continues, there are more outcroppings on the right. Small, sandy beaches occasionally line the shore.

In succeeding bends, the rock formations become increasingly beautiful—often covered with pines, ferns, and wildflowers. Periodically, streamlets can be seen flowing down the bluffs. Current grows slower, and the water deeper. In a left turn three old cabins appear on the right—the first dwellings of the trip.

After a long straightaway the river heads sharply right. Here gorgeous, undercut rock formations line both shorelines. Within sight is a tall railroad bridge, immediately followed by a large wooded island. Two sets of power lines cross after the island, and traffic noise from nearby Highway 12 can be heard. In the long left bend after the bridge the river starts looking more "civilized," with cabins and docks on both sides for a while. Rock formations almost disappear, but the environs are still heavily wooded.

In the straight stretch that follows, private landings appear opposite one another. Downstream the river heads to the right at an attractive, river-right stone outcropping near several wooden bears. The bridges of Interstate 94 follow, and soon you can see the dam in the distance. Cabins continue along the banks, but the shoreline remains wooded.

As you pass under another set of power lines, the last rock outcroppings of the trip appear on both sides. The flowage of the Black River Falls Dam is never wide. **Take out** at the concrete boat ramp on the left, just upstream from the warning buoys for the hydroelectric dam. A parking lot is located nearby. Before you leave, take a few minutes to look at the massive rock formations just below the dam; these were once part of the original Black River Falls.

BLACK RIVER 3

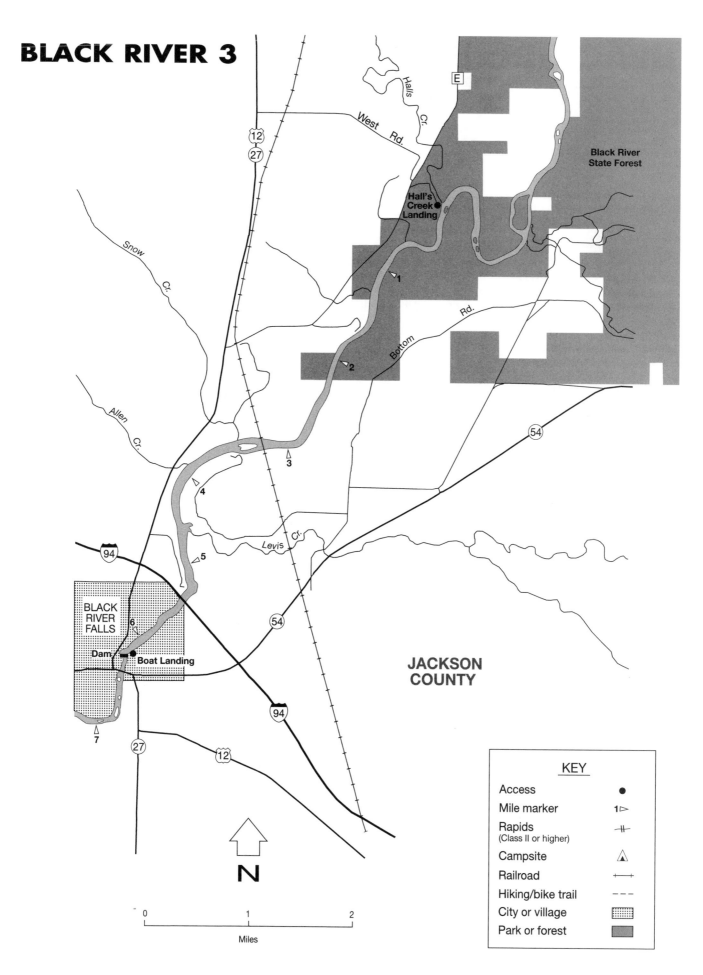

Black River
State Forest

Hall's
Creek
Landing

West Rd.

Halls Cr.

Snow Cr.

Allen Cr.

Bottom Rd.

Levis Cr.

BLACK
RIVER
FALLS

Dam

Boat Landing

JACKSON
COUNTY

N

| 0 | 1 | 2 |

Miles

KEY

Access	●
Mile marker	1▷
Rapids (Class II or higher)	╫
Campsite	△
Railroad	+++
Hiking/bike trail	- - -
City or village	▦
Park or forest	▨

BLACK RIVER 4
Black River Falls to Irving (12.2 Miles)

A Short Hike with a Spectacular View

There's a lot to do in the 66,000 acres of the Black River State Forest, including canoeing, skiing, camping, wildlife observation, biking, and horseback riding. You'll see part of the forest along the riverbanks (Black River 2, 3, 4), but for the most impressive overview of the area, head for Castle Mound. Accessed from Highway 12, two miles southeast of Black River Falls, the "mound" is actually a 200-foot-high, half-mile-long sandstone outlier—one of a series of striking buttes that rise from the countryside. A 1.5-mile hiking trail leads to the top of Castle Mound. To the east you can see several other rocky prominences (Belle Mound, Wildcat Mound, and The Ridge), and the area that was once the bed of Glacial Lake Wisconsin. An observation tower makes the view even better. If you have the time, you can hike or bike 4.5 miles from Castle Mound to the attractive gorge of Perry Creek, near its confluence with the Black.

Undercut rock walls along the lower Black.

Because it has relatively few of the big sandbars that make the downstream sections of the Black so popular, you won't see large numbers of fellow paddlers on this stretch. Most of the trip features the isolation and peacefulness that are typical characteristics of the Black. The surroundings are generally quite wild, with only a few dwellings during the second half of the trip. In addition to some small rock outcroppings along the way, there's a spectacular cliff. Multiple accesses make it easy to design trips of various lengths or to plan multiday paddling ventures.

For **camping** in the area, see Black River 3. On the sections of the river below Black River Falls, paddlers often camp on sandbars and beaches. Please stay off private property that is posted, however, and set up camp only in places where you'll be safe if the water rises. When wading, be careful of drop-offs downstream from sandbars.

Canoe rental and shuttle service are available at Lost Falls Resort and Campground south of Black River Falls (715-284-7133 or 800-329-3911), Riverview Inn at North Bend (608-488-5191), Wazee Sports Center and Black River Canoe Rental on West Highway 54 (715-284-5181), and Black River Express Canoe Rental at Melrose (608-488-7017). Flasher's Canoe Camping Trips (Wilton) offers guided trips on the Black (608-435-6802).

The **shuttle route** (8.4 miles) goes north on South Third Street; west, then south on Highway 54; east on John Deere Road; and south on Nichols Road across the Trout Run bridge. The shuttle is through attractive rolling terrain.

Gradient is 1.6 feet per mile.

For **water levels**, see Black River 3.

Put in at the Bruce Cormican Canoe Landing at the end of South Third Street in Black River Falls. A trail leads from the parking lot, over a levee, to a sandy beach. Heavily forested, the river begins with a long left bend past some modest rock outcroppings. The environment is wonderfully tranquil as the river straightens, then gently begins bending left again at some power lines. Keep an eye out for eagles.

In the long right arc that follows, a large stand of pines towers on the left. An attractive sandy shelf on the right is quickly succeeded by a small pine-covered cliff on the left. Soon thereafter there's a public boat landing at Perry Creek Park on the left—an excellent access. The park has toilets and picnic facilities.

Before long, the river divides around huge Hawk Island, where the main flow is on the right side. Compared to the 125-foot width upstream from the island, the right channel is narrow and riffly. One hundred yards downstream from an inlet on the right, Mason's Landing appears on the right shoreline—a convenient gravel access with a gravel parking area off Old 54 Road. Not far downstream from the landing is the tail of Hawk Island.

Spring Creek enters as the river swings left, then heads back to the right. There have still been no dwellings and few sandbars. When the long right bend ends at a sharp left turn, however, there's a huge sandy beach on the left, opposite erosion-retardant riprap on the high right shoreline. In the next turn, another big sand-and-gravel beach is found on the right. The first cabins and houses of the trip appear in the following turns, especially in a long right bend before Robinson Creek.

In the big left bend that follows the mouth of Robinson Creek, the river pulls alongside Highway 54, and, suddenly, gorgeous sandstone cliffs loom ahead. A wooded island and a high sandbank immediately precede the sheer rock formation, which is crowned with coniferous trees. The layered, multicolored cliffs are certainly a highlight of the trip. The river now straightens for a while, then starts heading back toward Highway 54 in another long right bend. The final left turn quickly takes you under some power lines to the **take-out** at Irving Landing—a small opening on the bank just downstream-right from the mouth of Trout Run. Undeveloped, the landing is easy to miss. There's room alongside the grassy shoulder of Nichols Road to park a few cars.

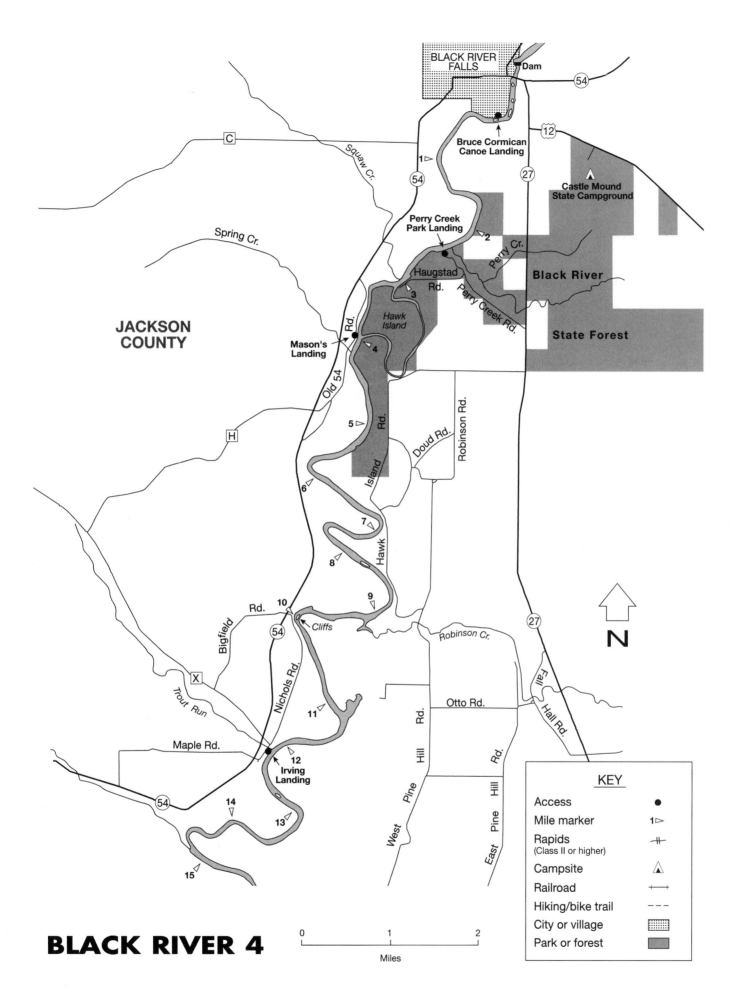

BLACK RIVER FALLS

Dam

54

Bruce Cormican
Canoe Landing

C

Squaw Cr.

Spring Cr.

54

1 ▷

Perry Creek
Park Landing

27

Castle Mound
State Campground

Perry Cr.

2 ◁

Haugstad
Rd.

Black River

3 ◁

Perry Creek Rd.

JACKSON
COUNTY

Hawk
Island

State Forest

Rd.

Mason's
Landing

4 ◁

Old 54

H

5 ▷

Island Rd.

Doud Rd.

Robinson Rd.

6 ◁

7 ◁

Hawk

8 ◁

9 ▽

27

Robinson Cr.

Bigfield   Rd.   10

54

Cliffs

Nichols Rd.

X

Trout Run

Otto Rd.

Fall   Hall Rd.

11 ◁

West   Pine   Hill   Rd.

East   Pine   Hill   Rd.

Maple Rd.

12
Irving
Landing

54

14 ▽

13 ◁

15 ▽

KEY

Access   ●
Mile marker   1 ▷
Rapids   ‖
(Class II or higher)
Campsite   △
Railroad   ┼─┼
Hiking/bike trail   - - -
City or village
Park or forest

N

0   1   2

Miles

BLACK RIVER 4

33

BLACK RIVER 5
Irving to Melrose (11.5 Miles)

The Mysterious Mounds of Aztalan

Although thousands of mounds constructed by prehistoric cultures in Wisconsin have been destroyed by plowing or development, many are still to be found in the southern part of the state. Built in linear, conical, or round form, or in the shape of animals (effigies), these fascinating structures served a variety of purposes: ceremonial, astronomical, political, religious, and funereal. As many as 15,000 mounds were painstakingly built in Wisconsin over several millenia, mostly by the people of the Woodland culture. Despite a century and a half of archaeological research and field work, much is still unknown about the mounds.

The most mysterious of all are the unique structures discovered in 1836 on the banks of the Crawfish River a few miles northwest of Jefferson. Between 900 and 1200 A.D. there was a thriving community here, partly within a high stockade with huge mounds at the corners. The inhabitants hunted, cultivated corn, beans, and squash, and fished; the remains of a rocky fish weir can still be found in the Crawfish at low water. Uniquely, archaeological digs have shown a relationship not only to the Woodland culture but also to the Middle Mississippians who created the magnificent mounds at Cahokia near St. Louis. No one knows why the people of Aztalan disappeared around 1200 A.D. Today, if you visit the site, you can take a self-guided walking tour, using a free guidebook provided by the park.

For the next 24 river-miles, you're likely to see many other canoeists on warm, sunny weekends. Plentiful sandbars for relaxation and camping, beautiful scenery, and the ready availability of rental canoes are a big draw for paddlers, whether beginning or experienced. Big, gentle bends, steady current, and the absence of rapids make this part of the river ideal for lazy float trips, including multiday canoe-camping ventures. Sandstone cliffs and a delightful box canyon make the setting even more picturesque. Houses are quite sparse on this section. In addition to the adequate landing at the put-in and the splendid boat ramp near Melrose, there's an excellent intermediate landing and a riverside campground. Numerous accesses on the Black make it possible for you to design trips ranging from a couple of hours to several days.

For **camping**, see Black River 3 and 4. On this section, riverside camping is available at Lost Falls Resort and Campground (715-284-7133 or 800-329-3911), which can also be used as a put-in or take-out.

For **canoe rentals**, see Black River 4.

The **shuttle route** (9.4 miles) goes north on Nichols Road, west on John Deere Road, south on Highway 54, and south on Highway 108 to the bridge.

Gradient is 2.2 feet per mile.

For **water levels**, see Black River 3.

Put in on river-right near the small community of Irving, immediately downstream from the mouth of Trout Run. The landing is an undeveloped bank, with room to park a few cars along the grassy shoulder of Nichols Road. After the put-in, the river is 125 feet wide and curves left past a stand of pine trees and high sandbanks on the right. In the long right bend that follows, big beaches begin to appear. A large cedar home comes into view when the

Sheer cliffs are a frequent highlight of the Black.

river heads left. Then as soon as you turn right, the Lost Falls Resort and Campground canoe landing can be seen on the right, quickly followed by a sharp left turn at a very high sandy bank.

At the river-right mouth of Roaring Creek, just upstream from a log cabin, you won't regret beaching your canoe(s) and walking upstream. There you'll find a couple of lovely 10-foot cascades in a steep-walled sandstone canyon. Downstream the river environs become quite wild and remote-feeling. Side sloughs appear occasionally.

After winding around for a while, the river comes to a tall bluff covered with red pines. At the bluff's base is a beautiful, undercut rock shelf, the first rock formation of the trip. Deflected sharply to the left by the bluff, the river quickly approaches an excellent public landing on the right, off River Road.

After the landing the river continues past numerous sandbars and through a wonderfully isolated setting, interrupted only by a set of power lines that cross within view of some silos. Finally, in the long right bend toward Highway 71, there are additional rock formations like the previous one. The big highlight, however, comes a few minutes before the take-out. A few hundred yards upstream from the long island that precedes the bridge is a spectacular 80-foot cliff—sheer and multicolored.

Take out downstream from the Highway 108 bridge at the river-left boat ramp, a busy place on weekends. The village of Melrose is 1.5 miles to the north.

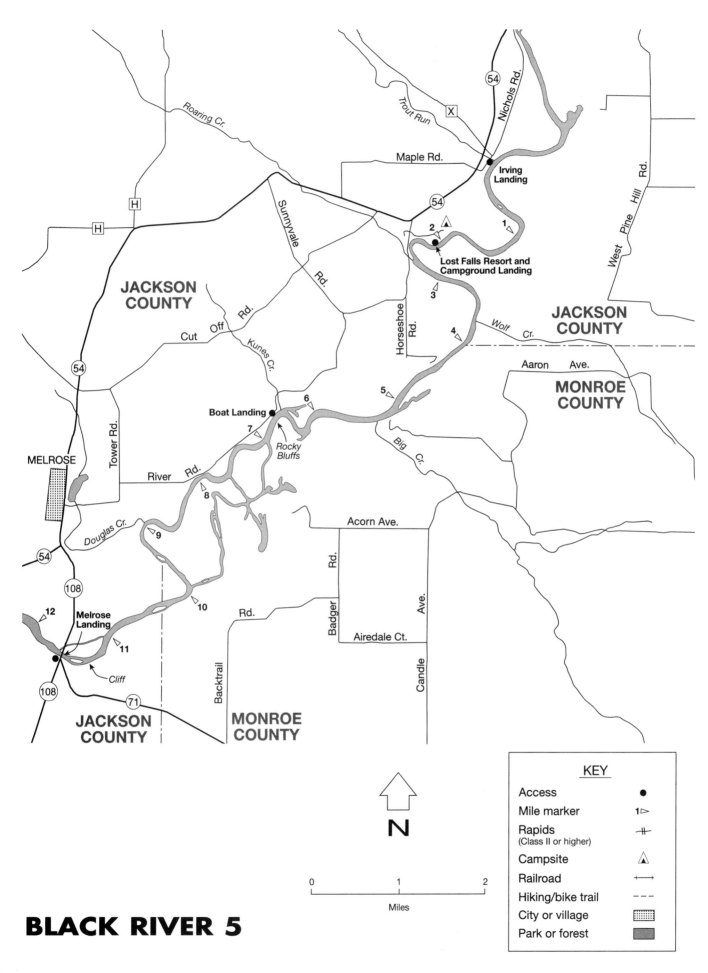

BLACK RIVER 5

Roaring Cr.

54

Trout Run

X

Nichols Rd.

Maple Rd.

Irving Landing

54

West Pine Hill Rd.

H

H

Sunnyvale Rd.

JACKSON COUNTY

2

Lost Falls Resort and Campground Landing

1

3

Cut Off Rd.

Kunes Cr.

Horseshoe Rd.

4

Wolf Cr.

JACKSON COUNTY

Aaron Ave.

MONROE COUNTY

54

Tower Rd.

Boat Landing

6

5

Big Cr.

7

MELROSE

Rocky Bluffs

River Rd.

8

Douglas Cr.

9

Acorn Ave.

Rd.

54

108

10

Rd.

Badger Rd.

Candle Ave.

Airedale Ct.

12

Melrose Landing

11

Cliff

108

71

Backtrail

JACKSON COUNTY

MONROE COUNTY

N

| 0 | | 1 | | 2 |

Miles

KEY

Access ●

Mile marker 1▷

Rapids ―╫―
(Class II or higher)

Campsite ▲

Railroad ⊢―――⊣

Hiking/bike trail – – –

City or village ▦

Park or forest ▨

BLACK RIVER 6
Melrose to North Bend (9.4 Miles)

Like Old Wine

There are many excellent, recent books related to the rivers of Wisconsin (see Appendix 2 for a selective list of some of them). But in addition to these there are a few "antique" books that still make good reading and thus deserve special mention. In each, the charm lies not only in the historical detail and the river descriptions, but also in the marvelously quaint but elegant style of writing.

Especially recommended is *Down Historic Waterways* by Reuben Gold Thwaites, a noted historian and longtime head of the State Historical Society of Wisconsin. In 1887 Thwaites paddled 600 miles on the Rock, Fox, and Wisconsin Rivers and in 1890 published a delightful account of his experiences. In some ways the rivers have changed a great deal, but in other ways they sound exactly the same.

Another book that has aged well is *Wau-bun: Early Days in the Northwest* by Juliette Magill Kinzie, wife of the Indian agent at Fort Winnebago (Portage), then at Fort Dearborn (Chicago). Her autobiographical work—first published in 1885—is a classic account of daily life on the Wisconsin and Illinois frontier in the 1830s. The Fox and Chicago Rivers (among others) figure significantly in this engaging story.

Devotees of the Black sometimes describe it as "a little Wisconsin River." Like the Lower Wisconsin, the Black River downstream from Black River Falls is a wonderful place for scenic, relaxed float trips. Both rivers are blessed with sandbars, undeveloped surroundings, periodic rock formations, excellent accesses, and other inducements that keep paddlers coming back. The Black is by no means a small river, but compared with the Wisconsin it offers a relatively intimate experience.

The section from Melrose to North Bend is the single most popular stretch on the Black. Like all of the other sections downstream from Hall's Creek Landing, it is suitable for beginners. The river here is even more isolated, with lovely cliffs occasionally punctuating the forested shoreline. Width ranges from 70 to 200 feet.

For **camping**, see Black River 3 and 4. Camping is also available between North Bend and Galesville at the Pow Wow Campground located along the river upstream-right from the Highway 53 bridge (608-582-2995), and at Sandman's Campground a mile south of the Highway 53 bridge (608 526-4956).

For **canoe rental,** see Black River 4.

The **shuttle route** (8 miles) goes north on Highway 108, west on Highway 54 into North Bend, and south on North Bend Drive to the landing alongside the Riverview Inn. Highway 54 from Melrose to North Bend passes through beautiful, hilly and winding countryside.

Gradient is 2.7 feet per mile.

For **water levels,** see Black River 3.

Put in at the concrete boat ramp downstream-left from the Highway 108 bridge, 1.5 miles south of Melrose. A couple of low, bushy islands follow the bridge, together with some cabins on the right. When the river heads left, there's a long, steep 50-foot sandbank on the right, and Highway 54 traffic can be seen briefly on top. Huge, sandy beaches are frequent and invite stops.

Later, in a big left bend 20-foot cliffs appear on the right—layered, multicolored, and topped with coniferous trees. A cabin looks out from the top of the cliff at the end. At one point there is a narrow cleft in the cliff; if you beach your boat here and walk into the small gorge, you'll find water falling into a pool from a hanging canyon.

After the mouth of Davis Creek, the river bends to the right, and a more impressive line of cliffs begins on the right, often jutting out over the water. These unique and beautiful outcroppings, rough-hewn by wind and water, continue for a long time in a straightaway. A long right bend follows the straightaway, then a big left one. In the left arc, there are more rock formations on the right, but not as extensive as the last series. After another straight stretch the river bends right, then straightens again. The setting here is densely wooded and wild.

Eventually you come to the head of a huge island where a sign advises canoeists to keep right. (The narrow left channel leads to the County V bridge, but is often choked with deadfall.) The main (right) channel bends around to the landing at North Bend. **Take out** on the right immediately upstream from the Riverview Inn. The gravel-and-concrete landing is just downstream from the mouth of Mill Creek, and can be quite crowded on weekends and holidays. The buildings of North Bend are the first in a long time. Be careful of the tricky eddy and quick current at the landing. You can also continue to the County VV bridge and **take out** at the public landing 100 yards upstream-left, behind some small, grassy islands.

Other trips. Also pleasant is the 12.6-mile section from North Bend to Highway 53, about 3 miles east of Galesville. There's an excellent landing 50 yards downstream-left from the Highway 53 bridge.

Relaxing in a side canyon of the Black.

BLACK RIVER 6

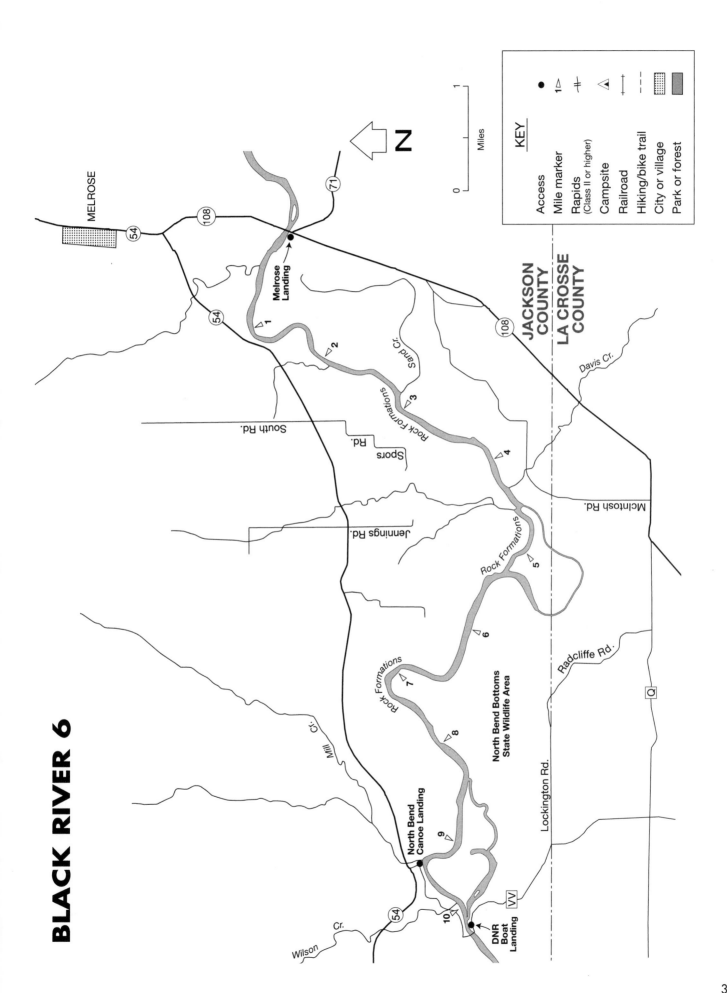

MELROSE

KEY

●	1△	╫	◁	╎	╌╌	▦	▨

Access

Mile marker

Rapids
(Class II or higher)

Campsite

Railroad

Hiking/bike trail

City or village

Park or forest

Miles

N

Melrose Landing

JACKSON COUNTY

LA CROSSE COUNTY

Sand Cr.

Rock Formations

South Rd.

Spors Rd.

Jennings Rd.

McIntosh Rd.

Davis Cr.

Rock Formations

Radcliffe Rd.

Q

Rock Formations

North Bend Bottoms
State Wildlife Area

Lockington Rd.

Mill Cr.

North Bend
Canoe Landing

VV

DNR Boat
Landing

Wilson Cr.

CHIPPEWA RIVER 1
Eau Claire to Caryville (12.8 Miles)

It would be difficult to overestimate the importance of the Chippewa River in Wisconsin's history. Together with its main tributaries—the Flambeau, Court Oreilles, Eau Claire, Red Cedar, Jump, and Yellow—its drainage basin covers one-sixth of the state's total area. A water highway for Native Americans, explorers, missionaries, traders, and settlers, it was part of an important seventeenth- and eighteenth-century route from Lake Superior to the Mississippi (via the Bad River and the West Branch of the Chippewa). The Chippewa became the state's largest and most important source of white pine during the logging era of the 1800s. In 1885 alone, more than 600 million logs were floated down the Chippewa to mills in Chippewa Falls and Eau Claire, and to other mills farther downstream on the Mississippi.

Except for a few important drops where power dams were developed for mills and other industries (e.g., at Chippewa Falls and Eau Claire), the lower half of the

The Chippewa is an excellent canoe-camping river.

Chippewa has a gentle but steady gradient that results in consistently brisk currents. Usually rather wide, it often resembles the Wisconsin River, including wild, wooded shorelines, sandbars, and beaches. If small streams are your sole source of paddling enjoyment, you probably should look elsewhere. But you might be pleasantly surprised and find that the Chippewa indeed is an unjustifiably neglected canoeing river.

The first recommended day trip begins in the city of Eau Claire but passes almost entirely through densely wooded countryside. An excellent bike trail—the Chippewa River State Trail—runs parallel to this route, making bike shuttles or peddle/paddle trips easy. Accesses are first-rate, including a good intermediate landing that makes it possible to vary trip length. There are relatively few sandbars on this stretch.

Camping is available at Elmer's Campground 4.5 miles east of Eau Claire (715-832-6277), Camp O'Klare a couple miles southeast of Eau Claire (715-832-7379), and at Lake Wissota State Park near Chippewa Falls, to the north (715-382-4574). For several additional campgrounds to the east, see Eau Claire River 3.

Canoe and kayak rentals and shuttles are available at Riverside Bike and Skate in Eau Claire (715-835-0088). Canoes also may be rented at GD Odds Inc. in Eau Claire (715-833-1942).

The **shuttle route** (9.2 miles) goes west on Menomonie Street, south on Ferry Street, west on Crescent Avenue, south on 960th Street, and south on County H

to the bridge.

Gradient is 1.6 feet per mile.

For **water levels,** check the Durand gauge (#05369500) on the USGS Web site. See "Water Levels" in the introduction. For general information on water levels (high, medium, low), call Riverside Bike and Skate (715-835-0088).

Put in on river-right at Hobbs Landing, a concrete ramp (with adjacent parking), not far from the Hobbs Ice Arena, off Menomonie Street in Eau Claire. Quickly, the river passes under a railroad bridge (now used for a bike trail), then the twin bridges of Highway 12 (Claremont Avenue). There are still a number of old wooden pilings to avoid under the bike-trail bridge. At a big island the river now bends left, and you can see the high mound called Mount Washington to the right. The Short Street bridge soon appears, followed by another large island. When the river heads to the right, the Interstate 94 bridges appear; by this time, houses and other buildings have stopped. Downstream on the left Lowes Creek enters near some unsightly concrete riprap.

The river now becomes wide and lake-like for a while, with a series of pretty islands. A long left bend begins, with a few houses, a set of power lines, and more islands. Eventually the Silver Mine Ski Jump appears on the right, several hundred yards from the river. Soon after a right bend begins, Highway 85 can be seen atop the high bank on the left. A couple of shelters mark the location of a wayside where you can take out (or put in) at a sandy landing, with picnic tables, parking, and water.

Soon after the wayside, there's lots of yellow on the left: a Caterpillar parts dealership. In the following left bend, the setting becomes quite wild as a high wooded ridge runs along the right shoreline. A couple of sets of power lines pass overhead, near rock outcroppings, in this quiet and beautiful part of the river. Several curves and a straightaway follow. In a left bend, an attractive 50-yard-long rock outcropping appears at the base of the bluff on river-right. Several hundred yards later is Yellow Banks, a high, 45-degree sandbank on the right; this landmark stands out because everything else is grassy or forested. Downstream from Yellow Banks, big sandbars and sand cut banks begin appearing, but not for long.

A very long and remote-feeling right bend leads to the County H bridge just north of Caryville. **Take out** at the boat ramp directly beneath the bridge on the right. A gravel road leads down to the landing from the downstream-right corner of the bridge.

Other trips. To combine part of this section with a trip on the Eau Claire River, put in at the Altoona Lake Dam and take out at Hobbs Landing or the Highway 85 wayside (see Eau Claire River 3).

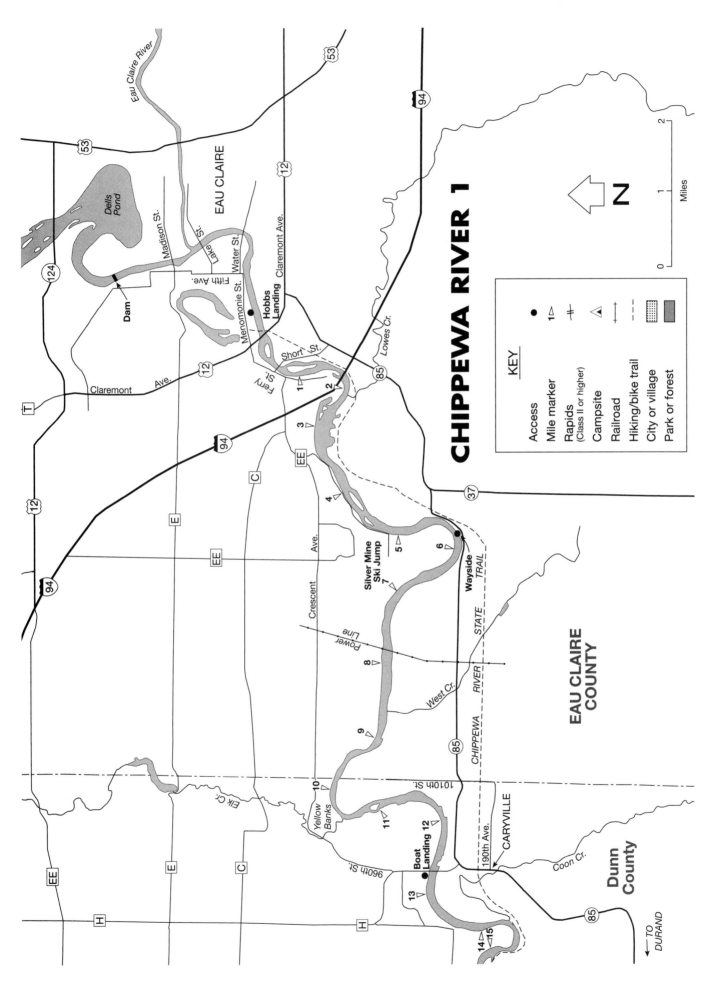

CHIPPEWA RIVER 1

KEY

●	Access
1△	Mile marker
≠	Rapids (Class II or higher)
◁	Campsite
┼	Railroad
- - -	Hiking/bike trail
▦	City or village
▨	Park or forest

N

0 — 1 — 2 Miles

EAU CLAIRE

Eau Claire River

Dells Pond

Dam

Madison St.
Lake St.
Water St.
Fifth Ave.
Menomonie St.
Hobbs Landing
Claremont Ave.
Short St.
Ferry St.
Claremont Ave.
Crescent Ave.

Silver Mine Ski Jump

Wayside

STATE TRAIL

Power Line

West Cr.

Lowes Cr.

Elk Cr.

Yellow Banks

960th St.

Boat Landing 12

1010th St.

190th Ave.

CARYVILLE

CHIPPEWA RIVER

Coon Cr.

EAU CLAIRE COUNTY

Dunn County

TO DURAND

39

CHIPPEWA RIVER 2 & 3

Caryville to Meridean (9.5 Miles)
Meridean to Dunnville (9.3 Miles)

Rails to Trails

A haven for bicyclists, Wisconsin is a national leader in converting abandoned railroads into recreational trails. Many of the rivers described in this book are crossed or paralleled by such trails, making it possible to combine peddling and paddling in the same trip. A good example is the Chippewa River State Trail, which runs westward 23 miles from downtown Eau Claire, through the communities of Caryville and Meridean, to an old railroad bridge where it joins the Red Cedar River State Trail, which in turn heads north for 14.5 miles into the city of Menomonie. The Chippewa Trail occupies the bed of the Chippewa Valley Railroad Line, built in 1882 and abandoned in 1980. The old railroad line originally extended from Eau Claire to Red Wing, Minnesota.

Wide, wild, and remote, this part of the Chippewa is not heavily canoed, so your only company is likely to be assorted wildlife and an occasional motorboat. Except during periods of high water, the river is suitable for beginners; however, brisk currents and unexpected drop-offs —especially downstream from sandbars—require caution. Low, grassy banks and continuous trees line the whole stretch. Only occasionally can farm fields or roads be seen from the river. On much of this section the river splits into separate channels or sloughs, presenting navigational choices. Many beaches and sandbars provide pleasant stopping places. Paralleling the river to the south is the Chippewa River State Trail, which runs all the way from Eau Claire to the mouth of the Red Cedar, where it joins the Red Cedar River State Trail.

For **camping**, see Chippewa River 1 and 4.

For **canoe and kayak rentals,** see Chippewa River 1.

The easiest **shuttle route** (approximately 20 miles) for the whole 19-mile trip goes north on County H, west on County C, and south on County Y to the Red Cedar landing at Dunnville. For a shorter trip to Meridean (i.e., Chippewa River 2), go south on County H, west on 150th Avenue, west on County O to Meridean, and north on 730th Street to the landing. For Chippewa River 3, the shuttle route is much longer (going east from Meridean to Caryville, then north, west, and south to Dunnville; see the map).

Gradient is 2.2 feet per mile.

For **water levels,** see Chippewa River 1.

Put in at the boat ramp at the County H bridge just north of Caryville. A gravel road leads down to the landing from the downstream-right corner of the bridge. Two big, gentle bends follow the landing—first left, then right. Then, after another left bend, the river straightens and passes a large wooded island. To the left of the island begins a long, narrow channel (sometimes called the South Channel) that flows to the south of huge Brush Island, then joins the wider Meridean slough to the south of Happy Island.

Continuing in the broad northern channel, the river bends to the right, passes the entrance to Meridean Slough (on the left), then comes to an excellent gravel boat landing on the right shoreline, at the western end of 240th Avenue. Back in the 1800s the original village of Meridean was located on Happy Island at this location, with a ferry connecting the two shores. Frequent flooding forced villagers to relocate Meridean to its present site. Incidentally, there are many stories that account for the unusual name of this once-bustling logging town. The most common version is that, when a Mrs. Dean came to visit her logger husband, their daughter Mary died of fever and was buried nearby. The community was then named in her honor.

The main (northern) channel now gently loops left, then right, soon splitting around Pasture Island. Both forks are sizable. If you wish to take out at Meridean, go left (south). Just downstream from Happy Island, after the mouth of the Meridean Slough, a concrete boat ramp and picnic shelter appear on the left—the best **take-out** for a relatively short trip from Caryville.

After Meridean the wide main channel (south of Pasture Island) heads west, then north, passing the mouth of the smaller northern channel on the right. Here on the right shore, immediately after the confluence of the two channels, there are huge, beautiful sand-and-gravel beaches, followed by a sandy boat landing alongside a dirt road. This area is popular with sunbathers and fishermen, but the road can get messy after rain.

Long, wide bends follow. Eventually, in a big right bend, a couple of Chippewa River State Trail bridges can be seen on the left, crossing feeder creeks. Immediately after the second bridge, a trail bench sits on the shoreline. Physically fit paddlers who don't mind the extra effort can take out here, walking up a short path to the bike trail, then continuing about 50 yards up through the woods to a dirt turnaround alongside 650th Street. There's plenty of room to park here, at the site of Old Tyrone, once an overnight stopping place for steamboat and stagecoach travelers.

Two more bends carry the river under an old railroad bridge, where the Chippewa River State Trail joins the Red Cedar River State Trail. Soon thereafter is the mouth of the Red Cedar on the right. Only a mile upstream is a splendid **take-out** at the County Y boat ramp, downstream-right from the bridge.

The "Chip" is a smaller version of the Wisconsin River.

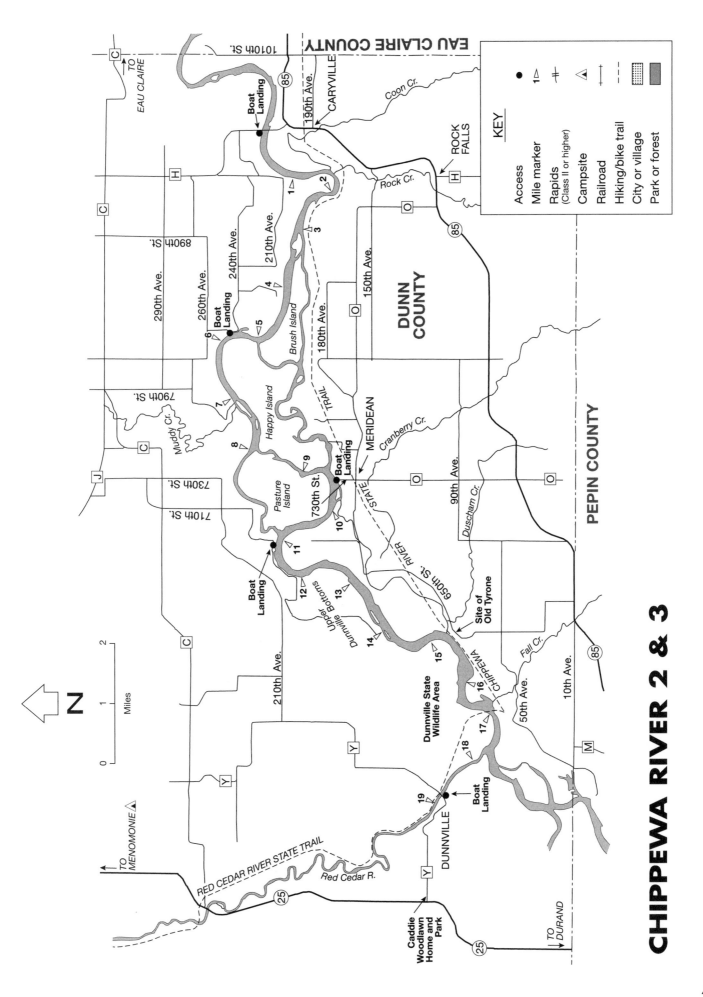

CHIPPEWA RIVER 2 & 3

CHIPPEWA RIVER 4
Dunnville to Durand (9.2 Miles)

"War" in Wisconsin

In the early years of logging, the mill owners in Chippewa Falls and Eau Claire dominated the processing of timber cut in the richly productive Chippewa River valley. After the Civil War, however, mill owners on the Mississippi increasingly looked toward the Chippewa for raw material. To take advantage of this opportunity, a group of speculators from Michigan, Oshkosh, and Fond du Lac formed the Beef Slough Manufacturing, Booming, Log Driving, and Transportation Company in 1868 with the express purpose of driving and delivering logs to mills on the Mississippi. The newly formed company built a "boom" (a log-catching structure) on the Chippewa several miles below Durand and directed their logs down a long side channel known as the Beef (or Buffalo) Slough to Alma, Wisconsin (see Chippewa River 5 and 6). There the logs were bound together into rafts for transport down the Mississippi.

Upstream, however, the Chippewa Falls and Eau Claire lumbermen had their own booms and storage ponds, and used various pretexts to hold up the logs of the Beef Slough Company. In retaliation, the new company sent men northward to cut the booms at Eau Claire and elsewhere, thus releasing huge quantities of logs. There was no bloodshed during the so-called Beef Slough War of 1868, but the quarrel raged in the courts and legislature for years. The hostilities were finally resolved in 1880 when the famous lumberman Frederick Weyerhauser worked out a compromise.

Beginning on one of the principal tributaries of the Chippewa, this day trip features large sandbars and beaches, a long slough that is paddleable when the river is sufficiently high, and an attractive bluff. The whole stretch has a wild appearance, and only a few houses are seen. As usual, the banks are typically 4–8 feet high, grassy, and sandy, with occasional cut banks on the outside of bends. Eagles, osprey, hawks, geese, turtles, and other wildlife are often spotted. Current is usually brisk, sometimes creating unexpected eddies and "boils." Always be careful when wading on or near sandbars, and keep your PFD on. The combination of drop-offs and current can be dangerous for the unwary.

Camping is available at Edgewater Acres Campground (715-235-3291), the KOA Menomonie (715-235-0641), and Twin Springs Resort Campground (715-235-9321)—all just north of the city of Menomonie. To the south, the Bumblebee Inn and Campground (715-442-2592) and Lake Pepin Campground (715-442-2012) are located in Pepin, Holden Park (715-672-8665) is 2.5 miles south of Arkansaw, and the Stockholm Village Park Campground is a few miles west of Pepin.

Canoe and kayak rentals are available at Riverside Bike and Skate in Eau Claire (715-835-0088), Red Cedar Outfitters in Menomonie (715-235-3866), and Crystal's Landing in Durand (715-672-5606).

The **shuttle route** (approximately 11 miles) from Dunnville goes west on County Y, south on Highway 25, east on Highway 25/10 across the river into Durand, north (left) on Main Street, and west (left) on Second Avenue to the landing.

Gradient is approximately 3 feet per mile.

For **water levels**, see Chippewa River 1.

Put in on the Red Cedar River at the Dunnville State Wildlife Area, downstream-right from the County Y bridge, where there's a concrete boat ramp near a parking lot. Heavily wooded, the Red Cedar gradually widens as it bends right, then left, soon feeding into the broad Chippewa. Sandbars and sandy beaches are immediately apparent on the larger river.

Curving left, then right, the Chippewa passes the entrance to Nine-Mile Slough on the right; the slough is the small right channel of huge Nine-Mile Island, which was once a favorite nesting ground of the now-extinct passenger pigeon. After another left turn the river heads back to the right near some farm buildings and a small creek, just upstream from a modest rock outcropping on the left (the only one of the trip). A broad, straight stretch follows.

In one of the following bends you can see imposing Waubeek Mound rising in the distance. Soon a right turn leads into a westward channel that shortcuts past the big loop of Snaggy Bend. In the very long left bend that follows, the outlet of Nine-Mile Slough appears on the right. Look upstream into the slough to see a high, sandy cut bank that was called the Waubeek Yellow Bank by early river men. Soon a couple of homes high up on the wooded bluff on the right can be seen, together with a private boat ramp. When the river finally heads back to the right, there's a huge island toward the right shoreline.

At an old cabin on the right, the river curves left again, and the long bridge at Durand comes into view downstream. High wooded bluffs form an attractive backdrop for the city. **Take out** 75 yards upstream from the bridge at the concrete boat ramp on the left, behind a row of downtown commercial buildings. A large parking lot and toilets are nearby. Another excellent boat ramp is located a quarter mile downstream from the bridge, also on the left (off Madison Street, at the end of Eighth Avenue). This alternate take-out is located in a residential neighborhood. Park alongside Madison Street.

A few riffles appear in the Chippewa at lower water levels.

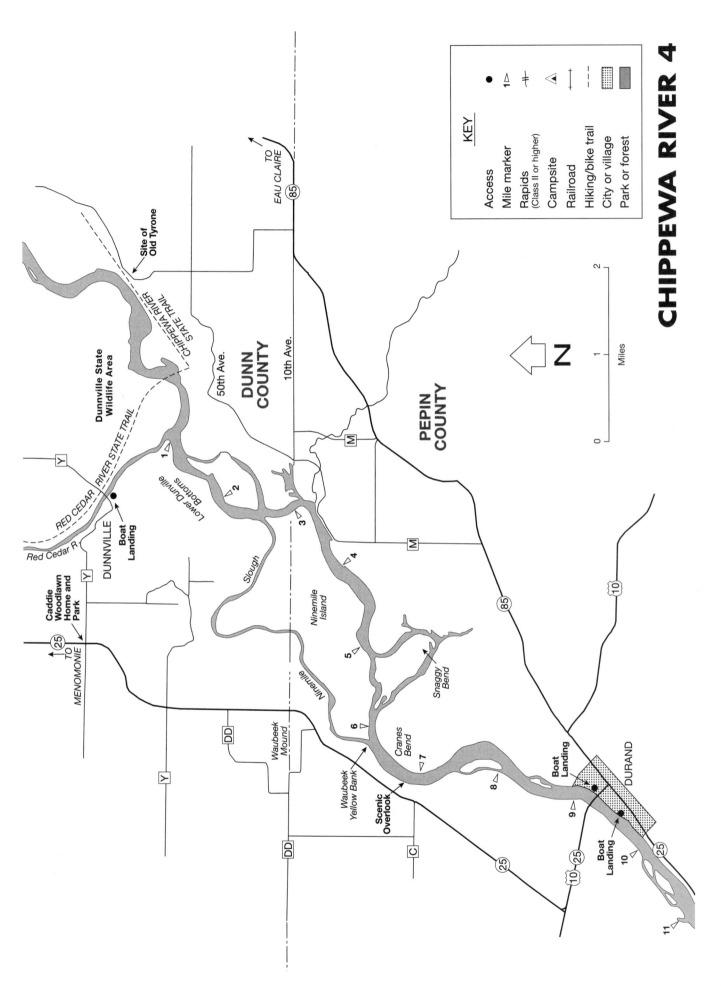

CHIPPEWA RIVER 4

KEY

- • Access
- 1△ Mile marker
- ‡ Rapids (Class II or higher)
- △ Campsite
- ┼ Railroad
- - - Hiking/bike trail
- ▦ City or village
- ▨ Park or forest

N

0   1   2
Miles

Site of Old Tyrone

TO EAU CLAIRE

85

CHIPPEWA RIVER STATE TRAIL

Dunnville State Wildlife Area

RED CEDAR RIVER STATE TRAIL

50th Ave.

10th Ave.

DUNN COUNTY

Y

DUNNVILLE

Boat Landing

Red Cedar R.

Caddie Woodlawn Home and Park

25
TO MENOMONIE

Y

1△

Lower Dunnville Bottoms

2△

3△

Slough

M

4△

Ninemile Island

85

M

10

5△

Snaggy Bend

Ninemile

DD

Waubeek Mound

6△

Cranes Bend

7△

Waubeek Yellow Bank

Scenic Overlook

DD

C

8△

PEPIN COUNTY

25

10
25

9△

Boat Landing

10△

Boat Landing

DURAND

25

11△

CHIPPEWA RIVER 5 & 6
Durand to Ella (7.7 Miles)
Ella to Pepin (7.6 Miles)

Beguiling Little River-Towns

While you're in the area, be sure to spend some time in nearby Pepin. Located on Highway 35 along Lake Pepin—a wide spot in the Mississippi caused by rock and sand washed out at the mouth of the Chippewa—this small town was the childhood hometown of Laura Ingalls Wilder, author of the famous *Little House* books. Heading the other direction (south) on Highway 35 takes you past a succession of breathtaking bluffs with huge exposed cliffs. Alma is another enchanting little Mississippi River town, only two streets wide but stretching several miles along Highway 35, between the river and Twelve-Mile Bluff. The town is filled with inviting shops, and an observation area provides an up-close view of lock and dam #4.

Scenery along the Chippewa

A rather long trip (five to eight hours for most paddlers), the final, 15-mile section of the Chippewa can easily be shortened by using the excellent intermediate landing at Ella as a put-in or take-out. After Durand the scenery is enhanced by a succession of beautiful wooded bluffs similar to those seen on the Lower Wisconsin. Overall, there aren't many rock outcroppings along the Chippewa, but on this section there are some undercut stone formations upstream from Ella. After Ella there isn't a single building, power line, bridge, or adjacent road, which makes this stretch one of the wildest and most remote parts of the whole river.

For **camping and canoe rentals**, see Chippewa River 4. The DNR allows camping in the Tiffany State Wildlife Area (which occupies much of the east side of the river from Ella to Highway 35), but requires prior permission (608-685-6225).

The **shuttle route** (15.5 miles) for the entire 15-mile trip goes south on Highway 25 and west on Highway 35. The shuttle (9.8 miles) for a shorter paddle from Durand to Ella goes west from Durand on Highway 25/10, west on Highway 10, and south on County N. The shuttle for Chippewa River 6 (approximately 13 miles) goes south from Ella on County N, then east on Highway 35. County N takes you through some gorgeous hill country, including the village of Arkansaw with its beautiful sandstone dells.

Gradient is 2.1 feet per mile.

For **water levels**, see Chippewa River 1.

Put in (1) at the public boat landing 75 yards upstream-left from the Durand bridge, off Main Street at the end of Second Avenue, or (2) at the public boat ramp a quarter mile downstream-left from the bridge, off Madison Street at the end of Eighth Avenue. As usual on the Chippewa, the 4- to 8-foot banks are grassy, often sandy, and there's dense tree cover on both sides. After the

mouth of the Eau Galle River on the right, the river heads left toward impressive Round Hill, opposite a huge sand beach that continues until the river heads to the right again.

Beautiful wooded hills now line the river on the left. Power lines cross near a large wooded island, and Highway 25 approaches the left bank. Huge Buffalo Island follows as the river begins curving left. The following straightaway heads toward a beautiful wooded ridgeline, which eventually diverts the river toward the left. It was in this area during the 1860s that the lumbermen of the Beef Slough Company diverted logs out of the main channel down a long side channel to the village of Alma, where rafts were formed for transport down the Mississippi.

After the mouth of Dead Lake Slough, County N runs along the river at the base of the bluffs, and a chalet-style house can be seen on the hillside. Attractive rock outcroppings are found on the right shoreline for a long time, 8 feet tall and topped with coniferous trees. In the long, gentle right bend that follows, the environs continue to be wild, quiet, and lovely, with only a few houses. Eventually the concrete boat ramp at Ella appears on river-right, with parking and picnic shelters, making it an excellent take-out or put-in for shorter trips.

Shortly after Ella, County N veers away from the river, and the remaining miles of the trip are far from roads and human habitation. The shorelines are more heavily forested than ever, and another long series of beautiful wooded hills begins on the right after the mouth of Plum Creek. Each wooded bluff comes all the way to the edge of the water. Suddenly, just before Wahcoutah Island, the high bluffs end. After heading right, the river goes into the longest straightaway of the trip, with a tall ridgeline looming in the distance. What you are seeing is the high bluff on the far side of the Mississippi, for you are now nearing the end of the trip, and of the Chippewa.

A sizable wooded island precedes the Highway 35 bridge, where the upstream **take-out** is on the left shore, in the left channel of the island. The boat ramp and adjacent parking lot are part of the Tiffany State Wildlife Area. From Highway 35, only 2 miles of the Chippewa remain. Another 3 miles of paddling on the Mississippi takes you to Wabasha, Minnesota; located in a side channel on the opposite (Wisconsin) shore is the Indian Slough Landing, downstream-left from the huge Highway 25 bridge.

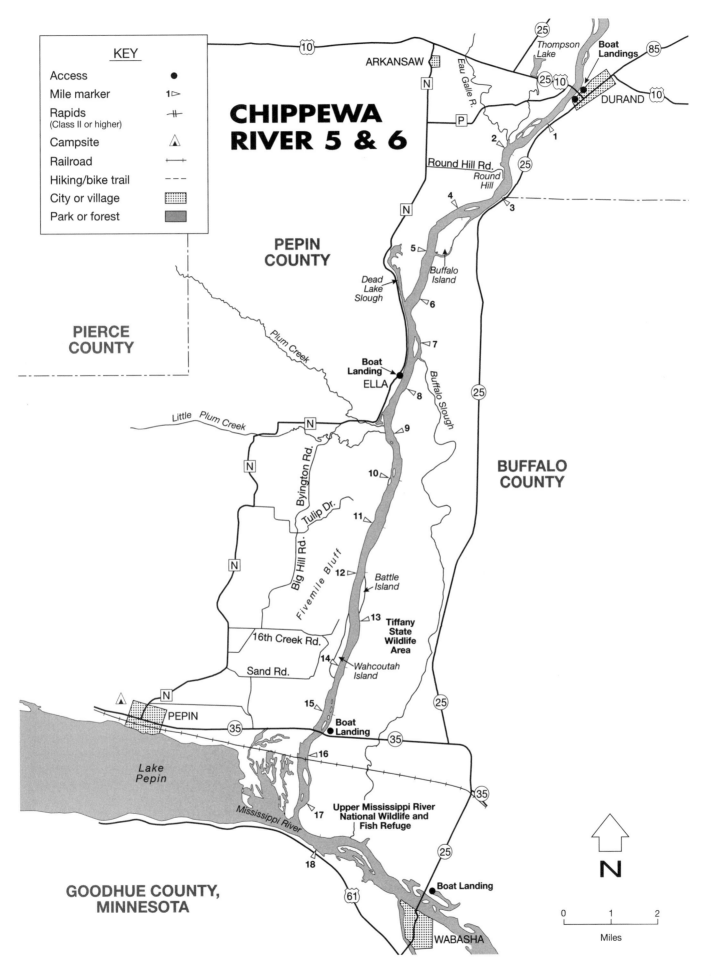

CHIPPEWA RIVER 5 & 6

KEY

Access ●
Mile marker 1▷
Rapids (Class II or higher) ⊣⊢
Campsite △
Railroad ⊢—⊢
Hiking/bike trail – – –
City or village ▦
Park or forest ▓

ARKANSAW

Thompson Lake

Boat Landings

DURAND

Eau Galle R.

Round Hill Rd.

Round Hill

PEPIN COUNTY

PIERCE COUNTY

Plum Creek

Dead Lake Slough

Buffalo Island

Buffalo Slough

Boat Landing
ELLA

Little Plum Creek

BUFFALO COUNTY

Byington Rd.

Tulip Dr.

Big Hill Rd.

Fivemile Bluff

Battle Island

Tiffany State Wildlife Area

16th Creek Rd.

Sand Rd.

Wahcoutah Island

PEPIN

Lake Pepin

Boat Landing

Mississippi River

Upper Mississippi River National Wildlife and Fish Refuge

Boat Landing

GOODHUE COUNTY, MINNESOTA

WABASHA

N

0   1   2
Miles

CRAWFISH RIVER
Milford to Jefferson (9.5 Miles)

An excellent stretch for beginners, this part of the Crawfish consists mainly of large, gentle bends and is generally free of obstructive deadfall. Averaging 90 feet wide, it passes through a quiet, almost entirely forested area with only a few houses. The surrounding countryside is rolling and mostly agricultural. A pleasant float trip, the section is easily shortened by using one of two alternate put-ins. Canoeing this stretch gives you a two-river day (barely!), taking out after a brief jaunt on the Rock. A big highlight of the trip is the proximity of two fascinating historic sites—one of which can be visited as you paddle down the river.

The mounds and stockade of magical Aztalan, as seen from the Crawfish.

Camping is available at Pilgrim's Campground 3 miles northwest of Fort Atkinson (800-742-1697).

Canoe rental and **shuttle service** on the Crawfish are available near Columbus at Crawfish Canoe Rentals (920-623-2047).

The **shuttle route** (8.9 miles) from Milford goes west briefly on County A, south on County Q, south on Highway 89, east on Highway 18 across the river into Jefferson, south on County W (Wisconsin Drive) across the river again, and east for a short distance on Riverview Drive to the boat ramp.

During the shuttle run, take a few minutes to stop at the pioneer village at the small community of Aztalan, on County Q just south of B. Settled in 1837, Aztalan was once the principal town of Jefferson County, but it declined after the railroad bypassed it. The original church, four log cabins, and a grainery make a charming side trip.

Gradient is only 0.5 foot per mile.

For **water levels**, check the gauge at Milford (#05426000) on the USGS Web site. See "Water Levels" in the introduction.

There are three possible **put-ins:** (1) in Milford at the County A bridge, downstream-right; a rough path leads down to the river, but there's barely room along the road to park a car for unloading; (2) at the County B bridge, where a short path leads to the river, downstream-left (unlike Milford, this access is easy, and there's room along the shoulder for several cars); and (3) at Aztalan State Park, where you can park in the large lot and carry boats down to the river-right shoreline. None of these is a designated boat landing; (2) and (3) are the safest and most convenient.

Immediately downstream from the Milford bridge, the river flows past a few homes and over a riffly shoal.

The shoreline soon becomes wooded on both sides; for the rest of the trip, there will be only a few clearings. Typically, the water is muddy-colored. The Interstate 94 bridges come in the midst of the first long right bend, and a couple of additional bends lead to the County B bridge.

Soon the wooden stockade walls of Aztalan State Park can be seen over the river-right tree line, and eventually the grassy mounds and picnic tables of the park appear in a clear area. The grassy, sometimes muddy shoreline can easily be accessed, not far from a large parking lot. Don't miss the opportunity to walk around this incredible site. (For more on Aztalan, see the sidebar for Black River 5.)

Big, sweeping curves continue below the park, leading to an old railroad bridge that is now used by the Glacial Drumlin State Park Bike Trail. A converted railroad line, this trail runs 47 miles from Waukesha to Cottage Grove, and crosses both the Crawfish and Rock Rivers. A straightaway immediately follows the bridge, and the first, brief open area of the trip. Sand becomes more conspicuous in the predominantly mud banks.

In the sharpest bend of the trip, the river narrows to 65 feet and turns to the right alongside Popp Road, where there's a bankside home with a private concrete ramp. A small rock-and-clay outcropping appears on the left just downstream from the home. As the river heads back to the left, a series of homes appears, with protective riprap shoreline. Downstream, an open field precedes the Highway 18 bridge, which is followed by a private, fenced-in game farm.

Houses become more numerous after Highway 18, all the way into Jefferson, where the river curves right. The junior high school—a tall, castellated building—looms over the trees in the distance. On the right, the grassy fields and picnic facilities of Riverview Park can be seen, with bare spots along the shoreline where people bank fish.

As soon as you paddle under the County W bridge, you're on the Rock River. The Jefferson dam can be seen several hundred yards to your left, at the upstream end of an island. **Take out** 100 yards downstream-right from the bridge at the concrete ramp alongside Riverview Drive, where there's room to park several cars on the gravel shoulder.

Other trips. (1) In Columbus you can put in behind the water treatment plant; Astico County Park off Highway 16/60 is a good take-out. (2) From the dam that forms the Danville millpond to Hubbleton, the river flows 20 miles through woods, marshes, farmland, rocky riffles, some wide spots, and a state wildlife area, with a couple of bridges as possible accesses. (3) For the 9-mile stretch between Hubbleton and Milford, put in at the public landing in Hubbleton or on river-left a mile downstream.

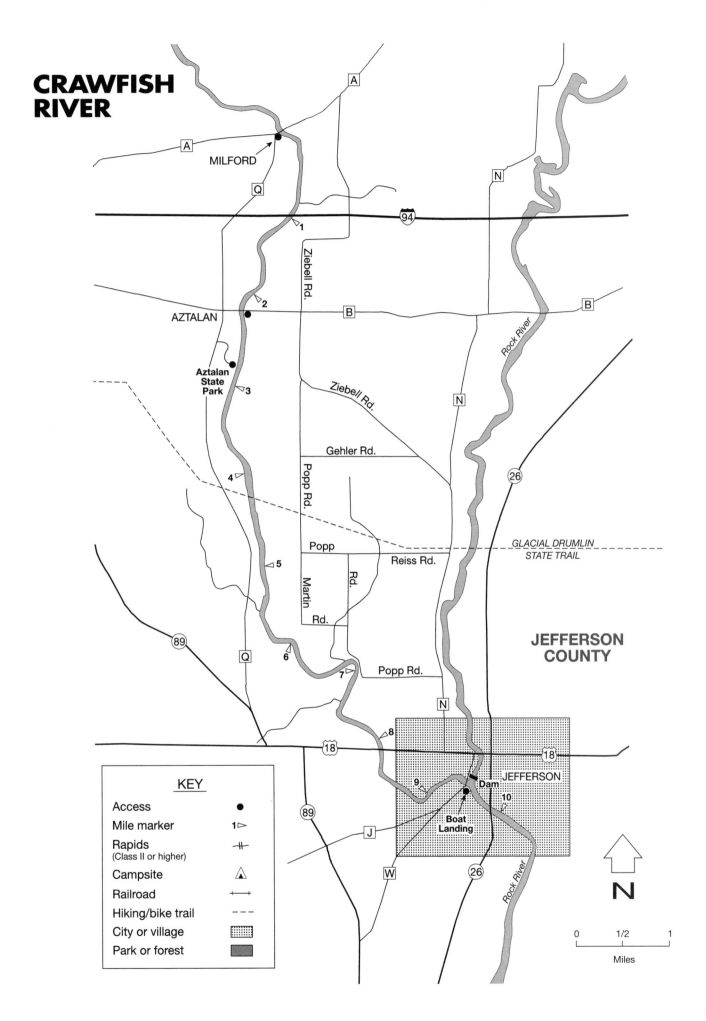

CRAWFISH RIVER

MILFORD

AZTALAN

Aztalan State Park

Ziebell Rd.

Ziebell Rd.

Gehler Rd.

Popp Rd.

Popp Rd.

Reiss Rd.

Martin Rd.

Popp Rd.

JEFFERSON COUNTY

JEFFERSON

Dam

Boat Landing

Rock River

GLACIAL DRUMLIN STATE TRAIL

KEY

Access	●
Mile marker	1 ▷
Rapids (Class II or higher)	─╫─
Campsite	◭
Railroad	─┼─
Hiking/bike trail	─ ─ ─
City or village	▦
Park or forest	▬

0   1/2   1

Miles

N

CRYSTAL RIVER
Rural to Shadow Lake Road (4 Miles)

The Magic of Old Mills

Nothing evokes the nostalgia and romance of the past more than a well-preserved old mill or covered bridge—and the tiny community of Lost Hope has both! Built on the Crystal River in 1855, the Red Mill ground flour for area farmers until 1959. Water from the nearby pond was channeled under the road (now County K) to power the huge, now-restored waterwheel. Today the well-maintained building houses a gift shop and the living quarters of the owners. Just downstream on the Crystal is a beautiful, wooden covered bridge built in 1970, a painstaking copy of an old bridge in New Hampshire. Lovely gardens and paths lead from the mill, across the bridge, to a pretty little Chapel in the Woods—a popular place for weddings. The whole setting is memorably scenic and often pictured on calendars.

If you like to paddle small streams, you'll love the Crystal. Seldom more than 20–30 feet wide, it's also a very short river. Originating as the outlet of the Waupaca Chain O' Lakes, it flows only 10 miles before joining the Waupaca River. Usually paddleable because of its source in the spring-fed lake system, the little river always earns its name with sparkling, clear water. Plentiful riffles and mild rapids add to the excitement. Two special treats for paddlers are the charming little village of Rural near the beginning, and the Old Red Mill and covered bridge farther downstream. There's a popular canoe-rental enterprise nearby, so you'll probably have to share the river with many other canoes on nice weekends.

For **camping**, see Tomorrow River.

Canoe rental and shuttles are available at Ding's Dock on Columbia Lake, off County Q (715-258-2612). Renters and unique little fiberglass canoes are towed on pontoon boats through Columbia and Long Lakes to the place where the river begins.

The **shuttle route** (3.5 miles) goes east on Main Street in Rural, east on Rural Road, east on County K, southeast on Crystal Road, and north on Shadow Lake Road.

Gradient is a riffly 5 feet per mile.

Water level. There is no USGS gauge, but you can visually check water level for paddleability by stopping at the Rural Road bridge, where the river's best rapids are located.

If you don't mind some lake canoeing, you can **put in** at the public landing on Columbia Lake (in the Waupaca Chain O' Lakes) and paddle to the southeast end of Long Lake, where the river begins. From here to Rural the Crystal is a tiny stream flowing peacefully through woodland, with a few riffles. The recommended put-in is near the bridge at the intersection of Main Street and Cleghorn Road in Rural, across from a couple of stores. There's room along the shoulder to park several cars. At this point, Main Street passes over a bridge and an earthen dam; some of the river's flow is diverted under the bridge into a higher left channel that once served as a mill race. As soon as you put in at the bridge (downstream-left), portage across a signed gravel path to the larger right channel. Incidentally, a sign on Main Street points out the site of the old mill; later, as you paddle by the mouth of the old mill race, you can still see the small dam where the waterwheel was located.

Shallow, clear, sand-and-gravel-bottomed, and nar-

The historic Old Red Mill at Little Hope.

row, the river winds through the attractive backyards of Rural's homes, and passes under three small bridges. Riffles are plentiful, with rocks to dodge. After you stop seeing houses temporarily, the river winds through a brief marshy area at Junction Lake, then narrows, goes under another bridge, and speeds up through some exhilarating riffles. A couple of wooden footbridges appear as the riffles turn into Class I boulder gardens. The setting is now tree-canopied and lovely. Limbs must be avoided occasionally, but the worst ones are usually cut out to allow passage.

Riffles stop before the Sanders Road bridge, and the water becomes consistently deeper in the densely wooded, winding stretch that follows. In the approach to the Rural Road bridge, the river narrows and drops through an exciting Class I+ rapid, about 75 yards long.

After a right bend the old metal bridge at Smith Road appears, followed by a couple of fast turns. Just before the next bridge, at Parfreyville Road, the private Ding's Dock landing is located on the right. The river now widens, deepens, and slows at the Little Hope Mill Pond. At the eastern end of the impoundment, portage around the narrow 8-foot-high dam. County K is immediately downstream; the attractive public park on the right after the bridge (with picnic tables and toilet) is a good place to **take out** if you wish to shorten your trip.

Another mile of paddling takes you past the delightful Old Red Mill, under a picture-book covered bridge, and through woodland to Shadow Lake Road, where there's an easy **take-out** at the bridge, upstream-left. Because rental canoes don't paddle this final stretch, there's a greater chance of encountering deadfall here. The next two bridges—at Highway 10 and County E—are poor access points. Soon after another impoundment at Highway 54/22 (Cary Pond), the Crystal flows into the Waupaca River a mile east of the city of Waupaca.

CRYSTAL RIVER

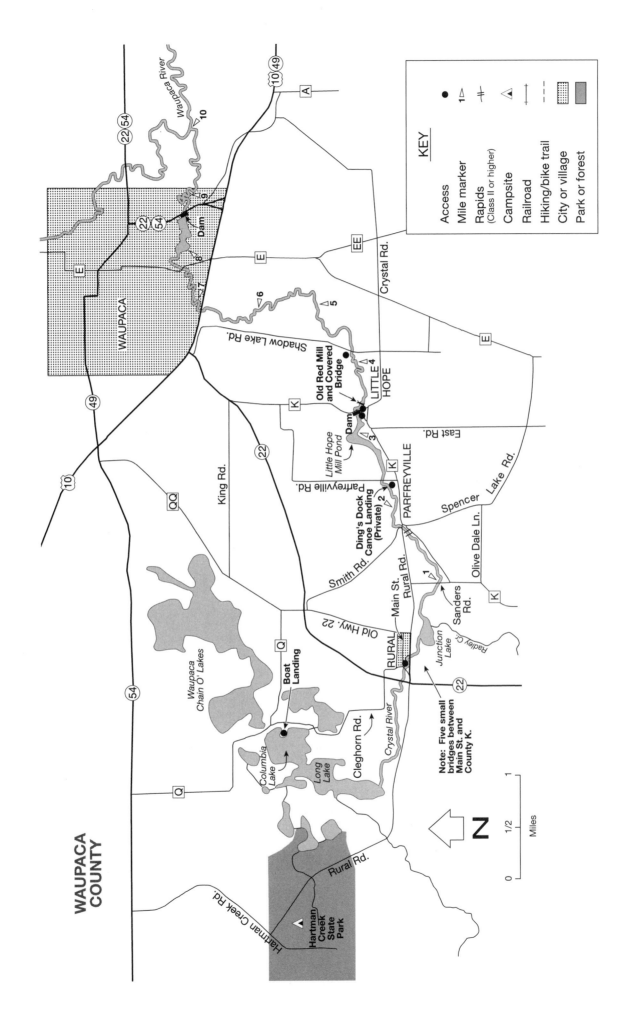

WAUPACA COUNTY

KEY

- Access
- Mile marker
- Rapids (Class II or higher)
- Campsite
- Railroad
- Hiking/bike trail
- City or village
- Park or forest

WAUPACA

Waupaca River

Dam

Shadow Lake Rd.

Old Red Mill and Covered Bridge

LITTLE HOPE

Dam

Little Hope Mill Pond

Crystal Rd.

East Rd.

Spencer Lake Rd.

Olive Dale Ln.

King Rd.

Ding's Dock Canoe Landing (Private)

Parfreyville Rd.

PARFREYVILLE

Smith Rd.

Main St.

Rural Rd.

Sanders Rd.

Radley Cr.

Junction Lake

RURAL

Old Hwy. 22

Note: Five small bridges between Main St. and County K.

Crystal River

Cleghorn Rd.

Boat Landing

Waupaca Chain O' Lakes

Columbia Lake

Long Lake

Hartman Creek Rd.

Hartman Creek State Park

Rural Rd.

N

Miles
0   1/2   1

49

DES PLAINES RIVER
Pleasant Prairie to Russell Road (6.5 Miles)

Drainage Mania

By the early 1900s the quest for new farmland in Wisconsin led developers to set their sights on huge areas of apparently fertile marshlands, especially in the central part of the state. Draglines were brought in to dig hundreds of miles of ditches to drain marshy peat beds, and drainage districts were organized to levy taxes. However, when the new land proved to be unproductive (coupled with high drainage district taxes and fickle growing seasons), most farmers were obliged to move out. In some areas, the dried-out peat beds caught fire, sometimes stubbornly smoldering for years. Eventually, beginning in the 1930s, federal, state, and county governments began buying and reflooding much of the marshland. One of the fortunate results has been the establishment of many well-managed wetlands such as the Horicon Marsh on the Rock River and the Necedah National Wildlife Refuge near the Wisconsin River.

Running a beaver dam on the Des Plaines.

An eminently historic river that once comprised part of an important and much-traveled canoe route from Lake Michigan to the Mississippi, the Des Plaines now travels through one of the most intensely urbanized areas in the Midwest. From its origin a few miles west of Racine to its northern reaches in Illinois, however, the river still flows through surroundings that are surprisingly wild, thanks to the foresight of those involved in overseeing forest preserves and park districts, and to a floodplain environment that discourages development. From Pleasant Prairie in Wisconsin, paddlers can head south for more than 30 river-miles before encountering the first of a series of dams. Along the way, the river is small, winding, and densely wooded (the name is derived from the French expression *eau pleine*, "full of water," in reference to the sap-filled maples that are still plentiful along the banks).

The section described here—almost entirely in Wisconsin—is a delightful day trip. Low, grassy banks provide plenty of places to stop for lunch or rest breaks. There are many limbs to dodge, but portages are seldom necessary. Although traffic noise can be heard from Interstate 94 for a while, the setting is generally quite remote-feeling and almost devoid of dwellings. The put-in and take-out are easy, and an alternate access facilitates shorter trips. Bird-watchers are sure to be kept busy.

Camping is available approximately 15 miles west of Kenosha at the Bong State Recreation Area (262-652-0377 or 262-878-5600) and 3 miles north of Bristol at the Happy Acres Kampground (262-857-7373).

Canoe rentals are available in Milwaukee at the Laacke and Joys downtown store (414-271-7878), in Chicago at Chicagoland Canoe Base (773-777-1489), and in Madison at Rutabaga (608-223-9300) and Carl's Paddlin' (608-284-0300).

The **shuttle route** (8.7 miles) goes north on the frontage road alongside I-94, east on Highway 50, south on County H/Kilbourne Road, and west on Russell Road to the bridge.

Gradient is negligible (less than a foot per mile).

For **water levels**, check the gauge at Russell, Illinois (#05527800) on the USGS Web site for Illinois: http://il.water.usgs.gov. See "Water Levels" in the introduction.

Put in downstream-right from the East Frontage Road near I-94, one mile south of Highway 50 (Seventy-fifth Street) in Pleasant Prairie. Carry boats a short distance across the grass between the shoulder and bank. There's room along the road for many parked cars.

Only 20 feet wide at the put-in, the river immediately passes a creek mouth on the left, then winds back and forth through a lightly forested floodplain, with lots of typical lowland vegetation. Maneuvering is required to get past occasional limbs in the water. The first houses of the trip appear on the left as you approach County C.

At times, the river widens to as much as 40 feet, with fewer obstructions. Beaver cuttings and lodges appear along the shoreline, and the industrious little animals occasionally create river-wide dams that are easy to run or to lift over. The environs continue to be wild, but adjacent farm fields can be glimpsed sometimes through the trees. In some areas the surroundings are savannah-like—open and grassy with scattered trees.

In the approach to Prairie Springs Park, the river turns right at a sizable, river-left tributary. Farther downstream another creek enters on the right just before the river bends left toward Highway 165. The environs are quite open at the bridge, where it's possible to access the river at several corners.

After Highway 165 the river widens, is much more open than it was upstream, and is less twisty. If the wind is blowing, you're more likely to be affected by it after Highway 165. In the approach to County ML a large game farm lies along the left shoreline. Before and after the bridge, where several houses are located, the river widens to 100 feet, then narrows somewhat.

Downstream, as the river curves right, railroad tracks follow the left shoreline, and before long, houses briefly appear in the vicinity of Russell. The river now curves left, narrows, and passes under the Russell Road bridge. **Take out** at the river-left canoe landing, alongside a paved parking lot. Just downstream is a floating snowmobile bridge, the center section of which is removed for boat traffic.

Other trips. For two more day trips, both in Illinois (Russell Road to Wadsworth Road, and Wadsworth Road to Oak Spring Road), see Des Plaines River 1 & 2 in my book *Paddling Illinois,* pp. 30–33.

DES PLAINES RIVER

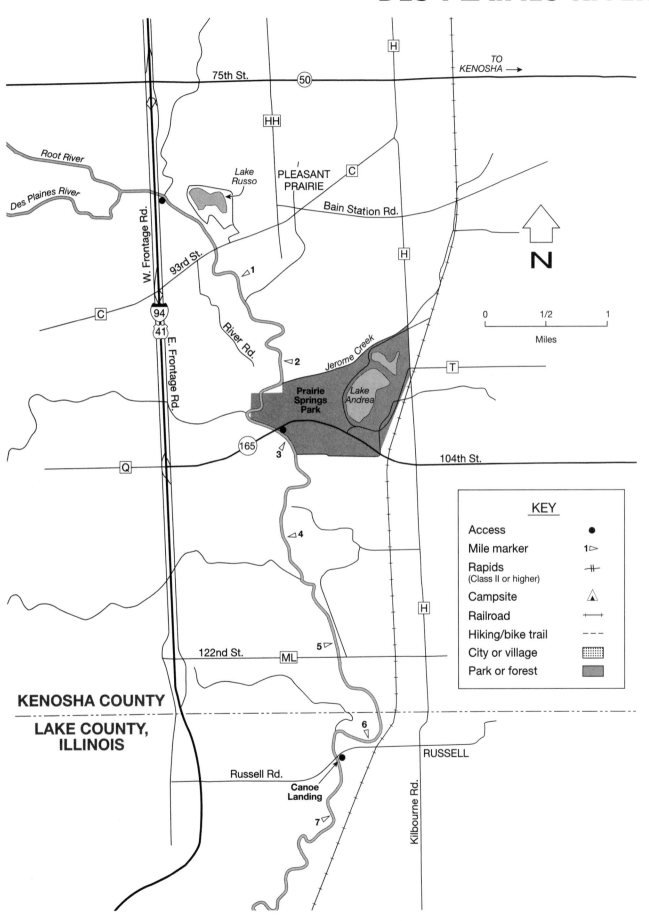

TO KENOSHA →

75th St.

Root River

Des Plaines River

Lake Russo

PLEASANT PRAIRIE

Bain Station Rd.

W. Frontage Rd.

93rd St.

River Rd.

E. Frontage Rd.

N

0   1/2   1
Miles

Jerome Creek

Prairie Springs Park

Lake Andrea

104th St.

KEY

Access	●
Mile marker	1▷
Rapids (Class II or higher)	─╫─
Campsite	▲
Railroad	┼─┼
Hiking/bike trail	– – –
City or village	▦
Park or forest	▰

122nd St.

KENOSHA COUNTY

LAKE COUNTY, ILLINOIS

RUSSELL

Kilbourne Rd.

Russell Rd.

Canoe Landing

51

EAU CLAIRE RIVER 1
Eisberner Memorial Park to County G (5 Miles)

High, wooded banks are characteristic of the Eau Claire.

A lovely and surprisingly uncrowded little river, the Eau Claire deserves the name given to it by early explorers who were impressed by its "clear water." Fortunately, the Eau Claire still delights paddlers with its clarity and its pristine sandbars and sandy beaches. Much of the shoreline lies within the Eau Claire County Forest, which preserves the river environs in an undeveloped, natural state. The wild surroundings are heavily wooded with a variety of deciduous and coniferous trees. As might be expected, accesses are not developed (i.e., no concrete boat ramps), but there are numerous designated canoe landings that are quite convenient for canoeists and kayakers. In the summer months, the river often gets too low for comfortable paddling, so it's always a good idea to call the Eau Claire County Parks and Forest Department for current water conditions.

The first recommended trip begins below the confluence of the North and South Forks, and thus has more volume than either of the Forks. Numerous riffles and low-level (Class I+) rapids add excitement and require some maneuvering.

Nearby **camping,** provided by the Eau Claire County Parks and Forest Department (715-839-4738), is available at: (1) Coon Fork Park (88 campsites, with electricity and showers) off County CF a few miles southeast of Lake Eau Claire; (2) Harstad Park (27 primitive campsites) off County AF a couple miles southwest of Lake Eau Claire; and (3) Beaver Creek Reserve (2 primitive sites) along the river just upstream from Big Falls. For (3), call the reserve at 715-877-2212 for campsite availability. Riverside camping is not allowed. For other camping available in the area, see Eau Claire River 3.

Canoe and kayak rentals are available at Riverside Bike & Skate in Eau Claire (715-835-0088). Canoes may also be rented at GD Odds Inc. in Eau Claire (715-833-1942).

The **shuttle route** (4.6 miles) goes north 1 mile on the Eisberner Memorial Park entrance road, west on Channey Road (a sand-and-dirt township road that is sometimes rather mushy and rutted in the spring), and south a short distance on County G to the bridge.

The **gradient** is only 2.4 feet per mile, but there are numerous riffles and Class I rapids.

Water levels. The only USGS gauge is located considerably upstream on the North Fork near Thorp (#05365707). For general information on water levels (i.e., high, medium, or too low to paddle), call the Eau Claire County Parks & Forest Department (715-839-4738).

Put in on river-right in Eisberner Memorial Park at the end of a loop drop-off road. Pool-like at the beginning, the river bends immediately to the left past the chimney of an abandoned cabin. Pines and other coniferous trees are plentiful from the outset, together with attractive rock formations. The bottom and shoreline are sandy, the banks often high, and the streambed 70–80 feet wide.

The first rapid, a relatively easy Class I+, comes soon in a brief left turn. For 25 yards the river drops a couple of feet through a boulder bed, followed by a long, scenic flatwater stretch. Then, just before Coon Fork Creek enters on the left, the river curves slightly to the right and through a couple of islands; the rapids located here necessitate some rock-dodging.

In the long, rather sharp left bend that follows Coon Fork Creek, a 35-foot-tall sandbank (known as Yellow Banks) looms impressively over the right shoreline, while sandy beaches occupy the left shore. Then, as soon as you make a sharp right turn, the first house of the trip—a log home—appears on the left, along with some pretty stone formations. In the wide stretch that follows, power lines cross, and another easy rapid occurs in a short right turn.

Take out downstream-right at County G (the Troubled Waters Bridge), where a rough, sandy road leads down to the bank.

Other trips. (1) When water volume is adequate, the North Fork is pleasantly narrow, winding, riffly, and isolated in the 8 miles from Hamilton Falls to Eisberner Memorial Park. Drive south to the end of Park Road, off County MM, and carry boat(s) along the river-right shoreline to put in below the falls. Putting in above the falls requires a 60-yard, river-left portage a few minutes into the trip. (2) For a longer version of Eau Claire River 1, you can put in on the South Fork at County H (upstream-left), if there's enough water; from County H to Eisberner is 3.5 river-miles. (3) Water levels permitting, Coon Creek is paddleable from Coon Fork Dam to the Eau Claire (2.5 miles).

After County G (take-out for Eau Claire River 1), the river soon flows into Lake Eau Claire. The next recommended trip begins 2 miles downstream from the Lake Eau Claire dam.

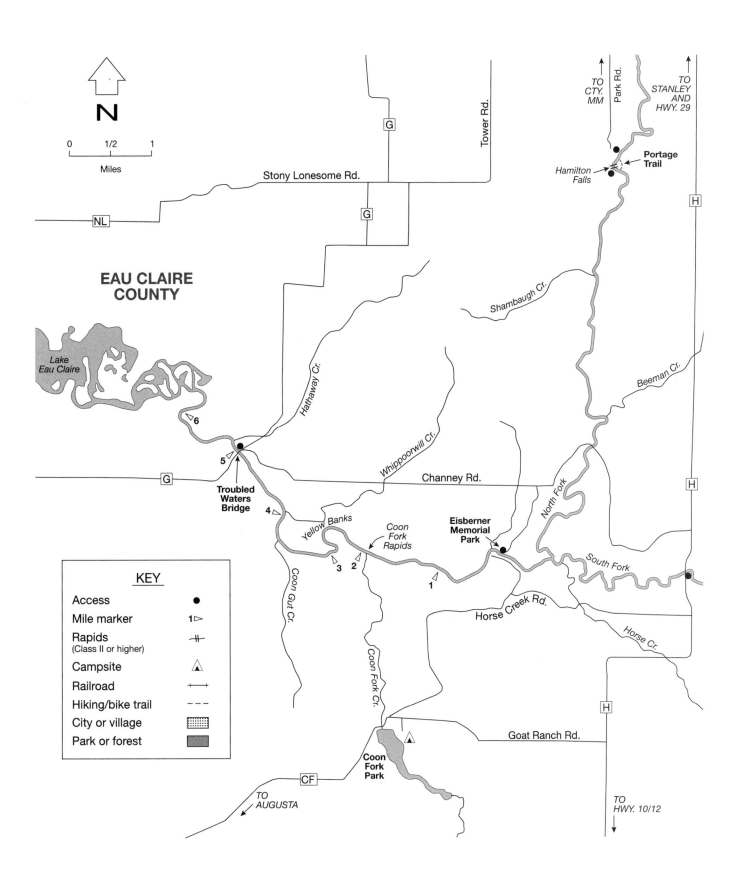

N

0   1/2   1
Miles

EAU CLAIRE
COUNTY

Lake Eau Claire

NL

Stony Lonesome Rd.

G

G

Tower Rd.

TO CTY. MM

Park Rd.

TO STANLEY AND HWY. 29

Portage Trail

Hamilton Falls

H

Shambaugh Cr.

Beeman Cr.

Hathaway Cr.

Whippoorwill Cr.

6

5

G

Troubled Waters Bridge

Channey Rd.

North Fork

H

4

Yellow Banks

Coon Fork Rapids

Eisberner Memorial Park

South Fork

3   2

1

Coon Gut Cr.

Horse Creek Rd.

Horse Cr.

KEY

Access	●
Mile marker	1▷
Rapids (Class II or higher)	—╫—
Campsite	◬
Railroad	┼———┼
Hiking/bike trail	– – –
City or village	▦
Park or forest	▨

Coon Fork Cr.

H

Goat Ranch Rd.

Coon Fork Park

◬

CF

TO AUGUSTA

TO HWY. 10/12

EAU CLAIRE RIVER 2
Harstad Park to County K (12.5 Miles)

Spending Time in the Augusta Area

Just 5 miles south of Lake Eau Claire, near Eau Claire River 1 and 2, is the small community of Augusta. As you drive through the rolling hills on the nearby county and township roads, you'll see that many Amish families have settled in the area in recent years. Here and there, signs indicate where you can purchase fresh farm produce or Amish craft items.

Just a few miles north of town, off Highway 27, is a remarkable building that you've probably seen on a calendar or in State of Wisconsin promotional literature. Built in 1864 and now a museum, the Dells Mill is a five-story grist mill in a beautiful setting. Everything is made of wood, including the waterwheel, gears, and pulleys.

Long, sweeping curves, huge beaches, and isolated surroundings abound on this beautiful section of the Eau Claire. For paddlers seeking a shorter day, the trip can easily be cut to 7.75 miles by taking out at County D. A scenic flatwater stretch through county forest, this part of the river has few of the riffles that are plentiful upstream. Bluffs, high sand banks, and rock formations add to the setting. Deep pools are frequent here, especially on the outside of bends. Eagles and other wildlife are often spotted. Nearby Big Falls, where the river drops 15 feet over magnificent rocky ledges, makes a fascinating side visit.

For **camping, canoe/kayak rentals,** and **water levels**, see Eau Claire River 1 and 3.

The **shuttle route** (approximately 10 miles) goes south from Harstad Park on County HHH, west on County AF, west on Highway 12 to Fall Creek, and north on County K to the bridge. The shuttle (7.1 miles) for a shorter trip to County D goes south on County HHH, west on County AF, north and then west on Lincoln Drive, north on Green Meadow Road, and north on County D to the bridge.

The **gradient** is 2.8 feet per mile.

Put in at the Harstad Park canoe landing, a river-left beach at the end of a loop drop-off road. Immediately after the put-in, the river bends to the right, past the picnic shelter and through some wavy riffles. The sandy banks are about 20 feet high, and pine trees are abundant in the wild, forested surroundings. Sandbars and beaches provide many places to stop for relaxation breaks.

Sand Creek enters on the right just before a sharp left turn. At this point a beautiful wooded bluff towers on the right, opposite a large sandy beach. After several additional bends, Bears Grass Creek enters on the left. In the right turn that follows, an attractive rocky bluff can be seen ahead. The environs of Sand Creek and Bears Grass Creek are two scenic highlights of the trip.

Downstream, a side channel appears on the right just before a sharp left turn. After a set of power lines crosses in a left bend (the first sign of civilization), the river runs into a tall bluff, then veers right. As the right bend continues, steep, 50-foot sandbanks rise on the left. Just before another sharp left turn, opposite the outlet of the side channel noted above, power lines cross again, then a third time as the left loop continues. This loop tends to collect dead trees along the right side, but there's plenty of room to paddle by them.

A couple of gentle bends now lead to the County D bridge. If you wish to end your trip here, you can do so upstream-left, where an access road leads to the river. Take out on the sandy beach and carry your boat(s) up the rather steep bank.

The next 4.5 miles of scenic paddling are through an equally remote, high-banked area, and end at the beautiful rock formations before and after County K. In the left bend approaching the bridge, there's a long, rocky Class I+ rapid (Little Falls). The rock outcroppings on both sides of the bridge are a preview of the more impressive formations 1.25 miles downstream at Big Falls. **Take out** at the County K bridge about 100 yards downstream-right; carry your boat(s) from the sandy beach up to a nearby parking area.

Other trips. (1) If you wish to continue downstream, you must take out upstream-left from Big Falls, a dangerous Class III–IV drop. There are falls on both sides of an island. The river-right falls is spread out over five separate drops, and is runnable by skilled whitewater paddlers at appropriate water levels. The left falls is a sheer drop, however, and should not be attempted. A parking lot is located on river-left a few hundred yards from the river, off the Big Falls Park south entrance road from County K. (2) Another enjoyable stretch starts downstream-left from Big Falls (accessed from the south entrance road) and ends 6 miles later at High Line Landing under the power lines off County QQ (6 miles) or at Altoona Lake Park on the south shore of Altoona Lake (8.75 miles).

The next recommended trip (Eau Claire River 3) begins at the Altoona Lake dam and ends on the Chippewa River.

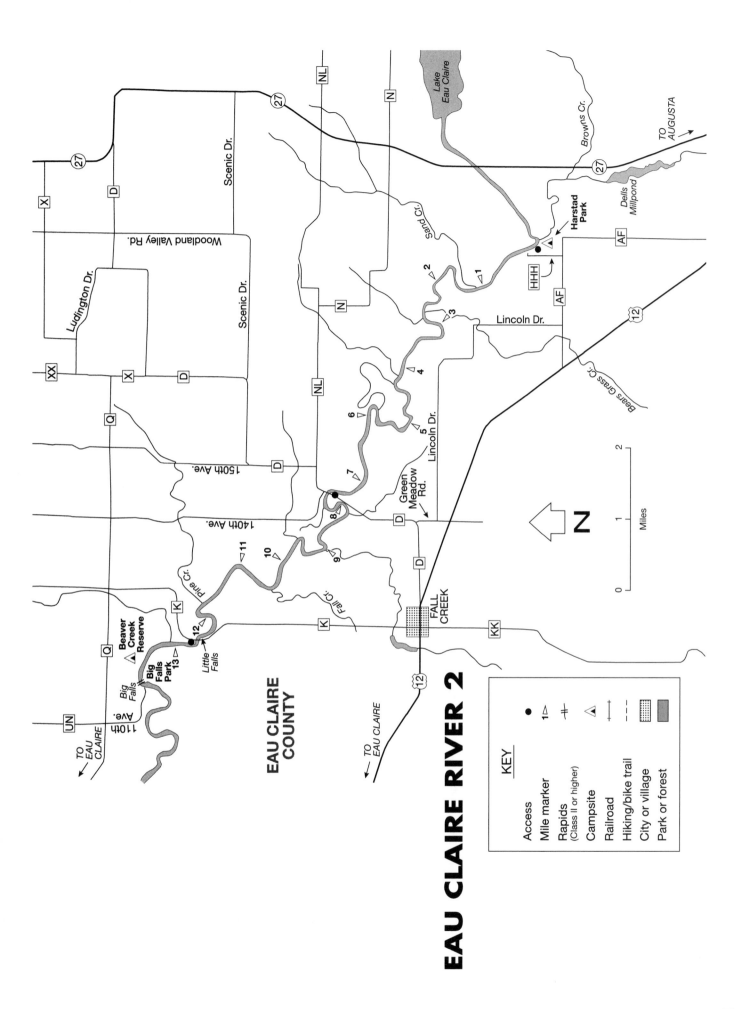

EAU CLAIRE RIVER 2

EAU CLAIRE
COUNTY

KEY

- Access
- 1△ Mile marker
- Rapids (Class II or higher)
- △ Campsite
- Railroad
- Hiking/bike trail
- City or village
- Park or forest

N

Miles

0   1   2

Lake
Eau Claire

Browns Cr.

TO
AUGUSTA

Dells
Millpond

Harstad
Park

HHH

AF

AF

12

Sand Cr.

Lincoln Dr.

Bear's Grass Cr.

2

1

3

4

5

Lincoln Dr.

6

7

Green
Meadow
Rd.

8

9

10

11

12

13

Little
Falls

Beaver
Creek
Reserve

Big Falls Park

Big
Falls

110th Ave.

Pine Cr.

Fall Cr.

FALL
CREEK

K

KK

D

D

D

Q

K

Q

K

UN

TO
EAU
CLAIRE

TO
EAU CLAIRE

12

NL

N

N

NL

27

27

27

X

XX

X

D

D

Scenic Dr.

Scenic Dr.

Woodland Valley Rd.

Ludington Dr.

140th Ave.

150th Ave.

EAU CLAIRE RIVER 3
Altoona Lake Dam to Hobbs Landing (5.1 Miles)

Sawdust City

Advantageously located at the confluence of the Chippewa and Eau Claire Rivers, the city of Eau Claire became an important boomtown during the height of the logging era—from the 1840s to the early 1900s. The Chippewa was the richest and most productive watershed in Northern Wisconsin's vast pinery, and hundreds of millions of logs were floated down the river to Eau Claire's 22 sawmills—hence the nickname "Sawdust City." Despite ongoing feuds with rival lumbermen upstream at Chippewa Falls and downstream on the Mississippi, great fortunes were made by such Eau Claire lumber barons as Joseph G. Thorp and Orrin H. Ingram, as evidenced by some of the grand old homes that still can be visited.

Fortunately, Eau Claire avoided the "bust" part of the boom-and-bust cycle that characterized most logging towns, and today is a large, prosperous, and diversified city. An agricultural and industrial center, it also boasts one of the prettiest campuses in the University of Wisconsin system.

In its final 3 miles before entering the Chippewa, the Eau Claire flows entirely within the large city of Eau Claire. Except for a few bridges and a factory, however, the surroundings are wild, wooded, and attractive. Rock formations and high embankments add to the scenery, and long riffles and rapids provide some excitement. When the water is high, large waves form, making the section dangerous for inexperienced paddlers. Herons, eagles, and other wildlife are often spotted. The put-in isn't easy, but the take-out is excellent.

Camping is available at Camp O'Klare a couple miles southeast of Eau Claire (715-832-7379), at Elmer's Campground 5 miles east of Eau Claire (715-832-6277), and at Lake Wissota State Park near Chippewa Falls (715-382-4574). For campsites farther upstream on the Eau Claire (at Coon Fork Park, Harstad Park, and Beaver Creek Reserve), see Eau Claire River 1.

Kayak rentals and shuttles are available at Riverside Bike and Skate in Eau Claire (715-835-0088). Canoes also may be rented at GD Odds Inc. in Eau Claire (715 833-1942).

The **shuttle route** (approximately 5.5 miles) from the Altoona Lake dam goes west on County QQ (North Shore Drive), west on County Q (Birch Street), south on Germania Street, west on Madison Street across the Chippewa, south on Fifth Avenue, west on Menomonie Street, and south at Tenth Avenue to Hobbs Landing.

Gradient is 2.9 feet per mile.

For **water levels,** see Eau Claire River 1.

Put in downstream-right from the Altoona Lake dam off County QQ, where an easy-to-miss gravel lane opposite Hotchkiss Street marks the beginning of the rough, rocky path down to the river bank. Be careful of your footing. The setting is attractive here, especially the rocky cliffs on the opposite shore.

More stone formations follow downstream, together with pleasant riffles over the sand-and-rock bottom. The river starts out 90 feet wide, with grassy, wooded banks, but soon widens to as much as 150 feet, bending left at a beautiful sandstone cliff on the right. When the river straightens, a railroad bridge appears downstream, followed briefly by a golf course on the left.

Immediately after a right turn, the bridges of Highway 53 loom ahead, with rock formations on the left. After Highway 53, high, densely wooded embankments lie on both sides of the river, which narrows, bends to the left, then straightens. A long succession of riffles and rapids soon begins. By the time you get to the former Uniroyal factory on the right, immediately preceded by a cable footbridge, the river is only 40 feet wide, with quickened current, waves, and some rocks to avoid. After a right bend, lovely rock outcroppings on the left lead to another railroad bridge. The best rapids of the trip follow, all the way to three vehicular bridges (Dewey, Farwell, and Barstow Streets).

The river now grows placid, heads left past some houses and commercial buildings, and flows into the Chippewa. Paddling left into the larger river, you quickly pass under a pedestrian bridge, then the Lake Street bridge. There are numerous commercial buildings along the river, but the shoreline is mostly covered with trees. Between the Lake Street and Water Street bridges on river-right lies Owen Park, with big, grassy areas, picnic facilities, and a gravelly beach.

In the right bend after Owen Park, the pedestrian bridge for the University of Wisconsin–Eau Claire campus soon follows. Just below the footbridge, where the river heads left, there's a gorgeous rocky cliff on the left. Nearby, Little Niagara Creek flows into the river over a drop. At this point in the left bend, 200 yards of wavy riffles and minor rapids begin, followed by a straightaway. Several hundred yards upstream from the next bridge, **take out** at Hobbs Landing on the right, a concrete boat ramp with adjacent parking.

Other trips. If you'd like a longer day on the river, you can continue down the Chippewa to the Highway 85 wayside or to the County H bridge near Caryville (see Chippewa River 1).

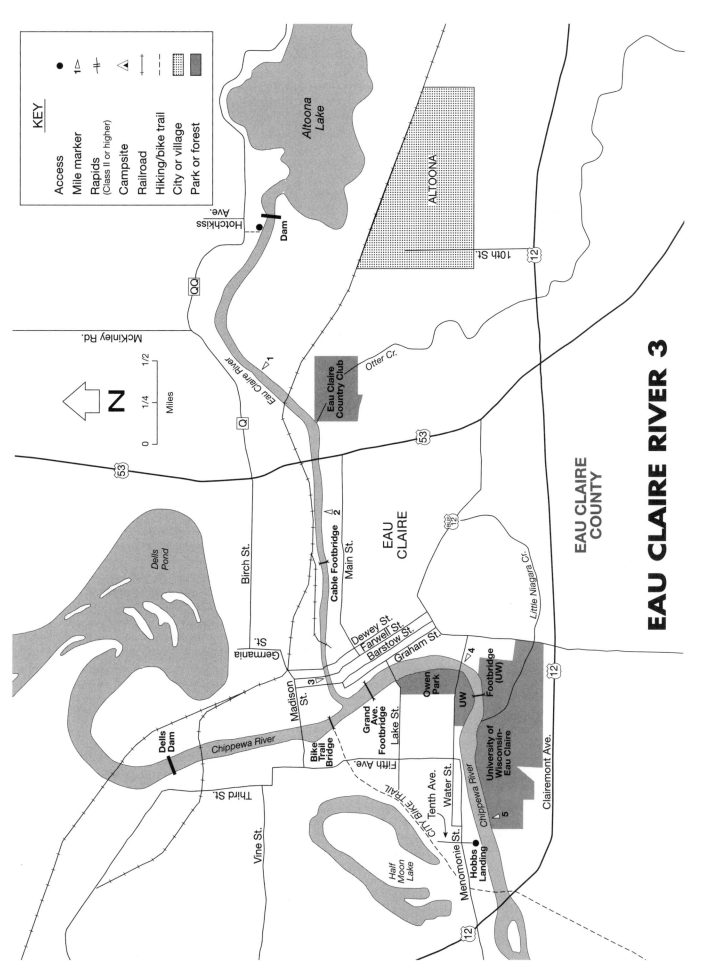

EAU CLAIRE RIVER 3

KEY

- **●** Access
- **1△** Mile marker
- **╫** Rapids (Class II or higher)
- **◁** Campsite
- **┼┼┼** Railroad
- **- - -** Hiking/bike trail
- City or village
- Park or forest

Altoona Lake

Hotchkiss Ave.

Dam

ALTOONA

10th St.

12

QQ

McKinley Rd.

Eau Claire River

1△

N

1/4 1/2

0 1/4

Miles

Q

53

Eau Claire Country Club

Otter Cr.

53

Dells Pond

Birch St.

Cable Footbridge 2△

Main St.

EAU CLAIRE

BUS 12

Little Niagara Cr.

EAU CLAIRE COUNTY

Germania St.

Dewey St.

Farwell St.

Barstow St.

Graham St.

4△

Madison St. 3△

Owen Park

Footbridge (UW)

UW

Dells Dam

Chippewa River

Bike Trail Bridge

Grand Ave. Footbridge

Lake St.

University of Wisconsin-Eau Claire

Third St.

Fifth Ave.

Tenth Ave.

Water St.

Chippewa River

5△

Clairemont Ave.

12

Vine St.

CITY BIKE TRAIL

Half Moon Lake

Menomonie St.

Hobbs Landing ●

12

FOX RIVER 1
Portage to County O (10 Miles)

Perhaps the chief allure of a trip on the Fox is the realization that you're paddling on one of the most historically significant rivers in America. For more than two centuries it was part of a major water highway between the populous eastern United States and the developing area west of the Great Lakes. Native Americans had long journeyed from Green Bay to the Mississippi via the Fox and Wisconsin Rivers, and in 1673 they guided Joliet and Marquette over the route. Thousands of missionaries, traders, and settlers soon followed—at first in canoes, later in steamboats. After 1876 the completion of a short canal between the Fox and Wisconsin, together with a series of dams and locks, made boat traffic easier. Since 1951, however, the waterway has been closed to commercial traffic, and canoes are again plying the waters of the Fox.

Originating about 20 miles northeast of Portage, the upper Fox comes within 1.25 miles of the Wisconsin River, then swings northwestward through the cities of Montello, Princeton, and Berlin before entering Lake Butte des Morts and Lake Winnebago, then heading toward Green Bay. In its 107-mile upper section the river flows through several large lakes and is quite slow, with an average gradient of only 4 inches per mile. In the remaining 39 miles, the lower Fox is wider, deeper, often dammed, and more urban/industrial.

The last remaining building of historic Fort Winnebago, at the put-in of Fox River 1.

The two stretches recommended here flow through peaceful, sometimes marshy areas of the rural upper Fox. In the first trip, which can be shortened by using a good intermediate access, you'll have an opportunity to see the canal close-up.

Camping is available at Pride of America Campground 3.5 miles southeast of Portage (800-236-6395), Sky High Camping Resort 4.5 miles southwest of Portage (608-742-2572), and Indian Trails Campground 1.5 miles northwest of Pardeeville (608-429-3244).

The **shuttle route** (7.5 miles) from Portage goes east a short distance on Highway 33, north on County F, and west on County O to the bridge.

Gradient is only 1 foot per mile.

For **water levels**, check the Berlin gauge (#04073500) on the USGS Web site. See "Water Levels" in the introduction.

Put in on the northeast side of Portage at the Highway 33 bridge, downstream-right. Launch your boat(s) from the grassy bank of an attractive riverside park, the approximate location where Joliet and Marquette started their portage to the Wisconsin River

in 1673. Directly across the road is the restored surgeon general's quarters of old Fort Winnebago, which was built in 1828 to protect the interests of fur traders.

Only 35 feet wide at the beginning, the river quickly turns several times through an open area, passing pastureland, farm buildings, and several sets of old wooden pilings. Soon after the river narrows and woods begin, the old canal appears on the left. Immediately upstream from the canal opening is a sandy landing that makes a good alternative put-in (reached from the nearby access road that leads from Highway 33 to the old lock and the restored Indian agent's house). The canal lock is only 100 feet from the river and well worth a short side trip; the old wooden gates have been unattractively replaced with rocks and steel pilings.

Woods don't last long after the canal as you enter a grassy, high-banked area. Here, as elsewhere on the trip, you see the effects of the nonstop dredging that occurred between 1876 and the 1930s. In order to maintain enough depth for navigation, dredgers went up and down the river removing silt and sand from the bottom and piling it along the sides. Occasionally in bends you can see tall cut banks where the river has eroded the shoreline, and a few drainage ditches are seen. Much of the bankside environment is marshy wetland.

After the Clark Road bridge, gentle bends lead to Governor's Bend, immediately preceded by several houses on the right. The big, grassy island at Governor's Bend—named after a visit to the location by the state's first governor, Nelson Dewey—is now a park that is popular with picnickers and fishermen. There was once a lock in the left channel (now filled in) and a dam in the right. The remnants of the dam—a pile of rubble—should be portaged; take out on the island and put back in below the rock pile. You can easily end your trip here by carrying your boat(s) to the footbridge over the right channel and across to the parking lot (at the end of Lock Road, off Fox River Road and County F).

Downstream, often-canoed Neenah Creek enters on the left, and French Creek soon follows on the right. The County CM bridge was the location of the Emancipation Ferry in the 1840s, so-called because of a nearby settlement of English potters who had come here in hopes of becoming free from the poverty they had known in England. After paralleling Fox River Road, the river winds around, past the mouth of Good Earth Creek, to the County O bridge. **Take out** at the gravel landing, downstream-left.

Within a few miles Buffalo Lake begins—10 miles long, half a mile wide, and extending all the way to Montello. Six miles after Montello, the Fox widens out into the even bigger Lake Puckaway. The next recommended section begins farther downstream at Princeton.

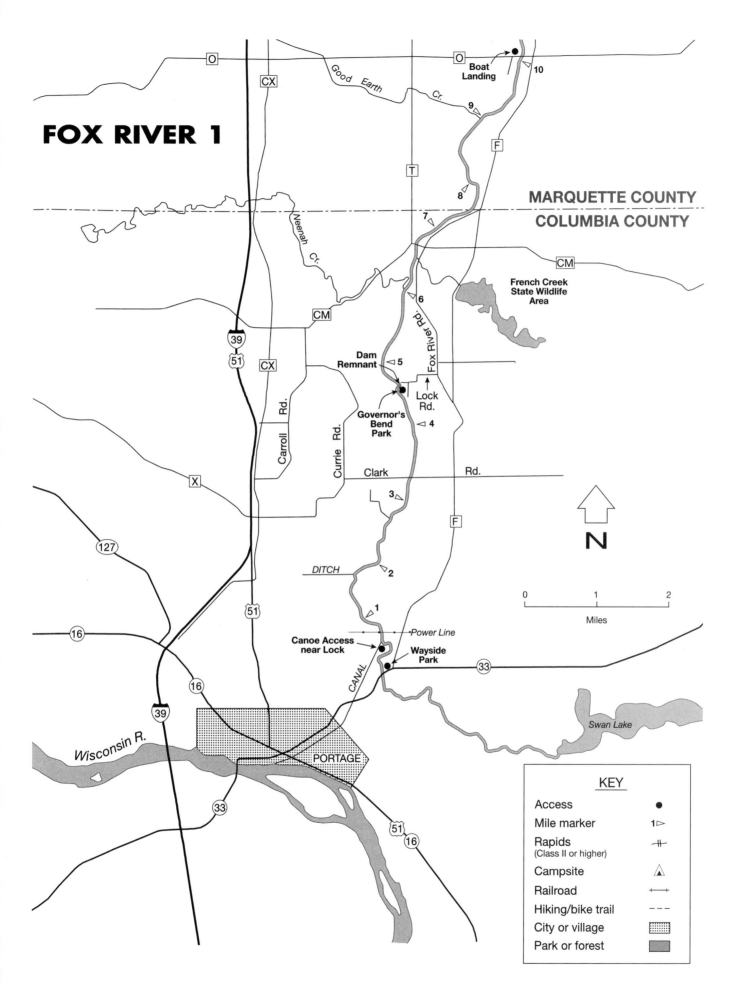

FOX RIVER 1

O

CX

Good Earth Cr.

O

Boat Landing

10

9

F

T

8

7

MARQUETTE COUNTY
COLUMBIA COUNTY

CM

Neenah Cr.

CM

French Creek State Wildlife Area

39
51

CX

6

Fox River Rd.

Dam Remnant ◁ 5

Carroll Rd.

Currie Rd.

Governor's Bend Park

Lock Rd.

◁ 4

X

Clark Rd.

F

3 ◁

127

N

2 ◁

DITCH

0   1   2
Miles

51

1 ◁

Power Line

16

Canoe Access near Lock

Wayside Park

33

16

CANAL

Swan Lake

39

Wisconsin R.

PORTAGE

33

51

16

KEY	
Access	●
Mile marker	1▷
Rapids (Class II or higher)	─╫─
Campsite	⚠
Railroad	┼─┼
Hiking/bike trail	- - -
City or village	▒
Park or forest	▓

FOX RIVER 2
Princeton to Berlin (15 Miles)

Quite different from the Portage-area stretch, this long section of the upper Fox flows lazily through big, gentle bends and varies in width from 80 to 200+ feet. Most of the surroundings are wild, and half the trip is through attractive marshland. There is an old lock and dam that must be portaged, but the carry-around is safe and easy, and provides an intermediate access that can be used for shorter trips. Unless you choose one of the shorter options, be ready for a long day because the current is weak and you'll have to depend mostly on paddle-power.

The scenery isn't varied—mostly wild woodland and open marsh—but the setting is quite peaceful, with houses sparse and only one bridge. The put-in and take-out are excellent, and Princeton and Berlin are charming small cities.

Camping is available at Riverside Park in Berlin, Mecan River Outfitters and Lodge 3 miles west of Princeton (920-295-3439), and Green Lake Campground 1.5 miles west of Green Lake (920-294-3543). There are also a number of campgrounds in the Montello and Puckaway Lake area.

Canoe rental and shuttles are available from Mecan River Outfitters and Lodge 3 miles west of Princeton (920-295-3439).

The **shuttle route** (13.6 miles) from Princeton goes east on Jefferson Street, south on Mechanic Street, east on Highway 23 (Main Street), north and east on County J, north on County A, and north on Landing Road. A longer, less winding shuttle route uses Highway 49 instead of County J.

Gradient is negligible (less than 1 foot per mile).

For **water levels,** see Fox River 1.

Put in in Princeton at the small city park downstream-right from the Highway 23 bridge. A concrete boat ramp, toilet, and parking area are provided. To get to the landing, turn off Main Street (Highway 23) onto Mechanic Street, then onto Jefferson Street. The river here is only 80 feet wide, curving to the right between wooded banks, then bending left under an old railroad bridge. Within a few minutes the docks and houses along the shoreline end. After widening to almost 200 feet, the river narrows and soon passes a public boat ramp on the left; located at the end of St. Marie Road, off County D, this is an alternative **put-in,** shortening your trip by 1.5 miles. Steep sandbanks follow on the left.

Heading north, the river is straight and narrow for

The lowhead at the White River Lock and Dam (Fox River 2): easily portaged.

a while, flowing through wild surroundings. Then the streambed widens in a very long right bend, followed by another straightaway and a sharp left turn. Along the way a couple of homes and farm buildings are passed. Eventually, in a gentle left arc, signs warn of a dam ahead. As you approach a large island—where the dam is in the left channel and the lock in the right channel—take out at the concrete boat ramp on the right shoreline. From here, portage along the gravel road and reenter the river at a gravel landing 50 yards downstream from the lock (which has been replaced with culverts and limestone blocks). The area of the White River Lock and Dam is a DNR public fishing ground. A path leads across the island to the dam.

In the long straightaway after the lock and dam, the setting becomes wild and deeply wooded again. When the river heads left, however, marshland begins on both sides, and the mouth of the White River soon appears on the left. For several miles the 10,000-acre White River Marsh State Wildlife Area continues along the left shoreline. Only 1.5 miles downstream from the mouth of the White, the Puchyan River enters on the right, also flowing through a vast marsh. Most of the rest of the trip is through very low, open marshland, but the channel of the Fox is always wide and distinct. The tree line is usually far off in the distance as the river winds through a long succession of bends, passing sloughs, a few cabins, and many deer stands.

In the last 1.5 miles, after a huge slough on the left, cabins and homes become more numerous, the river narrows, and woods appear sporadically. Finally, in the midst of some houses on the right shoreline and just before a left bend, **take out** at the boat ramp at the end of Landing Road (off County A). The Berlin Lock and Dam is only half a mile downstream.

Other trips. (1) It's 14 miles from Riverside Park in Berlin to Omro, but the Eureka Lock and Dam must be portaged. This stretch has several boat landings along the way, and considerable motorboat traffic. A few miles after Omro, the upper Fox ends as it flows into Lake Butte des Morts and Lake Winnebago (the state's largest inland body of water). (2) Another stretch that is sometimes paddled is a combination of the Mecan and Fox Rivers: put in on the Mecan at County C, float down to the Fox (at Devil's Elbow), portage the Princeton Lock and Dam around the river-left lock (the dam is very dangerous!), and take out at Highway 23 (downstream-right). You can shorten the trip by taking out upstream-left from the lock at the Princeton Lock and Dam (Lock Road runs south from Highway 23 to a DNR public fishing area alongside the lock and dam).

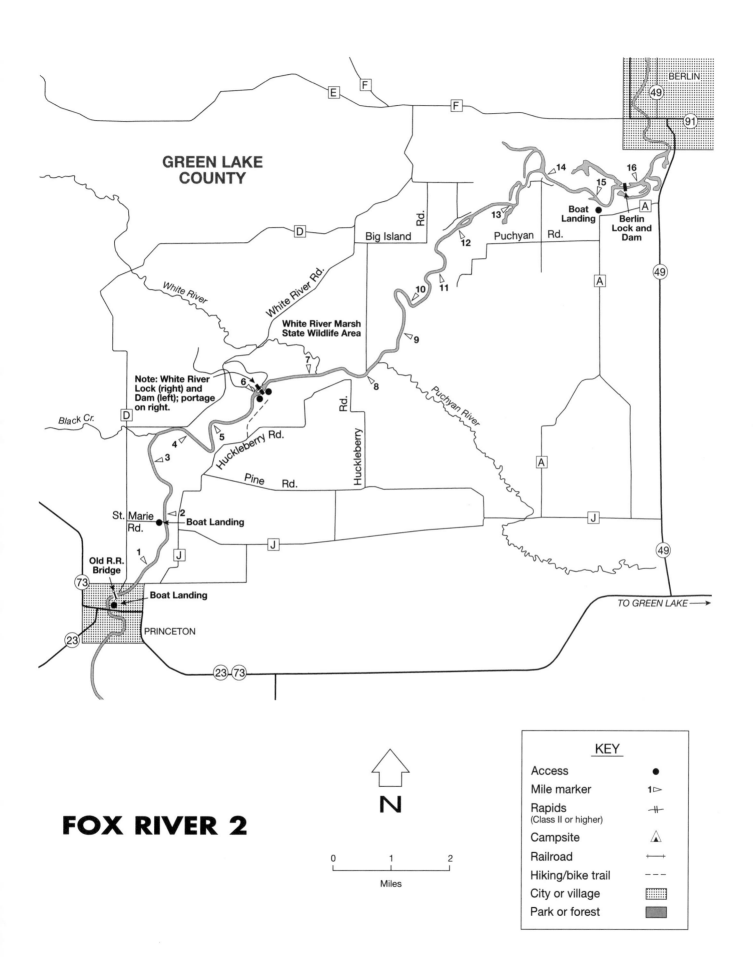

GREEN LAKE
COUNTY

BERLIN

White River

White River Rd.

White River Marsh
State Wildlife Area

Big Island

Rd.

Puchyan Rd.

Boat
Landing

Berlin
Lock and
Dam

14

15

16

13

12

10 11

9

Note: White River
Lock (right) and
Dam (left); portage
on right.

Black Cr.

7

6

8

Puchyan River

5

4

3

Huckleberry Rd.

Rd.

Huckleberry

Pine   Rd.

St. Marie
Rd.

2   Boat Landing

1

Old R.R.
Bridge

Boat Landing

PRINCETON

TO GREEN LAKE →

FOX RIVER 2

N

0   1   2
Miles

KEY

Access	●
Mile marker	1▷
Rapids (Class II or higher)	╫
Campsite	△
Railroad	⊢—⊣
Hiking/bike trail	- - -
City or village	▦
Park or forest	▬

GALENA RIVER
County W to Buncombe Road (5.8 Miles)

A Little Jewel of a Church

If you head east on County W a short distance from the Galena River, you'll come to the tiny community of New Diggings—once a thriving lead-mining town. Beginning in the 1820s, many prospectors from Galena, Illinois (the location of the "old," established diggings) headed north along the Galena River to find "new diggings." Soon other communities—including Benton, Shullsburg, and Platteville—sprang up in the area as the mining fervor spread. You won't regret taking a few minutes to visit the memorable St. Augustine's Church in New Diggings, a beautiful little wooden structure designed by the indefatigable missionary Samuel Mazzuchelli and built in 1844. For 30 years this talented priest served the lead-mining district, designing and constructing dozens of imaginative churches and other buildings. After his death in 1864, he was buried in nearby Benton. (For more on the lead-mining region, see the sidebar for Grant River 2.)

Designated the Galena River on some maps, the Fever on others, this delightful stream winds through the rugged hills of the Driftless Area. When water volume is sufficient (usually through May or after sustained rainfall), the river provides paddlers with multitudes of pleasant riffles, often in combination with lovely, wooded bluffs and rock formations. Flowing through the heart of the historic lead-mining district—Galena is the name of the lead ore extracted in the 1800s—the river generally has a remote feel, with few dwellings. The trip recommended here ends within 0.5 mile of the Illinois border. Averaging only 35 feet in width, the river is clear and flows over a rocky bottom. A highlight is an abandoned railroad tunnel that twice appears along the shoreline.

Camping. There are no nearby campgrounds, but see the Pecatonica River description for camping in the Darlington and Belmont areas. Camping is also available to the southeast in Illinois at Apple River Canyon State Park, north of Stockton (815-745-3302), and to the southwest near Galena at the Palace Campground (815-777-2466).

Canoe rentals are available in Madison at Rutabaga (608-223-9300) and Carl's Paddlin' (608-284-0300).

The **shuttle route** (4.8 miles) goes west, then south on County W, and south on Buncombe Road.

The **gradient** of 6.6 feet per mile produces countless riffles.

For **water levels**, check the Galena River gauge on the Interactive Weather Information Network. See "Water Levels" in the introduction. When the gauge is below 3.0 feet, some of the riffles become scratchy.

Put in at the County W bridge, downstream-left, near a small gravel pull-off that will accommodate two or three cars. Riffles begin immediately alongside tall cut banks. The river-right grain-storage structures at the beginning are the last buildings to be seen for some time. Soon the river is diverted to the right by

a wooded bluff, then flows alongside the bluff in a riffly, westward straightaway. The terrace on the left is the bed of an abandoned railroad. On the right are open fields.

As soon as the straight stretch ends at another bluff and the river veers left, the concrete abutments of an old railroad bridge appear on both sides, together with some wooden pilings in the streambed. Up on the hillside is the huge mouth of an old tunnel, followed by some brief but attractive cliffs. The river now arcs gently to the southeast—bluffs on the right, open fields on the left.

Eventually the long southeast stretch heads into another bluff and veers to the right amid good riffles. At the next sharp right turn, Kelsey Branch enters on the left, and farm buildings appear. An old metal truss bridge soon crosses the riffly streambed. A short distance downstream, the river runs straight into another tall bluff and abruptly turns right through a short, shallow rock garden that can result in a lot of scraping in low water. The river now proceeds in a long, gentle right bend, alongside the often-rocky bluff on the left. Power lines soon cross in the bend.

Once again a bluff deflects the river to the left, and the sharp, riffly left bend that follows heads south toward the Buncombe Station Bridge (named after an old railroad station). A concrete gauging station is located downstream-left from the bridge. Soon another bluff forces the river sharply to the right, and in the long right arc that follows there are some attractive rock formations and huge streamside boulders. Directly across from the mouth of Coon Branch is the gaping mouth of another railroad tunnel, carved through the rocky bluff.

After bending left alongside Buncombe Road, the river passes under a modern farm bridge. Then, a couple hundred yards upstream from where the river is sharply diverted to the left by more bluffs, the **take-out** landing appears on the right: a small, gravelly, easy-to-miss spot alongside the bank, just upstream from a creek that enters on the right. A short dirt road leads from Buncombe Road, near the bridge over the creek, to the landing, which the property owner generously allows paddlers to use.

Other trips. (1) Upstream, the gradient is considerably steeper; thus, the stretch from Benton to County W is difficult to catch with sufficient water. (2) After Buncombe Road the river soon heads south into Illinois. The 9-mile stretch to Buckhill Road is quite pleasant; another 4.5 miles leads to the charming city of Galena. (See Galena 1 and 2 in my book *Paddling Illinois*, pp. 50–53.)

Clear, riffly water on the Galena.

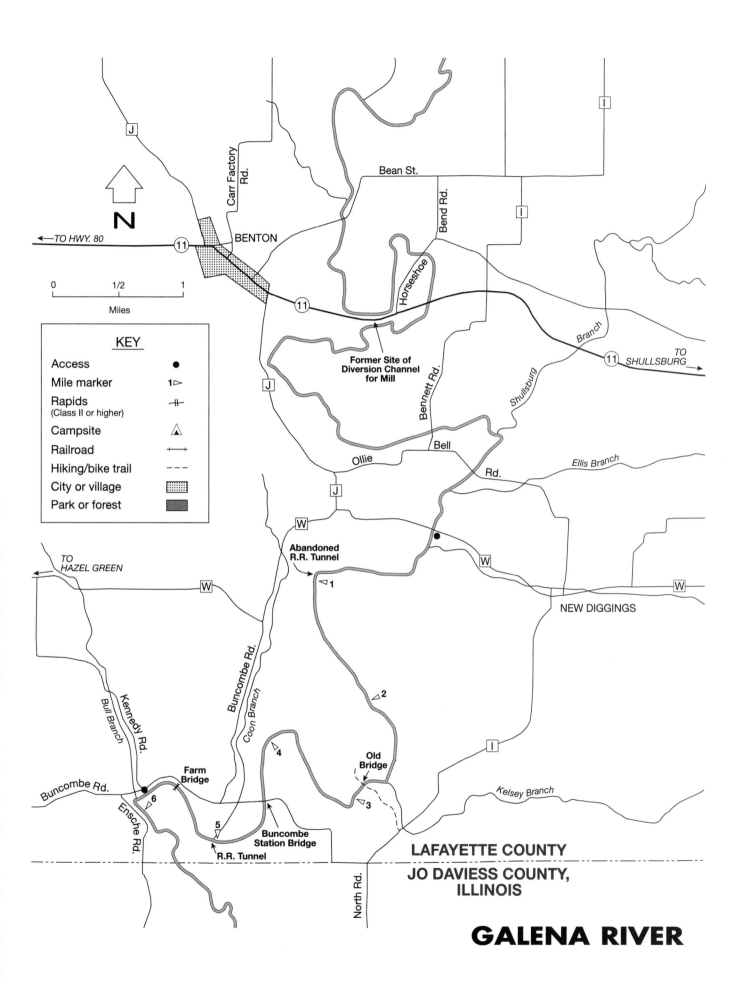

N

← *TO HWY. 80*

| 0 | 1/2 | 1 |
Miles

KEY

Access	●
Mile marker	1▷
Rapids (Class II or higher)	─╫─
Campsite	▲
Railroad	┼─┼
Hiking/bike trail	─ ─ ─
City or village	▨
Park or forest	▰

Carr Factory Rd.

BENTON

(11)

Bean St.

Bend Rd.

Horseshoe

(11)

Former Site of
Diversion Channel
for Mill

(11) *TO SHULLSBURG* →

Branch

Shullsburg

Bennett Rd.

J

Bell

Ollie

Rd.

Ellis Branch

J

W

Abandoned
R.R. Tunnel

●

W

W

NEW DIGGINGS

*TO
HAZEL GREEN*
←

W

▷ 1

Buncombe Rd.

Coon Branch

▷ 2

I

▷ 4

Old
Bridge

Bull Branch

Kennedy Rd.

Farm
Bridge

▷ 6

●

▷ 3

Kelsey Branch

Buncombe Rd.

Ensche Rd.

5

Buncombe
Station Bridge

R.R. Tunnel

North Rd.

LAFAYETTE COUNTY

**JO DAVIESS COUNTY,
ILLINOIS**

GALENA RIVER

GRANT RIVER 1
Porter–Hill Road to County U (11 Miles)

One of the most delightful paddling rivers in the state, the Grant winds circuitously between the hills of the rugged Driftless Area in southwestern Wisconsin. A small stream, only 25–40 feet wide most of the time, it provides a joyous experience of canopied foliage, striking rock formations, pleasant riffles, and unbroken solitude. Appropriate for "advanced beginners," the Grant has many sharp turns with tricky currents and eddies, together with trees and limbs that occasionally require maneuvering. Accesses are quite adequate. The two sections described here are similar, but the first has more rock outcroppings, while the second is somewhat more riffly. Relatively remote from the state's population centers, this beautiful stream isn't heavily canoed, but once you've paddled it, you'll definitely want to return.

Camping is available within a 15-mile radius at Klondyke Secluded Acres 2 miles west of Lancaster (608-723-2844), Mound View Park in Platteville (608-348-2313), Grant River Public Use Area 2 miles south of Potosi (608-763-2140), Big H Campground between Potosi and Cassville (608-725-5921), Nelson Dewey State Park on the Mississippi west of Cassville (608-725-5374), Jellystone Park 1 mile north of Bagley (608-996-2201), River of Lakes Resort and Campground 1 mile south of Bagley (608-996-2275), and the Rustic Barn Campground south of Dickeyville (608-568-7797).

If you pass through Dickeyville, take a few minutes to visit the famous grotto made of stone, mortar, and glass by Father Matthias Wernerus in the 1920s.

Canoe rentals and shuttle service are available in Beetown at Grant River Canoe Rental (608-794-2342).

The **shuttle route** (5.7 miles) for the first section goes west a short distance on Porter–Hill Road, west on Highway 81 to Beetown, and south on County U to the bridge.

Gradient is a riffle-inducing 3.6 feet per mile.

For **water levels**, check the Burton gauge (#05413500) on the USGS Web site. See "Water Levels in the introduction. For general information on water levels (high, medium, low), call Grant River Canoe Rental (608-794-2342).

Put in alongside Porter–Hill Road, at a river-right clearing 0.1 mile east of Highway 81. (To get to the put-in, turn south off Highway 35/81 just west of the bridge, then south on 81, and east on Porter–Hill Road.) Narrow and canopied, the river soon passes under an old metal truss bridge. The grassy banks are fairly steep, and riffles appear occasionally, especially beside small, grassy islands and in constrictions and shallows. At one point, gorgeous sandstone cliffs appear on the left, topped with both deciduous and coniferous trees and continuing for several hundred yards in a straightaway. Riffles initiate a long left bend where undercut rock outcroppings line the right shoreline. A barn near some power lines is the first building of the trip. Later in the curve a particularly beautiful cliff, topped with pines, goes on for a long time on the right in a series of tight turns.

The river now narrows to as little as 25 feet and twists back and forth through a mostly open area, passing under power lines four times. Heading straight toward a tall wooded bluff, the river suddenly veers right at a beautiful, radically undercut rock wall. The river here is straight, narrow, riffly, heavily wooded, and enchanting.

After the Grant River Road bridge—look for swallow nests on the bottom—the river curves left alongside wooded bluffs, with frequent, small riffles and more rock formations, including the largest cliff of the trip. Here, as elsewhere, house-size chunks of rock have fallen into the water. More curves lead to the Pigeon River Road bridge. Three farm fords cross the river downstream, but there are few rock formations until the riffly half-mile approach to the next bridge (also on Pigeon River Road).

The river is now relatively deep and slow as it arcs around toward County U. At the end, after an island in a right bend, Blackjack Road is seen on the right. **Take out** on river-right directly beneath the bridge. An upstream-right access road leads from County U to the landing, off Blackjack Road.

GRANT RIVER 1

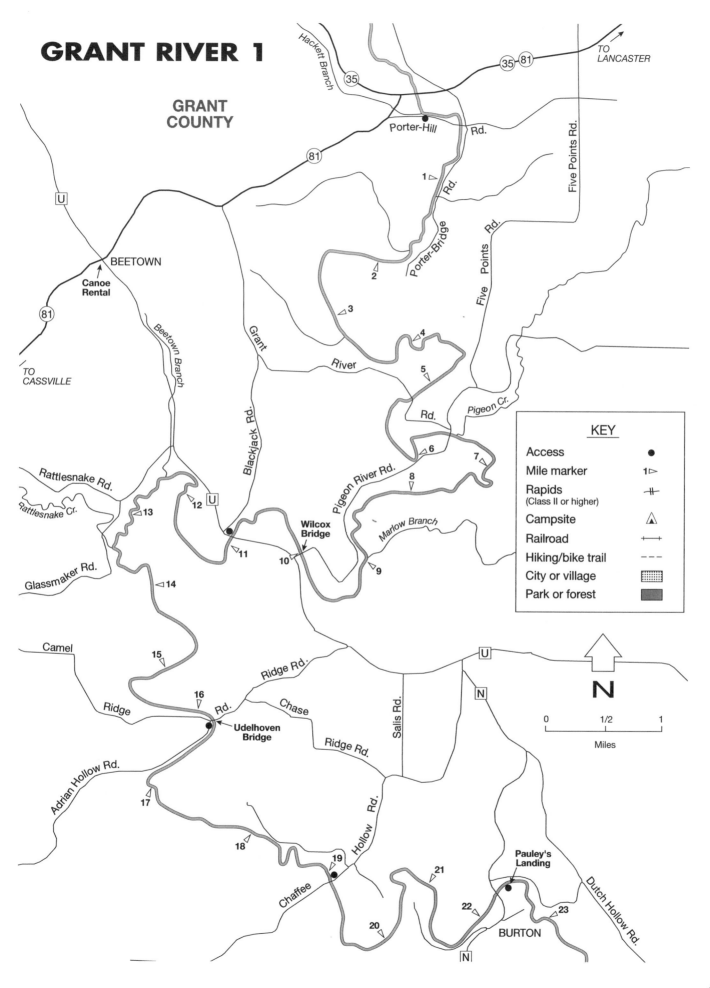

GRANT
COUNTY

GRANT RIVER 1

Hackett Branch

35 81

TO LANCASTER

35 81

Porter-Hill Rd.

81

Porter-Bridge Rd.

Five Points Rd.

1

2

3

Grant

River

4

Five Points Rd.

5

Rd.

Pigeon Cr.

U

BEETOWN

Canoe Rental

81

TO CASSVILLE

Beetown Branch

Blackjack Rd.

6

7

8

Pigeon River Rd.

KEY

Access	●
Mile marker	1▷
Rapids (Class II or higher)	╫
Campsite	⚠
Railroad	┼┼
Hiking/bike trail	- - -
City or village	▦
Park or forest	▨

Rattlesnake Rd.

Rattlesnake Cr.

13

12

U

11

10

Wilcox Bridge

Marlow Branch

9

Glassmaker Rd.

14

Camel

15

Ridge Rd.

Chase

Salis Rd.

U

N

N

0   1/2   1
Miles

Ridge

16

Rd.

Udelhoven Bridge

Adrian Hollow Rd.

17

18

Ridge Rd.

Chaffee

19

Hollow Rd.

20

21

22

Pauley's Landing

23

Dutch Hollow Rd.

BURTON

N

GRANT RIVER 2
County U to Chaffee Hollow Road (8 Miles)

Getting the Lead Out

The southwestern corner of Wisconsin was the first part of the state-to-be to experience a significant wave of immigrants, drawn to the rich deposits of lead in the Driftless Area. Beginning in the 1820s, thousands of miners—primarily from southern Illinois, Kentucky, and Tennessee, and later (in the 1830s) from Cornwall, England—headed for the Galena area of northwestern Illinois and for the region that would later become Grant and Lafayette Counties in Wisconsin. After an influx that began in 1825, the mining region was producing 12 million pounds of lead by 1829. Sometimes living in crude earthen dugouts that led to their being called "badgers," miners pocked the countryside with pits, shafts, and tailing piles—many of which are still visible. By the 1840s the price of lead had fallen precipitously and deposits had become less plentiful, so many miners turned to farming or headed for California in the gold rush of 1849.

Not far from the Grant, Platte, and Mississippi Rivers you can still get a feel for the lead-mining era. In Potosi, for example, St. John Mine gives visitors an opportunity to wind through the tunnels of a mine that dates back to 1690. In that year explorer/trader Nicholas Perrot was shown the lead-rich Snake Cave by Native Americans who mined the area until the Winnebago Peace Treaty of 1827 opened the region to white settlers. Owned by a man named St. John and later by the first governor of Wisconsin—Nelson Dewey—it became a very productive mine. In nearby Platteville, you can enter another lead mine from the 1820s and visit a museum that tells the story of the lead-mining years.

Although this section has fewer of the stunning rock formations that characterize the previous stretch, you'll find it to be equally enjoyable. In general, it's narrower, super-quiet, and very riffly. It has a little of everything, including a twisty stream-bed near the beginning, scattered rock outcroppings, high bluffs, swift water, and easy accesses (with an intermediate landing that makes shorter trips possible). Except for some pastureland and corn fields at the outset, the river feels quite remote here. You'll see only one bridge before the take-out, and few houses.

For **camping, canoe rentals**, and **water levels,** see Grant River 1.

The **shuttle route** (4.9 miles) goes southeast on County U, south on County N for a short distance, then southwest on Chaffee Hollow Road to the bridge. A slightly shorter route (4.1 miles) goes southeast on County U, south on Salis Road (gravel), and southwest on Chaffee Hollow Road.

Gradient is an exhilarating 6.2 feet per mile.

Put in at County U south of Beetown, directly beneath the bridge on river-right. A gravel road leads down to the landing, from nearby Blackjack Road. In the big right bend at the beginning, the river flows past high wooded bluffs on the left and pastureland on the right. After a left turn, close to County U, a long series of short, sharp bends begins. The banks are high and grassy in this winding area, and corn fields can be seen occasionally atop the banks, together with a couple of farm buildings.

Woods begin again near some pleasant riffles, and Rattlesnake Creek enters on the right. A straight stretch now follows toward the southeast—peaceful and tree-canopied, with an attractive rock outcropping and long riffles. When a long right bend begins, a ford crosses the streambed. Throughout the bend there are beautiful bluffs on the left, often displaying remarkably gnarled rock formations. Here and there huge slabs of rock have fallen into the water. Another ford crosses when the river turns sharply left, and riffles and rock formations occur in the approach to the Udelhoven

Riverside cliffs add to the beautiful scenery on the Grant.

Bridge on Camel Ridge Road. In the open area before the bridge there are a couple of houses.

Riffles begin below the bridge, the river swings to the right, and a lovely sand beach appears 25 yards after the bridge on the right—an excellent access with a nearby drop-off road and plenty of room to park vehicles. Soon a marvelous rock face appears on the left, covered with wet moss—a striking and beautiful example of a seep.

After a couple of sharp, riffly turns, the river heads toward the southeast along tall, sometimes rocky bluffs on the right. The last mile of the trip is one of the prettiest parts of the Grant: narrow, densely wooded, canopied, and placid. In the big gentle arcs of this area, the river is steep-banked and narrows to 25 feet; riffles are almost continuous. Eventually sharp turns to the left, then right, create a small oxbow. A few more sharp turns lead to Chaffee Hollow Road. After a final riffle in a left turn, **take out** 50 yards upstream from the bridge at a sand-and-gravel landing on the left. A dirt road leads back to the landing.

Other trips. Another 3.5 miles of paddling takes you to the small community of Burton, where Pauley's Landing (a dock, with steps leading up to the nearby tavern) is located on the right bank not far downstream from the County N bridge. The owners of Pauley Brothers Tavern allow camping in the nearby grassy area.

GRANT RIVER 2

GRANT
COUNTY

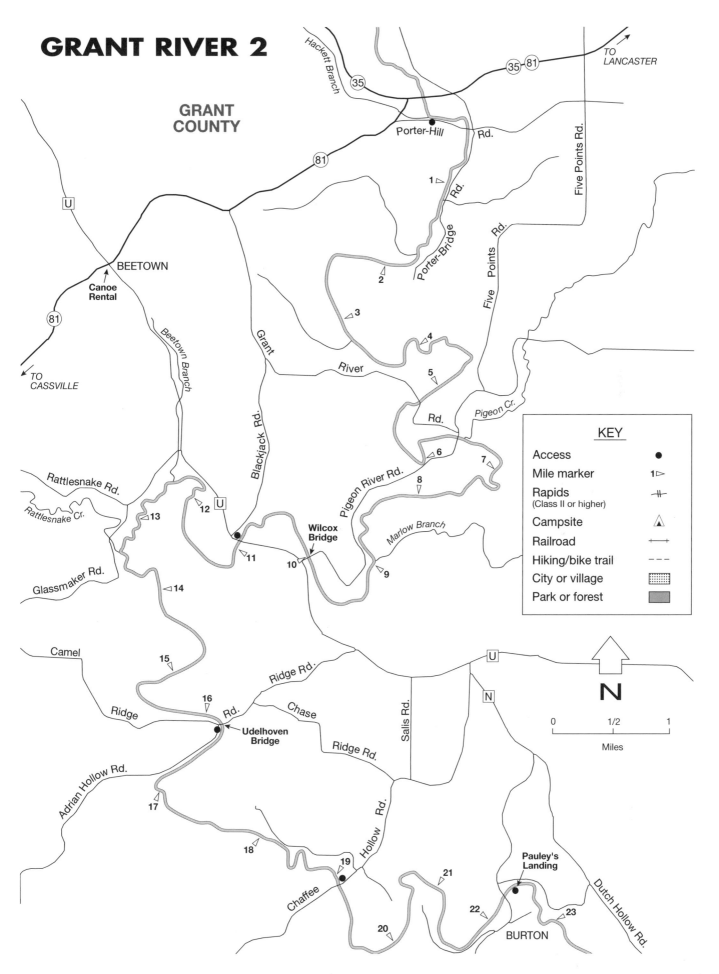

Hackett Branch

35
35 81
TO LANCASTER

81

Porter-Hill   Rd.

Five Points Rd.

U

1

BEETOWN

Canoe
Rental

81

TO
CASSVILLE

Beetown Branch

Grant

River

Blackjack Rd.

Porter-Bridge   Rd.

Five Points Rd.

2

3

4

5

Pigeon Cr.

Rd.

6

7

Pigeon River Rd.

8

Marlow Branch

KEY

Access	●
Mile marker	1▷
Rapids (Class II or higher)	╫
Campsite	△
Railroad	┼┼
Hiking/bike trail	- - -
City or village	▦
Park or forest	▨

Rattlesnake Rd.

Rattlesnake Cr.

13

12

U

Wilcox
Bridge

11

10

9

Glassmaker Rd.

14

Camel

15

Ridge Rd.

Chase

Salis Rd.

U

N

N

0   1/2   1

Miles

Ridge

16

Rd.

Udelhoven
Bridge

Ridge Rd.

Adrian Hollow Rd.

17

Hollow Rd.

18

19

21

Pauley's
Landing

Chaffee

20

22

23

BURTON

Dutch Hollow Rd.

ILLINOIS FOX RIVER 1
Mukwonago to Tichigan Lake (14 Miles)

Originating northwest of Milwaukee in the same area that spawns the Bark, Menomonee, and Oconomowoc Rivers, the Fox heads southward for 70 miles through Waukesha, Big Bend, Waterford, and Burlington before flowing into the popular Chain O' Lakes just below the Illinois border. After the state line the river still has 115 miles, many urban communities, and 15 dams to go before emptying into the Illinois River near Ottawa. Confusingly, there are two Fox Rivers in Wisconsin, so this one is often called the Illinois or Little Fox to distinguish it from the river made famous by Joliet and Marquette and those who followed them. The so-called Little Fox is not really a small river, and it's at least as paddleable as its namesake to the north. Except in times of high water, the Fox is a slow-moving river, winding through marshes, woods, and farmland and encountering dams at Waukesha, Waterford, and Rochester. Waterfowl and other wildlife are often observed, especially in the abundant wetland settings nearby. Bank fishing is popular.

Before the paddle.

The first recommended trip consists mostly of big, gentle bends, alternating between shallow areas and deeper pools. Never very wide, it presents a mixture of open, marshy shoreline and wooded banks, with only a few houses. It makes an excellent float trip for beginners. Shorter, more leisurely trips are easily arranged by using alternate accesses at Center Road or Big Bend.

Camping is available at Country View Campground near Mukwonago (262-662-3654), Bong State Recreation Area 6 miles southeast of Burlington (262-878-5600), and Meadowlark Acres near Burlington (262-763-7200).

Canoe rentals and shuttles are available at Fox River Landing near the take-out (262-662-5690), at Tichigan Trails on Tichigan Lake (262-662-5081), and at Tip-a-Canoe Rentals near Burlington (262-537-3227).

The **shuttle route** (5.8 miles) for a 7-mile trip from Mukwonago to Big Bend goes east a short distance on County ES, east on Edgewood Road into Big Bend, south on Highway 164, and west on County L (Milwaukee Avenue) to the bridge and park. For the full 13-mile trip (10.4-mile shuttle) continue west on County L, then south on Center Drive, east on Bridge Drive to the bridge, and south along the west side of the river to the Tichigan Lake Public Access.

Gradient is negligible (less than a foot per mile).

For **water levels**, check the Waukesha gauge (#05543830) on the USGS Web site. See "Water Levels" in the introduction.

Put in east of Mukwonago at the County ES bridge, upstream-left or downstream-right. The water usually has a muddy cast and flows with little current between low, thinly forested, mud-and-sand banks. Soon, within sight of the Interstate 43 bridges where some farm buildings can be seen upstream-left, the broad mouth of the Mukwonago River enters on the right. In the long straight stretch after the bridges, the woods grow thicker. Power lines run along the river for a while, and a game farm sign appears on the right. A series of bends, some with deep pools, carry the river back toward the traffic noise of I-43 before swinging toward the east again. Woods and open, marshy areas alternate, and farm buildings can be seen a few times. Once the sound of traffic has subsided, the setting is wonderfully quiet and peaceful.

Consistently about 50 feet wide, but sometimes as little as 30 feet, the streambed broadens in the open approach to the Center Road bridge, where there's an excellent gravel landing upstream-right. Soon power lines cross at some old bridge abutments. Downstream, a narrow, heavily wooded right bend is the prettiest part of the trip. Later, after a wide straightaway, another set of power lines cross in a long left bend, and eventually you can see far-off traffic on the right. After a short right turn, the Big Bend village park appears on the left, just upstream from the bridge. The concrete boat ramp is a first-rate access, with plenty of adjacent parking. This makes a good take-out or put-in for a short trip.

After Big Bend the river parallels Highway 164, past a few houses, before heading circuitously to the southwest. Numerous backwater sloughs occur in the series of bends that follow. At one point in a short straight stretch, a golf course can be seen on the right. The final mile is quite wide and marshy, with many cabins on the left shoreline. Take the deeper left channel of the long island before Bridge Road. **Take out** 0.1 mile downstream-right from the bridge at the excellent public boat ramp, which is in turn just downstream from the gravel access of Fox River Landing. Next to the public landing is an asphalt parking lot and a wildlife refuge with nature trails.

Other trips. Upstream from this section are two short trips that abound in wildlife: (1) Highway 59 to County I (5 miles) and (2) County I to County ES (6 miles). The latter passes through the wild environment of the Vernon Marsh State Wildlife Area. Considerably farther upstream, (3) the 5-mile section from Springdale Road (west of Brookfield) to Frame Park in Waukesha is narrow, marshy, and wooded and passes the mouth of the Pewaukee River, the location of a popular springtime canoe race.

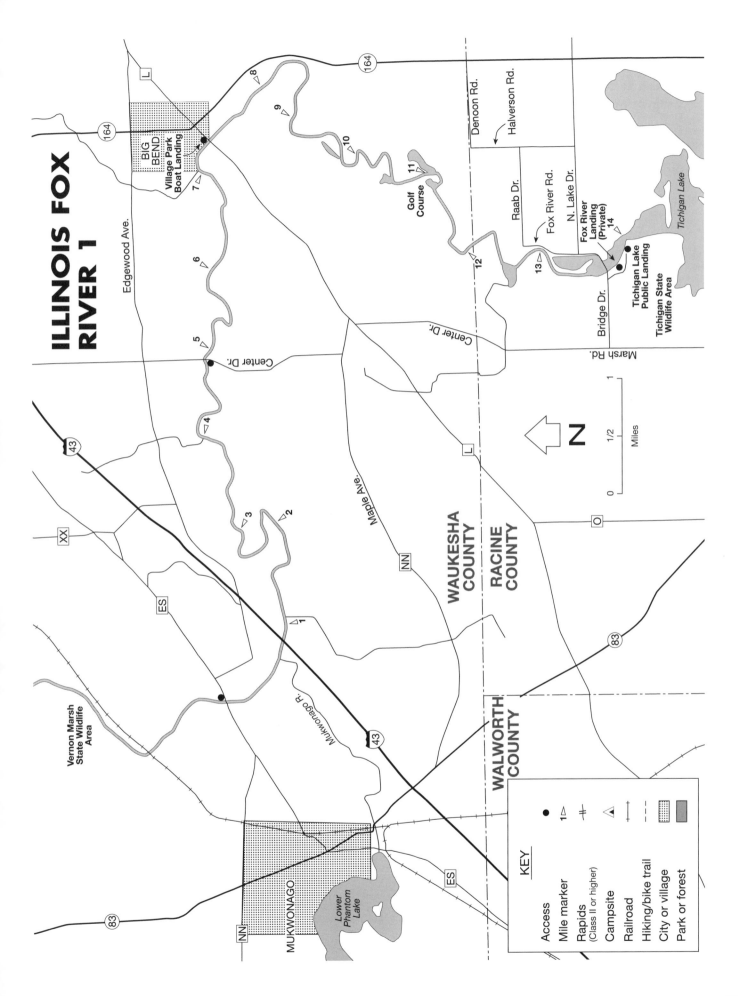

ILLINOIS FOX RIVER 1

164

L

BIG BEND
Village Park
Boat Landing

Edgewood Ave.

164

43

XX

ES

Vernon Marsh State Wildlife Area

Mukwonago R.

NN

MUKWONAGO

NN

83

ES

Lower Phantom Lake

Maple Ave.

Center Dr.

8
9
10
7
6
5
4
3
2
1

11
Golf Course

Center Dr.

Denoon Rd.
Halverson Rd.
Raab Dr.
Fox River Rd.
N. Lake Dr.

Fox River Landing (Private)
14
13
12

Tichigan Lake

Bridge Dr.
Marsh Rd.

Tichigan Lake Public Landing
Tichigan State Wildlife Area

WAUKESHA COUNTY
RACINE COUNTY
WALWORTH COUNTY

L
O
83

N

0   1/2   1
Miles

KEY

- ● Access
- 1△ Mile marker
- Rapids (Class II or higher)
- ◁ Campsite
- ┼┼┼ Railroad
- ─ · ─ Hiking/bike trail
- ▦ City or village
- ▨ Park or forest

ILLINOIS FOX RIVER 2
Waterford to Burlington (8 Miles)

Birding in Southern Wisconsin

Wisconsin's bountiful lakes, streams, and wetlands offer many opportunities for the observation and study of birds. Diverse habitats support a wide range of species, including not only familiar birds like great blue herons and Canada geese, but also less common ones such as trumpeter swans and golden eagles. Any of the trips described in *Paddling Southern Wisconsin* provides an occasion for bird-watching, but some settings are especially advantageous.

The following areas are practically guaranteed to be rich in bird sightings: (1) Avon Bottoms Wildlife Area (Sugar River 2); (2) Horicon Marsh Wildlife Area (Rock River 3); (3) Germania Marsh Wildlife Area (Mecan River 1); (4) Riveredge Nature Center (Milwaukee River 2); (5) Dunnville State Wildlife Area (Red Cedar River); (6) Tiffany State Wildlife Area (Chippewa River 6); (7) Avoca Unit and Mazomanie Wildlife Area of the Lower Wisconsin State Riverway (Wisconsin River 5 and 8); (8) Prince's Point Wildlife Area (Bark River 1 and 2); (9) Tichigan State Wildlife Area (Illinois Fox River 1); and (10) Vernon Marsh Wildlife Area (Illinois Fox River 1).

This trip is of a very different character than the often marshy, sparsely populated stretch from Mukwonago to Tichigan Lake. On the average, the river is a little wider here (typically 70–80 feet), has higher banks, and flows through an attractive wooded corridor. Near the beginning of the trip, roads are never far away, so houses are not infrequent. Buildings are generally screened by tree cover, however, so the setting remains natural. Beginning and ending in small, attractive cities, the trip passes through a third community where an old mill dam must be portaged. The nearby Racine County Bicycle Trail parallels the river from Burlington to Waterford, providing an opportunity to peddle and paddle on the same trip.

For **camping, canoe rentals,** and **water levels,** see Illinois Fox River 1.

The **shuttle route** (6.7 miles) from the village hall/library in Waterford goes south briefly on North River Street, west on Highway 20 (Main Street), south on County W, south on Highway 83/36 to Burlington, and east on Congress Street to Riverside Park.

Gradient is 1.2 feet per mile.

Put in on river-right at the city park behind the Waterford library and municipal building, off North River Street just upstream from the Highway 20 (Main Street) bridge. There is no designated canoe landing, but the rocky river bank is an easy place to put in. Before heading downriver, be sure to walk a couple hundred yards upstream to take a look at the dam, which consists of separate structures in the two channels of a large island. An old mill occupied the shore of the right channel, where a concrete dam with four metal gates now stands. A charming covered bridge crosses the left channel to a condominium community on the island.

From the outset, numerous houses and retaining walls are passed, but the banks are wooded and green. Soon the Waterford water tower looms overhead. South First Street, then River Road follow the left shoreline all the way to Rochester, an attractive little town with some historic old buildings.

One hundred yards downstream from the County D bridge at Rochester there's a small village park on the right—with room to park a few cars—where you can access the river. A short distance downstream is the old Rochester mill dam, similar in construction to the dam

at Watertown. Portage carefully on the left. Before your trip, it's a good idea to scout the dam while running the shuttle route. It's located directly behind a mini-mart in town, along County W. Local people often walk to the dam from J. I. Case Park on the east side of the river.

County W runs along the right shore in Rochester, but woods continue. After the dam a shallow, often rocky stretch begins, extending almost to Highway 83/36. This area can cause much scraping on your boat during low-water conditions. Before your trip, you can get an idea of how canoeable the river is by checking out the rocky area behind the supper club along County W in Rochester.

As you leave Rochester, J. I. Case Park lies along the left bank. Farther downstream, there's an excellent upstream-right access at the Highway 83/36 bridges. From the paved parking lot of nearby Saller Woods, a path leads to an undeveloped landing on the bank. Swinging toward the west, the river passes the St. Francis Friary and Retreat Center on the right and flows under the County W bridge, where a dirt road leads to an undeveloped, downstream-right access. The river continues to be tree-lined.

After gently curving to the left alongside Highway 83/36, the river passes the Browns Lake Golf Course, where there's a picturesque footbridge. In the approach to Burlington, the river makes an abrupt right turn into a short straightaway where Riverside Park is located. **Take out** anywhere along the grassy right shoreline, before the sharp left turn that carries the river southward along Highway 83. Riverside Park has picnic facilities, an attractive pedestrian bridge, and parking.

Lunch time.

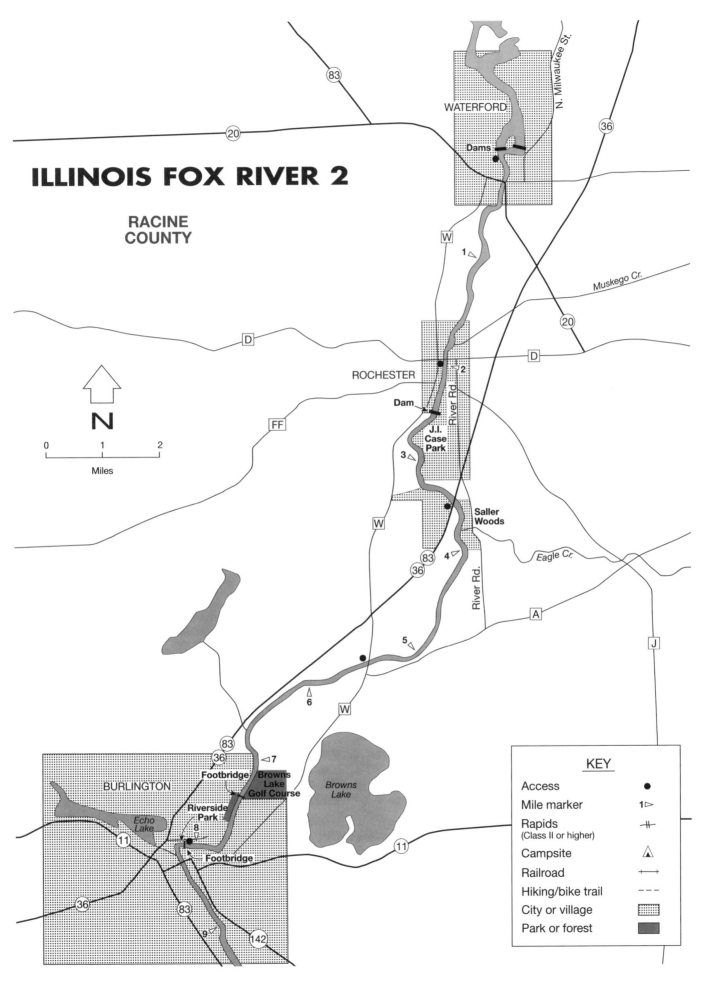

ILLINOIS FOX RIVER 2

RACINE COUNTY

WATERFORD

Dams

N. Milwaukee St.

83

20

36

W

1

Muskego Cr.

D

ROCHESTER

2

River Rd.

D

20

Dam

FF

J.I. Case Park

3

Saller Woods

W

83 36

4

River Rd.

Eagle Cr.

A

J

5

6

W

83
36

7

Footbridge

BURLINGTON

Browns Lake Golf Course

Browns Lake

Riverside Park

Echo Lake

8

11

Footbridge

11

36

83

9

142

N

0   1   2

Miles

KEY

Access	●
Mile marker	1▷
Rapids (Class II or higher)	─╫─
Campsite	△
Railroad	─┼─
Hiking/bike trail	- - -
City or village	▦
Park or forest	▨

ILLINOIS FOX RIVER 3
Burlington to Wilmot (17.2 Miles)

A long section that can easily be shortened by using alternate accesses, this is the southernmost part of the Fox before it crosses the Illinois border. Flowing slowly over a sand-gravel-silt bottom, the river is wide here, averaging 180 feet, and is a popular destination for local fishermen. Since the removal of a dam at Wilmot in 1992, there are now no artificial barriers between Rochester and McHenry in Illinois. From Burlington to County JB, the river environs are quite natural, but homes and cabins become numerous in the Wheatland area and beyond. The lower part of the river often has considerable motorboat traffic—much of it from the Chain O' Lakes area across the Illinois border. Spring flooding is usually a problem from Wheatland downstream.

The Fox River is named after the Native American tribe that originally lived along the Fox and Wisconsin Rivers. Known as mesquaki ("the red earth people") or outagami ("people of the other shore") in Algonquin, they were called Renards by the French and Fox by the English. These names (and others) are seen on early maps, where the river is also called the Riviere des Renards ("River of Foxes"), the Pistakee ("Buffalo"), and Riviere du Rocher ("Rock River").

Public **camping** is available at Meadowlark Acres near Burlington (262-763-7200), the Bong State Recreation Area 6 miles southeast of Burlington (262-652-0377 or 262-878-5600), and Chain O' Lakes State Park just across the border in Illinois (847-587-5512).

Canoe rental and shuttle service are available at Tip-a-Canoe Rental near Burlington (262-537-3227).

The **shuttle route** for the entire section (13.8 miles) goes west briefly on Commerce Street in Burlington, south on Highway 83, east on Highway 50, south on County W, east on County C, and finally south on the gravel road on the east bank of the river. Shorter trips use County JB, Highway 50, or County F as alternate accesses.

Gradient is negligible (less than a foot per mile).

For **water levels**, check the New Munster gauge (#05545750) on the USGS Web site. See "Water Levels" in the introduction. Springtime flows can be quite high (almost 6,000 cfs historically), but the river can fluctuate tremendously, having been as low as 50 cfs. For general information on water levels (high, medium, low), call Tip-a-Canoe Rental.

Put in at Riverside Park in Burlington alongside Congress Street, just off Highway 83/36. Immediately after launching on river-right, you pass under an arched pedestrian bridge, then turn sharply to the left past the outlet of Echo Lake and under the Jefferson Street bridge. Houses and other buildings quickly thin out, and the shoreline becomes densely forested.

Soon Bushnell County Park appears on the left, a large, grassy area with picnic facilities, playgrounds, playing fields, toilets, and a gravelly beach that is popular with bank fishermen. You could easily start your trip here. A huge quarry follows the park on the left, across from the mouth of Spring Brook. Before a railroad bridge crosses the river, some houses can be seen along Brever Road, but the surroundings are still pleasantly wooded.

Farther downstream, where Hoosier Creek Road comes alongside the river, there's a sizable gravel pull-off; a run-down, concrete-and-gravel landing is located here on river-left, an alternate take-out for a short trip. Half a mile downstream, at the County JB bridge, a rough road leads to an undeveloped access downstream-left.

After County JB the tree cover along the 4- to 6-foot banks grows thin and the environs are more open. A quarter mile north of Highway 50, where County W runs close by on the left, concrete steps lead from the gravelly shoulder down to the river—another possible access, but not an easy place to carry canoes or kayaks.

The river now curves through a series of long, sharp bends where cabins and homes are thick along the left shoreline. Slight tree cover continues, with occasional marsh vegetation. Passing the community of Silver Lake, the river turns sharply left just before County F, then veers right to the bridge. The river is attractive here: relatively narrow and high-banked. A large and beautiful county park is located to the right of the County F bridge, upstream and downstream, with a first-rate boat ramp and parking lot downstream-right. This is by far the best access on the whole section, and the most convenient **take-out.**

Two more river-miles lead to the village of Wilmot, where County C crosses the river. Downstream-left a gravel road follows the river bank 0.1 mile to where the dam used to be. There's no designated landing, but you can easily take out on the low shoreline, with plenty of room nearby to park cars.

Other trips. If you don't mind the company of numerous motorboaters, you can continue downriver from Wilmot, past Gander Mountain (to the west) into Illinois, and take out at the boat landing in Chain O' Lakes State Park south of Highway 173.

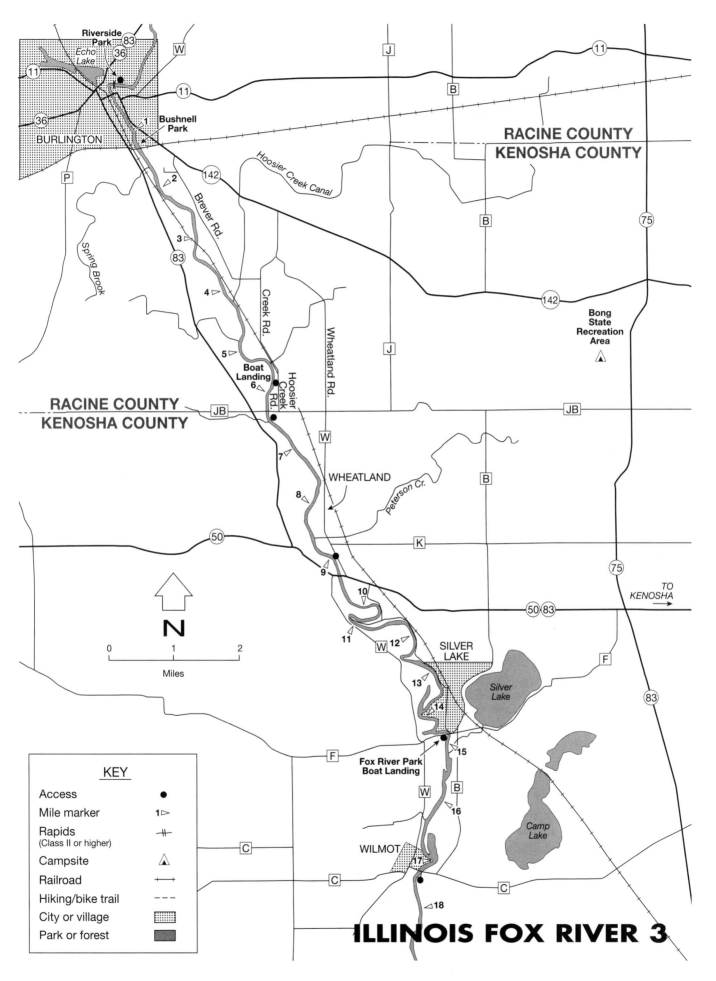

Riverside Park
Echo Lake
BURLINGTON
Bushnell Park
RACINE COUNTY
KENOSHA COUNTY
Hoosier Creek Canal
Spring Brook
Brever Rd.
Creek Rd.
Wheatland Rd.
Boat Landing
Hoosier Creek Rd.
RACINE COUNTY
KENOSHA COUNTY
WHEATLAND
Peterson Cr.
Bong State Recreation Area
SILVER LAKE
Silver Lake
Camp Lake
Fox River Park Boat Landing
WILMOT
TO KENOSHA

KEY

Access	●
Mile marker	1▷
Rapids (Class II or higher)	╫
Campsite	▲
Railroad	┼┼
Hiking/bike trail	- - -
City or village	▦
Park or forest	▓

N
0   1   2
Miles

ILLINOIS FOX RIVER 3

KICKAPOO RIVER 1
Ontario to Rockton (11.5 Miles)

Once you've had a taste of this enchanting little river, you'll be hooked for life. Traveling through one of the most rugged portions of Wisconsin—the heart of the unglaciated Driftless Area—the Kickapoo is incredibly twisty. Indeed, area tourist hype calls it "the crookedest river in the world." In its small, flood-prone water-shed—only 60 miles long and 10–15 miles wide—the river winds repeatedly past spectacular bluffs and sandstone cliffs. Its flat-bottomed, steep-sided valley is a good example of what the French called a coulee. After La Farge, cliffs are fewer but the course no less bending as the river flows through Viola, Readstown, Soldiers Grove, Gays Mills, and Steuben before joining the Wisconsin River near Wauzeka.

The 20-mile section between Ontario and La Farge is the best that the river has to offer. Good current, a narrow streambed, fantastic rock formations, and a wild setting make this part of the river truly memorable. In the first half you'll paddle under many bridges and are likely to have to share the river with rental canoeists, especially on warm weekends. Downstream from Rockton, however, the river is equally beautiful, but there are only a couple of bridges and relatively few paddlers.

Camping is available at Wildcat Mountain State Park 1.5 miles east of Ontario (608-337-4775), the La Farge Village Park at the north edge of town (608-625-4422), the Kickapoo Valley Reserve north of La Farge (608-625-2960), Brush Creek Campground 3 miles west of Ontario (608-337-4344), Crooked River Resort near Readstown (608-629-5624), and West Fork Campground near Avalanche (608-634-2303).

Canoe rentals and shuttles are available in Ontario at Drifty's Canoe Rental (608-337-4288), Mr. Duck Canoe Rental (608-337-4711), Kickapoo Paddle Inn (608-337-4726), and Titanic Canoe Rental (608-337-4551); Drifty's also rents canoes at Rockton (608-625-4395). Flasher's Canoe Camping Trips (Wilton) offers guided trips on the Kickapoo (608-435-6802).

The **shuttle route** (approximately 6 miles) from Ontario goes south briefly on County P, west briefly on Highway 33, then south on Highway 131 to Bridge 10 about a mile north of Rockton.

Gradient is 3.5 feet per mile.

For **water levels,** check the La Farge gauge (#05408000) on the USGS Web site. See "Water Levels" in the introduction.

Put in at the excellent boat landing alongside County P in Ontario, upstream-left from the Highway 33 bridge (Bridge 1). You'll notice that bridges on the Kickapoo have numbers stenciled on them; there are gaps in the numbering system because of the removal of a number of abandoned bridges. Six of the 10 bridges on this section are on Highway 131.

Modest cliffs begin almost immediately on the right, topped with coniferous trees. Narrow at the beginning, the river will be only 15–30 feet wide all day. The banks are typically grassy, steep, and 6–8 feet high. After the initial rock formations, one of the trip's infrequent clearings appears on the left. Undercut cliffs precede Bridge 2, which is followed by some pleasant riffles and another open area.

In the bends that follow the bridge, very impressive cliffs rise on the left side, then give way to wooded banks until the approach to Bridge 3. A series of riffly shoals follows the bridge, but there are no more cliffs until a huge undercut one appears on the right as Bridge 4 draws near (access downstream-left).

Fantastic, overhanging cliffs follow on the right, then on the left. As usual, mosses, ferns, lichens, and coniferous trees grow on the rock. Small, sandy beaches become more frequent—pleasant places to stop for a break. Occasionally, fallen limbs require dodging, but the canoe-rental companies do a good job of keeping the river unobstructed.

Eventually, in the long stretch between Bridges 4 and 5, a very tall, wooded bluff can be seen ahead, crowned by a dolomite precipice; hikers in Wildcat Mountain State Park can sometimes be seen atop this height. After a series of cliffs on the right, the canoe landing of the park appears on the left, near a picnic area with tables and toilets. This is a great place to stop for lunch. Intricately carved cliffs follow on the left, deeply undercut, with cave-like openings. Dense woods and more cliffs lead to Bridge 5, where there's a good landing upstream-left.

Interesting cliffs are found periodically all the way to Bridge 6. By now you've noted that each cliff on the trip is unique in shape, length, height, and color. There are few rock formations between Bridges 6 and 7, and the setting is mostly woods and grassy banks until Bridge 8 (access downstream-left). In the approach to Bridge 9 some of the largest and most beautiful cliffs of the day tower over the river on the left.

The final leg of the trip is extremely winding, with some limbs to avoid here and there. Lower cliffs accompany the river through much of this last portion, ending at Bridge 10 (Highway 131). **Take out** upstream-left. Like most of the accesses on the Kickapoo, this is an undeveloped bare spot along the shoreline. If you'd like a longer trip, you can continue to the site where Bridge 12 once stood (see Kickapoo River 2). After that, there are no more accesses for 8 miles.

Other trips. On days when there are hordes of rental canoes on the river, paddlers who want some tranquility put in at Bridge 5 and take out at Bridge 10 or "Bridge 12."

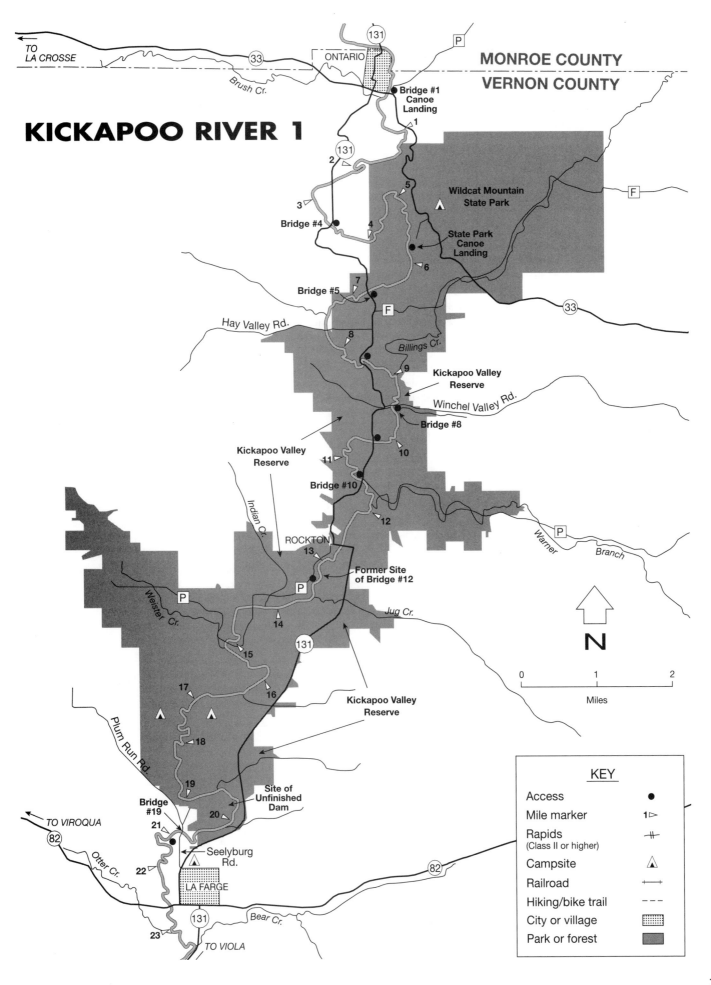

KICKAPOO RIVER 1

TO
LA CROSSE

ONTARIO

MONROE COUNTY
VERNON COUNTY

Bridge #1
Canoe
Landing

Brush Cr.

Wildcat Mountain
State Park

State Park
Canoe
Landing

Bridge #4

Bridge #5

Hay Valley Rd.

Billings Cr.

Kickapoo Valley
Reserve

Winchel Valley Rd.

Bridge #8

Kickapoo Valley
Reserve

Bridge #10

Indian Cr.

ROCKTON

Former Site
of Bridge #12

Warner

Branch

Jug Cr.

Weister Cr.

Kickapoo Valley
Reserve

Plum Run Rd.

Site of
Unfinished
Dam

Bridge
#19

TO VIROQUA

Otter Cr.

Seelyburg
Rd.

LA FARGE

Bear Cr.

TO VIOLA

N

0   1   2
Miles

KEY

Access	●
Mile marker	1▷
Rapids (Class II or higher)	╫
Campsite	⚠
Railroad	┼┼
Hiking/bike trail	- - -
City or village	▦
Park or forest	▨

75

KICKAPOO RIVER 2
Rockton to La Farge (9.5 Miles)

Less frequently paddled than the extremely popular upstream stretch, the second section of the Kickapoo has at least as many sandstone cliffs, several of which are quite spectacular. Because there are fewer bridges and only one intermediate access (near the beginning), this trip seems wilder and more remote. The only signs of human habitation are three bridges, a set of power lines, a brief glimpse of Highway 131, and a few buildings at the end. There's more deadfall in the sharp turns, but usually this poses no problem for experienced paddlers. Accesses can be a bit muddy but are quite adequate. Like the first section, the river here is seldom very deep under normal water level conditions, except on the outside of bends.

Appropriately, the name of the river is derived from a Native American expression meaning "he who stands now here, now there" (i.e., wandering about).

For **camping, canoe rentals,** and **water levels**, see Kickapoo River 1.

The **shuttle route** (approximately 6 miles) from Bridge 10 goes south on Highway 131 almost to La Farge, then north on Seelyburg Road 0.3 mile to a gated access road that leads westward a short distance to the old powerhouse building.

Unlike the Ontario-to-Rockton section of Highway 131, which crisscrosses the river six times, the Rockton-to-La Farge section is straight and bridgeless. This southern portion of the highway was relocated as part of the ill-fated Kickapoo dam project; "Old 131" and its bridges (numbers 12, 15, 16, 17, 18) were removed.

Gradient is 2.1 feet per mile.

Put in at Bridge 10 on Highway 131, upstream-left. (If you'd like to shorten your trip by 2 miles and enhance the remoteness factor, you can start south of Rockton at the "Bridge 12" landing.) A mile downstream from Bridge 10, after a deeply wooded stretch with a couple of small cliffs, the river passes under a very high, modern structure—unlike the small, low, older bridges between Ontario and Rockton.

Soon after Bridge 11, County P runs alongside the right bank. Be on the look out for the "Bridge 12" landing on river-right, immediately after a right turn (the bridge has been removed for a long time). This easy-to-miss access is a dirt-and-sand bank leading to a short drop-off road from County P. A campsite is located next to the access.

Downstream, fallen trees and limbs are often seen along the water's edge, but getting around them is no problem. The river is consistently about 30 feet wide, the water is clear, and the bottom is sandy. In the long right bend after the access, a series of lovely cliffs rise on the left. Occasionally, large chunks fall off, exposing the fresh, white, unoxidized sandstone beneath the weathered, darker stone. In the left bend after Bridge 13 (County P), there's a glorious, severely undercut cliff on the right.

Just downstream from Bridge 14 (also County P), in a sharp left turn, Weister Creek enters on the right near a tall cliff. In the bends that follow, boat control is required to get around the dead trees. When the river narrows, to as little as 15 feet at one point, cliffs appear on the right. After a sharp right turn the rock formations on the left are even more magnificent—60 feet tall, with many shapes and colors and complex effects of weathering—and continue for several hundred yards.

Where a small creek enters on the left, deadfall tends to accumulate. Just downstream, the remnants of the piers of Bridge 16 can be seen on the left shoreline, followed by the only straight stretch of the trip. Veering left past a long, low, undercut cliff, the river now passes the old piers of Bridge 17 on the right. Now begins a long series of very sharp turns where rock formations are sparse until a low, fern-covered cliff on river-right—the longest of the day—in a big left bend toward the east. By now the tree line has become rather thin.

Bending around to the right, you can briefly see the traffic on Highway 121 high up on the left. Soon a concrete tower appears on the right, part of a dam project that was terminated in 1975. Stretching to the west of the tower is an immense earthen structure that was intended to form a huge reservoir of impounded water. You can get out of your boat opposite the small cliffs near Highway 131, climb up the right bank, and get a good view of the partially completed dam.

In the continuing right bend, power lines cross, the river widens, trees grow even thinner, and there are a few modest rock outcroppings. After a couple of turns you can see a cemetery on the right hillside and some farm buildings (the first of the trip). After Bridge 19 (Seelyburg Road), the river bends left past the mouth of Plum Run. Just before the river heads right, the old block building of the powerhouse can be seen on the left shore. **Take out** at an open spot along the left bank and carry your boat(s) up to the dirt-and-gravel road alongside the powerhouse. From the powerhouse a dirt road leads farther downstream to the site of the old Seelyburg dam, removed in 2000.

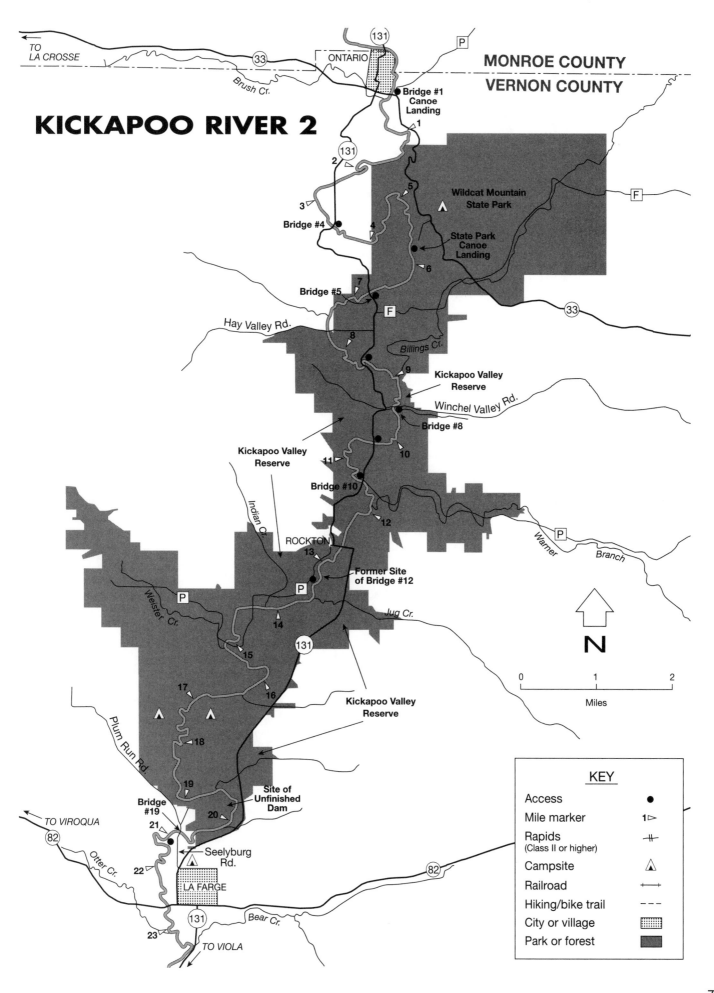

KICKAPOO RIVER 2

TO LA CROSSE

33

Brush Cr.

131

ONTARIO

P

MONROE COUNTY
VERNON COUNTY

Bridge #1
Canoe
Landing

1

131

2

3

Bridge #4

4

5

Wildcat Mountain
State Park

State Park
Canoe
Landing

6

F

7

Bridge #5

F

Hay Valley Rd.

8

Billings Cr.

9

Kickapoo Valley
Reserve

Winchel Valley Rd.

Bridge #8

10

Kickapoo Valley
Reserve

11

Bridge #10

12

Warner

Branch

P

Indian Cr.

ROCKTON

13

Former Site
of Bridge #12

P

P

Weister Cr.

14

Jug Cr.

131

Kickapoo Valley
Reserve

N

0   1   2

Miles

15

17

16

18

19

Site of
Unfinished
Dam

Bridge
#19

20

21

TO VIROQUA

82

Plum Run Rd.

Otter Cr.

22

Seelyburg
Rd.

LA FARGE

82

131

Bear Cr.

23

TO VIOLA

KEY

Access	●
Mile marker	1▷
Rapids (Class II or higher)	+++
Campsite	⋀
Railroad	+−+
Hiking/bike trail	- - -
City or village	▦
Park or forest	�

KICKAPOO RIVER 3 & 4
Viola to Readstown (11.6 Miles)
Readstown to Soldiers Grove (6.3 Miles)

After La Farge, riverside rock formations are infrequent, but the Kickapoo continues to be good for paddling all the way to its confluence with the Wisconsin. Unfortunately, the 11-mile stretch from La Farge to Viola has been blocked by a couple of large logjams in recent years; therefore, paddlers are advised to begin their next jaunt on the Kickapoo at Viola. The two popular day trips described here pass through a wooded corridor, with occasional openings for farm fields. There are many obstructions to contend with, but usually you can maneuver around them without getting out of your boat. Roads are never far away from the river, and high, wooded ridges are almost constantly in view. Twists, turns, and limbs in the water make quick trips impossible, so paddlers are advised against attempting the whole 17.9 miles in a single day.

Camping is available at Banker Park in Viola, the village park in Readstown, Anderson Park in Soldiers Grove, and Crooked River Resort just south of Readstown (608-629-5624).

Canoe rental and shuttle service are available near Readstown at Crooked River Resort (608-629-5624) and Voyager Canoe Rental (608-629-5745 or 888-730-6134).

Rock formations line the Kickapoo from Ontario to La Farge.

The **shuttle route** for the first trip (7.5 miles) goes west briefly on Highway 131/56 in Viola, then south on Highway 131 to the village park in Readstown. For the shorter second trip, the shuttle (5.1 miles) goes west briefly on Highway 131/14, then south on Highway 131 to Anderson Park in Soldiers Grove.

Gradient is 2.2 feet per mile.

For **water levels**, see Kickapoo River 1.

For the first trip, **put in** at Banker Park in Viola, upstream-right from the Highway 131 bridge. Banker Park is a pleasant, grassy area with picnic facilities and campsites. After the park, the 35-foot-wide river bends gently to the left alongside Highway 56, then heads south between West River Road on the right and Highway 131 on the left. High bluffs rise on both sides of the valley, usually several hundred yards from the river. Occasionally, exposed rock faces are seen near the top of the ridge line. Unseen by paddlers, wetlands occupy part of the area between the river and nearby roads. Homes and farm buildings periodically appear on high ground as the river executes a long series of sharp turns. At Kickapoo Center, where the river flows beneath Highway 131 and then makes an extremely tight, right turn around a narrow neck of land, there are several houses near the banks.

East River Road now runs along the left bank as the river heads west. At times the streambed narrows to 30 feet, and deadfall can be a challenge. Tree cover along the banks alternates between dense and sparse. A short distance upstream from the next Highway 131 bridge, the river passes under an old metal truss bridge.

After coming alongside Larson Road in a sharp left turn, the river swings back alongside Highway 131. Approaching the river-right bluffs, the river now swings right (south) to Readstown. Soon after floating under the Charles Street bridge, **take out** at the village park upstream-left from the Highway 131/14 bridge.

Because the stretch from Readstown to Soldiers Grove is more frequently paddled than the above section, deadfall tends to be cleared out more frequently after Readstown. Width here averages 40 feet. Massive wooded bluffs continue to rise on both sides of the valley. More than once the river swings close to Highway 131/61 and Day Creek Road before flowing under the highway bridge. A long left bend then carries the river alongside Tavern Road, which runs on top of a river-right bluff.

Soon after an old truss bridge near Trout Creek Road, houses begin to appear in the approach to Soldiers Grove, a town named after an encampment during the Black Hawk War of 1832. In Soldiers Grove, Highway 131 crosses the river twice in short order; Anderson Park is located in the bend between the two bridges. **Take out** 25 yards downstream-right from the second bridge at the designated canoe landing.

Other trips. (1) From Soldiers Grove, it's twelve river-miles to Gays Mills, where paddlers must take out upstream from a dangerous 7-foot dam. In 2000, there was a large logjam on this section. (2) A long stretch of 16 miles leads from Gays Mills to Steuben, where camping is allowed at a small park. (3) From Steuben, an 11-mile section ends at Plum Creek Landing (the put-in for Kickapoo River 5, described below).

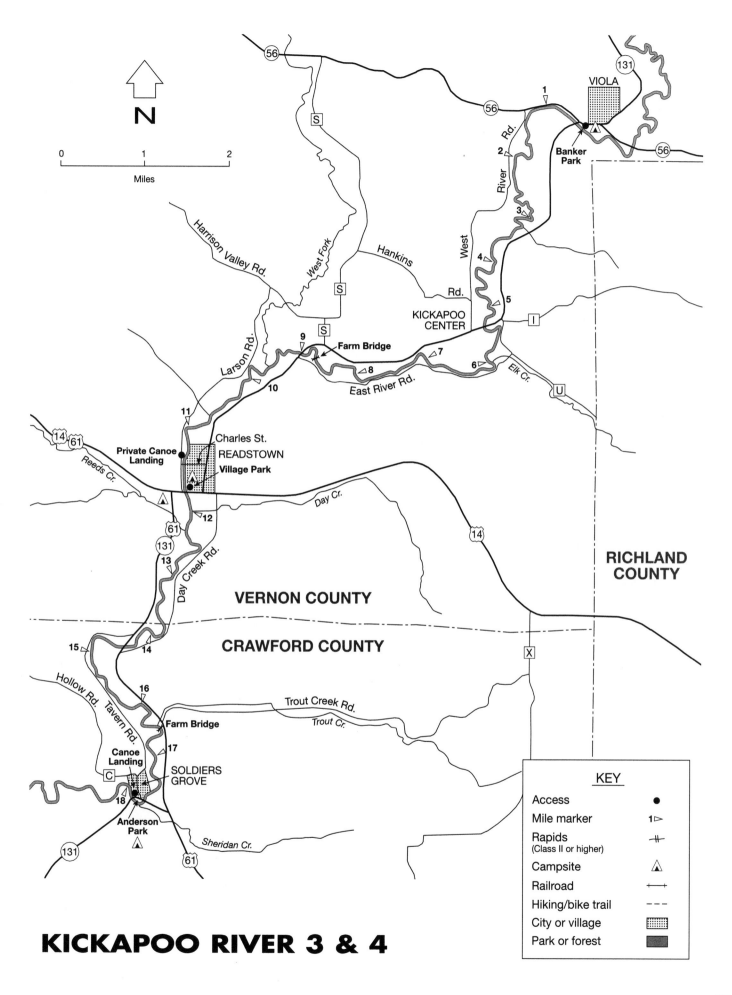

KICKAPOO RIVER 3 & 4

KICKAPOO RIVER 5
Plum Creek Landing to Wauzeka (8.6 Miles)

The Dam That Wasn't Meant to Be

Proponents of a dam aimed at controlling flash flooding in the Kickapoo Valley and enhancing tourism in the region were able to obtain congressional authorization in 1962 for the La Farge Dam. After 140 farms were purchased in the proposed reservoir area (with much resistance from unhappy property owners), the U.S. Army Corps of Engineers began construction in the early 1970s. By 1975 half of the dam had been completed, but a host of concerns (water-quality issues, endangered species habitat, etc.) brought the project to a halt. An attempt in 1983 to scale down the project in order to save it failed also. In the midst of continuing bitterness, frustration, and second-guessing, in 1992 the grassroots Kickapoo Valley Citizens Participation Project began addressing the issue of what to do with the now-idle La Farge Dam property. Eventually their recommendation of transferring the land to the state of Wisconsin and establishing a local management group—the Kickapoo Reserve Management Board—was approved by Congress.

The 8,569-acre reserve has tremendous recreational potential and is being developed for off-road biking, hiking, snowmobiling, cross-country skiing, horseback riding, fishing, hunting, snowshoeing, and other activities. Immediately to the north of the reserve is Wildcat Mountain State Park; thus, most of the land along the Kickapoo from Ontario to La Farge is publically owned and protected from development. You can obtain maps and additional information at the reserve office, located on the northern edge of La Farge.

In its final miles before joining the Wisconsin River, the Kickapoo flows almost entirely through the Kickapoo River State Wildlife Area Wauzeka Unit, a wild region with few signs of civilization. Quite different from the extremely popular Ontario-to-La Farge section, where a narrow streambed and numerous cliffs are featured, the last part of the Kickapoo looks more like a typical prairie river. The river is usually slightly muddy in color, flows between steep 4- to 8-foot banks, and is relatively wide (60–70 feet). Dead trees are often encountered, but there is almost always plenty of room to get around them. For canoeists the principal attraction of this part of the river is its isolation. Another draw is its proximity to the Wisconsin. Putting in at Highway 60 or Wauzeka (or even farther upstream at Plum Creek Landing), you can paddle out to the larger river and take out at several locations, depending upon how long you want to be on the water.

Primitive public **camping** is available near the river at the Wauzeka and Steuben village parks.

Canoe rental is available from Marshview Canoe Rental 1 mile west of Wauzeka (608-875-6203) and Crooked River Resort near Readstown (608-629-5624).

The **shuttle route** (3.1 miles) goes south on Plum Creek Road, south on County N, east on Highway 60 to Wauzeka, and south 1 block on Dousman Street to the landing. From Plum Creek Road you get a good bird's-eye view of the river, including a dramatic vista of an oxbow.

The **gradient** is 0.6 feet per mile.

For **water levels,** check the Steuben gauge (05410490) on the USGS Web site. See "Water Levels" in the introduction.

Put in on river-right alongside Plum Creek Road downstream from the mouth of Plum Creek, at the point where the river loops to the left beside the road. A short access road leads to the grassy landing (no ramp). After an initial straightaway, the river begins bending back and forth, never far from Plum Creek Road, high up on the river-right bluff. Old wooden pilings—first on the left, later on the right—are some of the few signs of human activity. Some of the turns are quite sharp, including the unusually tight oxbow that can be seen from the road. The surroundings are densely wooded.

The next intrusion of civilization is a set of power lines in the approach to Highway 60, where there's a boat ramp at the bridge (upstream-left), with a sizable parking lot. This is an excellent **take-out** for a shorter trip.

After Highway 60 the river swings to the west alongside the road, which can be seen for a while. Trees continue, but the Highway 60-to-Wauzeka stretch has more open areas than the upstream section. Power lines cross soon after Highway 60, and railroad tracks later pull alongside the left bank.

As the river approaches Wauzeka, houses begin to appear some distance from the river. Finally, in town, homes are located close to the banks, and an excellent boat ramp is located on the right in a small city park with plentiful parking. This is the last **take-out** before the Wisconsin River, which lies a mile downstream.

Other trips. Continuing downstream from Wauzeka onto the Wisconsin River and taking out at the Millville Landing (see Wisconsin River 11) adds 6.5 miles of paddling.

One of the many numbered bridges over the Kickapoo.

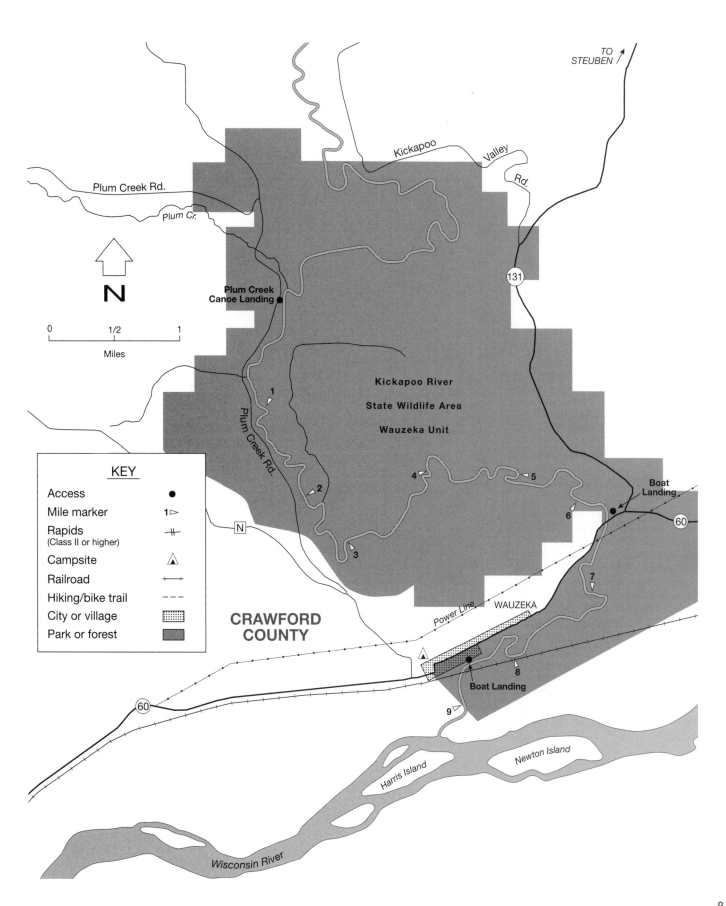

TO
STEUBEN

Kickapoo Valley Rd.

Plum Creek Rd.

Plum Cr.

N

0   1/2   1
Miles

Plum Creek
Canoe Landing ●

131

Plum Creek Rd.

Kickapoo River

State Wildlife Area

Wauzeka Unit

1

2

3

4   5

6

Boat
Landing

60

7

KEY

Access	●
Mile marker	1▷
Rapids (Class II or higher)	‡
Campsite	△
Railroad	+‡+
Hiking/bike trail	- - -
City or village	▦
Park or forest	▨

N

Power Line   WAUZEKA

CRAWFORD
COUNTY

8

Boat Landing

9

60

Harris Island

Newton Island

Wisconsin River

LA CROSSE RIVER 1
Sparta to Rockland (9 Miles)

The Great Wisconsin Swamp

Except for the Driftless Area in the southwestern corner of the state, marshes and bogs are found in most parts of Wisconsin—a product of the latest wave of glaciation, which ended as recently as 10,000 years ago. But the biggest marshland of all is the so-called Great Swamp of Central Wisconsin. Lying roughly in a triangle between Black River Falls, Camp Douglas, and Wisconsin Rapids, these 300,000 poorly drained acres were left behind by clay and sand deposits from Glacial Lake Wisconsin. Not surprisingly, much of the area is used for wildlife refuges and cranberry bogs. The La Crosse and Lemonweir Rivers originate on the southern edge of the Great Swamp.

A huge cyclist towers over the Sparta put-in on the La Crosse.

Sparta is best known as a trailhead of the famous Elroy-Sparta State Trail, a mecca for bicyclists in the Midwest. But it's also an excellent starting point for many miles of pleasant paddling on the La Crosse River all the way to the Mississippi River. Originating in the Fort McCoy Military Reservation, the La Crosse is dammed at Angelo, then again at Sparta and West Salem. Its clear water flows over a mostly sandy bottom, and passes through a variety of settings. Beaver, muskrat, and many kinds of birds are plentiful.

Upstream and downstream from the Neshonoc Lake dam at West Salem, the river lends itself to two very different day trips. Alternate accesses allow paddlers to vary the length and character of both trips. Virtually the entire route of the two trips is paralleled by the La Crosse River State Trail, which is linked with several other recreational trails.

Quite isolated, the first section averages 40 feet in width and is heavily wooded, including several beautiful stands of pine and cedar. Banks are generally grassy and low, making portages easy if you have to carry around a downed tree or two. Continual maneuvering is required by the circuitous streambed and the frequency of limbs in the water. Accesses are excellent.

Camping is available at the Neshonoc Lakeside Camp and Resort 2 miles northeast of West Salem (608-786-1792 or 888-783-0035), Leon Valley Campground south of Sparta (608-269-6400), and McMullen County Park north of Sparta (608-269-8737 or 608-378-4913). Also see La Crosse River 2.

Canoe rentals and shuttle service are available through Lloyd Larson, 1212 North Street in Sparta (608-269-3894.) Kayaks (no shuttle) may be rented at Buzz's Bike Shop in La Crosse (608-785-2737).

The **shuttle route** (6.3 miles) goes west from Sparta on Highway 16, then south on County J to the bridge north of Rockland.

Gradient is 5.5 feet per mile.

Water level. Spring-fed, the La Crosse is usually paddleable during most of the canoeing season. For current and historical levels, check the gauge at Sparta (#05382325) on the USGS Web site. See "Water Levels" in the introduction.

Put in at the designated canoe landing in Sparta, downstream-right from the Highway 16 bridge. In the right bend between the Highway 16 and Water Street bridges, there's a charming little park highlighted by the huge fiberglass figure of a bicyclist. A left turn after Water Street leads quickly to an old mill, on the right, and a small riffle. Just downstream is a USGS gauge on the left, then an old rock dam with an easily run 18-inch drop; select one of the tongues. The river now quickly turns right, passes under the Court Street bridge, goes by some trailer homes on the right, then heads left. Unfortunately, you're likely to encounter some trash in the water for a while after Court Street. After a few more houses, the river enters a wild area where there are no dwellings for a long time. Fallen limbs frequently necessitate tight squeezes.

The Highway 27 bridge is a high, modern structure with no access. By now the river has widened to 50 feet, but the environs remain quite wild. There are many low, grassy banks and occasional sandbars for "pit stops." Steep, sandy cut banks are found on the outside of some bends, topped attractively with coniferous trees. Houses can be seen a few times, but always in the distance.

Drawing closer to Hammer Road, the river briefly opens up and flows within view of Highway 16, then narrows and twists through a long series of very tight turns. A rare straightaway of 400 yards leads to the bridge, where there's an adequate access downstream-left. Downstream, the banks are consistently lower and the streambed wider (up to 60 feet). Thinner woods and increased width make this part of the trip less prone to deadfall. Power lines cross the river several times in sharp bends.

A river-right house—the first in a long time—announces the approach of the Icarus Road bridge, where the river can be accessed upstream-left. After a quarter-mile straightaway, the river bends gently back and forth, 50–60 feet wide. Obstructions here are rare, but there is a sharp left turn near the end of the trip that is easily blocked. The County J bridge comes at the end of a short straightaway; **take out** 25 yards downstream-left at an excellent gravel landing with adjacent parking lot.

Other trips. Six miles of additional paddling—through wooded corridor and marshland—leads to the Seventeenth Avenue bridge near Bangor. There is a gravel boat landing upstream-right from the bridge. After Bangor, the impoundment of Neshonoc Lake soon follows.

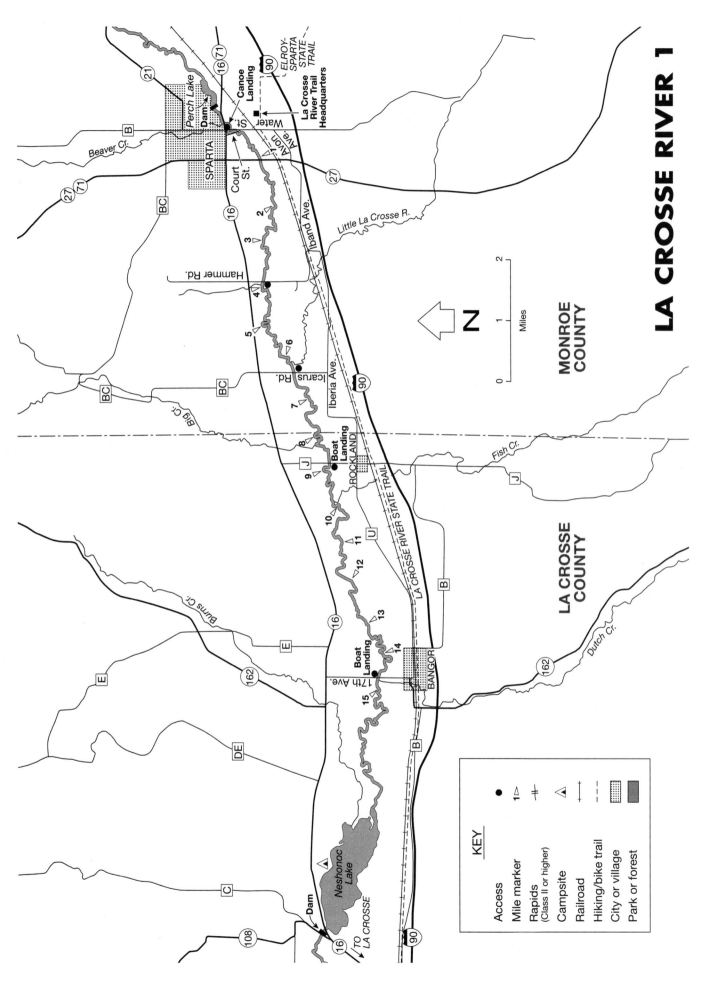

LA CROSSE RIVER 1

MONROE COUNTY

LA CROSSE COUNTY

N

Miles
0   1   2

KEY

- ● Access
- 1△ Mile marker
- ⌒ Rapids (Class II or higher)
- ◁ Campsite
- ┼ Railroad
- ┊ Hiking/bike trail
- ▦ City or village
- ▓ Park or forest

ELROY-SPARTA STATE TRAIL

La Crosse River Trail Headquarters

Canoe Landing

Water St.

Avon Ave.

Perch Lake

Dam

SPARTA

Court St.

Beaver Cr.

Iband Ave.

Little La Crosse R.

Hammer Rd.

Icarus Rd.

Iberia Ave.

Big Cr.

Boat Landing

ROCKLAND

LA CROSSE RIVER STATE TRAIL

Fish Cr.

Burns Cr.

Boat Landing

17th Ave.

BANGOR

Dutch Cr.

Neshonoc Lake

Dam

TO LA CROSSE

21 16 71 27 90 27 16 B BC 16 BC BC 90 J J U B 16 E 162 E DE C 108 16 B 90 162 B

2 3 4 5 6 7 8 9 10 11 12 13 14 15

83

LA CROSSE RIVER 2
West Salem to La Crosse (13.3 Miles)

Son of the La Crosse

Many famous authors spent their formative years near rivers covered in this book. The list includes environmental writer Aldo Leopold, whose seminal *A Sand County Almanac* grew out of his experiences near the Wisconsin River southwest of the Dells; internationally known poet Lorine Niedecker, who spent most of her life along the Rock River near Lake Koshkonong; Laura Ingalls Wilder, whose childhood years in the Pepin area near the Chippewa River provided material for her immensely popular Little House series; and the prolific author and lifelong resident of Sauk City, August Derleth (one of whose 150 published books is an excellent study of the Wisconsin River).

Hamlin Garland, who occupies a prominent role in the history of American literature, was born near the La Crosse River at West Salem in 1860, and spent his boyhood years at the family farm in the valley of Greens Coulee near Onalaska. A Pulitzer Prize winner, he is best known for his realistic novels portraying the bleak side of life on the frontier, especially *A Son of the Middle Border* and *A Daughter of the Middle Border*. Later in life, he purchased a home in West Salem, which is now open to the public. He was buried in Neshonoc Cemetery.

Wider and less sinuous than the section east of Neshonoc Lake, this portion of the river is seldom obstructed. The banks are considerably higher than upstream, and the woods thinner. Open pastureland occasionally adjoins the river, and huge wooded bluffs sometimes loom in the distance. Suitable for beginning paddlers, the section is quite tranquil except for a couple of minor riffles, and a small drop that can easily be avoided by using an alternative put-in. There are no accesses at most of the bridges, so you're in for a long day unless you shorten the trip by starting at Veterans Memorial Park, where there's a first-rate canoe landing; most paddlers put in here.

Whether you paddle this section or not, don't leave La Crosse without visiting Grandad Bluff, a 570-foot bluff that towers over the city and provides a fantastic view of the confluence of the Mississippi, Black, and La Crosse Rivers. To get to the bluff, go east on Main Street, which becomes Bliss Road; at the top, turn right (east) on Grandad Bluff Road.

The name La Crosse was given to the river by early Frenchmen who saw Native Americans playing a game with sticks resembling the racquets used to play the European game of lacrosse.

Camping is available near the put-in at Veterans Memorial Park one mile west of West Salem (608-786-4011), Goose Island County Park 5 miles south of La Crosse (608-788-7018), Bluebird Springs Recreational Area 4 miles east of La Crosse (608-781-2267), and Pettibone Resort in La Crosse (800-738-8426). Also see La Crosse River 1.

For **canoe** and **kayak rental** and **water levels,** see La Crosse River 1.

The **shuttle route** (9.5 miles) goes south briefly on County C, west and south on Highway 16, and west a short distance on County B.

Gradient is 4.5 feet per mile.

Put in along the sand-and-gravel shoreline downstream-left from the County C bridge, which crosses the river immediately after the Neshonoc Lake dam. The dam and adjacent mill are all that remain of the nineteenth-century village of Neshonoc. Eighty feet wide at the put-in (typical of this section), the river passes woods

and hills downstream. One hundred yards after the County M bridge the river constricts along a stone wall at the former site of a grist mill, then drops 2 feet over the remnant of a rock dam. At some levels, big waves form here; to run the drop, pick a tongue of water.

Downstream, after swinging sharply to the south, the river flows in quick succession beneath an abandoned truss bridge, then the Highway 16 bridge. Veterans Memorial Park—a spacious and popular area—occupies the left bank after Highway 16. Downstream several hundred yards, alongside the campsites, is an asphalt canoe landing—a splendid alternate put-in.

Soon, in a long, relatively straight stretch the river closely parallels the La Crosse River State Trail and Interstate 90 before flowing under the interstate. The immediate surroundings remain wooded in the long series of twists and bends that follow, leading to still another Highway 16 bridge.

As the river swings to the south, a long line of steep bluffs rises on the left, occasionally topped with beautiful rock outcroppings. This is the impressive bluff line that lends a special scenic touch to the city of La Crosse and that prevents the city from expanding to the east. The next bridge is at County B (Gillette Street), where you can **take out** on the bank upstream-right, near a small parking area.

Other trips. After County B the river flows alongside Highway 16 for a mile before turning westward, passing through marshland and some urban surroundings before joining the Mississippi just below the mouth of the Black River. Those who wish to paddle this final leg of the river can take out near the mouth at Riverside Park along the shoreline riprap on river-left.

Some tree-dodging is likely on the La Crosse.

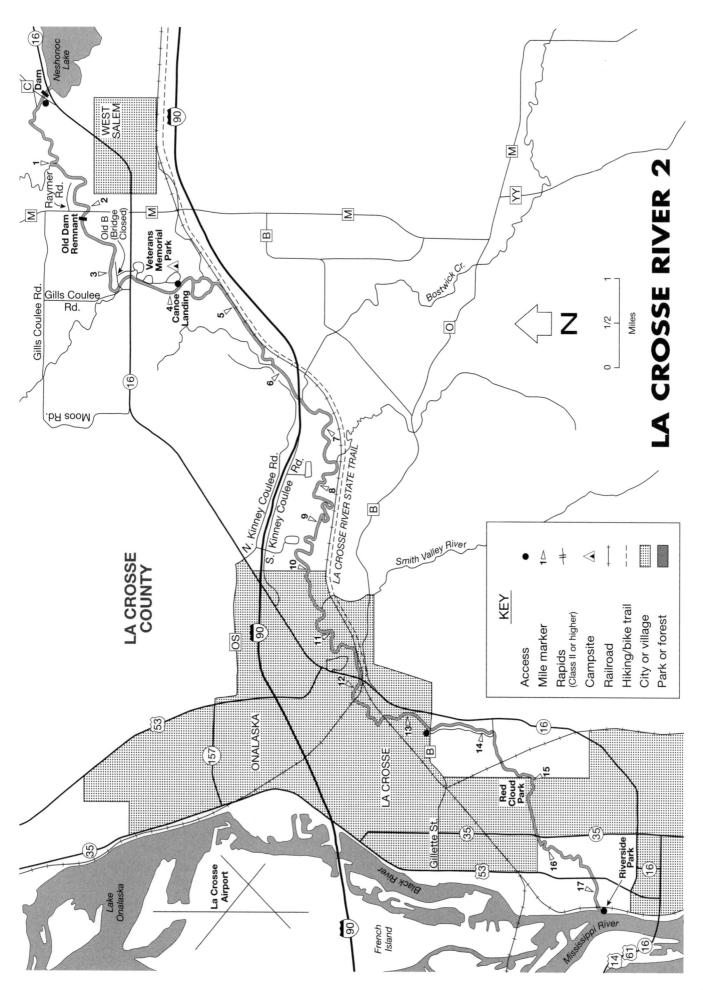

LA CROSSE RIVER 2

KEY

●	Access
△ 1	Mile marker
‡	Rapids (Class II or higher)
◁	Campsite
┼	Railroad
– –	Hiking/bike trail
▦	City or village
▰	Park or forest

N

Miles
0   1/2   1

LA CROSSE COUNTY

WEST SALEM

Neshonoc Lake

Dam

Raymer Rd.

Old Dam Remnant

Old B (Bridge Closed)

Gills Coulee Rd.

Gills Coulee Rd.

Moos Rd.

Veterans Memorial Park

Canoe Landing

N. Kinney Coulee Rd.

S. Kinney Coulee Rd.

LA CROSSE RIVER STATE TRAIL

Bostwick Cr.

Smith Valley River

ONALASKA

LA CROSSE

Gillette St.

Red Cloud Park

Riverside Park

La Crosse Airport

Lake Onalaska

French Island

Black River

Mississippi River

LEMONWEIR RIVER 1
River Road to Sixth Avenue (4.6 Miles)

Wildlife You Can Count On

Ask an experienced canoeist what animal he or she sees most frequently while paddling, and the answer is likely to be the heron. Ducks, geese, eagles, hawks, muskrats, deer, and other wildlife are commonly spotted on Wisconsin's rivers and streams, but none is as ubiquitous as the great blue heron. On days when other wildlife are nowhere to be seen, you can usually count on one or more herons to keep you company—allowing you to get close, then flying downriver, then repeating the process again and again.

Standing 4 feet high and displaying a wingspan of 6 feet, this regally colored wading bird is found throughout North America. Zoologists say that great blues have been around for about 2 million years. If you didn't know better, you'd still swear they're prehistoric when they swoop off, looking like pterodactyls while rasping and croaking to voice their annoyance. If you ever get a chance to see a heron breeding colony, don't miss the opportunity. Nesting atop the highest trees available, they create a marvelously raucous scene as they swoop in and out of their nests built of sticks.

A tributary that joins the Wisconsin River a few miles north of the Dells, the Lemonweir has few of the scenic riches and historic associations that make the larger river so popular with paddlers. What the Lemonweir does have in abundance, however, is wild peacefulness, a sense of truly "getting away from it all." Originating near Wyeville in Monroe County, it meanders southeastward through New Lisbon and Mauston before its confluence with the Wisconsin, almost always surrounded by dense tree cover. Reminders of civilization are seldom encountered.

The two day trips presented here represent the upper and lower parts of the river and provide different kinds of paddling experiences. Whereas the lower section is relatively wide, less sinuous, and free from deadfall, the first stretch is only 20–45 feet wide, never straightens, and is often blocked by fallen trees and limbs that can usually (but not always) be maneuvered around. Wending through the obstacle course of the upper section is fun for experienced boaters, but can be miserable for beginners.

Camping is available at Mill Bluff State Park 3 miles northwest of Camp Douglas (608-427-6692), Buckhorn State Park 11 miles north of Mauston (608-565-2789), Juneau County Castle Rock Park on the eastern shore of Castle Rock Lake (608-847-7089), Riverside Park in New Lisbon (608-562-3534), Kennedy Park 3 miles north of New Lisbon, and Lil' Yellow River Campground 4 miles north of New Lisbon (608-562-5355). Mill Bluff State Park is highly recommended for its fantastic views of the sandstone buttes and mesas that tower out of the otherwise flat countryside. Also see Lemonweir River 2.

Canoe rental is available east of Mauston at Country Corners Bait and Tackle, Campground, and Canoe Trips (608-666-2717) and Country Cruisin' Canoes (608-847-2663), and near Castle Rock Lake at North Country Canoes (608-847-6649).

The **shuttle route** (4 miles) goes north, then east on River Road, east on Twenty-eighth Street, south on County M, and south on Sixth Avenue to the bridge.

Gradient is negligible (less than 1 foot per mile).

Water levels. There is no working gauge on the Lemonweir.

Put in on River Road at the Freeborn Bridge northwest of New Lisbon, upstream or downstream right.

There's room to park a few cars along the road. Only 30 feet wide at the beginning, the river flows between grassy, 4-foot mud-and-sand banks, and deadfall can be seen along the edges immediately. The surroundings are utterly wild as you make one sharp turn after another, frequently maneuvering around, over, or through fallen limbs.

The environment is a hardwood floodplain—mostly maples—with occasional grassy banks or small mud/sandbars where you can stop for lunch or relaxation. Generally the bottom is sandy, with some silt along the shoreline here and there, and the water is clear, with a tannic hue. Deer, heron, muskrat, ducks, and sandhill cranes are often spotted by paddlers.

The river occasionally widens to as much as 45 feet and deadfall temporarily ceases to be a factor, but soon the streambed narrows again and the limb-dodging resumes. Side sloughs are passed, especially where the river makes sharp turns; some of these sloughs are quite large and invite exploration. Only a few cabins and farm buildings are seen on the trip, all on river-right.

Take out upstream-left at the wooden Lone Rock Bridge on Sixth Avenue. There's room on the shoulder for a few cars.

Other trips. Immediately upstream and downstream from this section, the obstructions are often too frequent for enjoyable canoeing. (1) Frequently paddled, however, is the short stretch from Kennedy County Park (alongside County M, 2.3 miles north of Highway 12/16) to New Lisbon; take out at Riverside Park to the left of the dam. (2) Years ago, the section from the New Lisbon dam (downstream-left) to Mauston (take out on Decorah Lake along Highway 12/16) was the scene of an annual canoe race. Expect lots of deadfall in this section! (3) Lemonweir River 2 starts downstream from Mauston.

Maneuvering is required on the upper Lemonweir.

LEMONWEIR RIVER 1

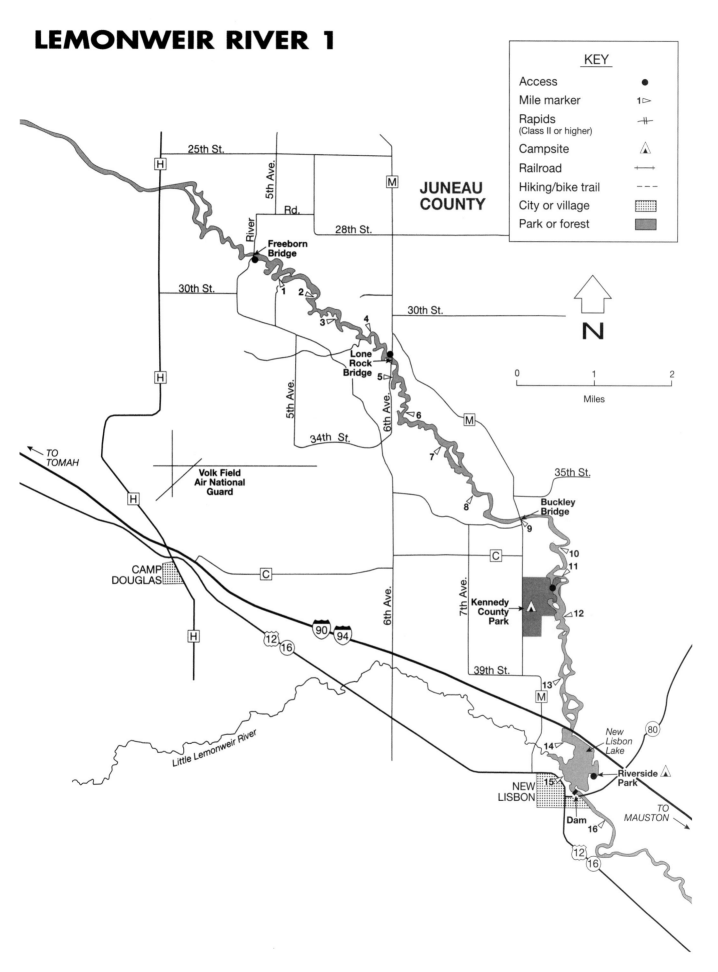

KEY

Access	●
Mile marker	1▷
Rapids (Class II or higher)	╫
Campsite	△
Railroad	┼┼┼
Hiking/bike trail	- - -
City or village	
Park or forest	

JUNEAU COUNTY

N

0   1   2
Miles

25th St.

5th Ave.

Rd.

River

Freeborn Bridge

28th St.

30th St.

30th St.

1 2

3 4

Lone Rock Bridge

5

5th Ave.

6th Ave.

6

34th St.

M

7

TO TOMAH

Volk Field Air National Guard

8

35th St.

Buckley Bridge

9

10

11

C

C

7th Ave.

Kennedy County Park

12

CAMP DOUGLAS

H

90 94

12 16

39th St.

13

M

Little Lemonweir River

14

New Lisbon Lake

80

NEW LISBON

15

Riverside Park

Dam

16

TO MAUSTON

12

16

LEMONWEIR RIVER 2
Nineteenth Avenue to County HH (10.8 Miles)

The Evolution of River Crossings

Before white settlement, rivers were crossed by fording through shallows or by paddling across in a canoe. Beginning in the early 1800s, however, ferryboats began to appear at trail crossings. Originally they were poled or rowed, but later many operators connected their craft to a cable strung across the river, allowing the current to push the ferry across. Some even used horse-operated treadmills to power their boats. As the movement of goods and people increased, ferries became extremely important to travelers, farmers, and commercial interests. Operators rendered a vital service, made a good income from tolls, and generally became significant members of their community.

Gradually, ferries were replaced with bridges—constructed initially of wood and built by entrepreneurs who charged for every crossing. Often bridges were built at locations already well established by ferries. Later, government took over the task of bridge building, especially after the establishment of the Wisconsin State Highway Commission in 1911.

Although this section is continuously wooded from start to finish, it is usually free of the deadfall that makes the upper river an obstacle course. A little maneuvering is necessary here and there to avoid occasional limbs, but nothing that most paddlers can't handle. This is a thoroughly pleasant part of the river, with many sandy beaches, few houses, and no bridges until the take-out. There are plenty of places to stop and relax. The river continues to be quite curvy, with almost no straightaways. Flatwater all the way, this section presents no riffles but moves along steadily with good current. Except for some traffic noise from I-90/94 for a short time near the beginning of the trip, the stretch is isolated and quiet. Accesses are excellent.

The origin of the river's unusual name is explained in various ways: (a) from *la memoire*, the French word for "memory"; (b) from a Native American phrase meaning "river of memory"; or (c) from a logger named Lenonair.

For nearby **camping**, see Lemonweir River 1. There are also three campgrounds near Lyndon Station: Yukon Trails Camping 1.5 miles to the northeast (800-423-9577), Bass Lake Campground 2 miles to the southeast (608-666-2311), and Crockett's Resort Camping 3 miles to the northeast (888-621-4711).

For **canoe rental** and shuttle service, see Lemonweir River 1.

The **shuttle route** (8.7 miles) goes north on Nineteenth Avenue, east on Highway 82, south on County HH, and south on Old HH to the river.

Gradient is 0.9 foot per mile.

For **water levels**, see Lemonweir River 1.

Put in at the public boat ramp at the Nineteenth Avenue bridge, downstream-right, near the site of the old Lemonweir Mill and stone quarry. A mill race was once located on the right side of the river here, below a dam. Now, huge, attractive sandbanks are found downstream from the bridge. There's room to park a number of cars on the flat, rocky area alongside the boat landing.

Sandy beaches continue downstream, often sprinkled with clam shells. Herons, hawks, and eagles are not uncommon. The initial right bend is followed by many more turns, some quite abrupt. Often, large sloughs are

Outliers near Camp Douglas—rock formations rising from the ancient lake floor.

found at the tip of sharp bends. Never less than 40 feet wide, the river sometimes widens to as much as 70 feet.

Not until an hour into the trip do the first farm buildings appear, on the right. A few minutes later there's an attractive stand of pines on the right, together with a brief outcropping of rock. Before long, a couple of cabins stand on the right shore in another pine grove, soon followed by more cabins just before a second rock outcropping. After thinning out for a while, the woods become dense again. The river continues to bend back and forth, but with fewer sharp turns for a couple of miles.

Eventually the river narrows, and sharp bends begin again. Several cabins appear on the right just before a rare, straight quarter-mile stretch, and soon the river widens again to 60–70 feet. When you encounter a series of homes on the right—the most developed setting of the trip—you're not far from the County HH bridge.

After County HH the river bends gently to the left and soon approaches the location of the Old HH bridge (now removed). **Take out** at the gravelly embankment on the left near the steel railing of the former bridge site. There's room to park several cars along the road near the access.

Other trips. (1) Paddling from the Mauston dam to Nineteenth Avenue takes about two hours. (2) Only a few miles of the Lemonweir remain after County HH before the confluence with the Wisconsin. There are numerous channels in the Lemonweir in the last mile before the mouth, where there's an excellent public access (the Two Rivers Boat Landing) on river-right a few hundred yards before the river meets the Wisconsin. To get to the landing, go east on Fifty-sixth Street off County HH, then northeast to the river (see the facing map). If you wish to continue downstream on the Wisconsin River, you can take out at the Plainville boat landing or at several other locations in the Dells area (see Wisconsin River 2).

LEMONWEIR RIVER 2

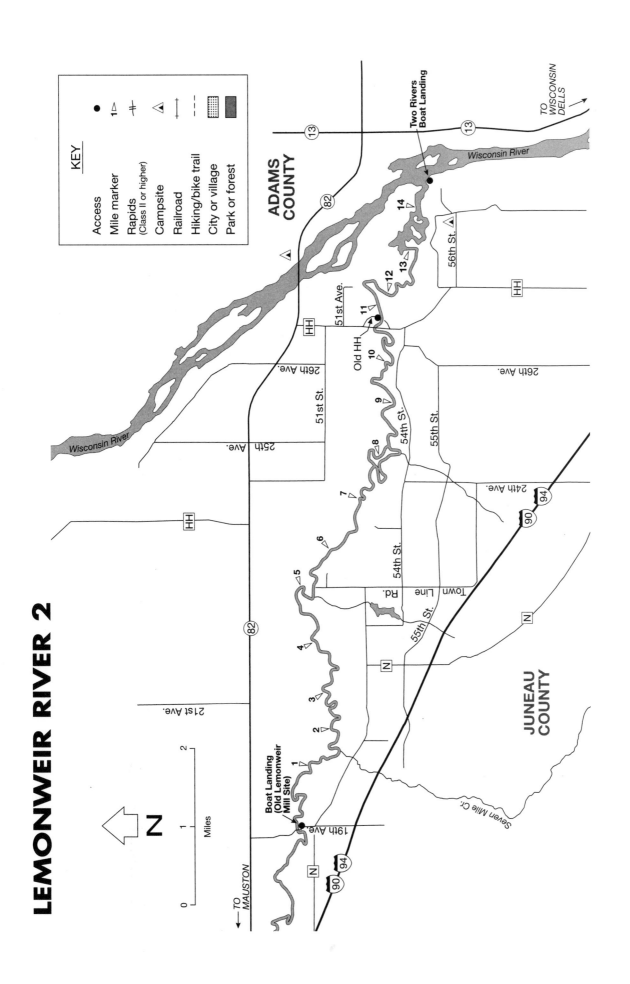

KEY

- Access
- 1△ Mile marker
- ‡ Rapids (Class II or higher)
- △ Campsite
- Railroad
- Hiking/bike trail
- City or village
- Park or forest

ADAMS COUNTY

JUNEAU COUNTY

Wisconsin River

Two Rivers Boat Landing

TO WISCONSIN DELLS

Boat Landing (Old Lemonweir Mill Site)

TO MAUSTON

N

Miles

0   1   2

Seven Mile Cr.

LITTLE WOLF RIVER 1
Wolf River Road to Big Falls (7.5 Miles)

Good rapids on the Little Wolf, upstream from County J.

Definitely not appropriate for paddlers who get upset over boat scratches, the Little Wolf is small, rocky, clear, and delightful. Surprisingly, most of the river is not heavily paddled. Arising 17 miles east of Stevens Point, it flows southeastward through woods, farmland, and marsh to its confluence with the Wolf River near New London. Dams block its progress at Big Falls and Manawa. Like most of the rivers in the area, it was heavily logged in the 1800s, with several "driving dams" that built up heads of water to carry logs over rock gardens and send them on their way to the sawmills of Oshkosh.

The river lends itself to paddling in three parts: Wolf River Road to Big Falls, Little Falls to Symco or Manawa, and Manawa to County X near the mouth. The first is a good whitewater run, the second a peaceful, often riffly trip, and the third a popular section with lots of riffles and Class I rapids.

Camping is available on the river at Wolf River Trips and Campground 4 miles west of New London (920-982-2458), Bear Lake Campground 3.5 miles south of Manawa (920-596-3308), and Iola Pines Campground near Iola (715-445-3489).

The **shuttle route** (7.4 miles) goes south, then east on Wolf River Road, and east on County C to the take-out just past the intersection of County C and County E.

Gradient is a steep 10.7 feet per mile.

Water levels. There is no gauge listed on the USGS Web site, but you can check the Royalton gauge on the Interactive Weather Information Network. See "Water Levels" in the introduction.

Put in downstream-left at the Wolf River Road bridge, near a small DNR parking area. Only 25 feet wide here, the river flows placidly over a sand-gravel-rock bottom in a wild, wooded setting. Boulders appear sporadically in the streambed. Just upstream from the mouth of Comet Creek several homes appear on the left, followed by a straight stretch. Later, after the river drops a little at a row of big boulders near a cabin, there's a short Class I rapid.

Within a few minutes, a long, twisting Class II boulder garden begins. After a brief pool, another long, exhilarating Class II rapid has a couple of good drops. In the midst of the whitewater an old cable foot bridge passes overhead, followed by a home on the left. For a while the rapids grow less intense, but remain continuous.

Finally, the 2-mile stretch of whitewater leads to another Class II rapid, in the middle of which is a rock shelf on the left that makes a good place to stop for lunch. At the end of the rapids is the County J bridge, where there's a good access upstream-left alongside another DNR parking area. Like the upstream bridge, this is a popular spot for trout fishermen. For paddlers who want a short whitewater run, County J is a good **take-out.**

After J the river widens a little and passes through a very peaceful, forested setting highlighted by occasional cedar groves. The quietwater is briefly interrupted twice by boulder clumps and fast water. In a straight stretch, County C runs along the river on the right. Another straightaway follows an old, private bridge. Not long after some farm buildings and old bridge abutments, the McNinch Road bridge appears. Short Class I rapids are found under the bridge and a hundred yards downstream.

After a long, quiet left bend, a sharp S-turn takes you to the scenic high point of the trip: a 150-yard mini-canyon known as the Dells. Paddle into the left channel of the small wooded island that immediately precedes the canyon, and take out at an eddy on river-left to scout the Dells and make sure there's no deadfall. A clearly established trail runs along the left wall of the canyon, not far from a river-left cabin. Granite walls rise over the water here, compressing the width to as little as 15 feet. The Dells is a fairly straightforward run—swift, with big waves, and some boulders to avoid.

Downstream from the Dells, huge granite outcroppings continue, cedars abound, and the setting is wonderfully peaceful—one of the prettiest parts of the trip, reminiscent of the wilds of Ontario. Gradually the current slackens and the river widens as you approach Big Falls on the dam flowage, but the impoundment never gets very wide and the environs are undeveloped. **Take out** at the boat ramp 100 feet upstream-right from the County C bridge, alongside a small park with picnic tables and parking.

Just around the bend after the bridge is the Big Falls dam, built on top of an awesome 30-foot drop over gigantic boulders. If you'd like to get an idea of how the falls looked before being dammed, you can follow a long path through the woods to the shoreline downstream-right from the dam (park at the turn-in about 100 yards south of the take-out, along County E at the small community of Big Falls).

Other trips. A tamer but scenic trip—mostly winding through woodland, farmland, and marsh—starts downstream near Little Falls at the Kretchmer Road bridge or at the Little Falls Resort alongside County C (ask permission at the nearby bar) and ends at Symco or at Bridge Road upstream from Manawa.

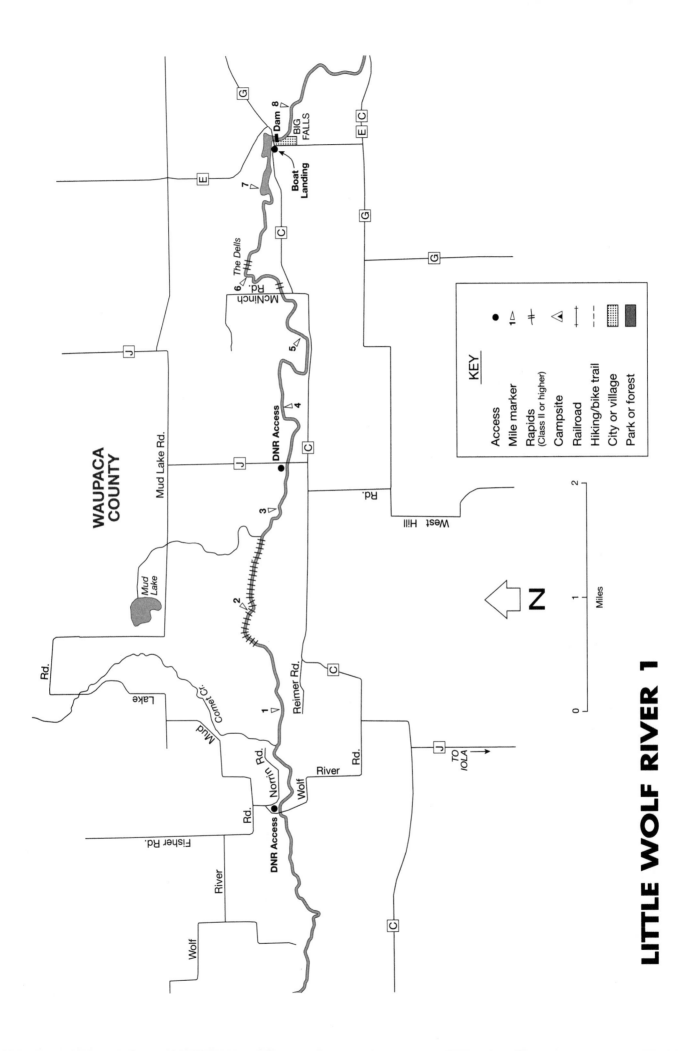

LITTLE WOLF RIVER 1

WAUPACA COUNTY

KEY

- Access
- 1 △ Mile marker
- ⊩ Rapids (Class II or higher)
- ◁ Campsite
- ╫ Railroad
- ┆ Hiking/bike trail
- City or village
- Park or forest

N

Miles
0   1   2

Mud Lake Rd.

Fisher Rd.

DNR Access

Mud Lake

The Dells

McNinch Rd.

DNR Access

Dam 8

BIG FALLS

Boat Landing

West Hill Rd.

TO IOLA

LITTLE WOLF RIVER 2
Manawa to County X (12 Miles)

A Heartening Comeback

Fortunately, sightings of bald eagles are no longer a rarity in Wisconsin. In fact, paddlers often see them soaring over many of the rivers in this book. It wasn't long ago, however, that the state's eagle population was almost wiped out. During the 1800s and early 1900s, habitat destruction and illegal shooting led to the virtual disappearance of eagles in southern Wisconsin. Then, beginning in the 1950s, the eagle population in the northern part of the state fell prey to widespread use of such pesticides as DDT.

Since the ban of DDT in 1972 and the implementation of other measures, eagle populations have slowly improved. Nevertheless, neither eagles nor those who thrill at their regal grace are "out of the woods" yet. The DNR's Bureau of Endangered Resources urges citizens to help increase the eagle population by reporting active nest locations, avoiding nests during breeding season, participating in the winter eagle survey, and discouraging the shooting of eagles. The BER sponsors an Adopt an Eagle Nest Program (608-266-7012).

Not as dramatic as the section upstream from Big Falls, this final segment of the Little Wolf nevertheless is quite popular with paddlers. Often you're likely to see no one else on the first stretch, but after Manawa you'll have plenty of company. Good accesses, myriads of riffles and relatively nonthreatening rapids, and the presence of a canoe-and-tube rental enterprise at the take-out make Little Wolf River 2 a busy place on weekends. In its last hurrah before flowing into the Wolf near New London, the river is a nice mixture of deep, wide, scenic stretches, riffly boulder gardens, and Class I rapids. For most paddlers it's an easy trip, but beginners without maneuvering skills can get in trouble with boulders and occasional limbs. The length is suitable for a leisurely day trip, but good intermediate accesses can be used for shorter trips. Eagles are often seen along the river.

For **camping** and **water levels**, see Little Wolf River 1.

Canoe and tube rental and shuttle service are available at Wolf River Trips and Campground at the County X take-out (920-982-2458).

The **shuttle route** (8.6 miles) goes south on Highway 22/110, south on County B, west briefly on Highway 54 in Royalton, and east on Ostrander Road across County X.

Gradient is 3.3 feet per mile.

Put in downstream-left from the Highway 22/110 bridge in Manawa. Turn west onto the road along the south bank of the river and go 0.15 mile to the gravel boat landing near the athletic fields. There's plenty of room to park. After the put-in the river winds back and forth over a sand-and-gravel bottom, alternating between pools and relatively shallow areas. Banks are wooded and the water clear. After a railroad bridge, large boulders begin appearing in the streambed, and the river soon passes under County B.

A deep pool follows the bridge, then a boulder garden near a couple of homes. When the river splits around a rocky island, there are easy Class I rapids on both sides. The streambed widens now and passes a pretty pine grove as the shoreline becomes more open. There's an excellent

Boats aren't the *only* way to enjoy the Little Wolf.

landing at the next bridge, Highway 22/110 (upstream-right). Again deep pools follow the bridge, especially in a big right bend with a beautiful oak-and-pine grove on the left. A long, deep, relatively straight stretch ends at a brief rapid under some power lines. Boulders and occasional riffles continue as the river narrows and winds around in a wild setting. A small rapid immediately follows the County BB bridge, where there's a good access downstream-left.

Gradient increases for a quarter mile after County BB through scattered boulders. After the river deepens again, the sizable South Branch enters on the right near a pine grove. Another rapid is followed by a wide, peaceful stretch.

Highway 54 at Royalton has an excellent gravel landing upstream-left, and a rapid directly beneath the bridge. Another long, peaceful stretch follows, sometimes interrupted by boulders and mild riffles. Then a mile-long stretch of boulder-garden riffles leads to the Ostrander Road bridge, which has another splendid landing (upstream-left). The best rapids of the day are found 100 yards after the bridge. Once again a deep, quiet stretch follows, ending at a long, Class I rapid within sight of the County X bridge, an old metal truss structure. Before the bridge, the river splits around a couple of islands.

Take out at the Wolf River Trips and Campground landing at the bridge, downstream-left. If you plan to use this take-out, be sure to stop by in advance to pay your landing-and-parking fee. From County X, the Wolf River is only a short paddle away; after the mouth, Shaw Landing is 2 miles downstream-left. Because of heavy motorboat traffic, the lower Wolf is not generally considered to be a good canoeing stream.

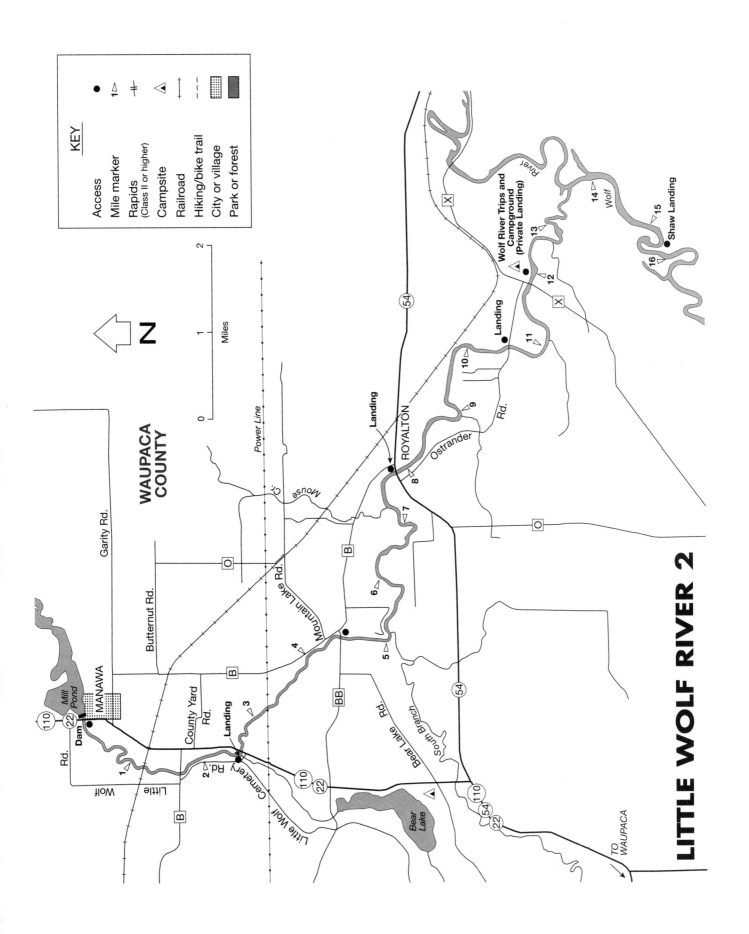

LITTLE WOLF RIVER 2

KEY

- **●** Access
- **1△** Mile marker
- **⌗** Rapids (Class II or higher)
- **△** Campsite
- **┼** Railroad
- **– –** Hiking/bike trail
- City or village
- Park or forest

N

Miles
0   1   2

WAUPACA COUNTY

Garity Rd.

Butternut Rd.

Mill Pond

MANAWA

Dam

110
22

Wolf Rd.

Little Wolf

County Yard Rd.

Landing

1△

2△

Cemetery Rd.

B

Little Wolf

3△

B

Mountain Lake Rd.

4△

5△

Power Line

Mouse Cr.

B

6△

7△

O

Landing

8△

ROYALTON

Ostrander Rd.

9△

10△

Landing

11△

54

O

BB

Bear Lake Rd.

South Branch

54

Bear Lake

△

110
22

110
54
22

TO WAUPACA

Wolf River Trips and Campground (Private Landing)

△

13△

12△

X

X

River

14△ Wolf

15△

16△

Shaw Landing

MANITOWOC RIVER 1

Collins to Clarks Mills (10.7 Miles)

The seldom-paddled Manitowoc begins just to the east of Lake Winnebago, flowing through marshland in most of its upper reaches. A few miles east of the Collins Marsh, however, it changes character completely, passing through woodlands, riffles, and rapids before entering the city of Manitowoc and emptying into Lake Michigan. Indeed, the Manitowoc upstream and downstream from County JJ near Collins is almost like a tale of two rivers. The former tends to be open, wide, marshy, and suitable for beginners, while the latter is generally narrower, steeper, and more appropriate for experienced paddlers. The section described here displays both aspects of the Manitowoc. Novices often have difficulty in the S-curve after Leist Road, where a challenging rapid is located.

The wide–open upper Manitowoc near Collins.

Camping is available at Rainbows End Campground near Reedsville (920-754-4142), Point Beach State Forest north of Two Rivers (920-794-7480), Devil's River Campground northwest of Manitowoc (920-863-2812), and Seagull Marine and Campgrounds in Two Rivers (920-794-7533).

Canoe rental is available at the Collins Marsh Nature Study Center on County JJ (920-772-4258) for trips on the lake and creek upstream from the dam, but not for trips on the river.

The **shuttle route** (7.1 miles) goes north on County W, east on County JJ, and north on County J to the bridge in Clarks Mills.

Gradient is 0.9 foot per mile.

For **water levels**, check the gauge at Manitowoc (#04085427) on the USGS Web site. See "Water Levels" in the introduction.

Put in (1) at the County W bridge south of Collins, where there are low, grassy banks but no designated landing; or (2) downstream-right from the Mud Creek dam in the Collins Marsh State Wildlife Area. Located directly across County JJ from the buildings of the Collins Marsh Nature Study Center, the small dam is situated next to a sizable parking lot. After put-in (2)—probably the more interesting of the two—Mud Creek meanders back and forth through marshland, then empties into the Manitowoc less than a mile east of the County W bridge.

Whichever put-in you select, the Manitowoc begins with a long right bend where the river is wide and the surroundings open. The first home and farm buildings of the trip are passed on the left, on high ground away from the floodplain. When the river heads left, a creek enters on the right and a thin line of trees begins, together with a series of duck blinds and deer stands. After heading back to the right, the river narrows considerably (to as little as 40 feet), and the bankside trees and bushes become thicker.

In the approach toward Quarry Road, the streambed is quite twisting. Downstream from the bridge, the environs open up, the river widens again, and many farms can be seen on the hillsides. After a long right bend, a metal-truss railroad bridge crosses the river; off to the right, in the distance, are a huge quarry operation and the water tower of Valders. Soon thereafter the river passes under the County JJ bridge, which is preceded by heavily vegetated banks. The river can be accessed upstream-right at the bridge.

Now begins the prettiest part of the trip. In most of the northeast stretch from County JJ to Leist Road, the river is narrow and high-banked. Tall bushes are plentiful along the shoreline, and lovely cedars and pines begin to appear in the woods. In contrast with the first part of the trip, the surroundings are decidedly unmarshlike. When Clarks Mills Road pulls alongside the left bank, homes appear, but the setting is still quite attractive.

After Leist Road the river narrows and passes through Class I rapids in a right turn. Then, quickly, a rock formation on the right swings the river back to the left; here the river constricts to 25 feet and drops over a couple of ledges that require caution (Upper Cato Falls). Portage on the left if in doubt. A succession of pleasant riffles follows between steep, wooded banks, and the setting continues to be wild, undeveloped, and beautiful.

By the time you pass under a set of power lines, the current has slowed and the river has begun to widen for the Clarks Mills Pond. After a large, wooded island, the river veers right, then left under the County J bridge in the village of Clarks Mills. **Take out** at the river-left boat landing immediately after the bridge. Be careful, because the 8-foot dam is a very short distance downstream!

Other trips. (1) For another 8 miles of slow paddling through predominantly marshy lowland, you can put in farther upstream on the North Fork at the County PP boat landing in the small community of Potter (downstream-left). Take out at County W near Collins. (2) In the 2.5-mile stretch from Clarks Mills to County S, the river continues to be high-banked, wooded, and narrow. The highlight of this short stretch is a beautiful dells where limestone cliffs form a minicanyon. Rocky ledges here form a Class II+ drop called Lower Cato Falls, which can be quite pushy at higher levels and should be attempted only by skilled paddlers. To scout and/or portage, take out on river-right upstream from the falls. Before running this section, you may wish to visit Lower Cato Falls County Park, off County JJ.

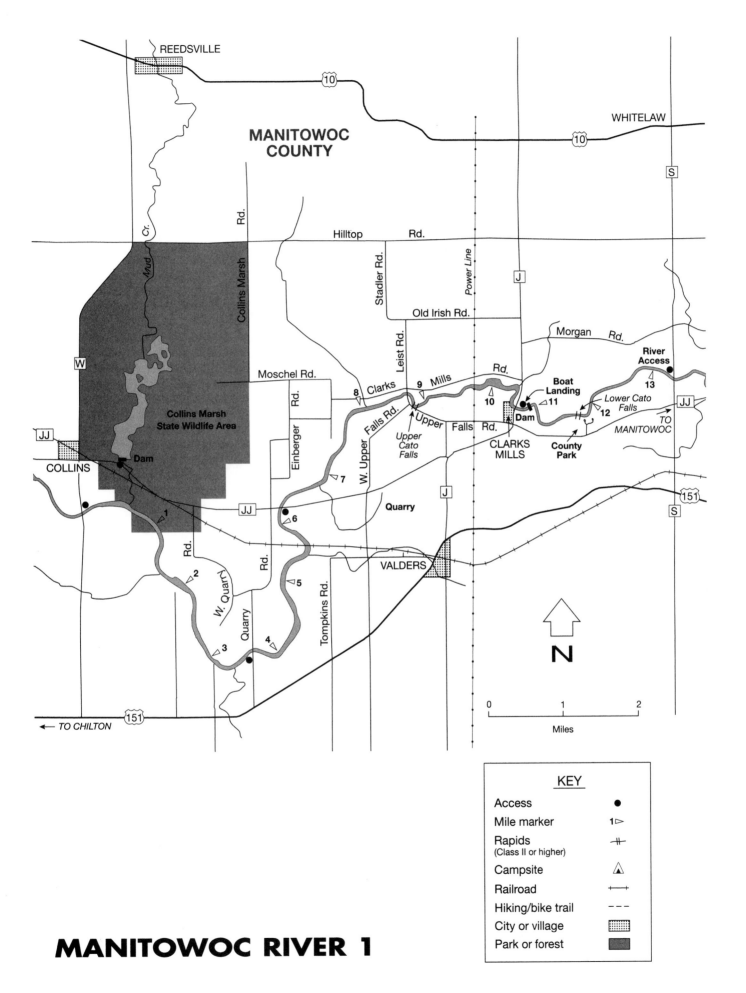

REEDSVILLE

MANITOWOC COUNTY

WHITELAW

10

10

S

Hilltop Rd.

Mud Cr.

Collins Marsh

Collins Marsh Rd.

Stadler Rd.

Power Line

J

Old Irish Rd.

Morgan Rd.

W

River Access

Collins Marsh State Wildlife Area

Leist Rd.

Moschel Rd.

Rd.

8 Clarks

9 Mills

Rd.

13

JJ

Boat Landing

10

11

Lower Cato Falls

12

JJ

Einberger Rd.

W. Upper Falls Rd.

Upper Falls Rd.

Dam

TO MANITOWOC

Dam

Collins

JJ

Upper Cato Falls

CLARKS MILLS

County Park

1

JJ

7

Quarry

J

151

Rd.

6

S

2

W. Quarry

Rd.

5

VALDERS

Quarry

Tompkins Rd.

3

4

151

← TO CHILTON

N

0   1   2

Miles

MANITOWOC RIVER 1

KEY

Access	●
Mile marker	1▷
Rapids (Class II or higher)	‒╫‒
Campsite	⚠
Railroad	+—+—+
Hiking/bike trail	- - -
City or village	▦
Park or forest	▰

MANITOWOC RIVER 2
County S to Manitowoc (13.8 Miles)

A little-known gem, this section of the Manitowoc is a springtime delight for experienced paddlers. When there's sufficient water (at least 200 cfs on the USGS gauge), the river offers an exhilarating succession of riffles, ledges, and boulder-strewn rapids. Tall, scenic bluffs often direct the river into long bends and sharp turns. Wild in appearance, the banks are heavily wooded most of the way, including many cedar and pine groves; not until the very end of the trip do the environs begin to look "civilized." Current is usually brisk. An added bonus is the city of Manitowoc itself, famed as a shipbuilding center (everything from yachts to submarines).

The Native American name of the Manitowoc has been variously translated as "spirit of the land," "abode of the spirit," "river of bad spirits," and "devil's den."

For **camping** and **water levels**, see Manitowoc River 1.

The **shuttle route** (8 miles) goes south on County S, east on County JJ, east on Highway 10/42, south on County R past the bridge, and north a short distance on Mill Road.

Gradient is 10.9 feet per mile.

Put in at the fishermen's access upstream-left from the County S bridge. The old Oslo Dam, removed in 1991, was located just upstream from the access. Only 35 feet wide at the beginning, the stretch begins with pleasant riffles, then widens somewhat. Flowing over a rock-and-gravel bottom, the river winds between wooded banks, with many beautiful cedars. Be on guard for boulders concealed in the many riffles. Eventually a tall wooded bluff, topped with houses, diverts the river to the right, and the Old County H Road bridge soon follows. Class I boulder gardens begin at the bridge and continue for several hundred yards, ending at a log home on the left. The river now narrows and pulls alongside a cedar-covered bluff on the right, then is deflected to the right by an attractive, river-left bluff.

The next bridge, at Union Road, is preceded by farm buildings and riffles, and is the last place to take out before Manitowoc. After the bridge, houses continue periodically on the left for a while as the river winds through one riffle-filled turn after another. Now begins a series of big, gentle bends in which tall, beautiful bluffs lie on one side—with plentiful pines, cedars, and birches—and wooded lowland on the other. Houses become infrequent, and the river has a remote feel to it. After a creek enters on the left, the river widens and becomes less riffly. There are plenty of low, grassy banks where you can get out to relax or have lunch.

Finally, at the end of one especially long, gentle left bend, where cabins appear on both sides, the gradient increases, boulder gardens begin, and the river heads toward Highway 43; this is the beginning of the best rapids of the trip. Nonstop Class I–II rapids continue for a few hundred yards in the right curve, including a series of exciting, river-wide ledges, then subside within view of the highway bridges. Immediately after the bridges, a more demanding Class II rapid begins with a couple of ledges followed by a seemingly interminable mass of boulders to maneuver through. After an abrupt S-turn (right-then-left), the rapids lessen, and the environs become quite wild again, deeply wooded on both sides.

A long right bend now begins, filled with boulders, riffles, and Class I rapids. In the bends that follow, many houses can be seen along the banks. The river narrows, and rapids continue, especially in the turns. Only after some power lines pass overhead in a right turn does the river calm down, splitting around a long island, then flowing alongside Highway 10/42. The river here is narrow, peaceful, and lined with cedars.

Mild riffles follow the Highway 10/42 and Michigan Avenue bridges, with large boulders scattered here and there in the streambed. Although the river is now approaching Manitowoc, the surroundings remain undeveloped, with attractive wooded bluffs. After the second set of power lines downstream from Michigan Avenue (at a sharp left turn), the river widens and the current becomes noticeably slacker. Houses begin to appear again, and the last riffle of the trip occurs in a very sharp turn to the left. At higher water levels, this 90-degree turn can be difficult, especially if deadfall is located there. In the three bends that quickly follow, the banks look increasingly urban.

Finally, after a sharp right turn, you can see a charming old truss bridge upstream from County R. **Take out** on the grassy bank 150 feet upstream-right from the old bridge, and carry your boat(s) through the grass to the adjacent parking lot. This public access, located at the end of Mill Road, is a small park maintained by Manitowoc County.

Other trips. If you wish to paddle farther into the city, you can continue another 1.5 miles to Manitou Park, where the take-out is on river-left. The river becomes much wider and more shallow in this stretch. Years ago there was an annual springtime canoe race down this section of the river, beginning at County S and ending at Manitou Park.

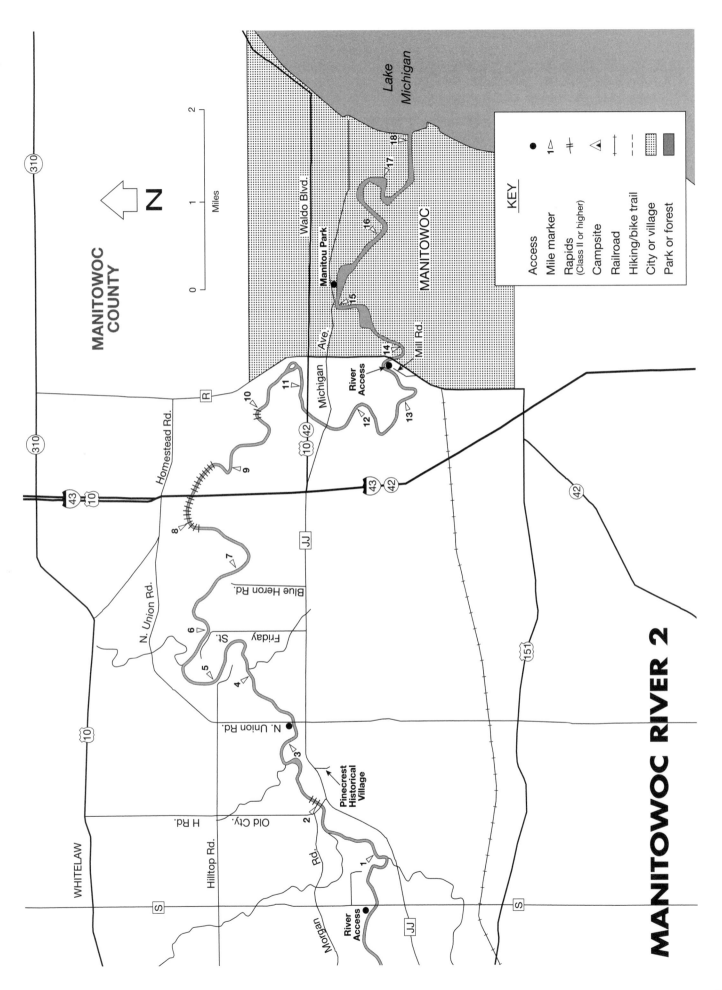

MANITOWOC RIVER 2

MANITOWOC COUNTY

N

Miles
0   1   2

KEY

Access
Mile marker
Rapids
(Class II or higher)
Campsite
Railroad
Hiking/bike trail
City or village
Park or forest

Lake Michigan

Waldo Blvd.

Manitou Park

MANITOWOC

Michigan Ave.

Mill Rd.

River Access

Homestead Rd.

N. Union Rd.

Blue Heron Rd.

Friday St.

WHITELAW

Hilltop Rd.

Old Cty. H Rd.

Morgan Rd.

Pinecrest Historical Village

N. Union Rd.

River Access

JJ

S

MECAN RIVER 1
Dakota to Germania (11.8 Miles)

Several of the Fox River's tributaries are canoe-able—including Neenah Creek, the Montello River, and the White River—but the most delightful of all is the Mecan. From its source at Mecan Springs between Coloma and Wautoma, this clear, narrow stream twists through isolated surroundings for 30 miles. Sharp turns, good current, and protruding limbs require considerable maneuvering.

The remote, wooded setting and nearby wetlands make the river a good place to observe wildlife, including greater sandhill cranes, black cormorants, and wild turkey. In its journey to the Fox, the Mecan passes through the Germania Marsh, one of the best waterfowl habitats in the state. Except for the marsh (which can be avoided by taking out upstream), the river is ideal for small-stream enthusiasts. Numerous accesses make it easy to design trips of varying length.

Camping is available nearby at Mecan River Outfitters and Lodge 3 miles west of Princeton (920-295-3439), Lake of the Woods Campground 1 mile south of Dakota (920-787-3601), and Oak Grove Campground a few miles northwest of Germania Marsh (920-293-4476).

Canoe rentals and shuttles are available at Mecan River Outfitters and Lodge (920-295-3439) and Lake of the Woods Campground (920-787-3601). The Mecan River Discovery Center offers nature education programs that include canoe trips (920-293-8404).

The **shuttle route** (approximately 13 miles) for the first trip goes east on County JJ, south on Highway 22, east on Duck Creek Avenue, south on County N, and west on the gravel access road to the dam. Many paddlers shorten the trip by using alternate accesses at Dixie Avenue, Dover Avenue, or Dike Road.

Gradient is 2.5 feet per mile.

Water levels. There is no USGS gauge on the Mecan. For information on general water conditions (high, medium, low), call Mecan River Outfitters and Lodge (920-295-3439).

Put in at the County JJ bridge near Dakota, downstream-left, where the river is only 15 feet wide, winding, riffly, and overhung with birch, oak, and pine. The bottom is sandy, with rocks here and there in the streambed, and the environs are intimate and beautiful. Tight turns can be tricky because of occasional limbs and stumps in the water, but experienced boaters will have no problem. About half an hour into the trip there's a wooden vehicular bridge. By the time you get to the Fourteenth Avenue bridge, you are likely to have encountered a couple of fallen trees blocking the river; however, the low banks and often-shallow water make portages easy.

Like many of the bridges on the Mecan, the new Fourteenth Avenue structure is low, necessitating a carry-around if clearance is insufficient. The upstream end is lower than the downstream end, in order to help prevent entrapment. After the bridge the streambed is somewhat less circuitous and the environs are more open for a while before the woods close in again. Immediately after a couple of homes, the river veers to the right under a small plank bridge (low clearance: carry on the right if necessary). Shortly afterward is the Dixie Avenue bridge (a large culvert), which can be accessed on the steep bank downstream-left.

The river now becomes narrow and winding again and passes the mouth of Chaffee Creek. At the Dover Avenue bridge there's a gravelly landing upstream-left, a good access for shorter trips. Another bridge follows within a quarter mile, the river widens, and the setting is more open for a while. A couple of farms and three old farm bridges are passed before you come to three more bridges in short order: County E, Fifteenth Drive, and Highway 22 (where there's a downstream-left landing, another good alternate access).

After Highway 22 the river widens to 40 feet and is thinly wooded, with gentler bends and less deadfall. On the left a sign announces nearby Oak Grove Campground. After an old low-clearance footbridge near a house, the river briefly narrows. Two more bridges follow: a very rickety footbridge after a house on the left, then a low, floorless metal truss bridge.

The river now winds through a low, open area where trees are some distance away. Finally a power pole can be seen ahead over the marsh grass, indicating that you're approaching the electric barrier that precedes the Dike Road bridge and separates northern pike and other predators from trout in the upper river. Upstream-right from the barrier a 150-foot channel leads to a gravel landing. From here you can carry your boat(s) across the road and put back in downstream-right, or take out if you don't want to continue through the Germania Marsh. Dike Road is open only from May 1 to September 30, however, and is accessible only from the north.

Once you've reentered the water from Dike Road, you're in a different world: marsh grass, cattails, and a sometimes indistinct channel. After making the turn toward the southeast, look for several tall pines atop the tree line in the distance and head toward them. When you approach the dam, **take out** upstream-left and carry your boat up to the public parking area off County N. You can also **take out** upstream-right from the dam; a short gravel road leads northward from Germania to the dam.

Other trips. The section from County II to County JJ is comparable to the JJ-to-Dover-Avenue stretch: narrow, twisting, riffly, and intimate. Unfortunately, because it's less frequently paddled, obstructions are more likely.

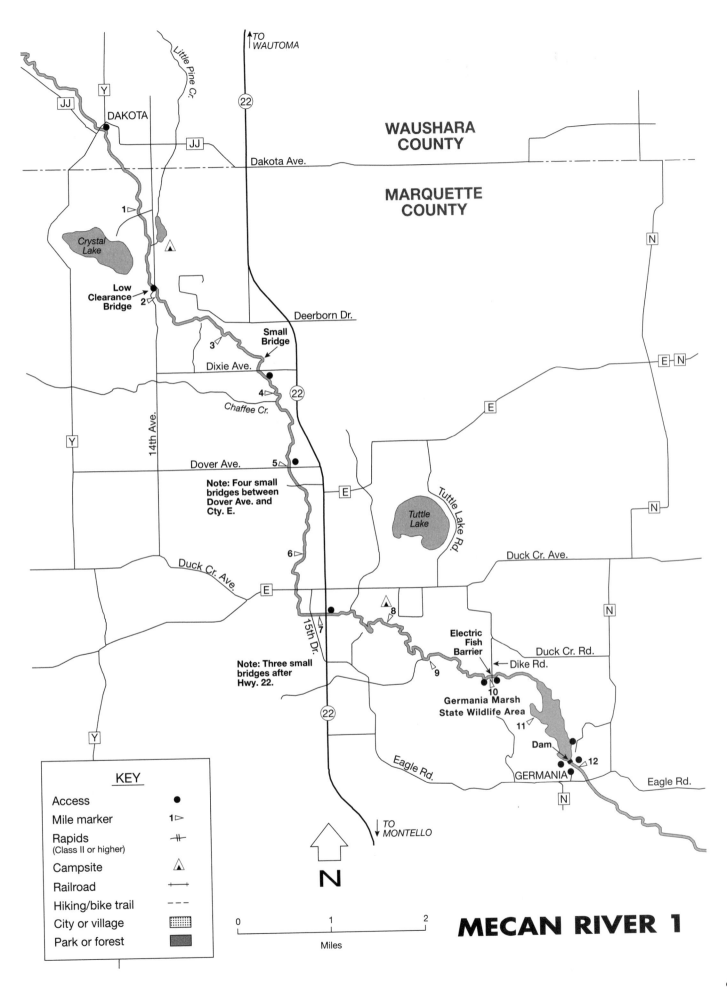

TO
WAUTOMA

(22)

Little Pine Cr.

JJ
Y
DAKOTA

JJ

WAUSHARA
COUNTY

Dakota Ave.

MARQUETTE
COUNTY

1▷

Crystal
Lake

△

Low
Clearance
Bridge
2▷

Deerborn Dr.

3▷

Small
Bridge

Dixie Ave.

(22)

4▷

Chaffee Cr.

14th Ave.

Y

Dover Ave.   5▷

Note: Four small
bridges between
Dover Ave. and
Cty. E.

E

Tuttle
Lake

Tuttle Lake Rd.

N

E N

E

N

Duck Cr. Ave.

6▷

Duck Cr. Ave.

Duck Cr. Ave.

E

15th Dr.

△
8

7▷

N

Note: Three small
bridges after
Hwy. 22.

(22)

9▷

Electric
Fish
Barrier

Duck Cr. Rd.

Dike Rd.

10

Germania Marsh
State Wildlife Area

11▷

N

Dam

12▷

GERMANIA

Eagle Rd.

N

Eagle Rd.

TO
MONTELLO

N

KEY

Access	●
Mile marker	1▷
Rapids (Class II or higher)	‖
Campsite	△
Railroad	+—+—+
Hiking/bike trail	- - -
City or village	▦
Park or forest	▬

0   1   2
Miles

MECAN RIVER 1

MECAN RIVER 2
Germania to County C (7.8 Miles)

Starting where the first section ends, this trip takes you within a mile of the Fox River. En route, the Mecan presents paddlers with a variety of settings. Much of the stretch tends to be a little wider, more open, and less twisting than the Dakota-to-Germania section, but there are a few parts that are narrow and meander back and forth relentlessly. Moreover, the only straightaways on the river are found here. The river continues to be incredibly peaceful and remote, seldom interrupted by reminders of civilization. Like the earlier section, this part of the Mecan requires boat control in negotiating tight turns and avoiding occasional limbs. It was on this section of the river that a 7-mile canal once diverted water from the Mecan to Princeton to operate a grist mill and generate electricity.

For **camping, canoe rental,** and **water levels,** see Mecan River 1.

The **shuttle rout**e (approximately 9 miles) from the Germania Dam goes east on the access road, south on County N, east on Highway 23, and south on County C to the bridge.

Gradient is 2.6 feet per mile.

Put in at the Germania Dam, downstream-left, near a public parking area accessed from County N. You can also put in on the south bank of the river, downstream-right, by driving to the end of a short gravel road from Germania (the road goes north from the small community's main east-west street, beginning alongside an old church near the fire number sign "Shields W1974"). The river below the dam is a popular fishing spot, often yielding sizable northern pike.

The Mecan: the quintessence of southern Wisconsin's charming little rivers.

Good current quickly carries you to the County N bridge, where the streambed constricts, drops about a foot, and creates a nice wave train. Narrowing a little, the river gently bends through a thinly forested area. When a barbed-wire fence appears on the left, a quarter-mile straightaway begins (the first on the river). As the river heads right again, there's a wooden retaining wall on the left. After a few bends, another straight stretch flows between the grassy banks in a rather open area. As soon as the river turns right and begins an even longer straight stretch, an attractive, arched metal-and-plank footbridge appears. When the river heads left after the latest straightaway, a concrete flow-control structure is found on the right.

After the County J bridge, the river meanders a great deal through mostly open country with trees interspersed here and there. Turns become progressively tighter and the river narrower, with overhanging trees and occasional deadfall to dodge. After a glimpse of the road, the river loops around to the County N bridge, which is rather low and may require a portage to the left.

A short distance after County N, the channel forks; make the sharp turn here into the right channel. After winding through the woods a while, the river passes through a wide, shallow, marshy area. Shortly after the woods resume, there is again a choice of two channels; take the right one, which is intimate and lovely and leads past a campsite atop the high right bank (the site must be reserved with Mecan River Outfitters and Lodge). In another marshy area the first houses of the trip can be seen. Look for swallow nests underneath the next bridge (County N again).

The river now winds through an isolated, often open area, where fallen trees and limbs continue. At one point, in a left bend, the first high, sandy cut banks of the trip appear on the right, pocked with swallow nests and topped with coniferous trees. Soon thereafter the river widens for a while to 80 feet, and houses can be seen in the distance. The farther you go, the more the setting takes on the appearance of a lowland hardwood forest.

After the Highway 23 bridge, the river narrows to about 50 feet and passes through a mixture of open and wooded areas. A quarter mile downstream from the bridge a home appears on the right, and later there's a marshy environment on the same side. Brisk stream flow and sharp turns continue to create interesting cross currents and strong eddies that call for attentive paddling.

Finally, when you begin hearing traffic from County C, start looking for the **take-out,** a gravel landing on the right, in a left curve. The landing appears before you see the bridge. A loop drop-off road leads from the bridge (upstream-right) to the landing, where there's room to park several cars.

Other trips. Less than a mile of the Mecan remains before it flows into the Fox River in the middle of a dramatic bend known as Devil's Elbow. Then a paddle of 5.5 miles takes you to Princeton, where there's a boat ramp at the Highway 23 bridge, downstream-right. Midway through the trip on the Fox, however, at the Princeton Lock and Dam, there's a potentially lethal low-head dam in the right channel of an island; to portage, take out upstream-left from the lock that is located in the left channel. You can also take out here for a short trip. Whether you portage or take out here, be very careful: The dam has claimed a number of lives. Lock Road leads from Highway 23 to the public fishing area alongside the lock and dam.

MECAN RIVER 2

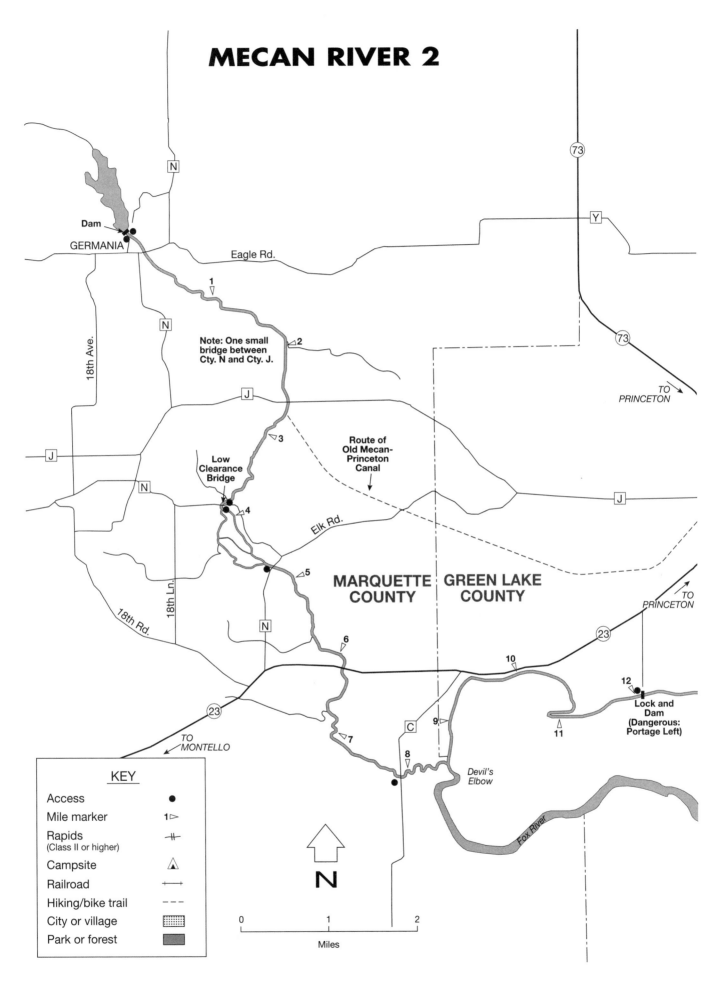

Dam

GERMANIA

Eagle Rd.

18th Ave.

Note: One small bridge between Cty. N and Cty. J.

Route of Old Mecan-Princeton Canal

Low Clearance Bridge

Elk Rd.

18th Ln.

18th Rd.

MARQUETTE COUNTY

GREEN LAKE COUNTY

TO PRINCETON

TO PRINCETON

TO MONTELLO

C

Devil's Elbow

Fox River

Lock and Dam (Dangerous: Portage Left)

KEY

Access	●
Mile marker	1▷
Rapids (Class II or higher)	─╫─
Campsite	▲
Railroad	┼─┼─
Hiking/bike trail	− − −
City or village	▦
Park or forest	▬

N

0   1   2
Miles

MILWAUKEE RIVER 1
West Bend to Newburg (11.2 Miles)

Like the Chicago River in northeastern Illinois, the Milwaukee River is associated by many people with the densely populated, urban environment of its final miles. Thus, visitors to its upper reaches are pleasantly surprised to discover a small, clear, rural stream that provides many miles of excellent paddling. Originating in marshland southeast of Fond du Lac—the same area that gives rise to the Sheboygan River—the Milwaukee is quite canoeable after the dam in Kewaskum. Although several dams have been removed from the river in recent years—sometimes with dramatic results—many remain, and each of the four sections recommended here essentially involves a trip from one dam to another.

Suitable for beginners, the first trip begins at the site of an especially successful dam removal. In 1988, the aged Woolen Mills Dam in West Bend was taken out, creating 61 acres of parkland that is a boon to the community. The streambed on this section ranges from 30 to 100 feet wide, flowing over a sand-and-gravel bottom and through several riffly areas. There is light tree cover along the banks most of the way. The trip can easily be shortened by using an intermediate access.

Camping is available 1 mile northeast of West Bend at Lake Lenwood Campground (262-334-1335), Lazy Days Campground 4 miles northeast of West Bend (262-675-6511), Timber Trail Camp Resort 4 miles northwest of West Bend (414-282-6394), Pike Lake State Park 10 miles southwest of West Bend (262-670-3400), and Waubedonia County Park 1 mile east of Waubeka.

Canoe rental is available at the West Bend Park, Recreation, and Forestry Department (262-335-5080).

The **shuttle route** (7.3 miles) from Riverside Park goes north on Indiana Avenue, east on Highway 33, northeast on Franklin Street in Newburg, and northwest on County MY to the parking area downstream-right from the bridge.

Gradient is 3.6 feet per mile.

For **water levels,** check the gauge near Cedarburg (#04086600) on the USGS Web site. See "Water Levels" in the introduction. Below 300 cfs, the shoals in the area of County M begin getting too shallow for comfortable paddling.

Put in at the river-left canoe landing in West Bend's Riverside Park. Until County G the river is quite open, narrow, and riffly, winding through the former lake-bed area and passing under several attractive footbridges. County G is a good alternate access, with adjacent parking (upstream-right).

After the bridge the setting changes completely: The shoreline is now wooded, with occasional high banks. Farther downstream, after a creek enters on the right in a sharp left bend, the river heads north and passes a fenced-in complex of water-treatment buildings before veering to the right and flowing beneath a bridge. In the many bends that follow, tree cover continues to be thin on both sides, with periodic openings, and at times the river widens to as much as 100 feet. Houses are sparse.

At one point the airport can be seen along the left shoreline. Soon thereafter the river twice loops to the north, and traffic can be seen briefly along Highway 33. The surroundings now become wilder, the river narrower, and the curves sharper. Eventually County I pulls alongside the right shoreline at the small community of Myra.

In the bends leading to County M, the gradient increases and the streambed becomes quite rocky. At medium levels this area is exciting, but shallow water necessitates some scraping and walking. Immediately downstream-left from the bridge is Goeden Park, where you can take out or put in on the grassy bank; parking and toilets are available here.

Rocky riffles continue in the left bend after County M past the Highway 33 bridge, then become infrequent. In the big bends that follow, Highway 33 appears once again on the right bank in a long left arc. Soon after passing a large, white-fenced horse farm on the right, then high wooded banks in a left bend, the river noticeably slows and widens at the head of the Newburg Pond. **Take out** alongside a cemetery on the river-right bank about 75 yards upstream from the dam, which is located directly beneath the County MY bridge. Don't get near the small mill race that flows to the right of the dam. Carry your boat(s) along the bank and across the road to the parking area downstream-right from the bridge, near Fireman's Park.

Other trips. Two dams block the river a short distance upstream from this section: one immediately north of Highway 33, alongside the West Bend Company, and another in neighboring Barton, 75 yards upstream from the Highway 144 bridge. The stretch from Kewaskum to Barton makes a very pleasant day trip. In Kewaskum, drive south from Highway 28 on Parkview Drive along the river and put in downstream-right from the dam. Flowing through the hills of the Kettle Moraine, the river here passes mostly through wooded countryside. Just north of Barton, there are rocky riffles before and after an abandoned metal truss bridge, near the site of an old mill dam that was removed in 1994. After a railroad bridge, the Barton impoundment begins. Hug the left shoreline and take out on river-left alongside the parking lot of the historic Barton Roller Mills building (now a private apartment building), and carry your boat(s) to the public parking along nearby Commerce Street.

MILWAUKEE RIVER 1

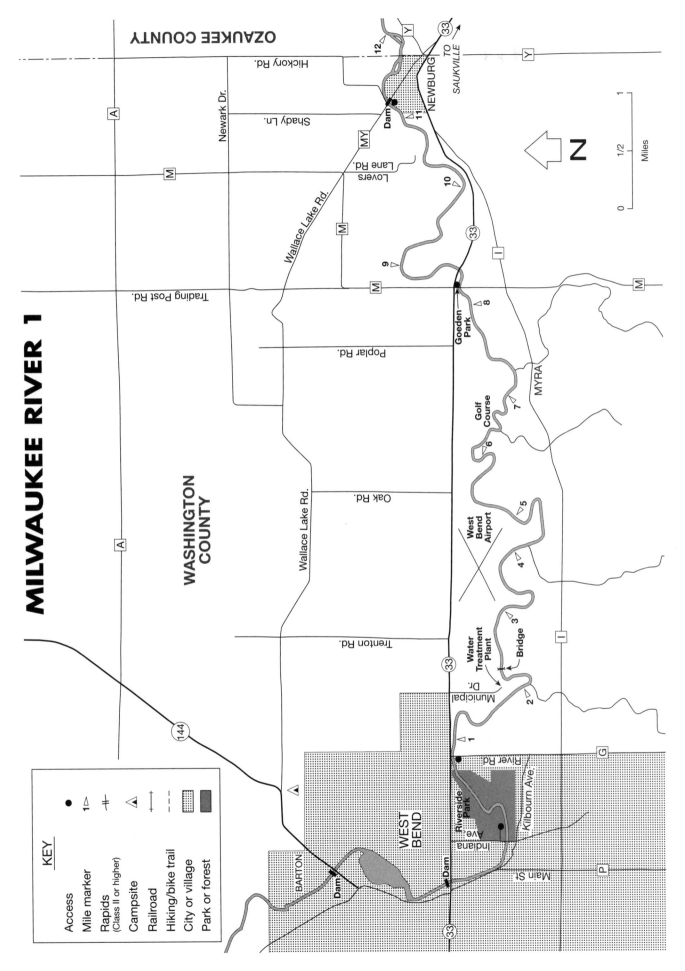

OZAUKEE COUNTY

WASHINGTON COUNTY

KEY

Access	●
Mile marker	1△
Rapids (Class II or higher)	⊬
Campsite	◬
Railroad	┼┼
Hiking/bike trail	┈
City or village	
Park or forest	

N
Miles
0   1/2   1

NEWBURG
TO SAUKVILLE
Hickory Rd.
Newark Dr.
Shady Ln.
Dam
Lovers Lane Rd.
Wallace Lake Rd.
Trading Post Rd.
Poplar Rd.
Goeden Park
MYRA
Golf Course
Oak Rd.
Wallace Lake Rd.
West Bend Airport
Trenton Rd.
Water Treatment Plant
Bridge
Municipal Dr.
River Rd.
WEST BEND
Riverside Park
Indiana Ave.
Kilbourn Ave.
Main St.
BARTON
Dam
Dam

MILWAUKEE RIVER 2
Newburg to Waubeka (8.8 Miles)

A Springtime Ritual

In southeastern Wisconsin, one sure sign of spring is the lineup of trout fishermen on the lower Milwaukee, Racine, and Menomonee Rivers. During the annual spawning run of steelheads, thousands of anglers are drawn to the area. Every year, about half a million steelheads are stocked by the DNR in the waters of Lake Michigan off the Wisconsin shore. Then, when the fish swim upstream to spawn in area rivers, legions of fishermen are waiting for them. When the spawning run is on, you can often see fishermen out in full force at such popular Milwaukee River locations as Maier Festival Park and Kletzsch Park.

Rock formations along the Milwaukee River

Overall, this may be the most pleasant section on the 100-mile length of the Milwaukee River. Most of it passes through a wild, sparsely populated setting, winding past high, wooded banks and occasional cedar groves. Steady gradient over a sand-gravel-rock bottom produces innumerable riffles, and large islands often split the flow of the river. Especially beautiful is the stretch that runs through the Riveredge Nature Center, a 350-acre natural sanctuary that provides a rich program of environmental education. The put-in and take-out are easy and convenient, and an intermediate access makes shorter trips possible. If the water level is much below 350 cfs on the Cedarburg-area gauge, you're likely to scrape a lot (and perhaps pull your boat) in the many shallow riffles.

In several Native American languages, Milwaukee means "good land" or "great council place." The area near the mouth, where the city of Milwaukee now stands, was a favorite gathering place for the Potowatomi, Winnebago, Ojibwa, Menominee, and other tribes.

For **camping, canoe rentals,** and **water levels,** see Milwaukee River 1.

The **shuttle route** (6.2 miles) goes southeast on County MY, east and north on County Y, east on County A, north on County H across the bridge, and west on River Drive.

Gradient is 6.8 feet per mile.

Put in at Fireman's Park in Newburg, downstream-right from the dam and the County MY bridge. Launch your boat(s) on the grassy bank just downstream from the small mill race. After a riffle-filled right bend alongside the park, there's a sizable island where the river turns left alongside a tall bank on the right. The river-right landing that soon follows on the right is a private access. Occasional riffles continue in gentle bends to the east, past another large island and several houses high atop the bank.

By the time the river heads to the left at a small island and enters the Riveredge wildlife refuge, both banks are densely wooded and the streambed has widened to 90 feet. Large boulders often line the banks. A long left bend now passes another large island; the high right shoreline here is beautiful, covered with cedars and birches. Huge willows cover the left shoreline after the sharp right turn that follows. At the end of the turn another large island can be seen in a straightaway, which eventually heads left near a house (the first building in a long time). After a modest rock outcropping on the right, a long succession of rocky riffles begins. A frame home appears on the left at the end of Highview Road.

After a couple of gentle bends, the river swings left around another island, past a lovely, cedar-covered bank on the right—one of the prettiest spots on the river. When the river heads back to the right, a row of boulders across the river creates a small, easy drop. The surroundings here are rather open, and farms can be seen in the distance. Farther downstream, Country Lane briefly appears on the right in a long left arc.

After a brick home, the river turns sharply to the right. In the long left bend that follows, there's another large island. In the ensuing curves, riffles become infrequent and the tree line thins out on both sides. Soon after a house with a tall wind-power generator the County A bridge appears, a good alternate access (upstream-right).

Immediately after the bridge the river bends right past a small island for the eastward leg to Waubeka. Riverside Road closely follows the left bank for almost a mile before heading north. A sizable tributary, the North Branch, soon enters on the left. Finally, in a long right bend, River Drive pulls alongside the left bank. Before long, just before the river begins heading to the left, there's an easy **take-out** along the low, gravelly shoreline. A large gravel pull-off beside the road provides plenty of room for parking. The take-out (located near the point where Section Line Road joins River Drive) is 0.7 mile west of County H in Waubeka.

The old dam at Waubeka, located alongside a mill that dates back to 1836, is in poor condition and is expected to be removed soon. Then, once the Newburg dam is taken out, canoeists and kayakers will be able to enjoy unobstructed paddling all the way from West Bend to Grafton—certainly one of the most attractive and enjoyable parts of the river.

Other trips. Downstream from Waubeka a long right bend leads to Waubedonia County Park, the put-in for the next recommended trip (see Milwaukee River 3).

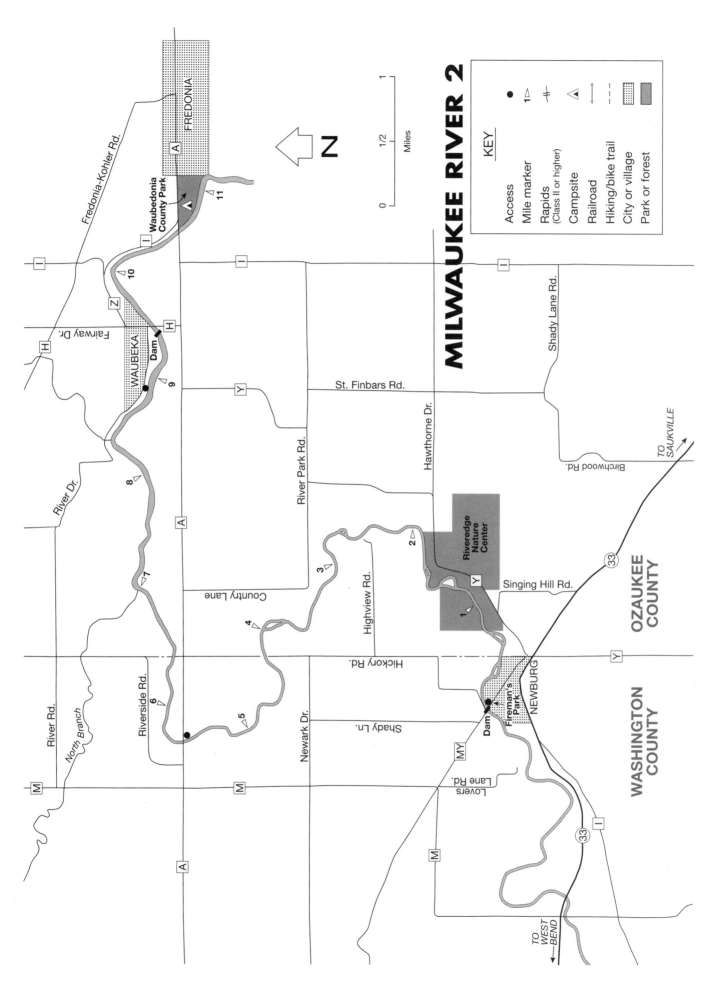

MILWAUKEE RIVER 2

FREDONIA

Waubedonia County Park

WAUBEKA

Dam

Fredonia-Kohler Rd.

Fairway Dr.

River Dr.

River Rd.

North Branch

Riverside Rd.

Newark Dr.

Shady Ln.

Lovers Lane Rd.

Highview Rd.

Hickory Rd.

Country Lane

River Park Rd.

St. Finbars Rd.

Hawthorne Dr.

Shady Lane Rd.

Birchwood Rd.

Riveredge Nature Center

Singing Hill Rd.

NEWBURG

Fireman's Park

Dam

TO WEST BEND

TO SAUKVILLE

OZAUKEE COUNTY

WASHINGTON COUNTY

KEY

- Access •
- Mile marker 1△
- Rapids (Class II or higher) ⊿
- Campsite
- Railroad
- Hiking/bike trail
- City or village
- Park or forest

N

Miles

0   1/2   1

MILWAUKEE RIVER 3
Fredonia to Grafton (13 Miles)

After Waubeka the river swings southward for its final 40 miles to Lake Michigan. Generally wider and less forested, it passes through Saukville and Grafton, then several suburban communities and the city of Milwaukee. Its decidedly urban surroundings at the end belie the fact that, for most of its length, the Milwaukee is a rural river. A number of dams remain after Waubeka, but several removals within the last decade have raised hopes that the river will again be free-flowing in the not-too-distant future.

Every spring the section from Fredonia to Grafton is the setting for the Downriver Canoe Run, sponsored by the Grafton Jaycees. For more leisurely paddlers, the trip can readily be shortened by using an alternative landing just north of Saukville. All three accesses are excellent, each with plenty of parking. Houses appear along the way, but most of the shoreline is wooded. In addition to some riffles here and there, there's a narrow, wavy drop at Saukville.

Waiting for the start of the annual Fredonia-to-Grafton canoe race.

Camping is available near the put-in at Waubedonia County Park (262-692-2825), Lazy Days Campground 3.5 miles northeast of West Bend (262-675-6511), Lake Lenwood Beach and Campground 1 mile northeast of West Bend (262-334-1335), Timber Trail Camp Resort 2.5 miles northwest of West Bend (414-282-6394), Kettle Moraine State Forest Northern Unit 7 miles northeast of Kewaskum (262-626-2116), and Pike Lake State Park 2 miles east of Hartford (262-670-3400).

Canoe rentals are available in Milwaukee at the Laacke and Joys downtown store (414-271-7878), and in Madison at Rutabaga (608-223-9300) and Carl's Paddlin' (608-284-0300).

The **shuttle route** (12.2 miles) for the full trip goes west a short distance on County A, south on County I, east on Highway 60 into Grafton, and north briefly on Washington Street to Veterans Memorial Park (upstream-right). Shuttling via County I and County O will take you through Saukville and closer to the river.

Located along the shuttle route (off County I north of Saukville) is the Ozaukee County Pioneer Village, in Hawthorne Hills County Park. The village features 20 log, stone, and wood-frame buildings from the nineteenth century.

Gradient is 3.1 feet per mile.

For **water levels**, see Milwaukee River 1.

Put in at Waubedonia County Park west of Fredonia. An attractive linear park, Waubedonia has river-left picnic facilities and a boat ramp downstream from the County A bridge. After a quarter-mile straightaway the river abruptly heads right, then turns left along a small bluff on the left side. The banks are heavily wooded, with many cedar trees, and the river is about 70 feet wide. A small willowy island appears after the first house of the trip.

The grassy area of the Hawthorne Hills golf course appears on the right, separated from the water by a narrow band of trees, and good riffles occur in the following bend. After a half mile of houses on the left and a set of power lines, the right shoreline is open for a while. A big metal railroad bridge and another set of power lines are followed by open area on the left, and County W now parallels the river. Soon the landing at grassy Ehlers County Park appears on the left, near a big red barn, off County W—a good place for lunch or for an alternate access. A third set of power lines crosses soon thereafter.

The road continues on the left as the river bends to the right past a big island, and houses are numerous on both sides in the approach to Saukville. At one point the river briefly constricts, drops a foot or two, and forms a wave train; look for the tongue of water and follow it, or portage on the right. Downstream more power lines cross, and the river turns sharply to the left at an apartment building.

After the metal truss bridge of Highway 33, the river loops to the right around Peninsula Park. In the left bend that follows, houses resume. Riverside Park on the right, off County O (Main Street in Saukville), has no landing but can be used as an access. Two more sets of power lines cross the river, which splits around a long island (main channel on the right). Following a very sharp right turn the river bends to the left and widens to 85 feet in a long, straight stretch. Houses appear periodically, but the setting is mostly wooded. Under the next set of power lines, another long island begins next to some old concrete bridge abutments.

Approaching Grafton, the river widens, and golfers can be seen on a big island. A foot bridge from the left shoreline crosses the attractive left channel to the island. **Take out** on river-right at Veterans Memorial Park, just upstream from the Highway 60 bridge. A few hundred yards downstream from the highway bridge is a very dangerous dam.

Until recently, two more dams followed within 1.5 miles. With the removal of the Grafton Chair Factory Dam in 2000, the next dam is just south of the city at Lime Kiln Park. A very pleasant trip begins at the park and ends 9 miles later at the Thiensville Dam (see Milwaukee River 4).

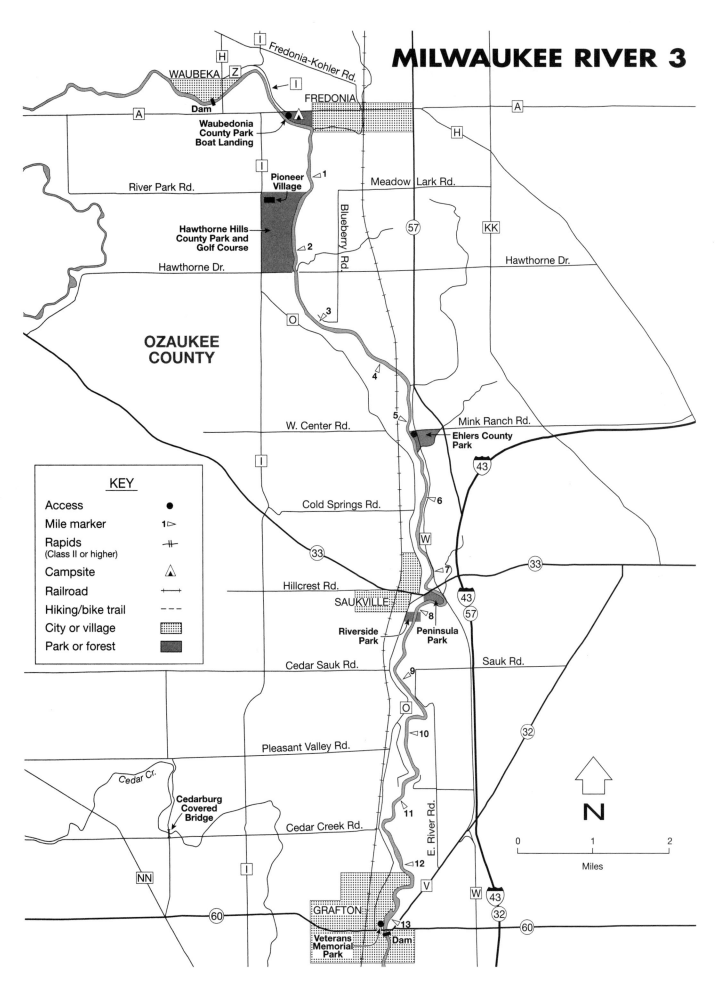

MILWAUKEE RIVER 3

WAUBEKA

Fredonia-Kohler Rd.

FREDONIA

Dam

Waubedonia
County Park
Boat Landing

River Park Rd.

Pioneer
Village

Meadow Lark Rd.

Hawthorne Hills
County Park and
Golf Course

Hawthorne Dr.

Hawthorne Dr.

Blueberry Rd.

OZAUKEE
COUNTY

W. Center Rd.

Mink Ranch Rd.

Ehlers County
Park

Cold Springs Rd.

Hillcrest Rd.

SAUKVILLE

Riverside
Park

Peninsula
Park

Cedar Sauk Rd.

Sauk Rd.

Cedar Cr.

Cedarburg
Covered
Bridge

Pleasant Valley Rd.

Cedar Creek Rd.

E. River Rd.

N

0   1   2

Miles

GRAFTON

Veterans
Memorial
Park

Dam

MILWAUKEE RIVER 4
Lime Kiln Park to Thiensville (10 Miles)

A Little-Known Wisconsin Industry

If asked what industries Wisconsin is best known for, you're likely to answer "dairy," "timber," and "paper." Few people will say "lime," but well into the twentieth century much of the nation's supply came from Wisconsin. Produced by heating limestone in huge, wood-fired kilns, lime was used for making mortar and plaster, whitewashing houses, reducing soil acidity, and treating leather. The first lime kiln in the Grafton area was built in 1846, and the industry grew until the 1920s when the Depression and other factors caused it to steadily decline. In its heyday from 1890 to the 1920s, the five-kiln operation at the present-day site of Lime Kiln Park was a major player in the lime business.

At Lime Kiln Park: sentinels of Wisconsin's once-thriving lime industry.

This trip begins and ends in very different environments. Starting out by braiding its way through a group of islands, with pleasant riffles and bankside rock formations, the river gets wider (averaging 80 feet), less riffly, and more developed as it approaches Thiensville and Mequon, eventually slowing and reaching the site where Joachim Thien built a mill and dam in the 1830s. The shoreline is wooded most of the time, and houses don't become numerous until the last few miles. Except for the initial islands, where narrow channels require some maneuvering, the trip is an easy one for beginners. Both the put-in and take-out are excellent: convenient boat ramps in attractive parks.

For **camping** and **canoe rentals**, see Milwaukee River 3.

The **shuttle route** (6.3 miles) goes south on Green Bay Road into Thiensville, and east on Elm Street to the village park.

Gradient is 4.6 feet per mile.

For **water levels**, see Milwaukee River 1.

Put in at the asphalt canoe landing in Lime Kiln Park (river-right). Just upstream is an old dam that is immediately followed by an island. The canoe landing is in the riffly right channel of this island. A unique place, the park has preserved several of the huge stone kilns that were once used to "burn" limestone, creating lime for various applications throughout the country.

After the put-in, there are rock formations on both sides for a while. For almost half a mile the river flows through a series of wooded islands where you must choose the channels with the most water and least brush. The water is quite riffly here. After the islands, the river widens to 80 feet, and riffles continue over the sand-and-gravel bottom.

The first houses of the trip are found in the area of the County T bridge, where current slackens somewhat and riffles become infrequent. In the first left bend after T, Cedar Creek—a historic stream where five dams and mills were built in the 1800s—enters on the right. The village of Cedarburg and its nearby covered bridge—the only original covered bridge left in the state—are quite popular with tourists, shoppers, and history buffs.

Downstream, tall wooded bluffs appear on the right for the first time, and large boulders are found along the shoreline. A long right bend leads to County C, where there's a series of pleasant riffles. In the right curve following the bridge, a row of cabins lines the shore. After County C, the river flattens and deepens, and a sizable, wooded island is located where the river turns sharply to the right. Limestone riprap periodically protects the right shoreline in a long, gentle left bend that leads to the Highland Road bridge, an attractive structure with decorative stonework.

After Highland Road the river is rather wide, with cabins and docks along the sides for a while; trees are still plentiful, however. In a big right bend the river narrows and passes a couple of nature preserves, then a huge shallow bay on the left. Bending sharply left, the river widens again at a large island. Just downstream from the island is the Mequon Villa Grove Park (off Freistadt Road), where you can use the river-right boat ramp for an alternate **take-out.**

After Villa Grove Park, the river widens again, and houses are more frequent. Soon warning signs and orange buoys indicate the approach of the Thiensville Dam. Just upstream from the dam is a rock wall alongside the village park. **Take out** 75 feet upstream-right from the dam at the concrete boat ramp; a large parking lot is nearby.

Other trips. A relatively short day trip (5 miles) begins at Thiensville (downstream-right from the dam) and ends at Brown Deer Road (downstream-left from the bridge, near a gravel parking lot). Dams follow at Kletzsch Park (north of Silver Spring Drive) and at Estabrook Park (south of Hampton Avenue), together with a sizable ledge at the south end of Estabrook Park (north of Capitol Drive). Farther downstream there are remnants of the former North Avenue dam. The river from Estabrook Park to the harbor is mostly urban—gradually being greened up, but with an abundance of commercial and industrial buildings, vertical walls, and wake-creating powerboats. Finding good accesses and getting back into your boat after a capsize can be significant problems. Negligible current allows out-and-back trips for experienced paddlers (e.g., from the Humboldt Avenue area southward toward the harbor and back). Such trips certainly provide a unique perspective of a great American city.

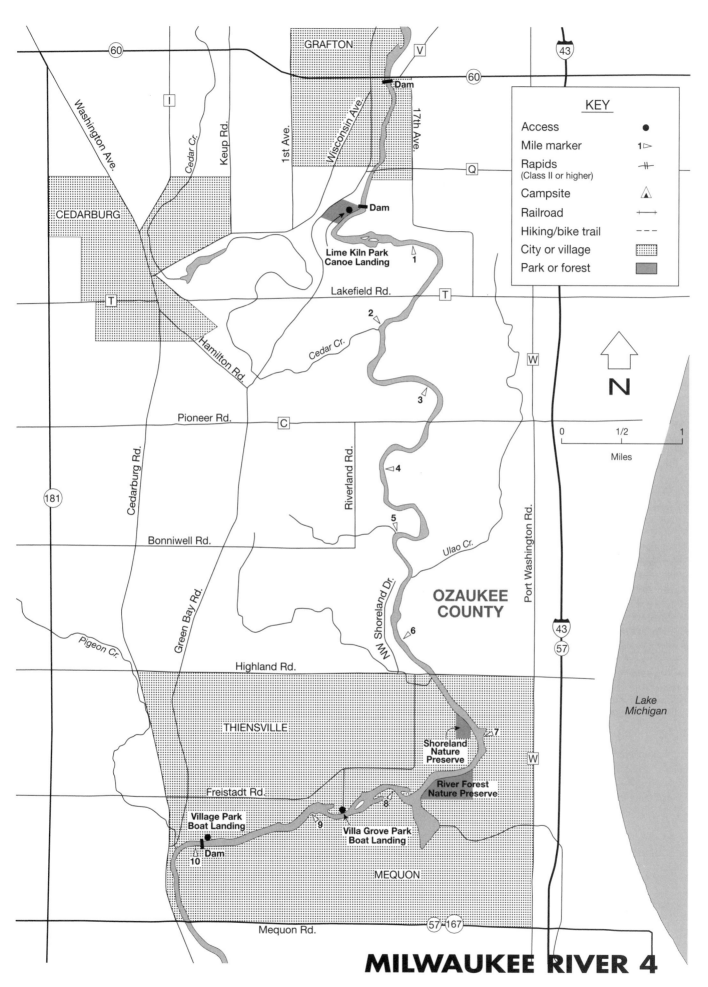

KEY

Access	●
Mile marker	1▷
Rapids (Class II or higher)	─╫─
Campsite	△
Railroad	─┼─
Hiking/bike trail	─ ─ ─
City or village	
Park or forest	

GRAFTON

CEDARBURG

Dam

Lime Kiln Park
Canoe Landing

OZAUKEE
COUNTY

Lake
Michigan

THIENSVILLE

Shoreland
Nature
Preserve

River Forest
Nature Preserve

Village Park
Boat Landing

Villa Grove Park
Boat Landing

Dam

MEQUON

N

0   1/2   1

Miles

MILWAUKEE RIVER 4

OCONOMOWOC RIVER
Oconomowoc to North Side Drive (11.2 Miles)

The Clamorous Big Birds

Once you've heard its unique call—a loud, guttural, rattling garooooo!—you'll always remember the sound of the sandhill crane. Visually, too, these birds are quite distinctive, standing 4 feet tall, with a bright red crown atop a gray body. Motorists commonly see flocks of sandhills gathered in harvested farm fields and marshes in the fall, foraging in preparation for their annual migration to Florida in September and October. In March and April they return to establish nests in Wisconsin's wetlands. For paddlers, they're a common sight and sound, especially on river trips near large marshy areas such as the Germania Marsh State Wildlife Area (Mecan River 1 and 2) and the White River Marsh State Wildlife Area (Fox River 2).

Now a thriving population, the sandhills came close to extinction in Wisconsin in the 1920s. However, when many farms failed in the Depression years, especially in former wetlands that had been drained for cultivation, huge acreages were turned into state and federal wildlife areas, and the cranes have made a steady comeback ever since.

A relatively short river with headwaters about 20 miles northwest of Milwaukee, the Oconomowoc drains the marshland of a north-south glacial moraine. In its southern route to the resort city of Oconomowoc, it passes through many lakes ranging from small ponds to 1,117-acre Lac La Belle. After its final control structure—a small dam that maintains water levels for Lac La Belle—the river swings to the west and peacefully winds through rolling hill country toward its confluence with the Rock River.

Banks are usually grassy and low throughout this stretch, with thin tree cover, occasional farm fields, and marsh vegetation. Generally there are sufficient bushes, trees, and topographical variations to prevent the surroundings from looking like a wide-open marsh. The whole section is pleasantly paddleable, and can easily be done in shorter segments by using alternate accesses. Note, however, that some of the bridges on this section have low clearance and warrant caution at medium-to-high water levels.

The name of the river derives from an Algonquin word variously translated as "river of lakes," "beaver dam," "waterfall," and "beautiful waters."

Camping is available 3 miles west of Eagle at the Kettle Moraine State Forest Southern Unit (262-594-6200) and 5 miles southwest of Oconomowoc at the Concord Center Campground (262-593-2707).

The **shuttle route** (approximately 8 miles) from the Concord Road put-in goes south on Concord Road, west on Allen Road, north on County F, and west on North Side Drive.

Gradient is 1.3 feet per mile.

Water levels. There is no USGS gauge on the Oconomowoc.

The usual **put-in** is at the Concord Road bridge, downstream-right, where there's lots of room to park along the road. Farther upstream, the river is narrow, riffly, and wooded as it flows through town. The only practical places to put in upstream from Concord Road are (1) immediately upstream-right from the old railroad bridge (there's a small city park here); and (2) upstream-right from the Second Avenue bridge, near a pumping station. Immediately downstream from the Concord Road

bridge a line of rocks makes an easily run 1-foot drop, and the streambed is rather shallow down to Champion Field. The river now heads through mostly open area to the new County BB bridge, where there's a downstream-right access next to another pumping station. The streambed widens here and is quite shallow when the water is low. Winding west past a subdivision on the right, the river passes through partially wooded lowland. Hills and distant farm houses can often be seen from the water.

The Morgan Road bridge can be accessed downstream-right on the grassy bank. Downstream, low banks and a thin tree line continue between rolling hills in a peaceful, attractive setting. A long series of sharp turns dominates the approach to Battle Creek, which is soon followed by the Elm Drive bridge (access upstream-right). Immediately downstream from the bridge is a nicely landscaped home with an elaborate rock retaining wall. The river now is rather narrow—about 35 feet—and relatively deep.

East River Road now runs closely alongside the right bank all the way to County F (access upstream-left). After approaching Interstate 94, the river shifts to the northwest, widens somewhat, and passes through increasingly marshy terrain to the old bridge at West River Road (access upstream-right).

Big, gentle bends through mostly open area lead to North Side Drive, where signs in the water warn of an electric fish barrier under the bridge (to prevent rough fish from swimming up the Oconomowoc from the Rock). **Take out** on the left bank where a well-established path leads to the road.

Other trips. If you wish to paddle the last leg of the Oconomowoc, you can put in at the North Side Drive bridge (downstream-left), negotiate a series of tight turns through a marshy area to the mouth, then float down the Rock to County P at Pipersville (see Rock River 1).

The usual grassy banks of the Oconomowoc.

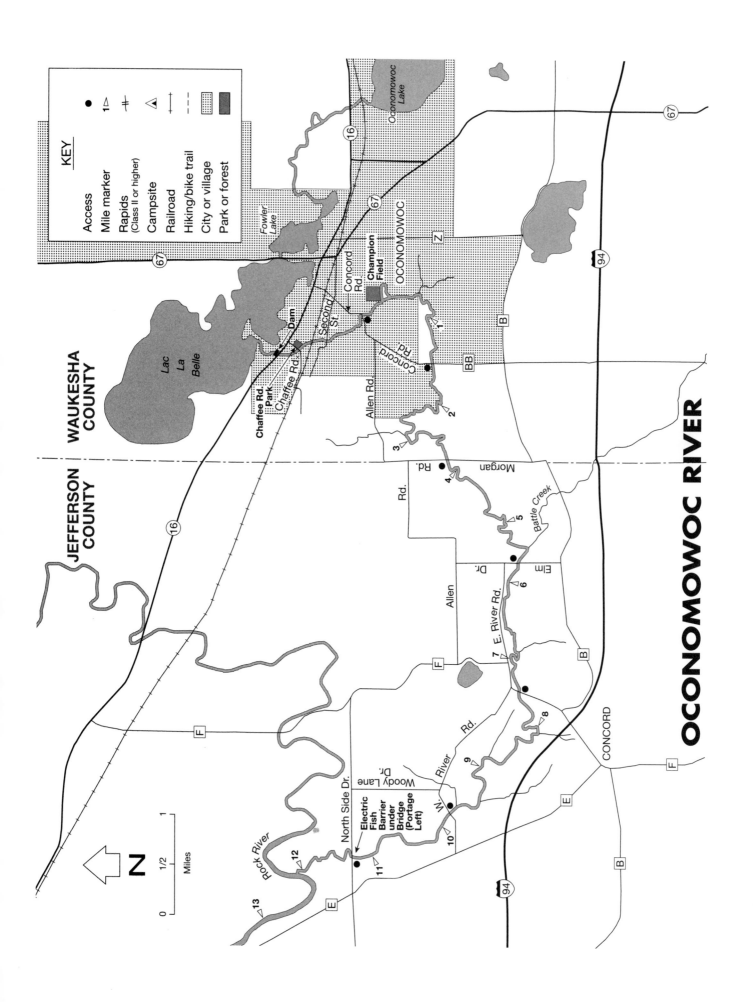

KEY

Access ●
Mile marker 1△
Rapids △ (Class II or higher)
Campsite ⊥
Railroad ┼┼┼
Hiking/bike trail ┄┄
City or village ▦
Park or forest ▓

WAUKESHA COUNTY

JEFFERSON COUNTY

Lac La Belle

Fowler Lake

Oconomowoc Lake

OCONOMOWOC

Chaffee Rd. Park
Dam
Second St.
Chaffee Rd.
Concord Rd.
Champion Field
Allen Rd.
Concord Rd.

Morgan Rd.
Battle Creek
Elm Dr.
Allen Dr.
E. River Rd.
CONCORD
River Rd.
Woody Lane Dr.
W. River Rd.
North Side Dr.
Rock River

Electric Fish Barrier under Bridge (Portage Left)

N

Miles
0   1/2   1

OCONOMOWOC RIVER

111

PECATONICA RIVER
Calamine to Darlington (8 Miles)

Originating west of Dodgeville, the Pecatonica winds its way southward through woods, farmlands, hardwood swamps, and marshes before crossing into Illinois, where it heads eastward to its confluence with the Rock River at Rockton. Obstructive deadfall tends to be a problem for canoeists on the Wisconsin portion of the river, but the section described here can be counted on to be brush-free. Prior to the annual Darlington Canoe Festival during the second week of June, the city makes sure that all obstructions are cleared from Calamine to Darlington. Nevertheless, considerable maneuvering is required as you make your way down the river. Incidentally, Pecatonica is derived from a Sauk word meaning "muddy," and the name is appropriate for this flood-prone river.

The Pecatonica here is small (averaging 35 feet wide), steep-banked, intimate, and often tree-canopied. There are only a few brief open spaces. Except for the very end of the trip, the setting is quite wild and remote-feeling. Accesses are excellent. To cap the trip, there's even an exciting riffle/rapid alongside one of the parks in Darlington.

Adding to the pleasure of the trip is Darlington itself, a charming little city that goes back to the lead-mining era and was named after a nineteenth-century land speculator who invested in the area. The city slogan, "Pearl of the Pecatonica," is based on the clams that were once harvested in the river, mainly to make "pearl" buttons. For bicycling enthusiasts, the Cheese Country Recreational Trail—a 47-mile Rails-to-Trails path from Mineral Point to Monroe—parallels the river.

Camping is available at Yellowstone Lake State Park between Darlington and Blanchardville (608-523-4427), Black Hawk Memorial County Park near Woodford (608-465-3390), Pecatonica River Trails Park in Darlington (608-776-4093), Lake Joy Campground near Belmont (608-762-5150), and Yellowstone Lake Chalet Campground near Blanchardville (608-523-4121).

Canoe rentals are available in Madison at Rutabaga (608-223-9300) and Carl's Paddlin' (608-284-0300).

The **shuttle route** (6 to 6.5 miles) from Calamine goes east a short distance on County G, east on Shortcut Road, and south on Highway 23 to Black Bridge Park or Pecatonica River Trails Park in Darlington.

Gradient is 1.2 feet per mile.

For **water levels**, check the gauge at Darlington (#05432500) on the USGS Web site. See "Water Levels" in the introduction.

Put in at the upstream-right landing near the County G bridge in Calamine. Immediately downstream is a metal bridge that is now used by the Pecatonica Trail,

The annual Darlington Canoe Festival is a good time to paddle the Pecatonica.

a 10-mile recreational path from Calamine to Belmont. If time permits, drive or bike to Belmont, the first capital of Wisconsin Territory. Two historic buildings date back to 1836.

From the beginning, the banks are steep and muddy, making it difficult to stop and get out of your boat. Trees line both sides and often hang over the river. In many places during the trip you can see where obstructive limbs or trees have been removed with chain saws.

The first open area occurs at 1.5 miles where there's a grassy hill and a creek mouth on the right. Occasionally the mud banks are briefly relieved by a small, water-level outcropping of crumbled rock. Farther downstream a creek enters on the left, with a bike-trail bridge over it. Immediately after the mouth of the Wood Branch, on the right, is an unspectacular rock formation, several feet high. The only comfortable place to stop to eat lunch or stretch your legs comes in a grassy area in a left bend after two large culverts in the bank.

The river turns sharply to the right after an old metal railroad bridge (now used for the bike trail). In the curves that follow, a great deal of deadfall is piled on the outside of bends. Pastureland lies along the left bank for a quarter mile, where a road runs parallel to the river, and another tributary enters on the left. Finally, after a sharp S-curve, Highway 23 comes alongside the river on the left.

As you approach the northwest edge of Darlington, there's a lovely little park on river-left alongside Highway 23—Black Bridge Park—with a gravel boat landing, toilets, and picnic facilities. A convenient place to **take out,** the landing comes immediately before a bike-trail bridge. Be on the lookout for old pilings and debris beneath the bridge (an old railroad span).

Looping left after the park, the river becomes quite wild again. But soon you can see some of the downtown buildings of Darlington and the magnificent old county courthouse. Just before the river makes a sharp left turn, Pecatonica River Trails Park appears on the left. As you make the left turn, there's an enjoyable 25-yard riffle/rapid where a dam was once located. A boat landing follows immediately on the left—an excellent **take-out** for paddlers who want a little taste of whitewater.

Numerous houses follow in the straight stretch between the park and the Highway 23 bridge. Downstream-left from the bridge, near a supermarket, is a landing used for the annual canoe race. Directly across from this landing is a spring and an interesting historical marker.

Other trips. (1) The river upstream from Calamine and downstream from Darlington is obstruction-prone, but canoeists sometimes paddle the East Branch, accessing the river at Blanchardville, Argyle, Black Hawk Memorial County Park, or Woodford. (2) For several trips on the Pecatonica in Illinois, see my book *Paddling Illinois,* pp. 108–113.

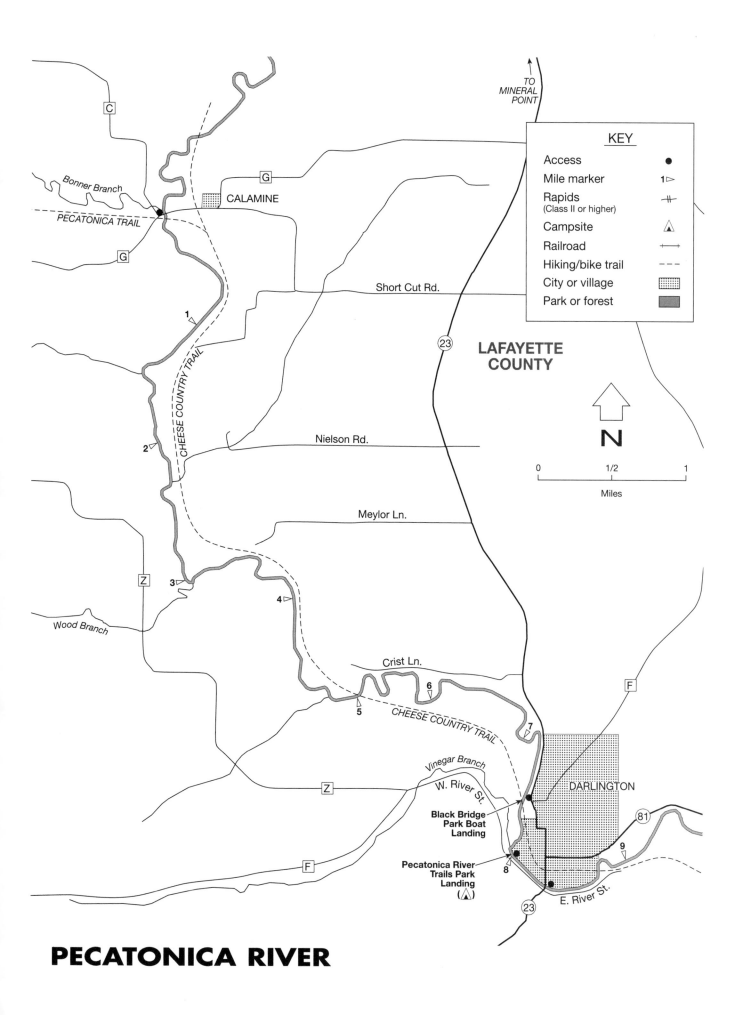

TO
MINERAL
POINT

KEY

Access	●
Mile marker	1▷
Rapids (Class II or higher)	╫
Campsite	▲
Railroad	┼┼┼
Hiking/bike trail	- - -
City or village	▦
Park or forest	▓

C

Bonner Branch

G

CALAMINE

PECATONICA TRAIL

G

Short Cut Rd.

23

LAFAYETTE
COUNTY

N

0   1/2   1
Miles

1

CHEESE COUNTRY TRAIL

2

Nielson Rd.

Meylor Ln.

Z

3

Wood Branch

4

Crist Ln.

6

F

5

CHEESE COUNTRY TRAIL

7

Vinegar Branch

Z

W. River St.

DARLINGTON

Black Bridge
Park Boat
Landing

81

Pecatonica River
Trails Park
Landing
(▲)

8

9

F

E. River St.

23

PECATONICA RIVER

PLATTE RIVER 1 & 2
Ellenboro to Steinbach Bridge (12.4 Miles)
Steinbach Bridge to Banfield Bridge (8.4 Miles)

If you've paddled the Grant River, you've had a good preview of the Platte. Paralleling the Grant a few miles to the east in the unglaciated southwestern corner of the state, the 46-mile-long Platte follows a similarly crooked path, caroming off one bluff after another on its way to the Mississippi. It has few of the dramatic rock formations found along the Grant, but is otherwise comparable. Filled with riffles, it's small, clear, peaceful, and pleasant. Along the banks, wooded bluffs, bankside pastures, and cultivated fields are common, but houses are few. Wire stretched over the river must be squeezed under a couple of times.

The name of the river derives from the Native American practice of smelting lead into bowl-shaped masses called "platts."

For **camping,** see Grant River 1.

Nearby **canoe rentals** (without shuttle) are available in Beetown at Grant River Canoe Rentals (608-794-2342).

The **shuttle route** (8 miles) for the first trip goes a short distance east on Ellenboro Road, south on Highway 81, and south on Platte Road/Big Platte Road to Steinbach Bridge (the first bridge upstream from County O). For the second trip (8 miles), go south on Big Platte Road, west on County O, south on Highway 61/35, and south on Long Branch Road/West Banfield Road.

The **gradient** for the first trip—7.2 feet per mile—is reflected in continual riffles, while the second section is a placid 2.4 feet per mile.

For **water levels,** check the Rockville gauge (#05414000) on the USGS Web site. See "Water Levels" in the introduction.

Put in from the grassy bank upstream-right at the Ellenboro Road bridge, just east of the small community of Ellenboro. This access is a few hundred yards downstream from the Highway 81 bridge, where it's possible to put in downstream-left.

Only 30 feet wide at the beginning, the Platte is immediately riffly and flows over a sand-and-gravel bottom. Soon the river runs into a tall, wooded bluff and veers to the right into a riffle-filled straightaway with rock formations on the left and open fields on the right. In the southward leg that follows an abrupt left turn, sheer cut banks are found in curves alongside open pastureland, and riffles are frequent. In deep pools—especially in bends—the water has a beautiful, greenish cast,

like an Ozark mountain stream. Before the first bridge, wire passes overhead a couple of times—be careful squeezing under it—and the river is twice deflected to the side by bluffs. The first houses of the trip appear high atop such bluffs. At one point the abutments of an old bridge are passed. A couple of houses on the left precede the Platte Road bridge.

Downstream from the bridge the river heads toward another bluff and turns sharply to the right (south). After the Baker-Ford Road bridge, which soon follows, the river turns right again at Lee Branch and follows a river-left bluff to the southwest through a succession of pleasant riffles. An old rusty truss bridge, on Platte Road again, is followed by a long series of shallow riffles. Before veering to the right (northwest), the river approaches County B, which can be seen momentarily on top of the river-left bluff. In the long right bend toward Red Dog Road, the prettiest rock formations of the trip are found on the left.

After the rusty old truss bridge at Red Dog Road, the river passes a large dairy farm, then turns left at a tall, wooded bluff and soon comes to the new County B bridge. In the southeast stretch that follows, Big Platte Road approaches on the left, high up on the riverside bluff, and at one point considerable debris has been thrown down the hillside from the road. The river-left bluff recedes where Quarry Road meets Big Platte Road; some paddlers use this location as an access, but it's a difficult one, like most of the intermediate bridges on this section.

The river now becomes quite winding, with sharp turns and lots of riffles, and passes under some power lines just before veering sharply to the west near a home on the left bank. The river is narrow and riffly here, flowing past some old bridge abutments. In the long, final curve to the left toward the take-out bridge, the river passes some farm buildings on the left and beautiful, wooded bluffs on the right. **Take out** upstream-right at the Steinbach Bridge, a modern structure.

The 7-mile stretch from Steinbach Bridge to Highway 35 is much less riffly but attractive, often flowing alongside bluffs in sweeping curves. The County O bridge is a poor access, but the grassy bank at Highway 35 (upstream-right) is an easy place to **put in** or **take out.** The Platte and Little Platte Rivers join just upstream from Highway 35. Another 1.8 miles leads through a wide, marshy area to the Banfield Bridge, where there's an excellent boat ramp upstream-right, with plentiful parking. It's a short paddle from here to the Mississippi. Slow current makes it easy to paddle out and back from the Banfield Bridge.

Cautiously approaching barbed wire strung across the Platte—fortunately, a rare problem for Wisconsin paddlers.

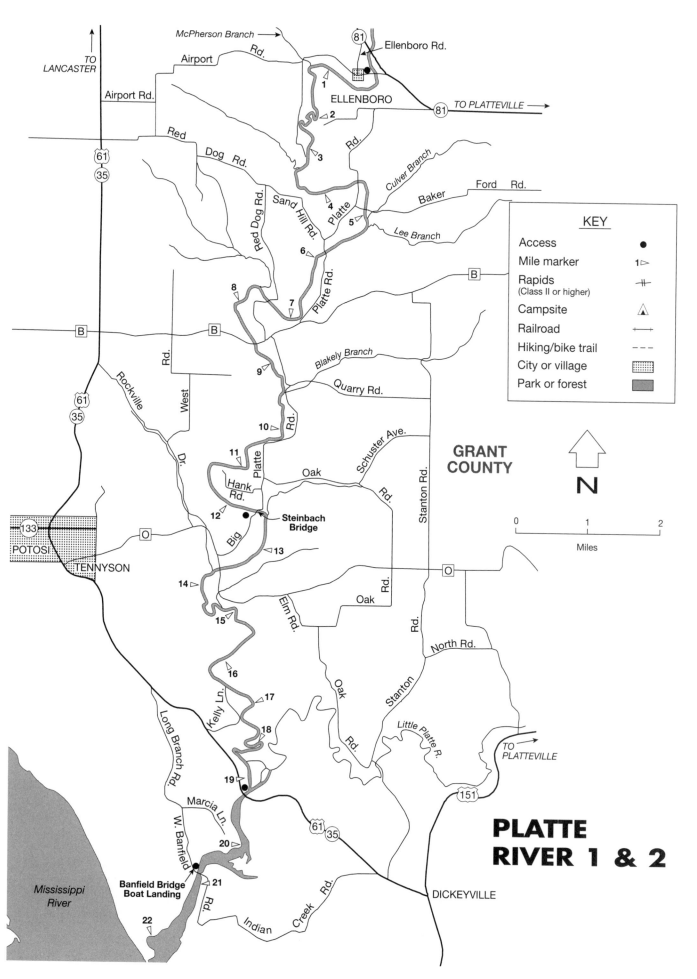

TO
LANCASTER

McPherson Branch →

Airport Rd.

Airport Rd.

81

Ellenboro Rd.

ELLENBORO

81   TO PLATTEVILLE →

Red

Dog   Rd.

Platte   Rd.

Culver Branch

Baker   Ford   Rd.

Sand Hill Rd.

Red Dog Rd.

Platte

Lee Branch

B

Platte Rd.

Blakely Branch

Quarry Rd.

Rockville

West   Rd.

Rd.

Platte   Rd.

Oak

Schuster Ave.

Stanton Rd.

**GRANT
COUNTY**

N

61
35

61
35

B

B

133

POTOSI

TENNYSON

O

Hank
Rd.

Big

Steinbach
Bridge

Elm Rd.

Oak   Rd.

O

Oak

Rd.

Rd.

Stanton

North Rd.

Little Platte R.

Kelly Ln.

Long Branch Rd.

Mississippi
River

Marcia Ln.

W. Banfield

**Banfield Bridge
Boat Landing**

Rd.

Indian   Creek   Rd.

TO
PLATTEVILLE

151

61
35

DICKEYVILLE

KEY	
Access	●
Mile marker	1▷
Rapids (Class II or higher)	╫
Campsite	△
Railroad	┼┼┼
Hiking/bike trail	– – –
City or village	▓
Park or forest	▓

0   1   2
Miles

**PLATTE
RIVER 1 & 2**

PLOVER RIVER 1
Bevent to Shantytown Road (8.7 Miles)

Like Strings of Pearls

Viewing southern Wisconsin from a satellite, you'd see many rivers that wend their way in and out of one "widespread" after another. Some get to be this way naturally, as a result of geological and glacial forces. The popular group of lakes on the Oconomowoc River near the city of Oconomowoc, for example, was formed by terminal moraines and buried ice blocks. Some lake chains are a combination of natural forces and human intervention, such as those on the Yahara River, where Mendota, Monona, Waubesa, and Kegonsa Lakes at Madison are followed by dammed flowages at Stoughton and Dunkirk. Most, however, are simply the result of a succession of dams: e.g., the Eau Claire, Fox, Milwaukee, Sheboygan, and Tomorrow/Waupaca Rivers. Fortunately, the removal of numerous dams in recent years has eliminated many of the man-made wide places in southern Wisconsin's rivers.

For devotees of little rivers, the Plover is a wonderful stream for a relaxing quietwater trip. Never very dramatic, it offers varied settings that include gentle riffles, wooded bluffs, lowland hardwood forest, some marshy vegetation, and almost unbroken tranquility. Clean and clear with a slight copperish tint, the river is seldom very wide, averaging 35 feet in the sections described in this book. Houses are infrequent, and wildlife is often spotted.

Beginning as a tiny rivulet a few miles south of Antigo (an area that is also the source of the Eau Claire, Embarras, and Red Rivers), the Plover flows to the southwest through an entirely rural environment until it joins the Wisconsin River at Stevens Point. In the three trips presented here, the river environs change considerably, offering choices to fit your preference for the day. On the first trip, there are three low farm bridges and a deadfall-prone area that are dangerous at higher water levels.

Camping is available at Jordan Park 6 miles northeast of Stevens Point (715-346-1433), Rivers Edge Campground 7 miles north of Stevens Point (715-344-8058), and Ridgewood Campground 3.5 miles southwest of Plover (715-344-8750).

The **shuttle route** (7.4 miles) goes west on Highway 153, south on County J, and east on Shantytown Road.

Gradient is 3.4 feet per mile.

Water levels. There are no gauges on the Plover. The river generally holds its water well, and becomes uncanoeable only after sustained dry periods.

Put in at the Highway 153 bridge (upstream-right) in the small community of Bevent, where the steeple of St. Ladislaus Church is a prominent landmark. A grassy path leads through a gate to a low bank; this is private property, so please be respectful of it. As soon as you put in, there are a couple of small, wavy drops. The river is gorgeous at the beginning—only 20 feet wide, with cedar, white pine, and white birch on the banks. The streambed winds back and forth in this intimate setting over many rocky riffles.

Widening, the river becomes more shallow and passes the first house of the trip, then splits around a large, bushy island. More houses follow. After passing under an old, low-clearance farm bridge in a relatively open area, the river narrows in a right curve and becomes more densely wooded. As it does, observe the tall white pine on the right with a huge eagle nest in it.

A few minutes downstream, the Bevent Drive bridge appears in a very open area. Dense woods resume after the bridge, and soon Pinery Road parallels the right shoreline. A couple of houses immediately precede the Pinery Road bridge, where the pile of boulders upstream-left provides an adequate access. Watch out for poison ivy at all of the accesses, however.

After Pinery Road the river narrows to about 30 feet, deepens, and again becomes heavily wooded. In the next mile a home and some farm buildings are passed, together with two old, low-clearance farm bridges. Just downstream from the second of these bridges, there's an S-curve where deadfall tends to accumulate. The river now passes through a very wild area where downed trees must be avoided. Then the river widens again and becomes more open after an old barn and some concrete abutments.

The wooden-piered County J bridge can be accessed downstream on either side. After County J the river narrows again and resumes its wooded, winding ways, twice crossed by fords. The banks continue to be low most of the time, but sometimes there are tall, attractive embankments. Near the end of the trip marsh vegetation becomes more plentiful on the shoreline: sedge grass, cattails, and bulrushes.

The Shantytown Road bridge appears shortly after a farm on the left, and is preceded by a clump of small, grassy islands. **Take out** downstream-right (opposite the abutment of an old bridge); there's a short carry up a grassy bank.

After Shantytown Road the Plover becomes increasingly marshy as it heads toward the old mill dam that forms Bentley Pond. Soon after the dam (which can be seen along County Y), the river approaches Bentley Road, the put-in for Plover River 2.

A typically peaceful stretch of the Plover.

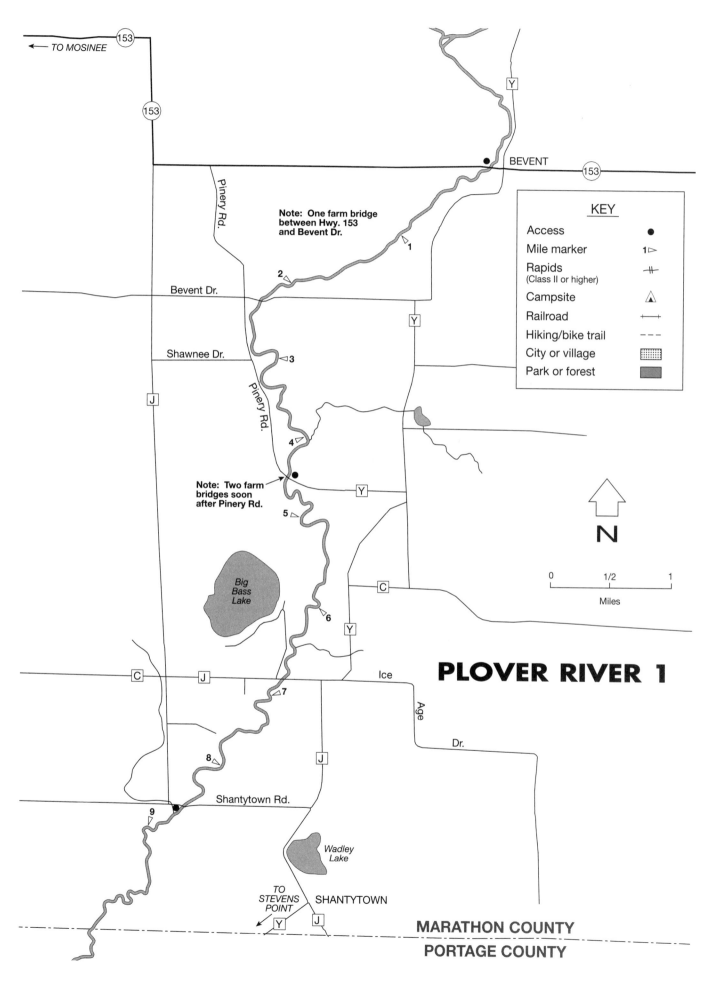

← *TO MOSINEE*

(153)

(153)

Pinery Rd.

Note: One farm bridge between Hwy. 153 and Bevent Dr.

● BEVENT   (153)

Y

1 ▷

2 ▷

Bevent Dr.

Y

Shawnee Dr.

3 ▷

J

Pinery Rd.

4 ▷

Note: Two farm bridges soon after Pinery Rd.

●

Y

5 ▷

Big Bass Lake

6 ▷

Y

C

C   J   Ice

7 ▷

Age

Dr.

8 ▷

J

●

9 ▷   Shantytown Rd.

Wadley Lake

TO STEVENS POINT   SHANTYTOWN

Y   J

MARATHON COUNTY
PORTAGE COUNTY

KEY

Access	●
Mile marker	1 ▷
Rapids (Class II or higher)	─╫─
Campsite	△
Railroad	─┼─
Hiking/bike trail	- - -
City or village	▦
Park or forest	▬

N

0   1/2   1

Miles

PLOVER RIVER 1

PLOVER RIVER 2
Bentley Road to Jordan Park (7.6 Miles)

Less intimate than the previous section of the Plover and more open than the following section, this middle stretch of the river is generally wider and less prone to deadfall than the other two. There are a couple of long, beautiful, heavily wooded segments as the river flows between a mixture of low, grassy shoreline and higher, forested banks. Most of the trip is wonderfully quiet and isolated. The woods continue to be quite varied, including maple, oak, white pine, red pine, balsam, and spruce. Current is usually brisk and the water clear as the river continues to flow over a sand-and-gravel bottom, with occasional boulders.

A few fallen trees may have to be paddled around and the remnants of an old dam must be portaged, but neither is difficult. One of the big highlights of the trip is the take-out at a lovely Portage County park, where canoe-campers can stay overnight. Shorter trips can be arranged by using County K as an access or by taking out at the old dam.

For **camping** and **water levels**, see Plover River 1.

The **shuttle route** (5.8 miles) from the Bentley Road bridge goes north briefly on Bentley Road, then south on County Y to the entrance of Jordan Park near the Highway 66 intersection. During the shuttle run, you may wish to stop briefly at the old mill building (where County Y pulls alongside the river) to scout the dam site.

Gradient is 2.6 feet per mile.

Put in at the Bentley Road bridge, downstream-right, where a short grassy path leads to the bank. There's room along the shoulder to park a couple of cars. Narrow at the beginning, the river winds between grassy banks, with occasional grassy islands. Fifteen minutes into the trip a house appears on the left in a pretty wooded grove, followed by a stand of white pines. The setting is quite peaceful. Relatively deep pools are found in the outside of bends as the river moves past a thin tree line.

Later the river widens to 40 feet and begins bending back and forth in a more heavily wooded area. Some homes are seen on the left in a pine grove. As high forested banks continue on the left, the woods become more dense and beautiful, lasting until the County K bridge

The old powerhouse on the Plover once provided Stevens Point with electricity.

(an earthen structure with three huge culverts). There's an excellent sandy landing downstream-right.

After County K the setting opens up somewhat, and soon a large farm appears on the right. Woods resume, and in a right bend there are 10-foot, sandy cut banks on the left near a beautiful pine grove. Tall banks continue on the left for a long time, while the right bank is consistently low and grassy. Winding around through the woods and passing a couple of houses, the river moves along with good current, occasionally narrowing briefly.

Suddenly the woods withdraw some distance from the grassy banks; this is where the Christensen Pond used to begin before the Van Order Dam was partially removed downstream. The narrow channel now winds through a pleasant marsh-like setting, past a group of houses on the right, to a clump of boulders in the streambed. Here County Y pulls alongside on the right. As soon as you turn left beside the road, you can see the red metal building on the site of the old mill, alongside the Van Order Dam. Signs warn boaters to take out upstream from the dam, either on the right near the mill parking lot (a good place to end your trip if you want a short paddle) or on the left, where a path leads through the grass over the earthen shoulder of the dam to a reentry point below the dam. Most of the dam has been removed, but there's still a turbulent drop of a couple of feet through a pile of rubble. A clean run is difficult, so paddlers are advised to portage on the left or **take out** on the right.

Beautiful woods begin again after the dam, and the Sharonwood Lane bridge soon follows. Then after a few riffles, a couple of houses, and a left turn, Jordan Lake opens up in front of you. Far ahead, at the end of the impoundment, traffic can be seen on Highway 66, where the dam is located. Before long, three designated canoe-camping sites appear on the right shore, alongside an aviary. Continue down the right shore past the swimming beach, and **take out** at the boat ramp, not far upstream from Highway 66.

The paddle down Jordan Pond, an attractive little lake ringed with wooded banks, is short and pleasant. From the boat ramp, a path leads through a tunnel underneath Highway 66 to South Jordan Park, where there's a canoe landing at the footbridge. In addition to the three campsites for canoeists, there's a campground located just across County Y to the west. Camping, picnic facilities, toilets, a large parking area, and other amenities make Jordan Park a great place to end (or begin) a trip.

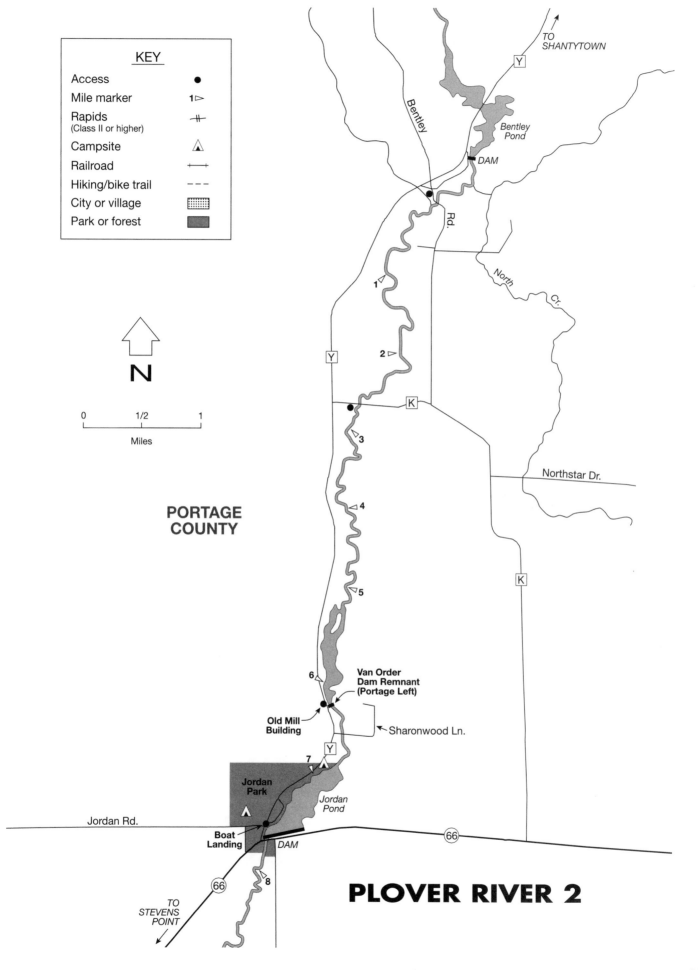

KEY

Access	●
Mile marker	1▷
Rapids (Class II or higher)	–|#|–
Campsite	▲
Railroad	–+–+–
Hiking/bike trail	– – –
City or village	
Park or forest	

N

0   1/2   1
Miles

PORTAGE COUNTY

TO SHANTYTOWN

Y

Bentley

Bentley Pond

DAM

Rd.

North

Cr.

1▷

2▷

Y

K

3▷

Northstar Dr.

K

4▷

5▷

6▷

Van Order Dam Remnant (Portage Left)

Old Mill Building

Sharonwood Ln.

7▷ ▲

Y

Jordan Park

▲

Jordan Pond

Jordan Rd.

66

Boat Landing

DAM

66

8▷

TO STEVENS POINT

PLOVER RIVER 2

PLOVER RIVER 3
Jordan Park to Stevens Point (6.4 Miles)

A Walk along the Glacier

Many of the rivers in this book—including the Plover, Manitowoc, Sheboygan, Milwaukee, Rock, Sugar, Wisconsin, Fox, and Mecan—are crossed or paralleled by the Ice Age Trail. Conceived in the 1950s, this ambitious project aims to establish a 1,000-mile pathway that follows the farthest advance of the last glacier in Wisconsin—a circuitous route from Potawatomi Park on Green Bay to Interstate Park at the St. Croix Dells. Approximately 500 miles of trail segments are now open for public use, covering an incredible variety of terrains: wooded moraines, kettle lakes, glacial outwash plains, dense forests, marshes, sandstone buttes, rocky gorges, rolling dairy country, etc. Many agencies and individuals have been instrumental in developing and maintaining the trail, which is administered by the National Park Service in cooperation with the Wisconsin DNR and the Ice Age Park and Trail Foundation. For an excellent fold-out map and brochures, contact the Ice Age National Scenic Trail, National Park Service, 700 Rayovac Drive, Suite 100, Madison, WI 53711-2476 (608-264-5610).

Because of its proximity to Stevens Point, this stretch of the Plover is often paddled. It is almost as wild a stretch as you'll find anywhere: dense lowland forest, few bridges or houses, no power lines, and no nearby roads most of the time. The almost constant need to maneuver in tight turns and past partial obstructions makes this a potentially frustrating stretch for beginners. There are splendid parks at the beginning and end, with convenient accesses. For 3.5 miles during the second half of the trip, the river is roughly paralleled by a hiking/biking path that is part of the Green Circle Trail that surrounds much of Stevens Point.

For **camping** and **water levels**, see Plover River 1. Camping is also available at two Portage County parks in the area: Collins Park near Rosholt (715-346-1433) and Du Bay Park on the west shore of Lake Du Bay north of Stevens Point (715-346-1433).

The **shuttle route** (5.8 miles) from South Jordan Park goes east briefly on Highway 66 across the river, south on Brilowski Road, west on Highway 10 across the river, and south on the Iverson Park entrance road.

Gradient is 3.1 feet per mile.

Put in at the canoe landing in South Jordan Park. Enter the park just west of the Highway 66/County Y intersection, and drive to the parking lot. From there a path leads to a footbridge, where the landing is upstream-right. Farther upstream between the highway and footbridge is the old Jordan Dam and Powerplant that produced electricity for the Stevens Point area from 1904 to 1965. Back in the 1800s a sawmill stood here to process logs floated down the Plover to the Wisconsin and Mississippi Rivers. At one time the town of Jordan surrounded the mill.

Densely wooded and narrow at the put-in, the river begins winding around in sharp turns over a sand-and-gravel bottom. Before long, high banks disappear and a lowland environment begins. Occasionally trees have fallen into the water, but there's usually no problem squeezing around or through them. Often you'll see places where previous paddlers have cut out limbs or trees that would otherwise block passage completely.

The first house appears atop a high right bank, soon followed by another home on top of a high, sandy cut bank. Occasional patches of marsh grass are seen along the shore, and small grassy islands appear here and there. Coniferous trees begin appearing, including a beautiful high bank covered in pines. At an even higher sandbank, a cable is strung across the river, soon followed by another lovely grove of white pines.

The consistently low, floodplain banks make it difficult to find a place to stop for lunch or a rest. In a couple of places, however, private picnic benches can be seen on the shoreline. The low, 1- to 2-foot banks continue for a long time, relieved only by sporadic pine groves on high banks. Sloughs are often found off the main channel, especially in bends. In one brief open area, a couple of houses can be seen on a left bluff; then lowland closes in again. Occasionally airplanes from the nearby Stevens Point Municipal Airport can be heard overhead. The river continues to be very twisty; there are no straightaways all day.

Eventually the river runs along Highway 39/51 in a left bend, then passes under the two bridges (look for swallow nests underneath). After the bridges the woods are less dense and the environs more open. Tight turns give way to gentle bends. As the Highway 10 bridge approaches, the river grows relatively wide, but there are still no houses.

A low, attractive stone wall lines the river on both sides after Highway 10 as you enter Iverson Park. **Take out** on the right along the low wall (there's a small dock here), and carry your boat(s) across the grass to the nearby parking lot. A component of the Stevens Point park system, Iverson Park has large grassy areas, toilets, picnic facilities, and plentiful parking.

After Iverson Park, the Plover flows into McDill Pond and meets the Wisconsin River about a mile thereafter.

A lake once covered this part of the Plover, upstream from Van Order Dam.

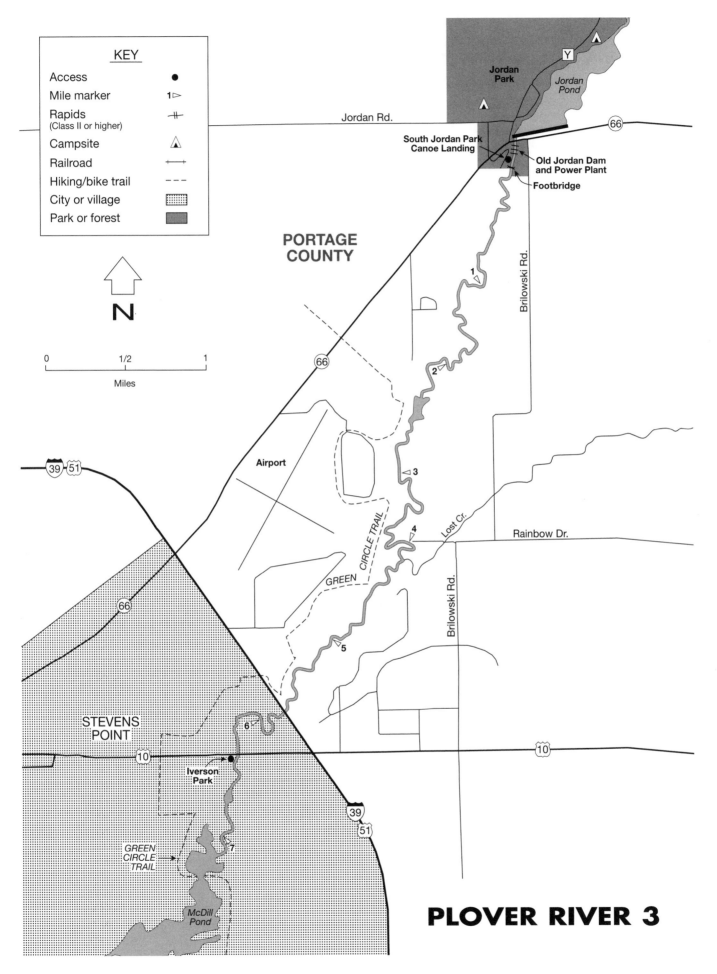

KEY

Access   ●
Mile marker   1▷
Rapids   ╫
(Class II or higher)
Campsite   ⛺
Railroad   +—+
Hiking/bike trail   - - -
City or village
Park or forest

N

0   1/2   1

Miles

PORTAGE
COUNTY

Jordan Park

Jordan Pond

Jordan Rd.

South Jordan Park
Canoe Landing

Old Jordan Dam
and Power Plant

Footbridge

Brilowski Rd.

Airport

GREEN CIRCLE TRAIL

Lost Cr.

Rainbow Dr.

Brilowski Rd.

STEVENS
POINT

Iverson
Park

GREEN
CIRCLE
TRAIL

McDill
Pond

PLOVER RIVER 3

RED CEDAR RIVER
Menomonie to Dunnville (15 Miles)

Peddling the Red Cedar

The crushed limestone surface of the Red Cedar River State Trail provides bicyclists some of the same pleasures as paddling the river. But the trail also offers some of its own delights. One is a close-up view of the sandstone quarries between Downsville and Dunnville. At Mile 10 along the 14-mile trail there's a cutoff that enables you to inspect an old quarry cut. Once widely used for construction throughout the country, Dunnville sandstone was shipped out on the railroad tracks that have been converted to the bike trail. Another feature that you won't readily see from your canoe is the broad floodplain of the Dunnville State Wildlife Area. The last 2.5 miles of the trail (south of County Y) expose you to the river bottoms and restored prairies near the confluence of the Red Cedar and Chippewa. If you're interested in bicycling even farther, you can peddle across the Chippewa on an old railroad bridge, then head east on the Chippewa River State Trail all the way into Eau Claire.

An ideal place for outdoor enthusiasts who enjoy both paddling and bicycling, this section of the Red Cedar is paralleled from beginning to end by a scenic, well-maintained bike trail. The river environs are quite wild, especially in the last few miles, and the setting includes wooded bluffs, sandstone cliffs, and pleasant riffles. Always at least 100 feet wide, the river is a good stream for beginners. Eagles, osprey, pileated woodpeckers, river otters, and other wildlife are frequently seen by paddlers. Downsville is an excellent intermediate point for shorter trips.

The Red Cedar figured prominently in Wisconsin's colorful logging history. Menomonie was an important mill town; in fact, the world's largest lumber company at the time, Knapp-Stout and Company, was located here from 1846 to 1901. Today there is much to see and do in the area. While shuttling, for example, stop at the Caddie Woodlawn Home and Park at the intersection of Highway 25 and County Y; the young woman who was the subject of the children's classic *Caddie Woodlawn* lived here.

Camping is available at Edgewater Acres Campground 2.5 miles northeast of the city of Menomonie (715-235-3291), Twin Springs Resort Campground 2 miles north of Menomonie (715-235-9321), and the Eau Galle Recreation Area 16 miles southwest of Menomonie (715-778-5562).

Canoe and kayak rentals and shuttles are available at Red Cedar Outfitters in Menomonie, near the put-in (715-235-3866).

The **shuttle route** (12.7 miles) for the full 14-mile trip goes east briefly on Highway 29, south on Highway 25, and east on County Y to the bridge. Shorter trips involve 7.3 shuttle-miles from Menomonie to Downsville, and 5.4 miles from Downsville to Dunnville.

Gradient is 2.7 feet per mile.

For **water levels,** check the Menomonie gauge (#05369000) on the USGS Web site. See "Water Levels" in the introduction.

Put in at the public boat ramp in Menomonie at the Highway 29 bridge, upstream-left. Immediately to the west of the bridge are Riverside Park (which has picnic facilities and toilets), the Red Cedar River State Trail Visitor Center and trailhead, and Red Cedar Outfitters. From the beginning of the trip, the bike trail can be seen along the right shore. At Riverside Park, the trail crosses Gilbert Creek on an old railroad bridge—the first of several such bridges on the trip. A few hundred yards downstream, there are mild riffles over the sand-and-gravel bottom. Then, in a long left bend alongside a river-left bluff, exhilarating riffles continue for several hundred yards.

The right bend that follows is also quite long, ending within view of the bridge at Irvington. If you wish to take out here, there's a river-right access 100 yards after the bridge alongside a wooden trestle, just upstream from a creek mouth. Downstream from Irvington, beautiful 75-foot sandstone cliffs (known as the Accordion Cliffs) tower over the water on the right. According to a persistent legend, a company of beleaguered French soldiers buried a treasure somewhere in this area of the river.

After a couple of small curves, the river is somewhat straighter for a while, passing several creeks and occasionally becoming riffly, including the best riffles of the trip in a short left bend. After splitting around a large island alongside a tall, sheer cut bank, the river bends right under the bike-trail bridge, then quickly heads left toward the Highway 25 bridge near Downsville. Fifty yards downstream-right is a boat ramp and parking area.

Narrowing to 100 feet after the bridge, the river curves past more cut banks, then a metal retaining wall on the right. Riffles become infrequent, and the setting is more open for a while, with a few islands along the way. The mix of woods and low, grassy shoreline continues until the final right bend, where the river narrows and tall wooded bluffs rise up on both sides. The impressive hillsides last all the way to the County Y bridge near the tiny community of Dunnville. **Take out** 50 yards downstream from the bridge at the Dunnville State Wildlife Area boat ramp on the right.

Other trips. (1) For four trips on the upper Red Cedar, north of Colfax, see my book *Paddling Northern Wisconsin,* pp. 124–31. (2) For the last mile of the Red Cedar, see Chippewa River 4.

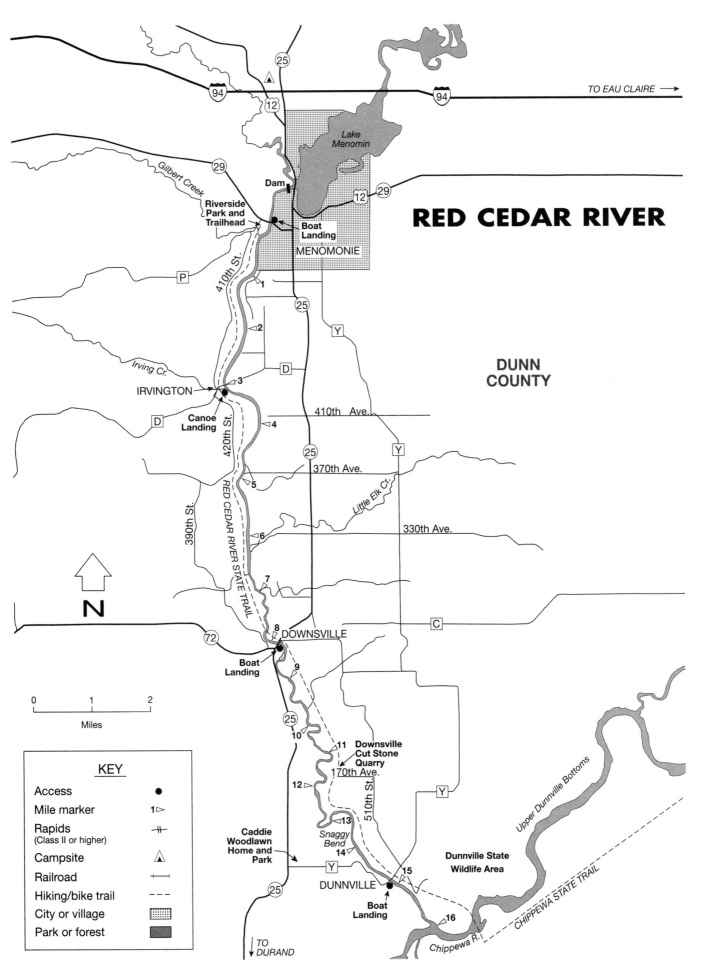

RED CEDAR RIVER

TO EAU CLAIRE →

Lake Menomin

Dam

Riverside Park and Trailhead

Boat Landing

MENOMONIE

DUNN COUNTY

Gilbert Creek

Irving Cr.

IRVINGTON

Canoe Landing

410th St.

420th 4th St.

390th St.

RED CEDAR RIVER STATE TRAIL

410th Ave.

370th Ave.

330th Ave.

Little Elk Cr.

DOWNSVILLE

Boat Landing

Downsville Cut Stone Quarry

170th Ave.

510th St.

Caddie Woodlawn Home and Park

Snaggy Bend

Dunnville State Wildlife Area

Upper Dunnville Bottoms

CHIPPEWA STATE TRAIL

DUNNVILLE

Boat Landing

Chippewa R.

TO DURAND

KEY

Access	●
Mile marker	1▷
Rapids (Class II or higher)	╫
Campsite	△
Railroad	┼─┼
Hiking/bike trail	- - -
City or village	▦
Park or forest	▓

0   1   2
Miles

N

ROCK RIVER 1
County CW to Pipersville (16 Miles)

Struck by its often-rocky bottom and the sandstone cliffs in its southern reaches, the Native Americans who hunted, fished, and lived along the Rock called it the Sinnissippi ("rocky river"). The river and the communities along it have an endlessly fascinating history. Perhaps the most famous story of all is that of Chief Black Hawk, whose people inhabited the valley and were defeated in the infamous "war" of 1832. Before his death the Sauk leader resignedly told his captors, "The Rock River was a beautiful country. I loved it. I fought for it. It is now yours. Keep it as we did."

Quite small where it emerges from Horicon Marsh (where the east, west, and south branches merge to form the main stem), the Rock flows approximately 120 river-miles in Wisconsin, gradually gaining volume from such major tributaries as the Oconomowoc, Crawfish, Bark, and Yahara Rivers. Ten dams block its course in Wisconsin. Just south of Beloit, the Rock enters Illinois, flowing to the southwest for another 163 miles and encountering seven more dams before joining the Mississippi at Rock Island. In its journey, the river passes through numerous cities of significant size.

The upper Rock is a good river for lazy float trips.

A number of sections on the river are unattractive for canoeists because of slack impoundments, developed shorelines, and motorized craft, but there are a number of other stretches that provide pleasant paddling opportunities. Three are presented here. On Rock River 1, there is little current, obstructions are rare, and houses are infrequent. The banks are usually wooded, and river width varies from 45 to 125 feet. Putting in at the Highway 16 wayside shortens the day's paddling to 9.5 miles.

Camping is available at Pike Lake State Park 2 miles east of Hartford (262-644-5248), Horicon Lodge Park east of Horicon (920-387-5450), Playful Goose Family Campground near Horicon (920-485-4744), and Concord Center Campground near Oconomowoc (262-593-2707).

There are no **canoe rentals** in the immediate area, but rentals are available at the Laacke and Joys store in downtown Milwaukee (414-271-7878), Rutabaga in Madison (608-223-9300), Carl's Paddlin' in Madison (608-284-0300), and Tip-a-Canoe Rentals near Burlington (262-537-3227).

The **shuttle route** for the whole section (7.4 miles) goes west on County CW, south on Gopher Hill Road, south on River Valley Road, west on Highway 16, south on County F into Ixonia, and west on County P to the take-out bridge. The shuttle (4 miles) for a shorter trip

starts at the Highway 16 bridge, goes west on Highway 16, south on County F into Ixonia, and west on County P.

Gradient is negligible (only 0.6 foot per mile).

For **water levels**, check the gauges at Hustisford upstream (#05424082) and/or Watertown downstream (#05425500) on the USGS Web site. See "Water Levels" in the introduction.

Put in at Kaul Park at the County CW bridge, upstream-right. A gravel road leads to a sizable parking area and a concrete boat ramp. About 75 feet wide at the outset, the river makes a couple of big loops, alternating between heavily wooded shores and open farmland. Where Rock River Road and Rock Valley Road meet, the river swings sharply left and comes close to the roadway—a popular spot for bank fishermen. Farther downstream, in a left bend, Kanow Park (a Jefferson County park) appears on the right bank; the river can be accessed here along the grassy bank.

After the park, a big right bend leads under the Rock River Road bridge to the Highway 16 wayside, a lovely little park that occupies an oxbow, with toilets, water, picnic shelters, parking lot, and concrete boat ramp (river-left). The wayside park makes an excellent alternate **put-in**. A historical sign at the wayside indicates that Wisconsin was the first state to identify highways by numbers, in 1917; Highway 16 was the first to be designated with a number.

A railroad bridge comes soon after Highway 16, followed by a long southward straightaway. Power lines cross at the site of some old bridge abutments and piers, and again at the Rockvale Road bridge. Low banks and floodplain forest continue, with a few buildings, as the river curves around to the County F bridge. Another long straightaway follows County F, toward North Side Drive, then a series of bends. In the second southward loop toward North Side Drive there's a prominent hill on the left with a house on top of it. This is the only hill of the trip.

A large marshy area now begins when the river swings left into the third and final loop to the south. When the river heads back to the right, the narrow mouth of the Oconomowoc enters through the marsh on the left. For a while the river is wide, open, and straight, with fields and houses on the left. But in the final 1.5 miles of the trip, the shores become heavily wooded again, and the river narrows, quickens, and becomes riffly over the rocky bottom.

Finally, the County P bridge appears, with a couple of small islands just upstream from it. **Take out** upstream from the bridge at the low grassy bank alongside a river-right clearing. A path leads to the road, where there's room for a couple of cars. The take-out is on private property, so you should ask permission and help keep the site clean.

ROCK RIVER 1

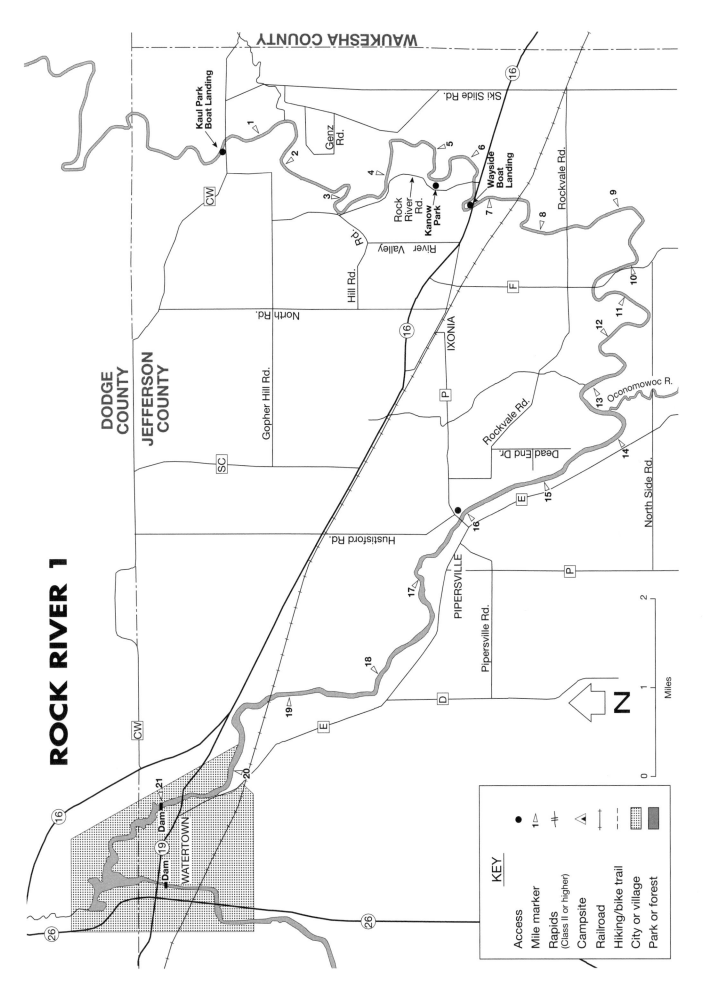

WAUKESHA COUNTY

DODGE COUNTY

JEFFERSON COUNTY

Kaul Park Boat Landing

Wayside Boat Landing

Kanow Park

Rock River Rd.

River Valley Rd.

Genz Rd.

Ski Slide Rd.

Rockvale Rd.

Hill Rd.

North Rd.

Gopher Hill Rd.

IXONIA

Rockvale Rd.

Oconomowoc R.

Dead End Dr.

North Side Rd.

Hustisford Rd.

PIPERSVILLE

Pipersville Rd.

WATERTOWN

Dam

KEY

Access ●

Mile marker ₁△

Rapids (Class II or higher) ≠

Campsite ◁

Railroad ⊥

Hiking/bike trail ┊

City or village ▒

Park or forest ▓

N

0 1 2

Miles

125

ROCK RIVER 2
Watertown to Johnson Creek (14 Miles)

One of the State's Most Unusual Houses

You're bound to be impressed by Watertown's famous Octagon House. Open to visitors from May 1 through Labor Day, this huge, beautiful dwelling is an architectural wonder. Completed in 1854 as a family residence for John Richards, a well-to-do mill owner, the eight-sided building has three above-ground stories, each with 2,500 square feet. Altogether the hilltop house contains 73 doors and 57 rooms, closets, and hallways. Among the highlights are a magnificent staircase that spirals from the basement to the third floor, a beautiful porch that completely surrounds the house on the first and second floors, and a rooftop cupola that provides a good view of the surrounding countryside. Other octagonal houses have been constructed elsewhere, but none is more impressive than this one. As a bonus for visitors, the building that housed the first kindergarten in the United States is located on the grounds of the Octagon House. The school was organized in 1856 by Margarethe Schurz, wife of the famed writer and political reformer Carl Schurz.

After the take-out of the previous trip, the Rock flows northwestward for several miles to Watertown, where the river makes an abrupt left turn toward the southwest. Back in the 1830's when settler Timothy Johnson built a cabin here, there were rapids in the bend, occasioned by a 30-foot drop from one end of the bend to the other. Two dams were soon built in order to harness the power of the river, and mills and other industries sprang up. After 1848 the growing city was popular with German settlers, one of whom was the famous political reformer Carl Schurz.

Beginning downstream from the second dam in Watertown, the second recommended trip on the Rock is good for a long, lazy trip. There's little current as the river flows through a mostly forested environment; one stretch of the trip is especially narrow, wild, and beautiful. Only a couple of areas are developed, and even these are not unattractive. Accesses are excellent, and there are a number of interesting bends with sloughs.

For **camping** in the area, see Rock River 1 and Bark River 1.

For **canoe rentals,** see Rock River 1.

The **shuttle route** (8.9 miles) from Schaller Park in Watertown goes 1 block east on Stimpson Street, south on Highway 26, south on County Y, and west on County B to the bridge.

Gradient is negligible (less than 1 foot per mile).

For **water levels,** check the Watertown gauge (#05425500) on the USGS Web site. See "Water Levels" in the introduction.

Put in at Schaller Park in Watertown, several hundred yards downstream from the Highway 26 bridge. To get to this small, grassy park in the middle of a residential neighborhood, turn west off Highway 26 onto Stimpson Street and go one block; then turn right onto a short dead-end street where you can park your vehicle(s). Put in from the low shoreline of the park on river-left.

The river here is rather shallow, with a rock-and-gravel bottom, and is only about 60 feet wide. From the beginning, trees are plentiful along the banks. On the right is the park-like setting of the Bethesda Lutheran Home. The initial left bend ends at the Watertown waste-water-treatment plant where there's an 18-inch broken-rock dam with a small island in the middle. The low dam can be run on the right (watch out for rocks) or portaged. Immediately downstream the water is deeper, houses resume on the left, and the streambed widens to 125 feet. Soon the river passes under a railroad bridge, then winds through several bends as houses grow sparse. High, wooded banks are found on one side, and low ones on the other. At one point the Watertown Outboarders boat ramp and clubhouse appear on the left.

A series of turns and straightaways follows, with cattails and marsh grass along the edge. After passing through a long, houseless, often marshy area for a while, the river comes to a very wide spot at Hahn's Lake. At this point, within view of some farm buildings on the right, the river narrows and begins a long, sharp left turn. The bends that follow are the prettiest part of the trip: narrow, densely wooded, wild, and peaceful. Marshy sloughs appear at the outside of bends as the river curves through the lowland hardwood forest; only a few buildings are seen.

Eventually, in a right bend, the river widens and County Y can be seen on the left. In this area, the most developed part of the trip, many houses appear on the left, with docks and private landings. After the houses thin out, the river swings left at a lake-like slough and cabins appear on the right; from here to Interstate 94 the river widens and flows through an open, marshy environment.

Immediately downstream from the I-94 bridges the banks become wooded again, and two gentle arcs lead to the County B bridge. **Take out** a few feet downstream-right, where there's an excellent gravel boat landing. Jefferson County maintains an attractive park here with toilets, parking area, picnic facilities, and an artesian well. Five miles downstream is the city of Jefferson, where there's a dam and no convenient access.

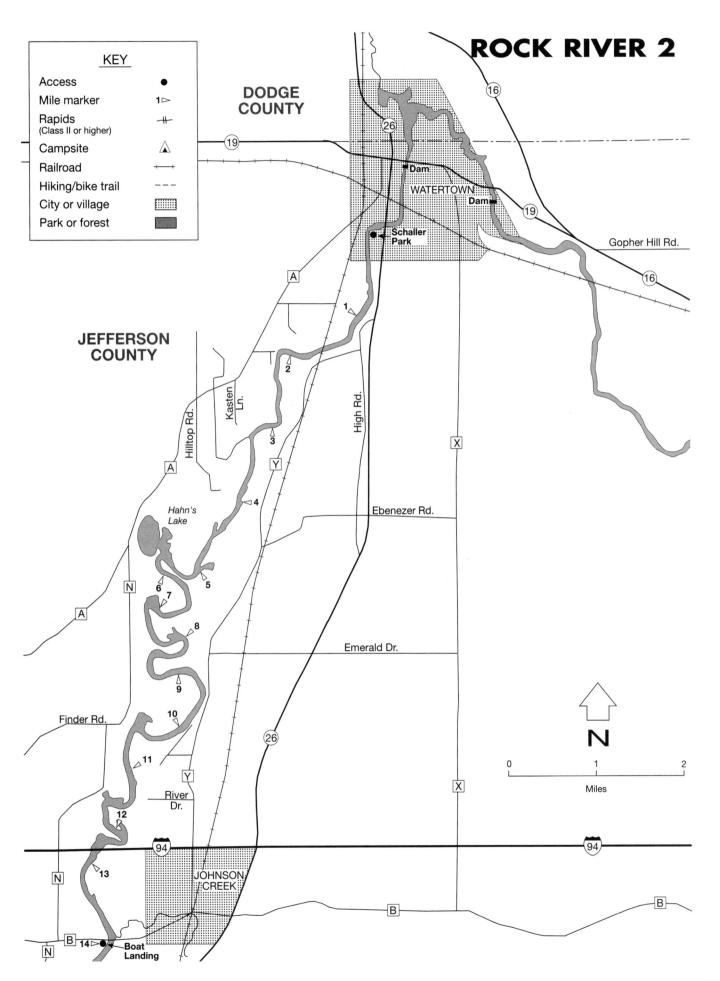

ROCK RIVER 2

KEY

Access	●
Mile marker	1▷
Rapids (Class II or higher)	―╫―
Campsite	▲
Railroad	―┼―
Hiking/bike trail	- - -
City or village	
Park or forest	

DODGE COUNTY

JEFFERSON COUNTY

WATERTOWN

Dam

Dam

Schaller Park

Gopher Hill Rd.

Hilltop Rd.

Kasten Ln.

High Rd.

Hahn's Lake

Ebenezer Rd.

Emerald Dr.

Finder Rd.

River Dr.

JOHNSON CREEK

Boat Landing

N

0   1   2

Miles

ROCK RIVER 3
Janesville to Happy Hollow Park (7 Miles)

Paddling in America's Largest Freshwater Cattail Marsh

Most of it doesn't qualify as moving water—a criterion for inclusion in this book—but the 32,000-acre Horicon Marsh is nevertheless a memorable experience for canoeists and kayakers. Fourteen miles long (north-south) and 5 miles wide, this unique wetland was once called the "Everglades of the North." Native Americans prized its rich wildlife for thousands of years—the Algonquin word Horicon means "land of pure water" – but the marsh has been much abused since the 1840s. A dam built in 1846 at the southern end created what was then the largest man-made lake in the world. Mills sprang up, and market hunters killed enormous quantities of geese and ducks. Worst of all, miles of channels were dredged in the early 1900s to drain the marsh for agriculture, which turned out to be a miserable failure.

In the late 1920s the state dammed the Rock River again to restore the marsh, and since the 1940s it has been owned and maintained by the federal government (the northern two thirds) and the state of Wisconsin (the southern one third). Paradise for migratory birds, the Horicon draws over 400,000 visitors annually, especially in the spring and fall, to watch the bountiful comings and goings of many migratory species. Canoeists can access the marsh in a number of places, including: (a) the boat landing on Chestnut Street and Nebraska Street in the town of Horicon, (b) the end of Greenhead Road, and (c) Burnett Ditch Road. In the town of Horicon, Blue Heron Landing (920-485-4663) provides canoe rental and shuttles. For more information, contact Dodge County Tourism (800-414-0101).

A short day trip on a mostly undeveloped part of the Rock, this relaxing section begins and ends with first-rate accesses and is paralleled by a biking/hiking trail. Suitable for beginners, the stretch gets progressively more attractive, especially in the final 2.5 miles, and there are small sandbars along the shoreline for relaxation stops. Like the previous trip, this section starts out within a city. Janesville calls itself the "City of Parks," with more than 2,000 acres of park land. Many lovely old mansions overlook the Rock River from the bluffs.

Two campgrounds are located 10 miles north of Janesville near Lake Koshkonong: Lakeland Campground (608-868-4700) and Lakeview Campground (608-868-7899). Also nearby are Black Hawk Campground a mile west of Milton (608-868-2586), Turtle Creek Campground 2.5 miles northeast of Beloit (608-362-7768), and Kamp Dakota east of Janesville (608-754-5282).

For **canoe rentals,** see Rock River 1.

The **shuttle route** (6.6 miles) goes south on County D, east on West Eau Claire Road, east on Happy Hollow Road, and south on the entrance road to Happy Hollow Park.

Gradient is 1.4 feet per mile.

For **water levels,** check the gauge at Afton (#05430500) on the USGS Web site. See "Water Levels" in the introduction.

The best **put-in** is at Trailhead Park in Janesville, where an asphalt landing is located upstream from the Willard Street bridge on river-right. Accessed from County D, this city park is the trailhead for the Rock River Parkway, a crushed limestone biking/hiking path that heads south along the river.

About 150 feet wide at the beginning, the river is tree-lined and relatively undeveloped. County D is nearby but can't be seen. Electrical transmission towers are visible on the right and parallel the river for most of the trip. In the left bend after the Willard Street bridge, 2 metal retaining walls appear along the right shoreline. A straightaway follows the second wall, and homes begin appearing behind the tree line on the left shore, alongside South River Road. Occasionally fishermen can be seen fishing at bare spots on the left bank. After power lines cross overhead, South River Road is more visible until the river heads right. In the following left turn houses appear on the right, the first of the trip. A right bend then leads to the West Eau Claire Road bridge.

Bending back and forth after the bridge, the river narrows considerably and is wild and beautiful. Trees are dense on both sides, and there are few signs of civilization. Eventually the river splits around a very large island, followed by several small islands. This is the only part of the river where you are likely to encounter downed trees or limbs, but you should have no difficulty if you follow the main channel. After the islands, the first dwellings since the last bridge appear, and in the following left bend you can see the smokestacks of a power plant downstream (at Town Line Road).

Before long, the bend leads to the **take-out** at Happy Hollow Park on the left: a Rock County park with picnic tables, toilets, parking lot, and a concrete boat ramp. About a mile downstream is the Town Line Road bridge. For the next 5 miles the river widens and straightens as it heads toward the next dam in Beloit.

Other trips. The 9 miles from Horicon to Hustisford are mainly lake-paddling, but the 21 miles between Hustisford (from Highway 60) to Highway CW provide good moving-water canoeing, with intermediate accesses at several bridges. Expect some deadfall in this section. The Rock between Jefferson and Janesville is not prime canoeing water, for a variety of reasons (considerable development, Lake Koshkonong, motorboats, etc.).

ROCK RIVER 3

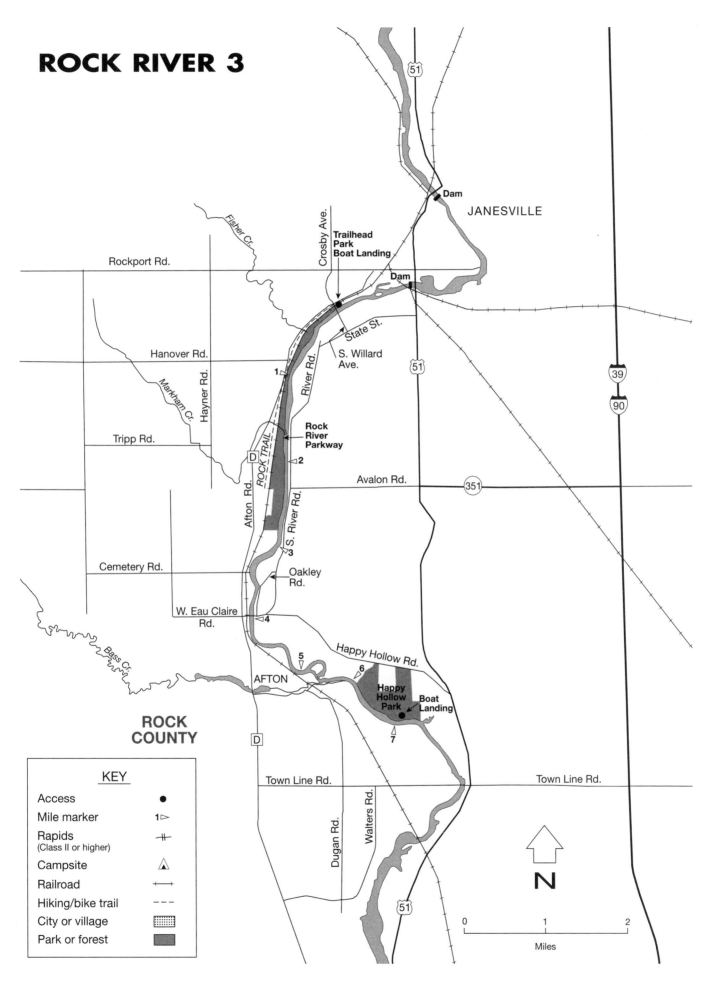

JANESVILLE

Dam

Crosby Ave.

Trailhead Park Boat Landing

Rockport Rd.

Fisher Cr.

Dam

State St.

S. Willard Ave.

River Rd.

Hanover Rd.

Hayner Rd.

Markham Cr.

1

Rock River Parkway

ROCK TRAIL

Tripp Rd.

Afton Rd.

D

2

Avalon Rd.

351

51

39

90

Cemetery Rd.

S. River Rd.

3

Oakley Rd.

W. Eau Claire Rd.

4

Bass Cr.

Happy Hollow Rd.

5

6

AFTON

Happy Hollow Park

Boat Landing

7

ROCK COUNTY

D

Town Line Rd.

Town Line Rd.

Dugan Rd.

Walters Rd.

51

KEY

Access	●
Mile marker	1▷
Rapids (Class II or higher)	╫
Campsite	△
Railroad	┼┼┼
Hiking/bike trail	-----
City or village	▦
Park or forest	▓

N

0   1   2
Miles

SHEBOYGAN RIVER 1
Johnsonville to Sheboygan Falls (16 Miles)

Despite the continuing presence of numerous dams that go back to the nineteenth-century mill era, the Sheboygan is a gem (largely undiscovered) for paddlers who like intimate little streams. With headwaters a few miles east of Fond du Lac—the same area that spawns the Milwaukee River—it flows for many miles through marshy lowland, including the ecologically and recreationally important 14,000 acres of the Sheboygan Marsh and Sheboygan Lake. At Kiel, however, it changes direction and heads southeast through attractive hill country toward Lake Michigan. Never very wide, even in impoundments, the Sheboygan after Kiel is generally clear, with a gravelly bottom, riffles, grassy banks, and mostly wooded surroundings. Although roads are never far away and buildings are not infrequent, the river has a decidedly rural atmosphere. Until the very end, there are no designated boat landings, but the river can be accessed at many locations.

On the first recommended section, boulders often line the shoreline, and frequently must be maneuvered around in the streambed. Because the upper Sheboygan is a narrow, wooded river, there's always a chance that you'll have to deal with deadfall obstructions.

Camping is available west of Elkhart Lake at Broughton Sheboygan Marsh County Park (920-876-2535), Plymouth Rock Camping Resort 3 miles southeast of Elkhart Lake (920-892-4252), Marsh Lodge Family Restaurant and Campground west of Elkhart Lake (920-876-2535), K-A Campground 3 miles northwest of Plymouth (920-893-0384), and Kohler-Andrae State Park 4 miles south of Sheboygan (920-451-4080).

Kayak rental (without shuttle service for this part of the river) is available in Sheboygan at Thill Marine (920-452-1814 or 877-844-0856).

The **shuttle route** from Johnsonville (approximately 9 miles) goes east on County JM, south on County M, and east on County PP into Sheboygan Falls to the parking lot behind the police station.

Gradient is a riffly 5.6 feet per mile.

For **water levels,** check the Sheboygan gauge (#04086000) on the USGS Web site. See "Water Levels" in the introduction.

Put in along the grassy bank upstream-right from the County JM bridge in Johnsonville, near the fire department parking lot. Launch your boat(s) well downstream from the dangerous low-head dam and the smaller concrete barrier that follows it. Better yet, you can avoid the dam altogether by putting in 0.6 mile downstream at the County J bridge (downstream-left); this is the recommended put-in.

After Johnsonville the river is narrow, wooded, and sometimes riffly, widening in the approach to County J. From here, most of the area down to Woodland Road is relatively open. In the long left bend that leads toward Rio Road, pines top the high ridge along the right shoreline. Sharp turns and riffles then lead to County M (access upstream-right). Swinging south alongside Hillside Road, the river then passes under the County O bridge. Downstream-right is a small park that makes an excellent access.

After a long series of gentle bends, tight turns, and occasional openings in the tree line, Alpine Road appears in a very riffly stretch, then the river heads north alongside wooded bluffs. County TT (access downstream-right) is quickly followed by Highway 23, then a separate metal bridge for the Old Plank Road Trail—a 17-mile asphalt-and-grass recreational path that runs from Sheboygan to Greenbush. After a long left bend, the river abruptly heads south near the intersection of Highway 23 and Meadowlark Road. Here on the left, at the top of the high, rip-rapped bank, is a trailside park with shelter, toilets, water, and parking lot—a wonderful stopping point.

Still riffly, the river parallels bluffs on the left before flowing under Meadowlark Road, then passes thin tree cover down to County C (access downstream-left). In the bends that follow, the river enters Sheboygan Falls, an old mill town with a charmingly restored historic district. The immediate environs are still mostly undeveloped, however. A couple of bends after the mouth of the Mullet River on the right, River Park appears, upstream from the Highway 32 bridge. Two pedestrian bridges cross the river at the park. **Take out** after the first pedestrian bridge at the river-right boat landing, alongside County PP (Monroe Street). A large public parking lot is located nearby.

Just around the bend from Highway 32 is a large dam, alongside a powerhouse. Riffles and rapids follow the dam down to the County PP bridge, where a series of dramatic 3- to 6-foot ledges begin (the "falls" that gave the city its name). Don't miss the opportunity to view the falls; the best vantage point is Falls View Park, which runs along Broadway Street in the business district. Only a couple of short bends downstream is Rochester Park, where the next recommended trip begins.

Other trips. The stretch from the Highway 57 bridge southeast of Millhome (downstream-right) to Johnsonville is comparable to the section described above, but there are two important caveats: (a) the decrepit old concrete dam at Franklin must be portaged on the right until its removal (scheduled for 2001); and (b) the upstream-right take-out (a concrete apron) at the hazardous Johnsonville Dam is much too close to the dam itself, only 25 feet. When the water is flowing briskly, paddlers can easily be swept over the edge. Consequently, it is recommended that inexperienced paddlers take out upstream at Franklin. Anyone contemplating a take-out at Johnsonville is advised to scout the location carefully beforehand.

SHEBOYGAN RIVER 1

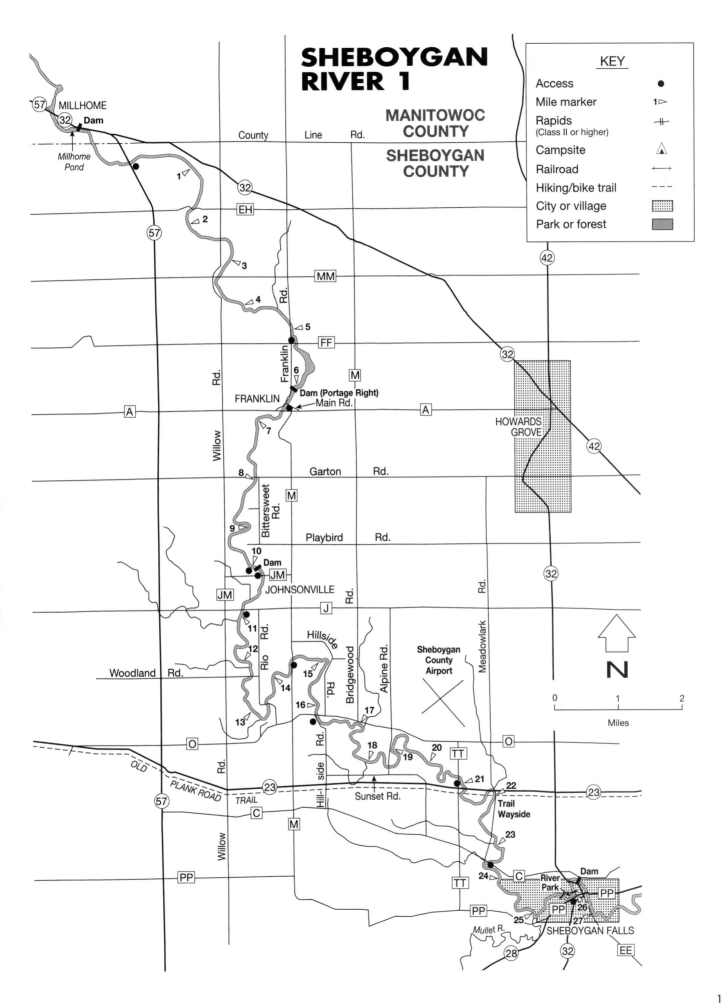

KEY

Access ●
Mile marker 1▷
Rapids (Class II or higher) ╫
Campsite △
Railroad ┼┼┼
Hiking/bike trail – – –
City or village
Park or forest

MANITOWOC COUNTY
SHEBOYGAN COUNTY

MILLHOME
Dam
Millhome Pond

County Line Rd.

FRANKLIN
Dam (Portage Right)
Main Rd.

Franklin Rd.

Willow Rd.

Garton Rd.

Bittersweet Rd.

Playbird Rd.

Dam
JOHNSONVILLE

Rio Rd.

Hillside

Woodland Rd.

Bridgewood Rd.

Alpine Rd.

Sheboygan County Airport

Meadowlark Rd.

HOWARDS GROVE

OLD PLANK ROAD TRAIL

Hill-side Rd.

Sunset Rd.

Trail Wayside

River Park
Dam
SHEBOYGAN FALLS

Mullet R.

N

0   1   2
Miles

131

SHEBOYGAN RIVER 2
Sheboygan Falls to Sheboygan (12.4 Miles)

The Underground River

The name *Sheboygan* comes from an Ojibwa word with a variety of meanings: "pipe stem," "hollow bone," "underground noise," "underground river," etc. Explanations range from a river bend resembling the shape of a pipe, to a Native American tradition of a loud rumbling sound that could be heard in the area of the river, perhaps emanating from a subterranean, hollowed-out channel. Sounds rather ominous, doesn't it?

This interesting trip provides tremendous variety. Beginning in one pleasant city and ending in another, the river is never very big and is extremely winding. At the take-out you're within a few paddle-strokes of Lake Michigan. Except for the open, grassy areas of a large and popular golf course, and an urban setting at the end, the section is wooded. Numerous riffles enliven the trip. Accesses are excellent, including intermediate landings for shorter floats. Deadfall is not a problem. The only negative aspect of the trip is the presence of two dangerous old dams that must be carefully portaged.

For bicyclists and hikers, the nearby Old Plank Road Trail is recommended. Starting from Sheboygan on the lakefront, it parallels Highway 23 for 17 miles to Greenbush.

For **camping,** see Sheboygan River 1. **Kayak rentals** and shuttles are available at Thill Marine in Sheboygan (920-452-1814 or 877-844-0856).

The **shuttle route** (5.1 miles) from Rochester Park in Sheboygan Falls goes north on Hickory Street, east on County PP (which becomes Indiana Street in Sheboygan), and north on Eighth Street to the bridge.

Gradient is 2.4 feet per mile.

For **water levels,** see Sheboygan River 1. For general information on water levels (high, medium, low), call Thill Marine (numbers above).

Put in at Rochester Park in Sheboygan Falls. From the parking lot at the end of the entrance road, carry your boat(s) to an open spot on the river-left bank. Forty feet wide at the put-in, the river bends to the right through gentle riffles with a few scattered boulders, past a series of weeping willows. After two more bends and some river-left homes, the river becomes slower, deeper, and wider. Then, in a long left bend you can hear the roar of the first dam. Get out on the concrete shelf upstream-left (as far upstream as possible) to portage. Be careful: The 8-foot, stone-block dam can be lethal.

In the sharp right bend after the dam the river narrows to 35 feet and County PP can be seen briefly on the left. The setting now becomes quite wild and beautiful. Soon the road can be seen again in another sharp right turn where a creek enters on the left. After a small brick pumping station, the river straightens and approaches the Waelderhaus Dam. Unlike the first dam, this one has no warning signs. Portage on the left on the concrete apron. On the left is your first glimpse of Kohler's acclaimed Black Wolf Run golf course, which will be seen intermittently for several miles.

Soon, when a handsome log clubhouse appears on the left, then a metal golf-course bridge, the river passes

A graceful footbridge at River Park in Sheboygan Falls.

over a long, enjoyable series of shoals and rocky ledges. At one point a large creek enters on the right, with a bridge made from a railroad flatcar over its mouth. In the tortuous sequence of bends that follows, dense woods and the open expanse of the golf course alternate; this is one of the prettiest parts of the river. Traffic noise from Highway 53 can be heard for a while, but then the river curves away from the road and silence reigns again.

In a sharp right turn, the next golf-course bridge is followed by the best riffles of the day. Wild, wooded sections, open grassy areas, and bends continue, and County PP eventually appears again on the left shore in a sharp right turn. After curving in quick succession under County A, then the Highway 43 bridges, the river runs through riffles alongside County PP and passes under two more closely spaced bridges (County PP and County TA). A gravelly shoreline just downstream-right from the County TA bridge is a good place to **take out.**

After a metal-truss railroad bridge, the river turns right abruptly, and industrial buildings follow on the left. The water now divides around a large island where the right channel is usually deeper. After the New Jersey Avenue bridge and an inverted-truss railroad bridge, Kiwanis Park appears on the left; its boat landing is another possible **take-out.** Boat slips and cabin cruisers are now lined up along the shoreline as the river bends to the right past the Fourteenth Street bridge; immediately downstream-right is an excellent public boat ramp (yet another alternate **take-out**). The boat landing downstream-right from the next bridge, Pennsylvania Avenue, belongs to a private boat club. A few hundred yards farther downstream, on the right, is Thill's Marine, the take-out for kayak renters.

The recommended **take-out** is at the Eighth Street bridge, upstream-left, where there's a concrete boat ramp with adjacent parking. Incidentally, the urban setting of the last part of the trip is not unattractive, and no-wake restrictions are generally effective in moderating motorboats. If you wish to eliminate the downtown component, plan to take out at County TA.

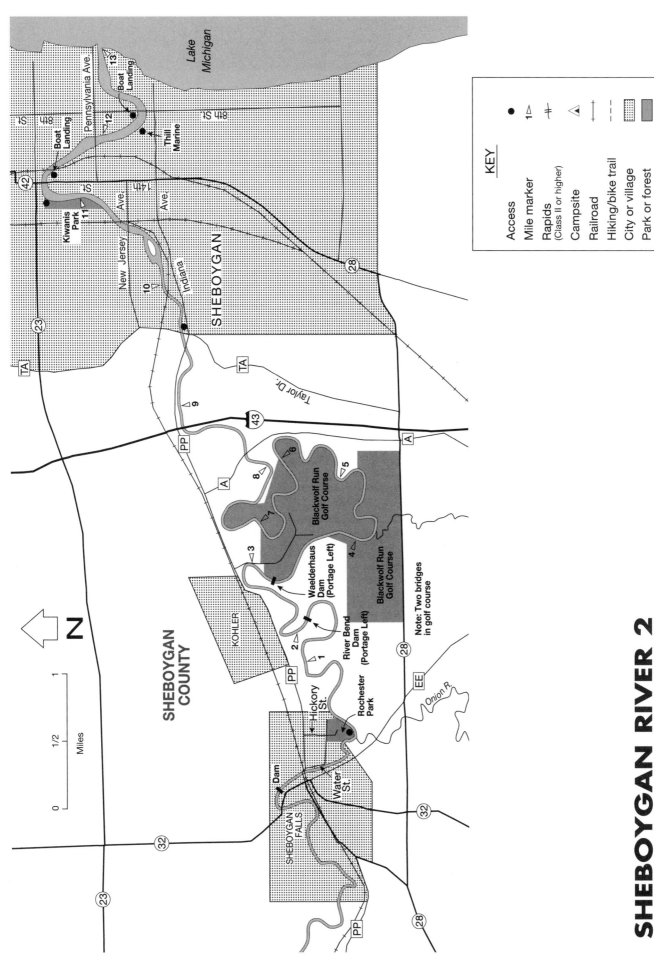

KEY

●	Access
1 △	Mile marker
╪	Rapids (Class II or higher)
◁	Campsite
┼	Railroad
┊	Hiking/bike trail
▒	City or village
▓	Park or forest

N

Miles

0   1/2   1

Lake Michigan

SHEBOYGAN COUNTY

KOHLER

SHEBOYGAN

SHEBOYGAN FALLS

Pennsylvania Ave.
Boat Landing
Thill Marine
Kiwanis Park
New Jersey Ave.
Indiana Ave.
14th St.
8th St.
4th St.

Taylor Dr.

Blackwolf Run Golf Course

Blackwolf Run Golf Course

Waelderhaus Dam (Portage Left)

River Bend Dam (Portage Left)

Hickory St.

Rochester Park

Water St.

Dam

Onion R.

Note: Two bridges in golf course

SHEBOYGAN RIVER 2

SUGAR RIVER 1
Attica to Albany (7.3 Miles)

Rural is the best overall word to describe the Sugar River. In its southeastward course through Dane, Green, and Rock Counties, it provides brief glimpses of only three small towns: Belleville, Albany, and Brodhead, where dams impound its waters. Elsewhere it travels peacefully past sparsely populated farmland, wooded hills, marshes, and hardwood swamps. Fairly steep in its headwaters area between Madison and Mt. Horeb, it begins leveling out as it passes through lower, less hilly country, and has very little gradient by the time it enters Illinois and joins the Pecatonica. In many places, trees and limbs in the water can be a challenge for paddlers, especially in the upper and lower reaches (i.e., above Dayton and below Avon). There is never anything particularly dramatic about the Sugar—no rock outcroppings, rapids, or big sandbars, for instance—but it's a great place for a quiet paddle through unspoiled, mostly wooded surroundings.

Paddling the Sugar in a hand-made cedar-strip canoe.

Waterfowl, muskrats, beavers, and turtles are common. An added bonus is the proximity of the Sugar River Trail, which parallels the river from Brodhead to Albany, then follows the Little Sugar River to New Glarus.

The name of the river comes from an Algonquin word meaning "sweet water"—perhaps (some say) because of the Native Americans' use of sugar maples to make syrup, perhaps (say others) because of the sand in the water.

Camping is available at the Sweet Minnihaha Campground between Albany and Brodhead (608-862-3769), Crazy Horse Campground west of Brodhead (608-897-2207), and New Glarus Woods State Park south of New Glarus (608-527-2335).

Canoe rentals and shuttles are available at Sweet Minnihaha Campground south of Albany (608-862-3769), and canoe rentals without shuttle at the River Bend Bar in Attica (608-862-3440). Canoes also may be rented in Madison at Rutabaga (608-223-9300) and Carl's Paddlin' (608-284-0300).

The **shuttle route** (approximately 7.5 miles) from Attica goes east on County C/Brooklyn-Albany Road, south on Attica Road/County E, south on Highway 59 into Albany, and north on Water Street to the public landing. The shuttle route (4.3 miles) for a shorter trip to the County EE bridge goes west, then south on County C, south on County X, and east on County EE.

Gradient is 2.7 feet per mile.

For **water levels,** check the gauge at Brodhead (#05436500) on the USGS Web site. See "Water Levels" in the introduction. For general information on water levels (high, medium, low), call Sweet Minnihaha Campground (608-862-3769).

Put in at the County C landing (upstream-left) just across the river from the small community of Attica. A dirt access road leads to the landing, where there's room to park several cars. Forty feet wide at the put-in, the river curves left away from Attica. Downstream, in a right bend, a sizable tributary enters on the left, with a bridge over its mouth.

Quite winding, the river flows past occasional sloughs and small islands, widening at times to 50 feet. Maple, willow, ash, basswood, and oak are thick atop the dirt banks, which become sandier as you go farther downstream. Limbs in the water sometimes require maneuvering. Gradually the banks become lower and the woods thinner. Farm buildings appear on the right, then pastureland. Here and there, small, sandy banks and sandbars are suitable for rest breaks. Widening to 60 feet, the river is quite open on the left for a while, but there's always some tree cover. Allen Creek enters on the left.

County EE is a good place to **take out** (100 feet downstream-right) if you want a shorter trip or wish to avoid the flowage of Albany Lake downstream. After EE the current slows in the winding approach to Albany. When you get into the marshy northern head of the lake, the channel makes an abrupt left turn. Once you're onto the main body of the lake, stay to the left. As you paddle into Albany, there's a city park on the left where you can **take out** at the concrete boat ramp. The park lies along North Water Street and is 0.1 mile upstream from the dam.

Other trips. (1) If you wish to continue downstream, take out at the concrete pad on river-right immediately upstream from the dam, carry your boat(s) up the steps over the dam shoulder, and reenter the water below the dam. After the shallow, rocky area below the dam, the river is winding and often more open in the 3 miles before Sweet Minnihaha Campground, where you can take out if you're camping or renting a canoe there. Minnihaha puts boats in at Attica, County EE, and Albany. (2) Another 3 miles of paddling takes you through Decatur Lake to the dam, where canoeists portage on the left and continue down the river. To the left of the dam, you can proceed down the old 3-mile millrace (where a head gate structure is soon found, and a small dam must be portaged in Brodhead). If you paddle down the millrace, intending to pass through the opening at the head gates, be sure that there is no obstruction and that your boat-handling skill is sufficient. If in doubt, portage around the head gates. See the map for Sugar River 2. (3) The upstream section between Dayton and Attica (with accesses at Highway 92, upstream- or downstream-right, and at County X, downstream-left) is attractive but more prone to deadfall.

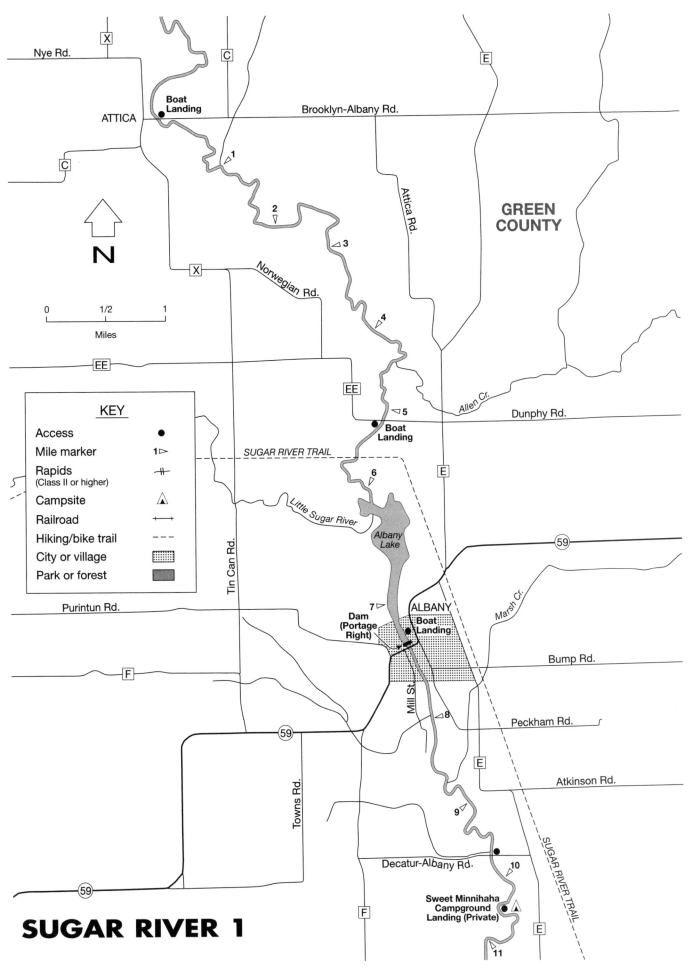

KEY

Access	●
Mile marker	1▷
Rapids (Class II or higher)	─╫─
Campsite	▲
Railroad	┼─┼
Hiking/bike trail	─ ─ ─
City or village	▦
Park or forest	▨

Nye Rd.

Boat Landing

ATTICA

Brooklyn-Albany Rd.

Attica Rd.

GREEN COUNTY

Norwegian Rd.

0   1/2   1
Miles

EE

EE

Allen Cr.

Dunphy Rd.

Boat Landing

SUGAR RIVER TRAIL

Little Sugar River

Albany Lake

59

Marsh Cr.

Purintun Rd.

Tin Can Rd.

Dam (Portage Right)

ALBANY

Boat Landing

Bump Rd.

F

Mill St.

Peckham Rd.

59

Towns Rd.

Atkinson Rd.

Decatur-Albany Rd.

Sweet Minnihaha Campground Landing (Private)

SUGAR RIVER TRAIL

59

F

E

SUGAR RIVER 1

SUGAR RIVER 2
Brodhead to Avon (10.3 Miles)

Historic Brodhead

When you're paddling Sugar River 2, nearby Brodhead invites a visit. Back in the Civil War years, a 3-mile millrace was dug from the Decatur dam into Brodhead to operate a grist mill at the end of the artificial waterway. Then, from the 1880s until 1963, the millrace was used to generate electricity for the city. The old powerhouse and dam are located near the city water tower and the trailhead of the Sugar River Trail.

Just north of Brodhead is a scenic replica of the historic Clarence Covered Bridge that once crossed the Sugar River at Highway 11/81. Now spanning a tributary of the Sugar, the bridge is on the Sugar River Trail but also can be reached by a combination of driving and walking. Go north on County E, then west on Golf Course Road 0.3 mile to the intersection with the trail; walk 0.25 mile north on the trail to the bridge.

Somewhat wider, on the average, than the previous stretch, this part of the river seldom obliges paddlers to thread their way between fallen limbs. Nevertheless, the setting is mostly forested, with few buildings or other signs of civilization. Not until the end of the trip do you begin to see some of the marshy lowland environment that begins to prevail after Avon. Accesses are excellent, and the trip can readily be shortened by putting in at an intermediate landing.

For **camping**, see Sugar River 1.

Canoe rentals and shuttles are available at Crazy Horse Campground a mile west of Brodhead (608-897-2207). Also see Sugar River 1.

The **shuttle route** (approximately 9 miles) goes east on County F into Brodhead, east on Highway 11, south on County T, and east on Beloit-Newark Road across the bridge. The shuttle route (5.6 miles) for a shorter trip from Highway 11 to Avon goes south on Mt. Hope Road and east on Town Center Road/Beloit-Newark Road.

Gradient is 1.9 feet per mile.

Water levels. For general information on water levels (high, medium, low), call Crazy Horse Campground (608-897-2207). Also see Sugar River 1.

Put in at the County F bridge, downstream-left. This is a first-rate gravel landing with an adjacent parking lot. Downstream the river is wooded and winding, with periodic openings for farmland. Banks are 4–5 feet high, and the water usually has a muddy cast. After the mouth of the millrace channel on the left, the Crazy Horse Campground (off County F) appears on the right; a sign indicates its canoe landing in a left bend. This is the take-out for Crazy Horse canoe-renters, who put in upstream at County EE, Albany, Decatur-Albany Road, or Head Gates Park north of Brodhead. Downstream, a railroad bridge and the Ten Eyck Road bridge appear in short order. In the next 2 miles the river becomes progressively less circuitous.

At Highway 11 there's an attractive park on the right (downstream), with a boat ramp, toilets, and parking lot. This makes an excellent alternate put-in for a leisurely 6-mile trip. The park is located on Mt. Hope Road, which now runs parallel to the river for a while; riprap guards the shoreline from erosion. In the many bends that follow, small sandy beaches make good stopping places. After a couple of creeks enter on the right, the river passes under an abandoned farm bridge. Periodically there are clearings where you can see crop-

land. The river widens somewhat, but there are sometimes limbs in the water to avoid. At one point in a left bend there are 6-foot cut banks on the right near some trailers.

In the last couple of miles before County T more creeks enter on the right, and the river is placid and often tree-canopied. In the last mile of the trip, there are several sloughs off the main channel. As Beloit-Newark Road nears, a big, grassy, open area appears in a left bend. **Take out** at the sandy landing 100 yards downstream from the bridge, on the left. There's plenty of adjacent parking.

Other trips. (1) In the 4 miles after Beloit-Newark Road the river flows through the swampy Avon Bottoms Wildlife Area, where blockages are common. The next access is at Sugar River Park 150 yards downstream-right from the Nelson Road bridge. (2) From Nelson Road, 6 twisting river-miles lead through densely wooded lowland into Illinois to the river-left landing at Colored Sands Forest Preserve. (See *Paddling Illinois*, pp. 142–43.) (3) For an interesting variation, put in on the millrace at Head Gates Park (take County E north from Brodhead, turn west on Golf Course Road, then south on a dirt access road just before you get to the Norwegian Creek bridge). There's a sandy landing upstream-left from the old millrace gates, one of which can be paddled through (or you can carry around). Caution: be sure that the gate opening is unobstructed and that you have enough skill to paddle through it safely. There's another (and safer) access on the millrace—a concrete boat ramp—in Brodhead at Putnam Park along West Third Street. In Brodhead you must portage the powerhouse dam, which is found immediately after a 90-degree right turn in the millrace. From a dock on the grassy right bank just before the turn, carry your boat(s) 50 yards and put back in below the powerhouse. Before long, the millrace channel rejoins the main channel.

Threading through some limbs on the Sugar.

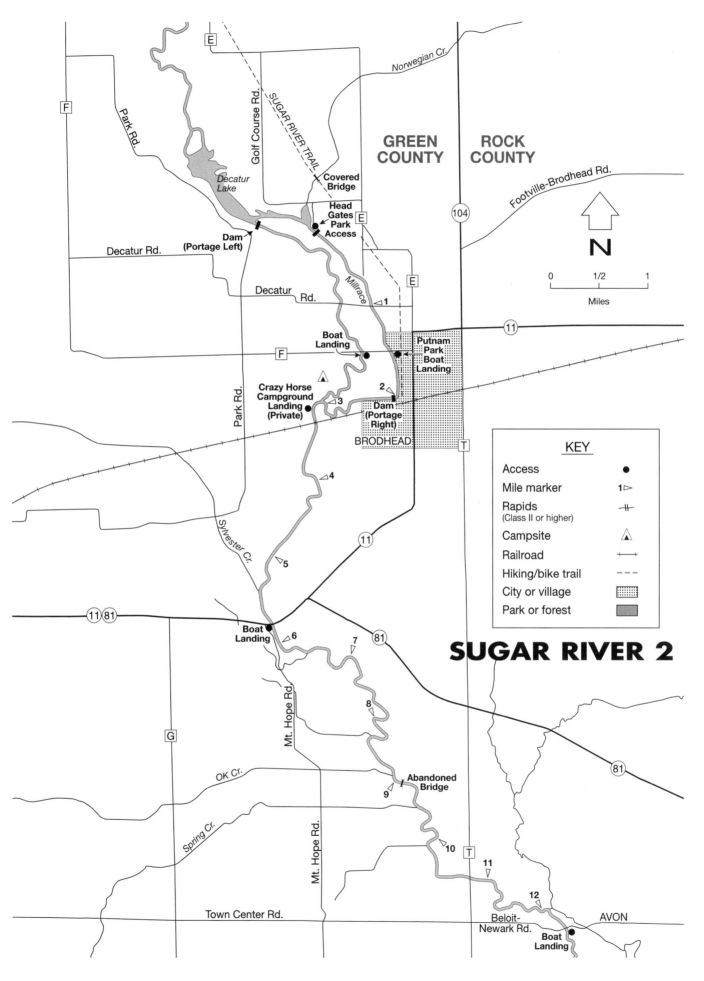

Park Rd.

Decatur Lake

F

Golf Course Rd.

SUGAR RIVER TRAIL

Norwegian Cr.

GREEN COUNTY

ROCK COUNTY

Footville-Brodhead Rd.

104

Covered Bridge

Head Gates Park Access

E

Dam (Portage Left)

Decatur Rd.

Decatur Rd.

Millrace

E

1

11

N

0   1/2   1

Miles

Boat Landing

F

Putnam Park Boat Landing

2

Crazy Horse Campground Landing (Private)

3

Dam (Portage Right)

BRODHEAD

T

KEY

Access ●

Mile marker 1▷

Rapids +++
(Class II or higher)

Campsite ▲

Railroad +++

Hiking/bike trail - - -

City or village ▦

Park or forest ▬

Park Rd.

4

Sylvester Cr.

5

11

SUGAR RIVER 2

11 81

Boat Landing

6

7

81

Mt. Hope Rd.

8

G

OK Cr.

Abandoned Bridge

9

81

Spring Cr.

Mt. Hope Rd.

10

T

11

12

Town Center Rd.

Beloit-Newark Rd.

AVON

Boat Landing

TOMORROW RIVER
Nelsonville to Amherst (4 Miles)

When you get your first glimpse of the Tomorrow River at Nelsonville, it's understandable if you misidentify it as a creek. Indeed, it is a tiny stream – only 10 feet wide at the put-in—and that accounts for much of its charm. Until it nears Amherst and broadens at the millpond, it remains small throughout this enchanting section. Except for the wide, somewhat marshy ending, the river twists through a heavily wooded area. Surprisingly, deadfall is seldom a problem, thanks to obstruction-removal by other canoeists. Because of its relative brevity, this trip is a good destination for paddlers who want a two- to three-hour outing. You'll certainly have a hard time finding a more intimate stretch of river.

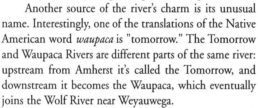

The old Nelsonville Mill on the Tomorrow River.

A bonus of the trip is the mill-to-mill aspect. You'll put in alongside the lovely old red mill at Nelsonville and will take out just upstream from the mill at Amherst. The latter still grinds grain, by the way, although electricity now does the grinding, not water power.

Another source of the river's charm is its unusual name. Interestingly, one of the translations of the Native American word *waupaca* is "tomorrow." The Tomorrow and Waupaca Rivers are different parts of the same river: upstream from Amherst it's called the Tomorrow, and downstream it becomes the Waupaca, which eventually joins the Wolf River near Weyauwega.

Camping is available to the east at Hartman Creek State Park 6 miles west of Waupaca (715-258-2372), Waupaca Camping Park (also known as Holmes Camping Park) 1 mile southwest of Waupaca (715-258-8010), and Rustic Woods Campground 5 miles south of Waupaca (715-258-2442).

The **shuttle route** (4.1 miles) from the bridge in Nelsonville goes north a short distance on Highway 161, east on County SS, and south on County A to the Amherst public boat landing.

Gradient is 2.5 feet per mile.

Water levels. The USGS Web site lists no gauges for the Tomorrow and Waupaca Rivers, but you can check the gauge reading for the Waupaca River (at Waupaca) on the Interactive Weather Information Network site. See "Water Levels" in the introduction.

Put in alongside the Nelsonville mill at the Highway 161 bridge, upstream-left. Carry your boat(s) from the parking lot in front of the mill down the grassy lawn to the low riverbank. Upstream 150 feet is a small bridge where the mill dam used to be.

From the start, the clear water flows over sand and gravel, with small boulders scattered in the streambed, widening to as much as 20 feet. Generally the banks are canopied with trees, including willow, cedar, and pine. A couple of houses are passed before long, and a rickety, old, low-clearance footbridge appears. As the river continues to wind around, the environs become a little marshy and more open for a while.

When a farm appears on the right, there's a low farm bridge that usually requires a portage on the right (this can be messy if cattle have been nearby). Shallow riffles immediately follow the bridge. Just downstream from the bridge is a beautiful pine grove on the left. On the right the shoreline clears enough to enable you to see Alm Road paralleling the river.

Soon after the farm bridge, the Lake Meyers Road bridge is a concrete-and-stone structure with four culverts running through it. A home follows downstream-left. The river now widens to 30–35 feet, but maintains good depth for paddling. Periodic pine groves continue to be a delight.

Eventually the river widens, slows, and deepens in the backup from the Amherst dam. Marshy vegetation begins to appear along the edges, and the setting becomes more open. As County A draws close on the left side, the houses of Amherst begin to appear. **Take out** on the left at the public boat ramp, where parking is available. Within sight of the landing (i.e, 0.2 mile downstream) is the old cream-colored mill that stands just to the left of the dam. If you wish to avoid most of the impoundment (which actually isn't very big), you can take out farther upstream at Cate County Park (0.6 mile before the public landing), also on the left. If you elect to take out here, you need to put a bandana or other temporary marker along the wooded shoreline; otherwise, you'll miss the tiny clearing. This is not a developed landing, and the public boat ramp farther downstream is recommended.

Amherst is a very pleasant little town—a good place to have coffee or breakfast before you paddle, browse in the antique and gift shops, or stay in a bed and breakfast.

Rivers don't get any smaller than the Tomorrow.

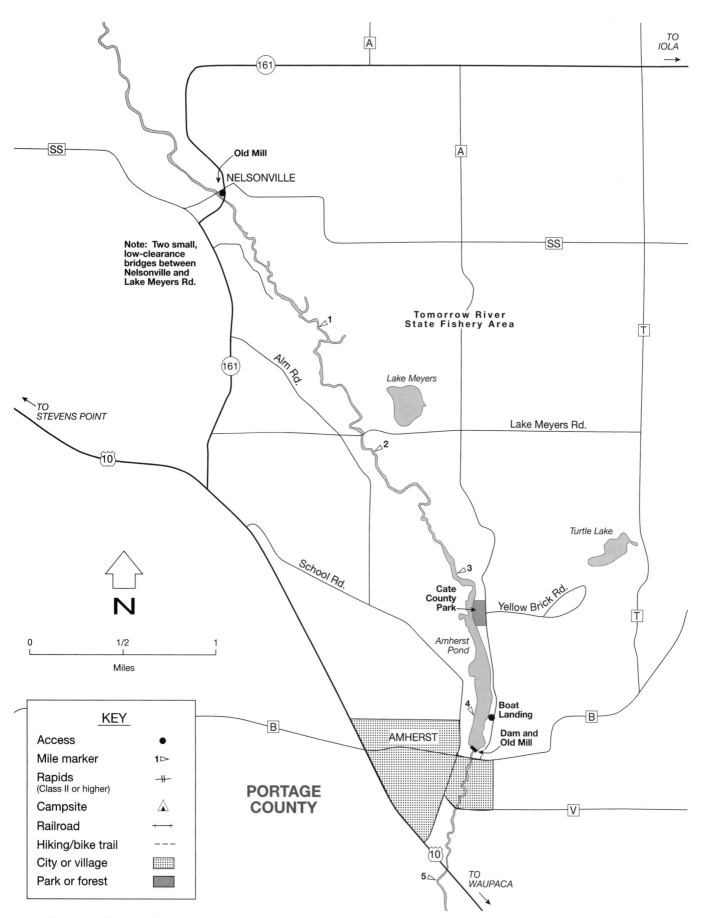

TO
IOLA

161

A

A

SS

SS

T

Old Mill

NELSONVILLE

Note: Two small,
low-clearance
bridges between
Nelsonville and
Lake Meyers Rd.

**Tomorrow River
State Fishery Area**

1

161

Alm Rd.

Lake Meyers

TO
STEVENS POINT

Lake Meyers Rd.

10

2

Turtle Lake

School Rd.

3

**Cate
County
Park**

Yellow Brick Rd.

T

*Amherst
Pond*

4

**Boat
Landing**

B

B

AMHERST

**Dam and
Old Mill**

V

**PORTAGE
COUNTY**

10

5

TO
WAUPACA

KEY

Access	●
Mile marker	1▷
Rapids
(Class II or higher)	╫
Campsite	▲
Railroad	+—+
Hiking/bike trail	- - -
City or village	▒
Park or forest	▓

0   1/2   1

Miles

TOMORROW RIVER

TREMPEALEAU RIVER 1
Whitehall to Independence (7.5 Miles)

What's a Coulee?

When Nicholas Perrot and other French explorers and traders came to the Mississippi River valley in the late 1600s, they were struck by the steep-walled valleys and ravines emptying into the Mississippi between the mouths of the Chippewa and Wisconsin Rivers. Their name for these rugged, stream-cut valleys—coulees—has stuck, and this part of Wisconsin is still known as Coulee Country. The heart of the region is bounded roughly by the Chippewa River to the north, the Mississippi to the west, Interstate 90 to the south, and Interstate 94 to the east. Thus, such rivers as the Trempealeau, Buffalo, Black, and La Crosse flow through Coulee Country.

The area owes its rough topography to the fact that it's part of the unglaciated Driftless Area in the southwestern corner of Wisconsin. Shuttle routes on the highways and back roads of Coulee Country are one of the best parts of a canoe trip, providing endless views of bluff-top scenery, wooded valleys, and sinuous streams.

Hard to spell but fun to paddle, the Trempealeau flows gently through the rolling hills of the Coulee Country of western Wisconsin. Emptying into the Mississippi 10 miles upstream from the mouth of the Black River, it takes its name from a beautiful, wooded bluff sitting in a bay near the confluence of the Trempealeau and Mississippi; early French explorers called the bluff *la montagne qui trempe a l'eau*, "the mountain that soaks in the water."

Upstream from Whitehall the Trempealeau is too small and brushy for good canoeing, but the rest of the river is quite paddleable. Especially popular is the easily accessed section from Whitehall to Arcadia. The entire 19 miles can be done in one long day, but it's much more enjoyable to paddle it in shorter stretches, using the excellent intermediate landings at Independence or Joe Pietrek Park.

Unlike the wider and less heavily wooded section after Independence, the first trip bends sharply back and forth in a narrow streambed that is often overhung with trees. This part of the river often necessitates maneuvering between or around fallen limbs, but portages are rare. Paddlers experience an intimate, wild, woodland environment, occasionally heightened by sightings of wild turkey, eagles, herons, deer, and other wildlife.

Riverside **camping** is plentiful: at Colonel Larson Park in Whitehall, Four Seasons Park in Independence, Joe Pietrek Park between Independence and Arcadia, and Memorial Park in Arcadia.

Canoe rentals are available near the put-in at Trempealeau River Canoe Outfitters in Whitehall (715-538-4833 or 715-538-2444).

The **shuttle route** (5.9 miles) from the Highway 121 bridge in Whitehall goes west on Highway 121, south on Highway 93 into Independence, and east on Elm Street to Four Seasons Park.

Gradient is 4.7 feet per mile.

For **water levels,** check the Dodge gauge (#05379500) on the USGS Web site. See "Water Levels" in the introduction. For general water level information (high, medium, low), call Trempealeau River Canoe Outfitters (715-538-4833 or 715-538-2444).

Put in at either of two locations in Whitehall: (1) at the Highway 121 bridge, upstream-left, next to the Oil Spot and Trempealeau River Canoe Outfitters; or (2) a short distance downstream at the boat landing of Colonel Larson Park. To get to the park, take Blair Street off Main Street (Highway 121) in Whitehall. The landing is on river-left at the end of the entrance road, near the ball fields. A short path leads over a dike to a small sandy beach. The park has campsites, toilets, a swimming pool, picnic facilities, and parking.

Narrow and tree-canopied at the Highway 121 put-in, the river flows over a sandy bottom. Banks are 3–8 feet high and grassy. Soon the landing at Colonel Larson Park appears on the left in the midst of an S-curve. From the beginning, the river is extremely winding, and averages 35 feet wide. There's considerable deadfall along the sides, but usually plenty of room for clear paddling. Here and there you can see where limbs have been sawed away to provide easy passage. In a right bend, the large grassy area on the left with lovely coniferous trees and stone riprap is a golf course. Later a metal snowmobile bridge is flanked by pine trees.

After the first house of the trip, on river-right, the Trempealeau widens to about 45 feet for a while, and the shoreline is occasionally open, allowing brief glimpses of farm fields. Eventually, after a sharp right turn, the river narrows and is again canopied with trees—a very wild, peaceful, and beautiful area. A straight stretch is followed by a series of turns that lead to the Highway 121 bridge. The river continues to be 90 percent wooded, but is consistently wider after the bridge, with less deadfall, and bigger, gentler bends.

In the approach to a metal-truss railroad bridge the river narrows and canopies over again. Downstream in a right bend a cable suspension bridge passes overhead. Then, after a long left bend and a short right turn, the river narrows once more at a small riffle. Before long, Elk Creek enters on the right. **Take out** at the small dock just upstream from the mouth, and carry your boat(s) to the parking area in the nearby park. Not far upstream Elk Creek is dammed to form Bugle Lake; the dam lies under the Highway 93 bridge in Independence.

Always a welcome sight: a dedicated canoe landing, on the Trempealeau.

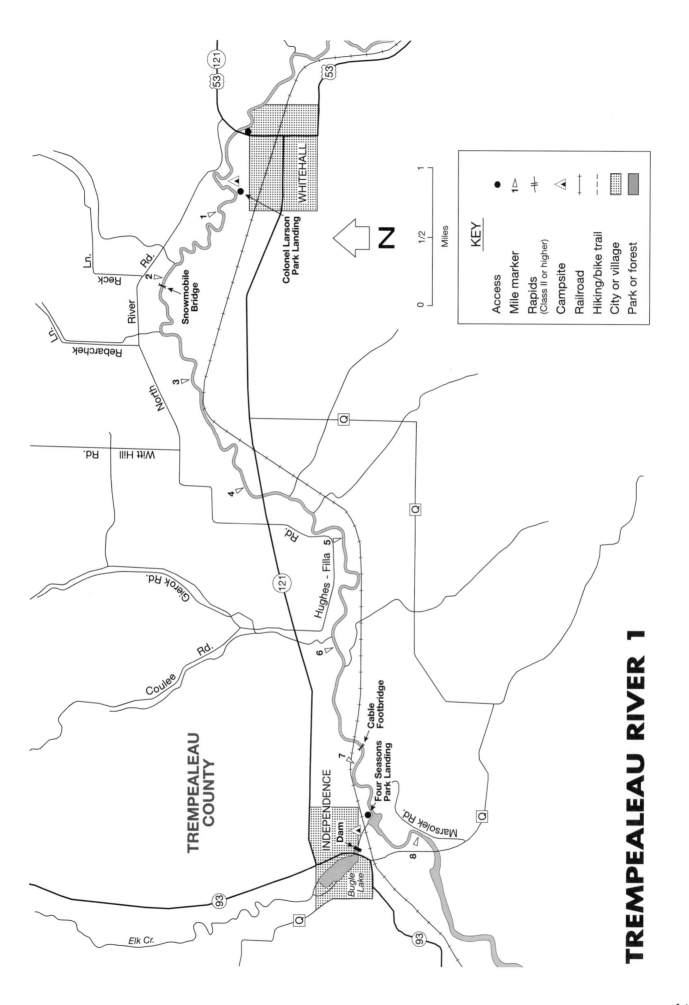

TREMPEALEAU RIVER 1

WHITEHALL

Colonel Larson Park Landing

Snowmobile Bridge

Reck Rd.

Reck Ln.

Rebarchek Ln.

River

North

Witt Hill Rd.

Gierok Rd.

Coulee Rd.

Hughes - Filla Rd.

TREMPEALEAU COUNTY

INDEPENDENCE

Dam

Bugle Lake

Four Seasons Park Landing

Cable Footbridge

Marsolek Rd.

Elk Cr.

N

KEY

Access

Mile marker

Rapids (Class II or higher)

Campsite

Railroad

Hiking/bike trail

City or village

Park or forest

Miles

0   1/2   1

TREMPEALEAU RIVER 2
Independence to Arcadia (11.6 Miles)

Exploring the Backwaters of the Mississippi

Someone has said that the heart of the Mississippi is its main channel, while the backwaters are its soul. If you'd like to try your hand at "soulful" paddling, a good place to do it is the Long Lake Canoe Trail, about 20 miles south of Arcadia. A circular out-and-back route through a network of sloughs and islands, this 4.5-mile trip begins and ends at a U.S. Fish and Wildlife Service landing 1.5 miles south of the town of Trempealeau. Canoe-trail signs help you to find your way, together with a descriptive brochure and map available from the Upper Mississippi River National Wildlife and Fish Refuge in Onalaska (608-783-8405) or Wisconsin DNR in La Crosse (608-785-9000).

Another popular backwater trail (also signed to keep paddlers on track) is found at Wyalusing State Park, at the confluence of the Wisconsin and Mississippi Rivers (see Wisconsin River 12).

A tamer part of the river, the section downstream from Independence is consistently wider and less circuitous. The setting is still mostly wooded, but there are more openings along the shoreline for farm fields. Because the turns are gentler and the deadfall is infrequent, this is a good stretch for beginners. Accesses are excellent, including a pleasant intermediate landing that makes shorter trips possible. Riverside camping at Four Seasons Park in Independence and at Joe Pietrek Park farther downstream are made-to-order for canoe-campers who'd like an overnight trip all the way from Whitehall to Arcadia.

For nearby **camping,** see Trempealeau River 1. Another outstanding campground is located about 20 miles south of Arcadia at Perrot State Park, at the mouth of the Trempealeau River (608-534-6409). The river views from the park's bluffs are spectacular, and the 24-mile Great River Bicycle Trail is nearby.

For **canoe rentals** and **water levels,** see Trempealeau River 1.

The **shuttle route** (10.3 miles) from Four Seasons Park goes west on Elm Street, south on Highway 93, west on Highway 95 (Main Street) into Arcadia, north on Park Street, west on River Street across the river, and north on Willow Street a short distance to Schultz Park. For a short trip from Independence to Joe Pietrek Park, the shuttle is 5.6 miles: west on Elm Street, south on Highway 93, and east on the park entrance road.

Gradient is 4.3 feet per mile.

Put in at the Four Seasons Park boat dock near the mouth of Elk Creek. Follow the park entrance road (off Elm Street) to the end; from there it's a short carry to the landing. Augmented by the flow of Elk Creek, the Trempealeau is heavily wooded and 55 feet wide at the beginning, quickly passing a few houses. Highway Q runs close on the left briefly, and soon crosses the river downstream.

After cornfields, pastures, and a small island, woods resume. Later, in a long left bend with stone riprap on the right shoreline, power lines cross and farm buildings can be seen in the distance. More cornfields appear in the long right bend that follows, and another set of power lines. As the river curves left sharply, past the mouth of Traverse Creek, traffic can be seen on Highway 93. A series of gentle bends follows.

Just upstream from Cross Road bridge, a sharp little S-curve tends to collect dead trees; be careful here. After the bridge, the river is wider, averaging 70 feet, with open fields on both sides. Farther downstream, in a left turn, you can briefly see Highway 93 again. The banks eventually become thinly wooded, and a couple of small islands are passed.

In a right bend, a 90-foot wooded bluff looms on the left, much of its clay-and-sand slope exposed by the action of wind and water. In the left bend following this sheer embankment, a creek enters on the right, and the river begins to widen even more—to as much as 80 feet. In the approach to Joe Pietrek Park dense woods resume on both sides. The park can be recognized by a shelter and picnic tables on the grassy right bank. Operated by Trempealeau County, the park offers camping, toilets, and nature trails. The canoe landing—a good place to **take out** for a short trip—comes at a point where the river bends left, then sharply right. A large grassy area provides plenty of room for parking.

After Joe Pietrek Park, the Trempealeau makes a series of gentle bends as it flows southwestward toward Arcadia, passing under Highway 93 along the way. In Arcadia **take out** at the concrete canoe ramp 50 yards upstream-right from the River Street bridge. Immediately to the west of the landing, across Willow Street, is Schultz Park, with a picnic shelter, playground, and parking area. On the east side of the river, directly across from the canoe landing, is Klink Deer Park.

Other trips. (1) It's a long haul from Arcadia to Dodge (13 miles), with no intermediate accesses, and (2) another 13 miles from Dodge to Perrot State Park at the mouth. (3) A very different kind of trip starts at Marshland (Highway 35), floats through the Trempealeau National Wildlife Refuge, and takes out at the Perrot State Park canoe landing or farther downstream at the Trempealeau Hotel. Canoe rentals and shuttles for this trip are available at the Trempealeau Hotel (608-534-6898).

Recreational kayaks work well on small rivers like the Trempealeau.

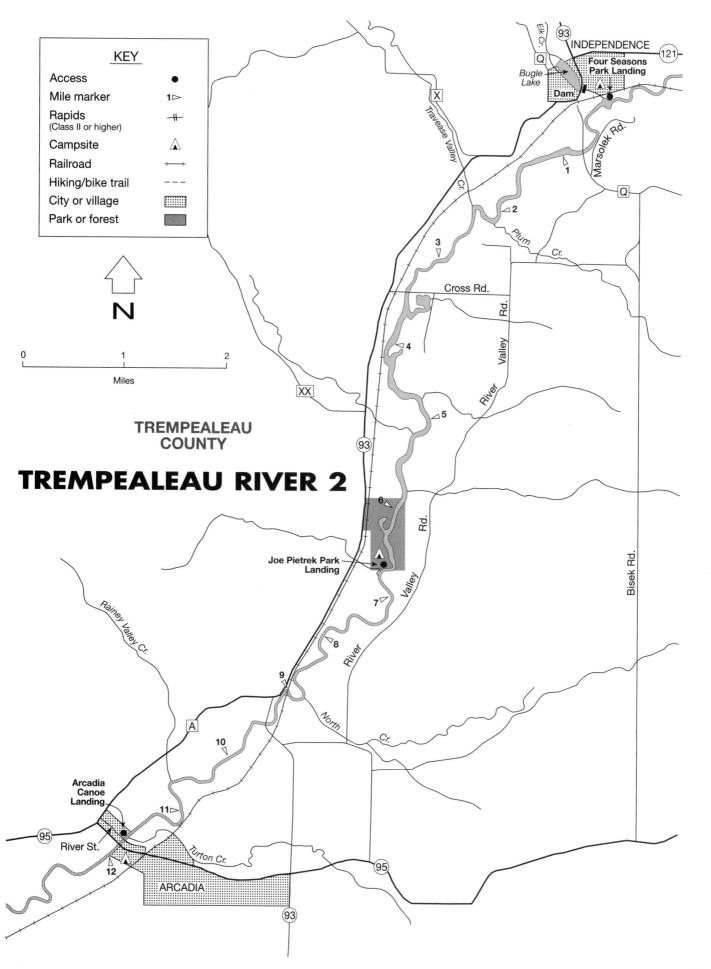

TREMPEALEAU RIVER 2

TREMPEALEAU COUNTY

KEY

Access   ●

Mile marker   1▷

Rapids (Class II or higher)

Campsite   ⚠

Railroad

Hiking/bike trail   - - - -

City or village

Park or forest

N

0   1   2

Miles

INDEPENDENCE

Four Seasons Park Landing

Bugle Lake

Dam

Elk Cr.

Travease Valley Cr.

Marsolek Rd.

Plum Cr.

Cross Rd.

River Valley Rd.

Joe Pietrek Park Landing

Valley Rd.

Bisek Rd.

North Cr.

Rainey Valley Cr.

Arcadia Canoe Landing

River St.

Turton Cr.

ARCADIA

93

121

Q

Q

X

XX

93

A

95

95

93

143

WAUPACA RIVER 1
Amherst to County DD (10 Miles)

Still isolated, winding, intimate, and clear, the Tomorrow becomes the Waupaca River downstream from Amherst. Not for beginning paddlers or those who have a low tolerance for occasional obstructions, this section requires some maneuvering around, over, and through downed trees and limbs. You're also likely to encounter wire strung from bank to bank in a couple of places. Only 30–40 feet wide, the river flows briskly over a sand-and-gravel bottom, often serving up riffles and low-level rapids, including an exciting 3-foot drop. Few houses are encountered, but there are numerous bridges. Rather long for most canoeists, this trip can easily be shortened by using alternate accesses.

"Are we having fun yet?" A carry-over on the upper Waupaca.

Paddlers who also enjoy off-road bicycling will be heartened by the development of a new biking and hiking route through the area. Beginning at Plover and following the old Green Bay and Western right-of-way, the Tomorrow River Trail will cross the river just north of Amherst and continue all the way to Manawa. Work began late in 1999. A connecting path will link the new bike route to the Green Circle Trail at Stevens Point.

For **camping** and **water levels**, see Tomorrow River.

The **shuttle route** (6.4 miles) for the full trip goes south from Amherst on County A, then east on County D to the intersection with County DD (where the take-out bridge is located).

Gradient is 10 feet per mile.

Put in at Nelson Park in Amherst, downstream-right from the County A bridge. Lower your boat into the water from a low stone wall along the riverbank. A public parking lot is located nearby. Soon after the put-in, the County V bridge appears, immediately followed by some rock debris where there's a small drop and wave train. One hundred yards later, after a short S-curve, a graceful, arching railroad bridge dating back to 1913 appears. Then, on the south edge of Amherst, Highway 10 crosses the river on a small concrete bridge. Later in the trip, Highway 10 will cross the Waupaca two more times, but on much larger bridges with long, square conduits to paddle through.

The environs now become very remote-feeling, with dense woods and few openings. Good riffles begin early in the trip and continue all day, with boulders scattered here and there. Paddling is necessarily slow because of the frequent need to wend your way through fallen trees and limbs. Like most of the bridges on this section, the County A span is an older structure. The river can be accessed here, downstream-right, where there's a short path to the bank and some room alongside the road to park several cars. Immediately downstream the river splits around a wooded island.

The next bridge, on Keener Road, is small and provides a thrill for paddlers, especially those who don't know what's coming. The river makes an abrupt left turn, just before the bridge, then drops 3 feet. Find the tongue in the middle and ride the wave train to the pool below.

A long, twisting stretch follows, eventually arcing twice under Highway 10 at the largest and most modern bridges of the trip. In between the two bridges is an attractive wayside on the right, a pleasant place for lunch or an alternate access. Toilets, picnic tables, and parking are provided. Some particularly long riffles are found in the area of the Highway 10 bridges, together with a bed of giant boulders that is very picturesque and easy to paddle through. Upstream and downstream from Otto Road (a small concrete structure with two metal culverts) the river is extremely riffly, with lots of boulders. Later a home precedes County T, where the bridge is an attractive stone structure with metal culverts. A series of bends now leads to Spring Creek—a significant tributary with a log cabin at its mouth—on the right. After Spring Creek, the river is a little wider for a while, with fewer obstructions. Soon a large home appears on the right near a small private bridge.

In the final leg of the trip the best riffles of the day occur: the gradient is a little steeper, there are more boulders, and the current is swifter. **Take out** about 100 feet upstream-right from the County DD bridge at a boulder-strewn pasture. This is private land, so you should obtain permission. Taking out downstream-right from County DD at Stedman County Park is also possible but not recommended; a couple of steep paths lead down to the river near some old abutments, but accessing the river here necessitates taking out in the middle of a rapid.

Other trips. The following section, from County DD to County Q, is much like this stretch: winding, riffly, and wooded, with many limbs and trees to get around and over. The next recommended section begins farther downstream at County Q.

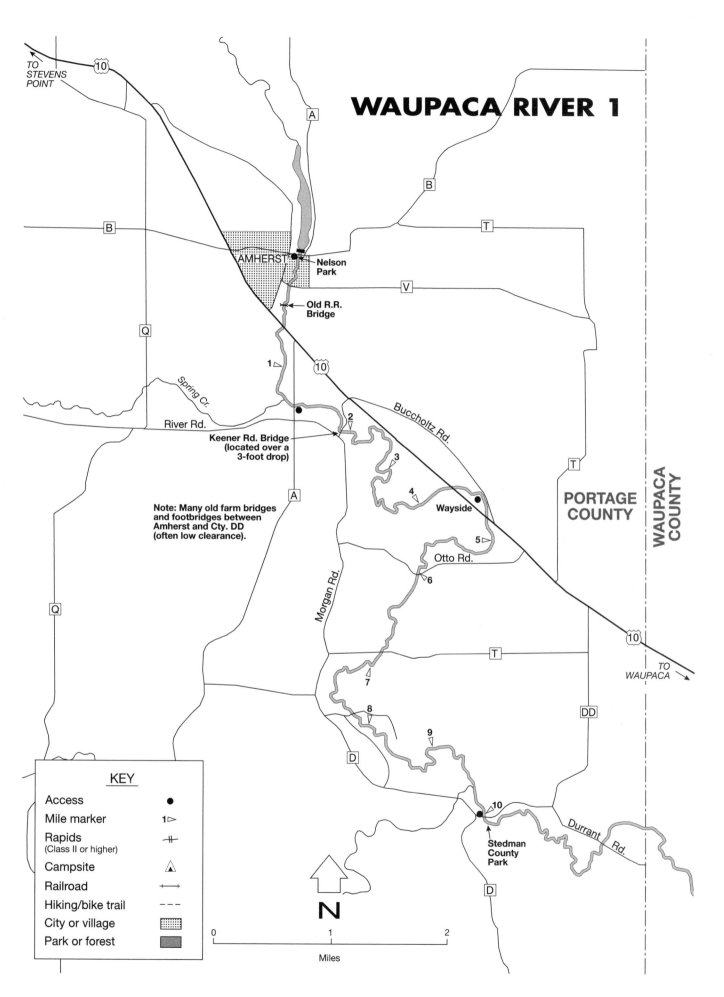

WAUPACA RIVER 1

TO STEVENS POINT

AMHERST

Nelson Park

Old R.R. Bridge

Spring Cr.

River Rd.

Keener Rd. Bridge (located over a 3-foot drop)

Buccholtz Rd.

Note: Many old farm bridges and footbridges between Amherst and Cty. DD (often low clearance).

Wayside

Otto Rd.

Morgan Rd.

PORTAGE COUNTY

WAUPACA COUNTY

TO WAUPACA

DD

Durrant Rd.

Stedman County Park

KEY

Access	●
Mile marker	1▷
Rapids (Class II or higher)	╫
Campsite	▲
Railroad	┼
Hiking/bike trail	- - -
City or village	▦
Park or forest	▬

N

0   1   2

Miles

WAUPACA RIVER 2
County Q to Brainards Bridge Park (7.2 Miles)

Covered Bridges of Wisconsin

Throughout the 1800s, thousands of wooden covered bridges were constructed over the rivers and streams of America. These picturesque structures served a variety of purposes: mainly protecting the often-intricate trusses of the bridge from the elements, but also affording shelter to travelers during inclement weather, and even providing an excellent meeting place for special occasions. Only a thousand of these scenic spans have survived, principally in Pennsylvania, Ohio, Indiana, Vermont, New Hampshire, and Oregon. Countless others have been lost to decay, replacement by modern structures, and vandalism.

Because its population was relatively late in developing, Wisconsin was not on the cusp of the nineteenth-century covered-bridge boom. Nevertheless, an estimated 60 covered bridges were built here—only one of which survives near Cedarburg. The best known were the massive structures that spanned the Wisconsin River at Mosinee, Portage, Boscobel, and Bridgeport. Six covered bridges crossed the Baraboo River, and there were three over the Rock. Other notable structures crossed the Sheboygan, Sugar, Chippewa, Black, and La Crosse Rivers.

Paddling under Covered Bridge Road on the Waupaca.

This pleasant trip on the Waupaca offers quietwater, riffles and rapids, boulder beds, good scenery, and a rare covered bridge. Demanding less exertion than the narrower, sometimes-obstructed section upstream (Amherst to County DD), this part of the river ends on an exciting note with Class I rapids in Brainards Bridge Park. Although considerably wider and thus less prone to deadfall, the river after County Q is nevertheless mostly wooded. Highway 10 comes alongside the river a couple of times, and there are some brief open areas.

The meaning of the name of the river is difficult to pin down, but all of the options are interesting. The Native American word *waupaca* is variously translated as "tomorrow," "place of clear water," "white, sandy bottom," "place to wait for deer," and "white earth." A local Potawatomi leader named Sam Waupaca (also spelled Waupuca) is reputed to have dissuaded his people from attacking white settlers.

For **camping** and **water levels**, see the Tomorrow River.

The **shuttle route** (5.7 miles) goes north on County Q, east on Highway 10, east on Highway 49 into Waupaca, east on Hillcrest Drive, north on Morton Street, west on North Street, and north on Bailey Street to Brainards Bridge Park.

Gradient is 6.2 feet per mile.

Put in from a grassy bank at the County Q bridge, downstream-left. Nearby is a pull-off with room to park a number of cars. For a while the river winds through a rather open area with grassy shorelines, light tree cover, and a couple of small riffles. Directly beneath some power lines, there's an ingenious little footbridge rigged from metal cable. The water is clear, flowing over a sand-and-gravel bottom with scattered boulders and occasional small, grassy islands. As the river widens to 50 feet, the setting is quite attractive, with many oaks and pines.

A few houses appear in the approach to Highway 10, where there's a rocky rapid directly beneath the bridge. Many big boulders continue in the streambed downstream from the bridge. Downed trees are occasionally seen along the sides, but the river's width makes them no problem. At one point, where Highway 10 is nearby, a number of

Class 1 rapids at Brainards Bridge Park.

houses appear on the right. In this area a small concrete bridge crosses the river, with a little drop and some waves under it, and an arched, old concrete bridge soon follows. Periodic riffles continue, but the streambed becomes less boulder-strewn. Downriver, a road runs close by on the left.

After the surroundings become heavily wooded again, the river constricts and flows briefly through a small boulder bed. Another sequence of riffles is found at an island, and shortly thereafter there's a small drop and wave train beneath a bridge.

As the city of Waupaca nears, Highway 10 can be seen on the right, and soon a lovely covered bridge appears—a modern evocation of the charming wooden spans that were common in the 1800s. After the bridge, houses continue on the left for a while, then the setting becomes wild again. Pleasant riffles and boulder gardens follow the bridge, then a series of Class I rapids as the river wends its way through small islands.

Widening to 45 feet, the river is placid for a long stretch. When riffles begin again at an island, you are nearing Brainards Bridge Park. At the park the river drops through boulder beds on both sides of a couple of islands, which are connected with the right shoreline by two lovely little footbridges. **Take out** on the bank in the park, upstream-right from the small one-lane bridge. The attractive 19-acre park has picnic facilities, toilets, and parking.

Soon after Brainards Bridge the river slows as it enters the backup from a large power dam (located in Waupaca off Elm Street between Highway 49 and Water Street). Immediately before the Water Street bridge (also in Waupaca) there's a very dangerous low-head dam. After Waupaca the river is augmented by the Crystal River, then flows southeastly through Weyauwega to the Wolf River 3 miles north of Fremont.

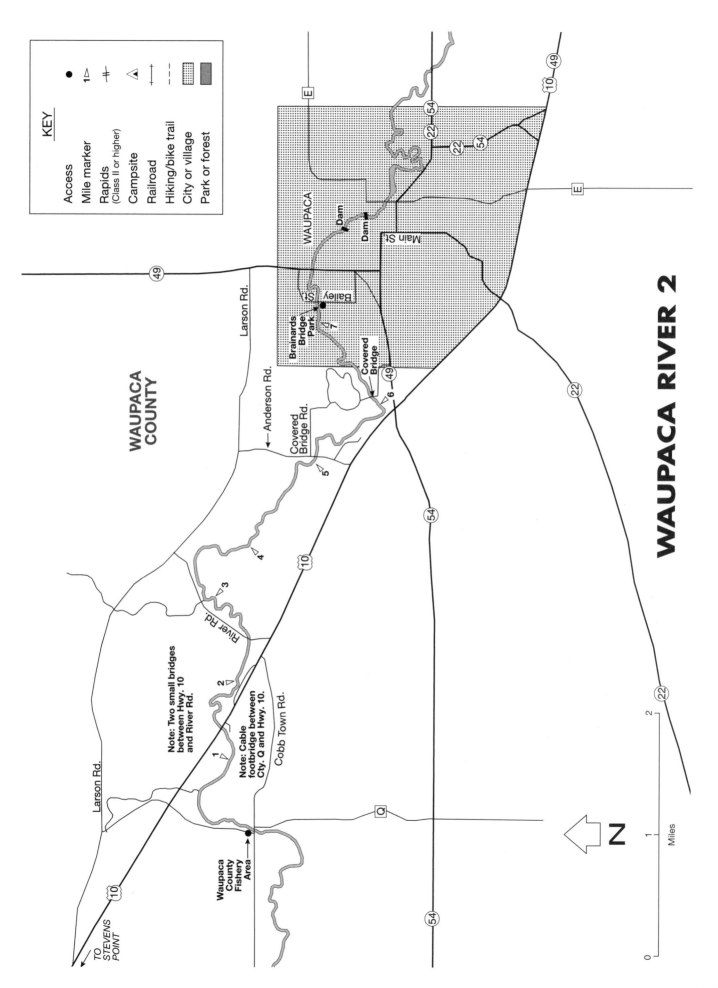

WAUPACA RIVER 2

KEY

- ● Access
- 1△ Mile marker
- ⊣ Rapids (Class II or higher)
- ◁ Campsite
- ┼ Railroad
- ┊ Hiking/bike trail
- ▦ City or village
- ▪ Park or forest

WAUPACA COUNTY

WAUPACA

Larson Rd.

Anderson Rd.

Covered Bridge Rd.

River Rd.

Larson Rd.

Cobb Town Rd.

Main St.

Bailey St.

Dam

Dam

Covered Bridge

Brainards Bridge Park

Note: Two small bridges between Hwy. 10 and River Rd.

Note: Cable footbridge between Cty. Q and Hwy. 10.

Waupaca County Fishery Area

TO STEVENS POINT

N

Miles

0   1   2

49   10   54   22   E   Q

147

WISCONSIN RIVER 1
Castle Rock Lake to Plainville (14 Miles)

After a humble origin as a small stream near the Michigan border, the Wisconsin flows south, then west for 430 miles before joining the Mississippi near Prairie du Chien. Augmented along the way by many tributaries, it drains a third of the state and is interrupted 26 times by hydroelectric dams. From the first dam (at Eagle River) to the last (at Prairie du Sac), much of the river involves flowage paddling, especially in the stretch from Wausau to Castle Rock Lake. Even in the often-dammed upper river, however, there are many pleasant places for canoeists and kayakers, and the free-flowing, final 92 miles of the Lower Wisconsin make it one of the most popular paddling destinations in the Midwest.

The first four recommended sections are in the long stretch between the last three dams. The availability of many accesses makes it possible for paddlers to plan trips that suit their preferences, skill level, and time available. It's just as easy, for example, to find short segments that can be done in two or three hours as it is to design two- or three-day trips involving camping along the river.

This trip, which can readily be shortened by using one of the intermediate landings, features sandy beaches and sandbars, numerous islands, and a long series of gorgeous rock formations. Accesses are excellent.

Camping is plentiful in the area, including Rocky Arbor State Park 1.5 miles northwest of Wisconsin Dells (608-254-8001) and Juneau County Castle Rock Park (608-847-7089) just west of the lake. Several campgrounds are located alongside the river between Castle Rock Lake and Wisconsin Dells: Point Bluff Resort (608-253-6181), Castle Rock Resort and Campground (608-847-6269), River Bay Resort and Campground (608-254-7193 or 800-443-1112), and Holiday Shores Campground and Resort (608-254-2717). Paddlers often camp on sandbars, beaches, and islands, but must be aware of the dangers of rising water and must respect private property.

Canoe rentals and shuttles are available at Point Bluff Resort at the Highway 82 bridge (608-253-6181), Wisconsin Dells Trout Farm and Canoe Trips near Plainville (608-589-5353), River's Edge Resort at Wisconsin Dells (608-254-7707), North Country Canoes near Castle Rock Lake (608-847-6649), and Country Cruisin' Canoes east of Mauston (608-847-2663).

The **shuttle route** (13.7 miles) from the Castle Rock Dam goes east on Edgewood Drive, south on County Z, east on Highway 82, south on Highway 13, and west on Gem Court a short distance to the boat landing.

Gradient is 1.4 feet per mile.

For **water levels,** check the gauge near Wisconsin Dells (#05404000) on the USGS Web site. See "Water Levels" in the introduction.

Put in at the canoe landing downstream-left from the Castle Rock Dam. Separate from the concrete boat ramp, the nearby canoe landing is on a creek that quickly empties into the river 100 yards below the dam. Big, sandy beaches are apparent from the beginning as the river heads left, then straightens. Both shorelines are densely wooded and wild. In a long, gentle right arc, County Z and some cabins can be seen along the left for a while, then the environs become quite wild again. Islands begin appearing when the river bends left.

There are no buildings until Castle Rock Resort and Campground appears on the right, opposite an island. The massive sandstone "outlier" or "sea stack" for which the resort is named is located here, but you can't see its exposed rock formations from the river. Castle Rock can be viewed by taking out at the resort and walking a couple hundred yards to it, or by driving to it via Highway 82 and Twenty-sixth Avenue. The resort landing is a good alternate access.

Islands become more numerous in the long, straight stretch to the Highway 82 bridge, where Point Bluff and an undercut cliff rise on the left. Two hundred yards upstream-left is Point Bluff Resort, which offers canoe trips on the whole stretch from the lake to Wisconsin Dells. Canoeists may use the landing for a fee. Downstream, there are even more islands. The narrow channels are fun, but when the water is low you must choose your course carefully to find sufficient depth over the sandy bottom. Once again the surroundings are wild.

Suddenly a huge, beautiful cliff—layered, undercut, and topped with coniferous trees—looms on the right. This massive formation marks the mouth of the Lemonweir River. Paddle 100 yards up the Lemonweir and take a look at the excellent access (Two Rivers Public Landing)—a good **take-out** or put-in for a shorter trip.

In the straight, narrower stretch that follows, wooded bluffs and beautiful rock formations are found on both sides, making this a strikingly scenic part of the river. At one point, a private boat ramp (off Sixtieth Street) appears on the right, quickly followed by a private dock on the left. After the bluffs and cliffs end, islands resume, together with cabins and homes.

When you come to a low, rocky shelf on the left, alongside several cabins, turn left into the easy-to-miss inlet. At this point, the river is approaching an immense, lake-like wide spot that leads to the Upper Dells. Follow the inlet channel around to the right, past the houses of Plainville, and **take out** at the gravel landing on the left.

WISCONSIN RIVER 1

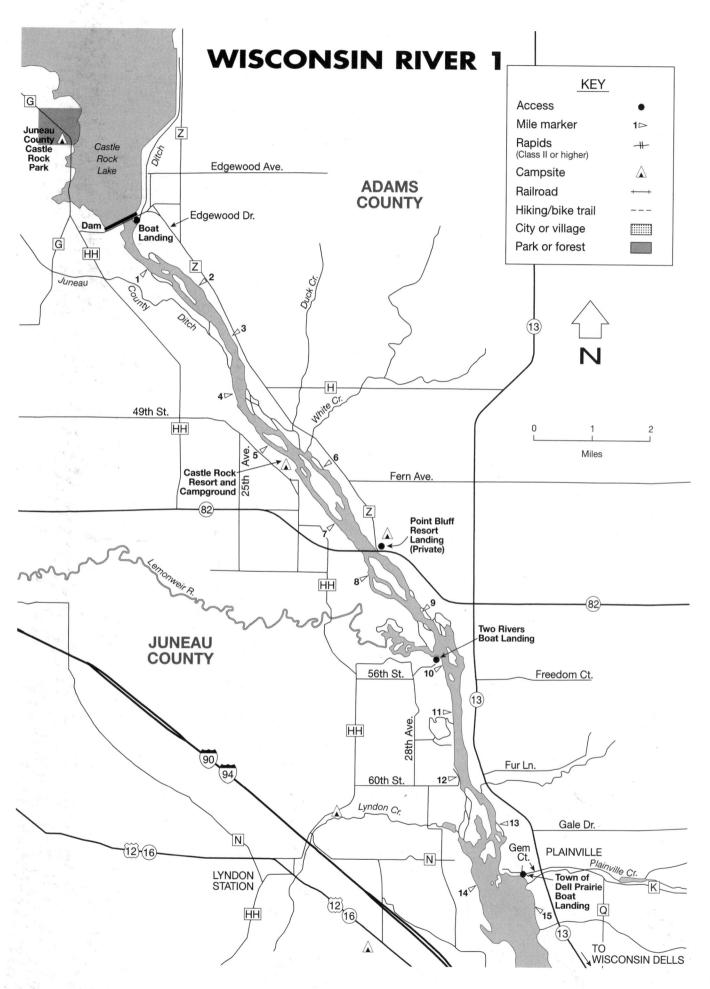

KEY

Access	●
Mile marker	1▷
Rapids (Class II or higher)	─╫─
Campsite	△
Railroad	─┼─
Hiking/bike trail	- - -
City or village	▦
Park or forest	▨

N

Juneau County Castle Rock Park

Castle Rock Lake

Ditch

Edgewood Ave.

Edgewood Dr.

Dam

Boat Landing

ADAMS COUNTY

Juneau

County Ditch

Duck Cr.

White Cr.

H

13

0   1   2
Miles

49th St.

HH

25th Ave.

Castle Rock Resort and Campground

Fern Ave.

82

Z

Point Bluff Resort Landing (Private)

Lemonweir R.

JUNEAU COUNTY

HH

82

Two Rivers Boat Landing

56th St.

Freedom Ct.

13

28th Ave.

11

HH

90 94

60th St.

12

Fur Ln.

Lyndon Cr.

13

Gale Dr.

12 16

N

Gem Ct.

PLAINVILLE

Plainville Cr.

LYNDON STATION

N

Town of Dell Prairie Boat Landing

K

Q

HH

14

12 16

15

13

TO WISCONSIN DELLS

WISCONSIN RIVER 2
Plainville to Wisconsin Dells (7 Miles)

In this relatively short section paddlers experience the extremes of a lake-like widening of the river and a long, narrow, rocky gorge. The latter—the spectacular Upper Dells of the Wisconsin—is extremely dangerous in high water, and should never be paddled by inexperienced boaters at any water level. Big tour boats and other motorized craft create hazardous wakes in the last 4 miles of the section. At the height of tourist season, as many as 5,000 people a day view the Dells from large motor launches and amphibious "ducks." Indeed, for most people the best way to see the Dells is from a tour boat. For experienced paddlers, a good time to venture onto the water is for a "crack-of-dawn" trip before the tour boats get started.

There are numerous accesses, allowing you to paddle all or part of the 7 miles. For skilled paddlers, the trip through the Upper Dells is a remarkable experience. A corridor along both sides of the river is owned by the DNR, and the rugged grandeur of the Dells has been preserved in a natural state. (Please bear in mind, however, that much of the riverside is still privately owned.)

For **camping,** see Wisconsin River 1. Other campgrounds in the area include Mirror Lake State Park (608-254-2333), Stand Rock Campground (608-253-2169), Wisconsin Dells KOA (800-254-4177 or 608-254-4177), and Eagle Flats Campground (608-254-2764). All are within 5 miles of Wisconsin Dells.

For **canoe rental** and **water levels,** see Wisconsin River 1. Glacier Valley Wilderness Adventures offers canoe/kayak trips on this section (608-493-2075).

The **shuttle route** (approximately 8 miles) from Plainville goes east on Gem Court, south on Highway 13, and south on River Road into Wisconsin Dells to the boat landing at the end of Indiana Avenue.

Gradient is 1.4 feet per mile.

If you wish to paddle the wide, 3-mile-long expanse that extends from Plainville to Witches Gulch, **put in** at the public landing maintained by the township of Dell Prairie. (To get there, go west on Gem Court a quarter mile off Highway 13.) Part of the "lake" paddling can be avoided by putting in farther downstream (for a fee) at the River Bay Resort and Campground on river-right or Holiday Shores Campground and Resort on river-left. The other option (an excellent one) is to **put in** at a pull-off alongside County N near the head of Blackhawk Island. From here you can paddle a clockwise route around the island and back again (thus, no shuttle), or continue downriver. The "old" (right) channel of Blackhawk Island is beautiful but too shallow for tour boats.

As the river spreads out near Plainville, Louis Bluff dominates the right shoreline. Named after Frenchman Louis Dupless, who settled here in 1846, this huge wooded prominence is fronted by lovely cliffs along the river. The huge "bay" in this part of the river was caused by backup from the dam constructed at Wisconsin Dells in 1908.

Farther downstream on the right are the Palisades, towering rock formations eroded by wind and water. They signal the beginning of the Upper Dells. Nearby—you can't see it from the river—is Stand Rock, made famous by photographer H. H. Bennett in the 1860s. On the other side of the river is Witches Gulch, a beautiful side canyon that is entered between two soaring cliffs known as Signal Point and Sunset Cliff. Like Stand Rock, Witches Gulch is leased from the DNR by Dells Boat Company.

After Witches Gulch the river narrows tremendously, with rock walls on both sides. Rood's Glen, another side canyon, enters on the left, with Steamboat Rock at its mouth. Note the Canadian hemlocks on top of the cliffs. Farther downstream, just before Cold Water Canyon on the left, a fallen rock shelf called the Giant's Shield lies near the waterline. Continuing down the main left channel of Blackhawk Island (the Narrows), the river is as little as 52 feet wide; swift current, powerful eddies, and big waves make this a ferocious place in high water. Lumbermen who floated rafts down the Wisconsin in the logging era understandably feared the Dells.

As you paddle through the sharp right turn at Devil's Elbow, look for an inscription on the river-right wall—"LEROY GATES, DELLS AND RIVER PILOT, 1849–1858"—carved there by a famous raftsman of the logging days. Soon the river briefly widens at the tail of Blackhawk Island, passes Blackhawk's Profile and Chimney Rock on the left, then narrows again at the Jaws (between Romance Cliff on the right and High Rock on the left). After the Jaws, where the depth is 120 feet, the river widens once more and you begin to see buildings downstream.

Before the river heads right, Crandalls Bay enters on the left. To **take out** at the municipal boat landing, paddle up the bay to the concrete ramp on your right.

The landing is alongside River Road at the end of Indiana Street, with an adjacent parking lot. If you prefer, you can paddle past the mouth of the bay, go under the railroad and highway bridges, and **take out** at the portage trail path immediately upstream-left from the warning buoys for the dam. From here, carry your boat(s) up to the parking lot alongside Finnegan Avenue.

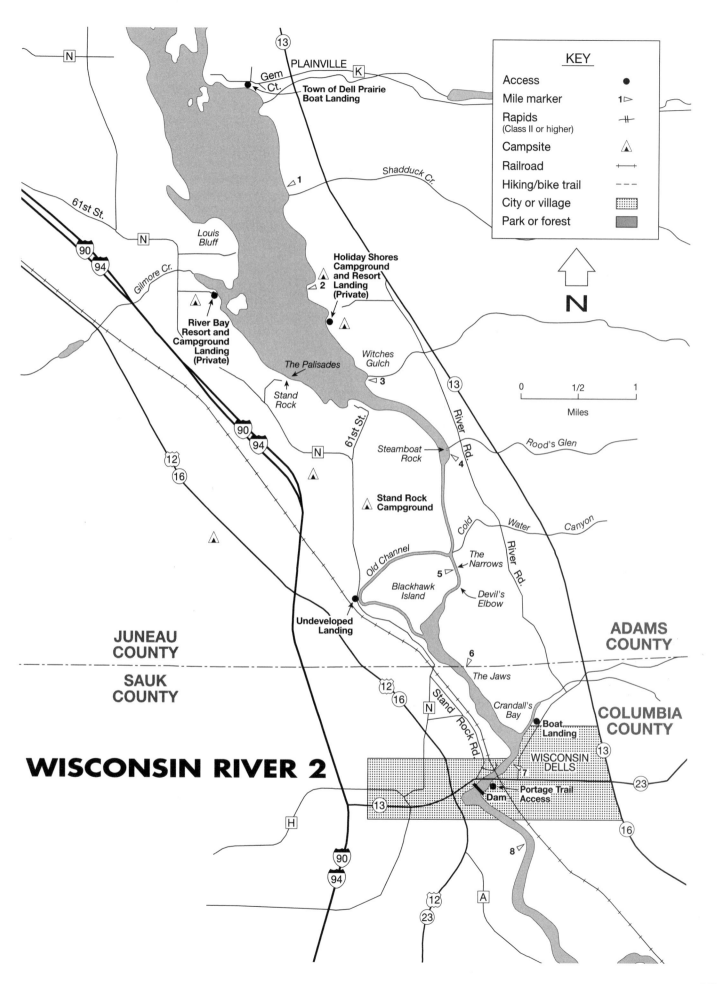

KEY

Access ●

Mile marker 1▷

Rapids ─╫─
(Class II or higher)

Campsite ▲

Railroad ─┼─

Hiking/bike trail ─ ─ ─

City or village

Park or forest

N

0   1/2   1

Miles

PLAINVILLE

Gem Ct.

Town of Dell Prairie
Boat Landing

Shadduck Cr.

Louis
Bluff

Gilmore Cr.

61st St.

Holiday Shores
Campground
and Resort
Landing
(Private)

River Bay
Resort and
Campground
Landing
(Private)

The Palisades

Stand
Rock

Witches
Gulch

Rood's Glen

Steamboat
Rock

Cold   Water   Canyon

Stand Rock
Campground

Old Channel

The
Narrows

Blackhawk
Island

River Rd.

Devil's
Elbow

Undeveloped
Landing

JUNEAU
COUNTY

SAUK
COUNTY

ADAMS
COUNTY

The Jaws

Crandall's
Bay

Boat
Landing

COLUMBIA
COUNTY

WISCONSIN
DELLS

WISCONSIN RIVER 2

Dam

Portage Trail
Access

Stand Rock Rd.

WISCONSIN RIVER 3
Wisconsin Dells to Pine Island (15.5 Miles)

After the hydroelectric dam at Wisconsin Dells, fantastic rock formations—known as the Lower Dells ever since the construction of the first dam in 1859—continue for a while. The original dam was a notorious obstacle for river pilots during the logging years. If they survived the tight quarters of the Upper Dells, they still had to get their rafts past the turbulent 60-foot slot of the dam; many perished in the attempt. Today's dam, completed in 1908, raised the river 20 feet upstream and covered part of the intricate formations of the Upper Dells.

Because large tour boats also frequent the Lower Dells, paddlers must be prepared to deal with wakes. Except for one brief Narrows, however, the river isn't nearly as tight below the dam as above it. In the first 4 miles, cliffs periodically line the shore, but the most memorable feature of the Lower Dells is the Rocky Islands area, a series of unique, towering structures that have been cut off from the mainland. Downstream, the surroundings are unpopulated and wild, with an excellent intermediate landing for shorter trips. There are many sandy beaches and islands. Sightings of eagles, herons, turkey vultures, hawks, migrating waterfowl, and turtles are frequent.

Rock formations in the Wisconsin Dells are awesome.

For **camping,** see Wisconsin River 1 and 2. Also available is riverside camping at the Fisherman's Luck 7 miles downstream (608-254-8082), the Dell Boo Campground 3 miles south of Lake Delton (608-356-5898), Yogi Bear's Camp-Resort near Lake Delton (608-254-2568 or 800-462-9644), Teepee Park Campground 2 miles southwest of Wisconsin Dells (608-253-3122), Bonanza Campground 1 mile south of Wisconsin Dells (608-254-8124), Arrowhead Resort Campground 4 miles west of Wisconsin Dells (608-254-7344), and several Portage-area campgrounds (see Fox River 1).

Canoe rental and shuttles are available at River's Edge Resort about 2 miles downstream from the dam (608-254-7707).

The **shuttle route** (13.5 miles) goes north on Finnegan Avenue in Wisconsin Dells, west across the river on Highway 23/13, southeast on County A, east on County T, and east on Levee Road.

Gradient is 1.3 feet per mile.

For **water levels,** see Wisconsin River 1.

Put in at the sandy shoreline several hundred yards downstream-left from the dam. To get there, go south on Finnegan Avenue (the first street east of the Highway 23/13 bridge) past the powerhouse entrance road to the fishermen's parking area. From here, carry your boat(s) down a long path to the bank. An alternative **put-in** is 2 miles downstream-right at the River's Edge, where you can put in for a fee.

Below the dam, the river is a couple hundred feet wide, with lovely cliffs and sandy beaches on both sides. Not far downstream, on the left, is Pulpit Rock; at its foot lies the Baby Grand Piano, a huge rocky shelf that has fallen to the water's edge. Farther downstream, the strikingly beautiful sandstone formations are called the Painted Rocks because of their different colors caused by oxidation.

Just upstream from the Narrows, where cliffs are close on both sides, you can see on the right some of the old stone foundations from the village of Newport—bypassed by the railroad in the 1800s and superseded by Wisconsin Dells (then called Kilbourn City). Immediately after the Narrows is the bridged outlet from Dell Creek/Lake Delton, on the right. As the river heads left, three resorts follow quickly on the right. River's Edge has a good landing.

A USGS gauging station can be seen on the river-right cliff as you approach the Rocky Islands. First to appear are the Sugar Bowl and Grotto Rock, near the right side of the river; you can paddle between them. The Inkwells follow on the left, and the largest of the islands—Lone Rock—is several hundred yards farther downstream, also on the left. Beautifully layered and undercut, each of the tree-topped islands is like a work of art. Tour boats usually don't go very far past the Rocky Islands.

Having completed its course through the Lower Dells, the river now makes a big left bend. The shoreline is heavily wooded, with frequent sandy beaches. In the long right bend that follows, there's a high wooded bluff on the left, with occasional houses. After the river straightens, an excellent asphalt landing appears on the left (off Fox Run Road); this makes a good **take-out** for a relatively short trip.

A few cabins are seen in the left bend that comes next, and coniferous trees begin to appear. When the river straightens out, a large sign on the left bank announces the Fisherman's Luck Resort, where there's a riverside restaurant and campground. Downstream is the first island—long and wooded—of the trip. Huge sandbars and beaches become more common.

Many islands follow, some with "No Trespassing" signs on them, and more cabins are situated on the right in a left bend. Channels are pleasantly narrow when islands are clumped together. Eventually, the **take-out** appears on river-right in the main (right) channel of Pine Island, just downstream from some power lines (the only ones of the trip). The landing is across from the head of a small island.

WISCONSIN RIVER 3

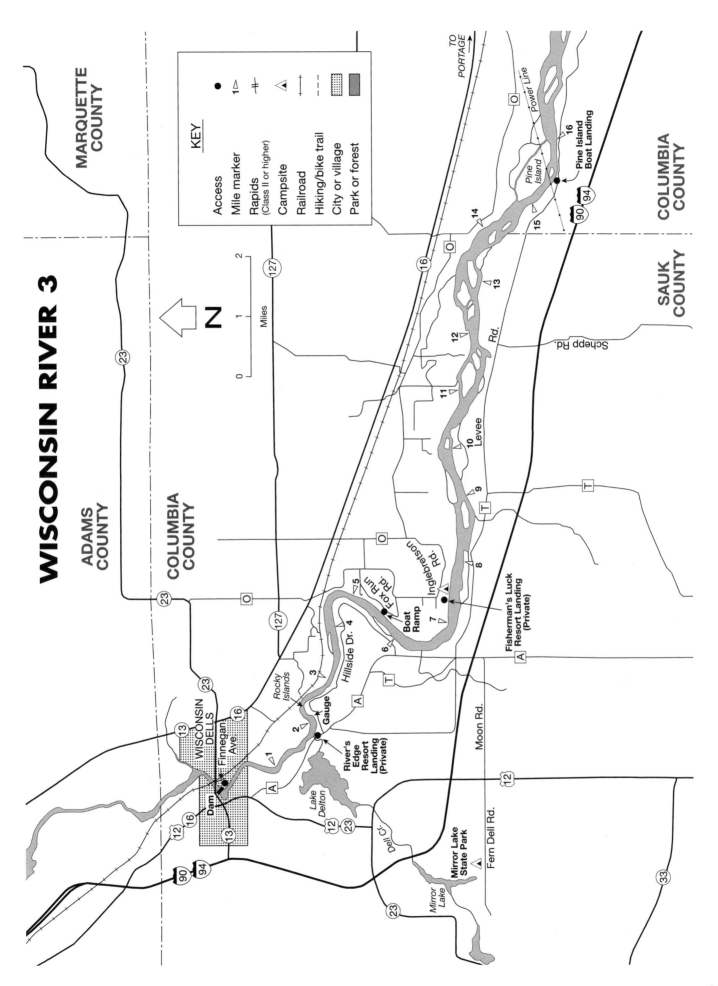

MARQUETTE COUNTY

ADAMS COUNTY

COLUMBIA COUNTY

COLUMBIA COUNTY

SAUK COUNTY

N

Miles

0   1   2

KEY

Access ●

Mile marker △1

Rapids ‡ (Class II or higher)

Campsite △

Railroad ┼┼┼

Hiking/bike trail ┊┊┊

City or village

Park or forest

TO PORTAGE

Power Line

Pine Island Boat Landing

16

Pine Island

14

15

13

12

Schepp Rd.

11

Levee

10

9

T

8

Ingleberson Rd.

Fisherman's Luck Resort Landing (Private)

7

Boat Ramp

Fox Run Rd.

6

5

Hillside Dr. 4

Rocky Islands

3

Gauge

2

1

River's Edge Resort Landing (Private)

WISCONSIN DELLS

Finnegan Ave.

Dam

Lake Delton

Dell Cr.

Mirror Lake

Mirror Lake State Park

Fern Dell Rd.

Moon Rd.

WISCONSIN RIVER 4
Pine Island to Dekorra (12.7 Miles)

Located downstream from the magnificent Dells and upstream from a long impoundment known as Lake Wisconsin, this section is loaded with sandbars and islands. About halfway through the trip the river flows past the historic city of Portage, where a boat ramp provides an excellent alternate access. Paddlers who wish to spend two or three days on the river canoe-camp on sandbars and on riverside beaches, starting as far upriver as Wisconsin Dells or the Fox Run Road landing. The setting is mostly wild but with no dramatic highlights. Accesses are first-rate.

For nearby **camping,** see Wisconsin River 3 and Fox River 1. Camping is also available at Devil's Lake State Park 15 miles west of Dekorra (608-356-8301), and Wunder Er'de Campground 6 miles west of Poynette (608-635-2059).

Canoe rentals and shuttles are available at Judd's Marina in Dekorra (608-635-4800) and River's Edge Resort south of Wisconsin Dells (608-254-7707).

The **shuttle route** (15.6 miles) from the Pine Island Landing goes east on Levee Road/Fairfield Street, east on Highway 33, south on Highway 51/16, west on County VJ, and west on County V to Dekorra. The portion of the shuttle route on Levee Road/Fairfield Street is quite attractive: narrow and canopied with trees.

Gradient is 1.6 feet per mile.

For **water level**s, see Wisconsin River 1.

Put in on river-right at the Pine Island Landing—part of the Pine Island State Wildlife Area along the river. A short access road leads over the levee to a sand-and-gravel parking lot near the landing, which is just downstream from a set of power lines.

In the 5 miles to Highway 78/39, there are sandy shoreline and forested banks everywhere as the river curves gently toward Portage. Occasionally through a break in the tree cover you can see the

Portage: a city proud of its voyageur heritage. The Fox and Wisconsin Rivers are only 1.25 miles apart here.

level, grassy top of the levee that runs 9 miles upstream from Portage. Islands aren't as frequent as in the 6 miles before Pine Island, but are still plentiful.

The river is quite wide in the approach to Highway 78/39. Several hundred yards downstream-left from the bridge is the Sunset Park Landing, tucked away behind an island 100 yards upstream from power lines crossing the river. There's nearby parking for several cars. To get to this excellent alternate access, go north on Pierce Street just north of the Highway 33 bridge, then west on West Conant Street 0.7 mile to the landing.

As soon as you clear the landing, the houses of Portage begin to appear on the left. At Portage, a strip of land only 1.25 miles wide separates the Wisconsin from the nearby Fox River. For centuries, Native Americans took advantage of the rivers' proximity in their travels from the Great Lakes area to the Mississippi, and it was here that the Portage Canal was dug in the 1800s. The locks at the two ends of the canal have been permanently closed, but the canal is still in fairly good condition and makes an interesting visit.

Downstream from the Highway 33 bridges a huge island splits the river, the main flow obviously being on the right. Stone riprap lines the left channel along Highway 51/16, but the main channel is deeply forested. Immediately after the island a radio tower appears on the left. Then, as a very long right bend begins, the two smokestacks of a power plant can be seen in the distance. Huge sandbars, beaches, and a large wooded island follow.

Cabins begin on the right alongside the big island and continue for a while. As you approach the power plant (on the left), the river is quite wide, with a few small islands. Downstream from the power plant a wooded bluff rises on the right, with a house on top. Nearby, the Baraboo River, a major tributary, enters alongside an island.

Huge Lib Cross Island follows, where the right channel is navigable only in high water. Farther down on the left shore is the concrete intake building where water is drawn from the river to serve as coolant for the Columbia power plant, then discharged into Columbia Lake nearby. The mouth of Duck Creek is just upstream from the intake. Islands now create slim channels as the river heads to the right for a while, making this a very pretty part of the river, with low banks and dense woods.

As the river straightens out, a tall wooded mound appears in the distance. At the base of the bluff the river has carved beautiful sandstone cliffs—craggy and undercut—that continue for several hundred yards to the public landing at Dekorra. **Take out** at the river-left boat ramp. A parking lot and toilets are located nearby. Dekorra Park (with picnic facilities and toilets) is a short distance downstream. A few hundred yards farther, also on the left, are Hooker's Resort and Judd's Marina.

After Dekorra the Wisconsin remains riverlike for 3 more miles, passes under the Interstate 90/94/39 bridges, and then broadens out into Lake Wisconsin. The 15-mile impoundment is a product of the hydroelectric dam at Prairie du Sac, the final dam on the river. At a relatively slim part of the lake, a popular and longstanding ferry crosses the river at Merrimac.

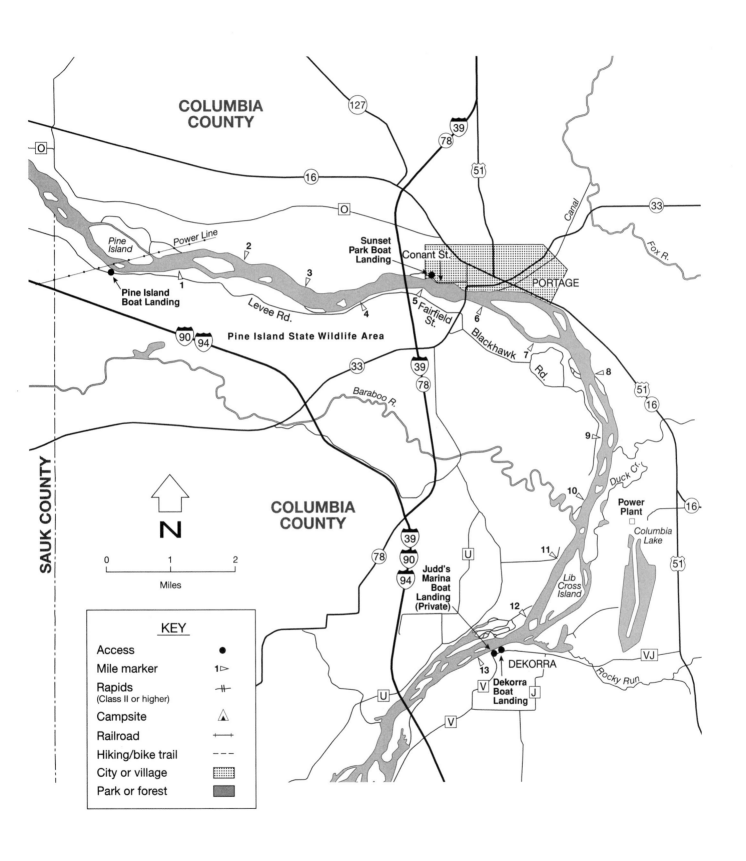

COLUMBIA COUNTY

Pine Island

Pine Island Boat Landing

Power Line

Levee Rd.

Pine Island State Wildlife Area

SAUK COUNTY

COLUMBIA COUNTY

Baraboo R.

Sunset Park Boat Landing

Conant St.

PORTAGE

Fairfield St.

Blackhawk Rd.

Canal

Fox R.

Duck Cr.

Power Plant

Columbia Lake

Lib Cross Island

Judd's Marina Boat Landing (Private)

DEKORRA

Dekorra Boat Landing

Rocky Run

N

| 0 | 1 | 2 |
Miles

KEY

Access	●
Mile marker	1▷
Rapids (Class II or higher)	╫
Campsite	△
Railroad	┼─┼
Hiking/bike trail	- - -
City or village	(dotted)
Park or forest	(shaded)

WISCONSIN RIVER 5
Prairie du Sac to Arena (14.3 Miles)

After Prairie du Sac there are no more dams on the Wisconsin River. In its final, free-flowing 92 miles the river flows through a wonderfully undeveloped landscape. Thanks to 1989 legislation creating the Lower Wisconsin State Riverway, the DNR owns more than half of the land along the river here and is steadily acquiring more. Thus the natural character of the river and its surroundings has been preserved, making the Lower Wisconsin one of the longest and most scenic stretches of river in the Midwest.

An abundance of splendid public landings maximizes accessibility for paddlers, and makes it possible to organize trips lasting a couple of hours or a whole week. In its final 92 miles the river drops only 162 feet, for an average gradient of 1.8 feet per mile. Islands and occasional rock outcroppings add to the scenery, and innumerable sandbars and beaches make great places to camp or relax. Eagles, osprey, sandpipers, turkey buzzards, herons, and hawks are frequent companions.

By far the most popular part of the Lower Wisconsin is the 24-mile stretch from Prairie du Sac to Spring Green; in fact, almost two thirds of the river use is here. Thus, if you're looking for solitude, you should paddle this section (or part of it) on a weekday to avoid the crowds, or select a stretch farther downstream.

A word of caution for canoe-campers: when choosing a campsite, be aware that the river can rise 2 or 3 feet overnight after heavy rainfall. Wear your PFD, and remember that water depth near sandbars and beaches can suddenly go from inches to many feet.

In addition to **camping** on sandbars, beaches, and islands, campgrounds are available at Devil's Lake State Park 9 miles north of Prairie du Sac (608-356-8301), Tower Hill State Park 3.5 miles southeast of Spring Green (608-588-2116), Veterans Memorial Park in Prairie du Sac, Cedar Hills Campground 4 miles northeast of Mazomanie (608-795-2606), Snuffy's Campgrounds in Sauk City (608-643-8353), and Bob's Riverside along the river south of Spring Green (608-588-2826).

Canoe rental and shuttles are available at Sauk Prairie Canoe Rentals in Sauk City (608-643-6589), Blackhawk River Runs north of Mazomanie (608-643-6724), Bender's Bluffview Canoe Rentals in Sauk City (608-643-8247), Trader's Canoe Rentals near Arena (608-588-7282), Bob's Riverside near Spring Green (608-588-2826), and DJ's Kwik Stop in Gotham (608-583-7922). Flasher's Canoe Camping Trips (Wilton) offers guided trips on the Wisconsin (608-435-6802).

The **shuttle route** (19 miles) from Veterans Memorial Park goes south on Highway 78 west on Highway 14, north on Village Edge Road at Arena, and north on River Road to the landing.

Gradient is 2.1 feet per mile.

For **water levels**, check the Muscoda gauge (#05407000) on the USGS Web site. See "Water Levels" in the introduction. For general water level information (high, medium, low) call one of the canoe-rental companies.

There are two public **put-ins:** (1) at the Veterans Memorial Park boat ramp on river-right in Prairie du Sac, half a mile downstream from the dam, off Highway 78 (Water Street); and (2) 4 miles downstream-right at the canoe landing on the south edge of Sauk City, off Lueders Road. The latter access, opened in 1999, avoids a potentially dangerous railroad bridge, and is the recommended put-in.

At the Veterans Memorial Park boat ramp, tall rounded bluffs can be seen to the east; near one (Sugar Loaf) is the Wollersheim Winery, started in the 1840s by a Hungarian count who later was instrumental in launching California's wine industry. After the Highway 60 bridge, Eagle Island is followed by August Derleth Park on the right, named for the prolific Wisconsin writer who spent most of his life in Sauk City.

Downstream from the Highway 12/78 bridge, the side channel of Kranzfelder Island heads off to the left, and a railroad bridge appears in the main (right) channel. Stay far to the right; fast, squirrelly current can sweep inexperienced paddlers into the piers on the left. Before long, the river canoe landing off Lueders Road is passed on the right (a sandy beach that is hard to spot from the river). A little over a mile away, in the hills to the left, the famous Battle of Wisconsin Heights occurred during the Black Hawk War of 1832.

The setting is now wild, with a sandy shoreline and forested banks, and campers' tents begin to appear along the river. When County Y approaches the river on the left, some cabins line the shore, together with two landings: the first is the town of Mazomanie's public boat ramp (an excellent alternate put-in).

Arcing left, the river now heads toward the impressive mass of Ferry Bluff, the first of several 300-foot hills along the right shore. Just upstream from the bluff, Honey Creek enters on the right; you can paddle up it to the Ferry Bluff canoe landing and nature preserve. The view from the top of the bluffs—reached by walking trails—is awesome. Quite wide and shallow after Ferry Bluff, the river passes many sandbars, beaches, and islands. This is an especially lovely and popular part of the river.

As the river bends right past large wooded islands, three more bluffs loom in the distance, followed by a left bend. Then, just before the river heads right again, **take out** at the Arena canoe landing on the left, after some cabins.

WISCONSIN RIVER 5

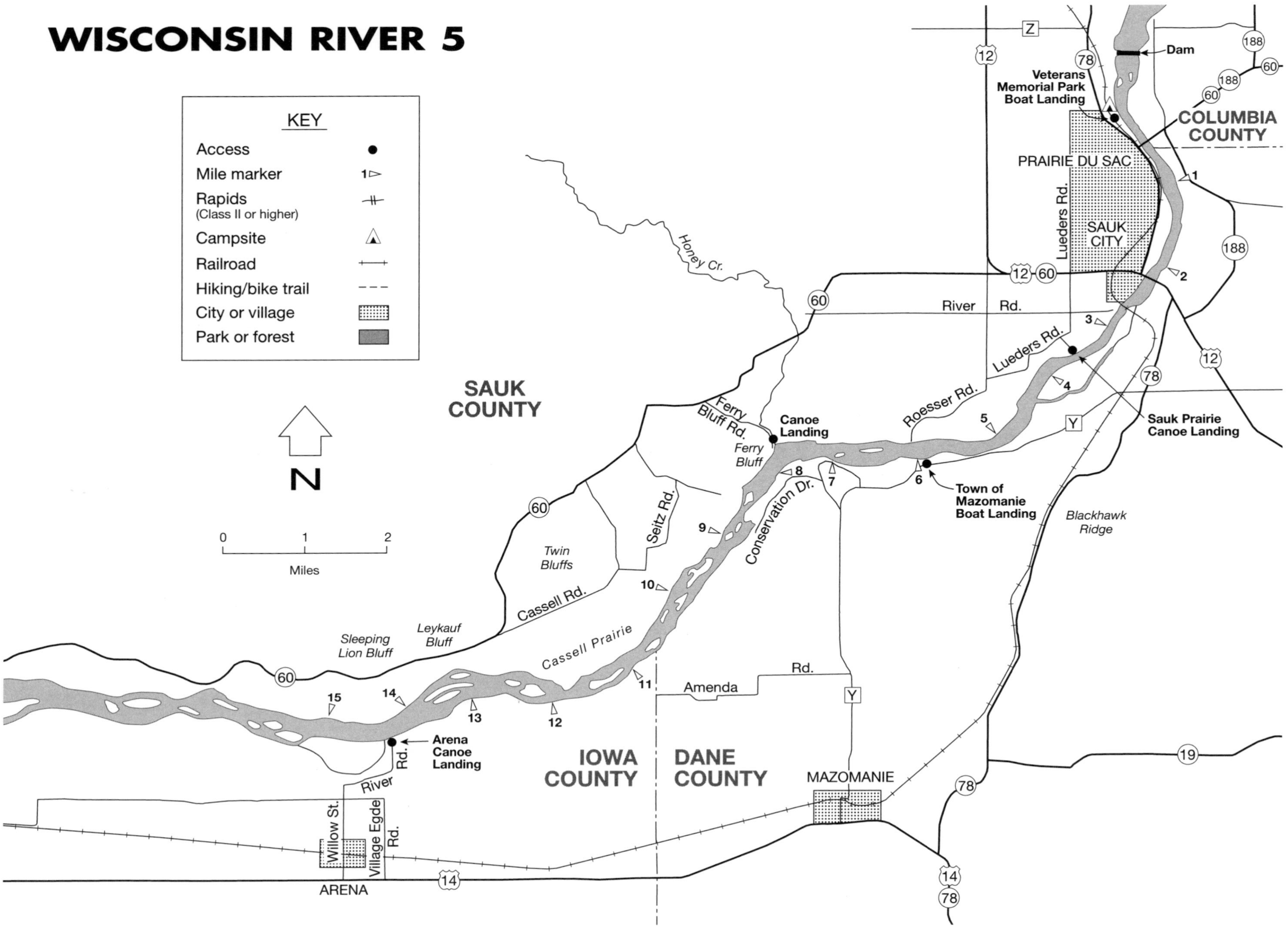

KEY

- ● Access
- 1△ Mile marker
- ⊣⊢ Rapids (Class II or higher)
- ◁ Campsite
- ┼ Railroad
- - - Hiking/bike trail
- ▦ City or village
- ▨ Park or forest

N

Miles
0   1   2

COLUMBIA COUNTY

Dam

Veterans Memorial Park Boat Landing

PRAIRIE DU SAC

SAUK CITY

Lueders Rd.

Sauk Prairie Canoe Landing

Blackhawk Ridge

Town of Mazomanie Boat Landing

MAZOMANIE

DANE COUNTY

Roesser Rd.

Lueper's Rd.

River Rd.

Canoe Landing

Ferry Bluff Rd.

Ferry Bluff

Honey Cr.

Conservation Dr.

Seitz Rd.

Twin Bluffs

Cassell Rd.

Cassell Prairie

Amenda Rd.

IOWA COUNTY

SAUK COUNTY

Leykauf Bluff

Sleeping Lion Bluff

Arena Canoe Landing

River Rd.

Village Egde Rd.

Willow St.

ARENA

WISCONSIN RIVER 6
Arena to Spring Green (10 Miles)

The Fine Art of Making Buckshot

Thanks to the lead rush of the 1820s, southwestern Wisconsin and northwestern Illinois were a magnet for lead miners, quickly becoming the most populated parts of the two states. Galena, Platteville, Schullsburg, Potosi, and many other small towns grew and prospered as miners scurried to extract the valuable deposits from the hills of the Driftless Area. One of the related industries that sprang up locally was the making of lead shot. Today you can still see how it was done by visiting Tower Hill State Park, where the shot tower and smelting house have been reconstructed.

Built in the 1830s, the shot tower was a remarkable construction project. Using only picks and shovels, workers carved a 120-foot vertical shaft down through the sandstone bluff, then a 90-foot horizontal passage from the side of the bluff to the bottom of the shaft. On top of the shaft sat a 60-foot wooden tower. The shot-making process was rather simple. Lead was melted, then poured through a sieve at the top of the tower, forming small spheres in its 180-foot descent to a pool of water at the bottom. Shot was then carried through the lateral tunnel to be sorted, packed, and shipped out to such destinations as St. Louis, Green Bay, and Milwaukee.

The nearby town of Helena prospered through the 1850s, but—like so many of Wisconsin's ghost towns—declined when the railroad bypassed it. The shot tower lasted until 1861. Twenty-eight years later, Frank Lloyd Wright's uncle bought the property, and in 1922 his widow gave it to the state. Trails now enable visitors to walk to the top of the bluff, where an exhibit explains the shot-making process. In addition, the park offers campsites, picnic facilities, a canoe landing, and a network of hiking trails.

Often combined with the previous section for a two-day canoe-camping trip, this relatively short stretch also makes a good day trip. Sandbars, islands, and bluffs continue as the river makes a big swing toward the southwest. The trip ends with a couple of historic and cultural highlights: Tower Hill State Park, the site of an important lead-shot manufactory in the 1800s; and the Frank Lloyd Wright Visitor Center, not far from the famed Wisconsin architect's home. Like most of the towns and cities located near the Lower Wisc-onsin, Spring Green is a charming community, favored by artists and craftspeople.

For **camping, canoe rental,** and **water levels,** see Wisconsin River 5.

The **shuttle route** (9.5 miles) goes south on River Road and Willow Street, west on Highway 14, west on County C, and north on Highway 23 to the bridge.

Gradient is 2 feet per mile.

Put in at the canoe landing at the end of River Road about a mile north of Arena. Just downstream from the sandy canoe landing is a ramp for motorboats. The river is quite wide at the beginning and heavily wooded (as usual) on both sides. About half a mile north of the landing (i.e., on river-right) is the bluff called Sleeping Lion. Large sandbars are abundant, and a string of big islands begins.

At 3.5 miles a creek enters on the left just upstream from several trailers, and the river begins bending left in a very long, gentle arc. On the left for several miles (hidden by trees) is the Arena Prairie, now farmland. Eventually another bluff appears on the right side, the last one until the end of the trip.

Downstream, when you come alongside the second of two large wooded islands, a railroad bridge can be seen in the distance, preceded by power lines. The Highway 14 bridge quickly follows, where there's an excellent canoe landing (and possible **take-out**) upstream-left, with plentiful parking.

After Highway 14 the left bend resumes, a couple of cabins appear on the right, and bluffs can be seen ahead. As soon as the river turns right, alongside the river-left bluffs, the Highway 23 bridge comes into view. Tower Hill State Park and the once-prosperous site of Helena are found on the bluff. You can get to the park and a canoe landing by paddling up Mill Creek.

Continuing past the Frank Lloyd Wright Visitor Center on the left hillside (usually screened by trees), the river approaches more power lines and the Highway 23 bridge, where Peck's Landing is an outstanding **take-out.** Named for a ferry operator who was once located here, the landing is upstream-right.

Beautiful wooded bluffs line the Wisconsin River all the way to the Mississippi.

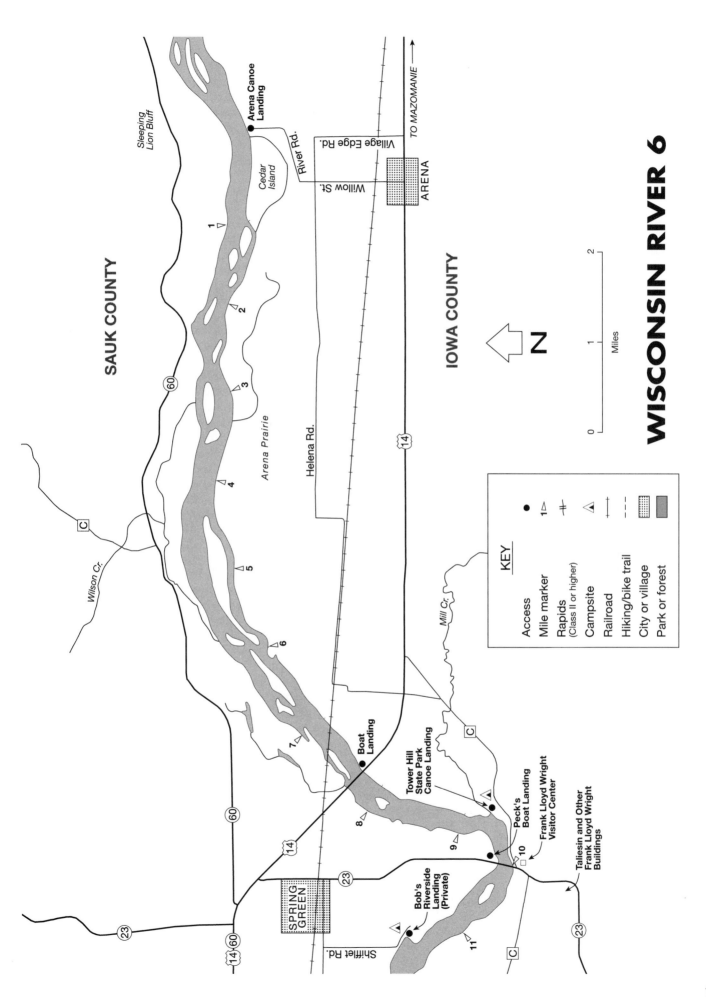

WISCONSIN RIVER 6

SAUK COUNTY

IOWA COUNTY

Sleeping Lion Bluff

Arena Canoe Landing

Cedar Island

River Rd.

Village Edge Rd.

Willow St.

TO MAZOMANIE →

ARENA

1 ▷
2 ▷
3 ▷
4 ▷
5 ▷
6 ▷

60

Arena Prairie

Helena Rd.

Wilson Cr.

C

14

N

Miles
0   1   2

KEY

●	Access
1 △	Mile marker
≠	Rapids (Class II or higher)
◁	Campsite
┼	Railroad
‒ ‒ ‒	Hiking/bike trail
▦	City or village
�	Park or forest

Mill Cr.

C

60

14

7 ▷

Boat Landing

8 ▷

Tower Hill State Park Canoe Landing

Peck's Boat Landing

9 ▷

Frank Lloyd Wright Visitor Center

10 ▷ □

Taliesin and Other Frank Lloyd Wright Buildings

SPRING GREEN

23

Bob's Riverside Landing (Private)

Shifflet Rd.

14/60

23

11 ▷

C

23

159

WISCONSIN RIVER 7 & 8

Spring Green to Lone Rock (8 Miles)
Lone Rock to Muscoda (13 Miles)

In this long section—which can easily be broken into shorter day trips by using the intermediate access near Lone Rock—the Wisconsin is peaceful, studded with islands, and loaded with inviting sandbars and beaches. Bluffs often tower over the shoreline, and a unique, relatively open area is one of the most beautiful places on the river. An annual canoe race covers most of this section in July; the rest of the year, you'll see far fewer paddlers here than in the Prairie-du-Sac-to-Spring-Green stretch. Most of this section's 21 miles flow through remote areas, but highways are nearby for several miles.

For **camping**, see Wisconsin River 5. Excellent camping is also available at Victora Riverside Park in Muscoda (608-739-3786), upstream-left from the bridge.

For **canoe rental**, see Wisconsin River 5. Also renting canoes and providing shuttle service on this part of the river is Rent-a-Canoe in Boscobel (608-375-5130).

The **shuttle route** (23 miles) for the full 22-mile trip goes north on Highway 23 into Spring Green, west on Madison Street/Kennedy Road, south on Highway 130/133 through Lone Rock and across the river, west on Highway 133, and north on Highway 80

Sometimes shuttle routes are almost as attractive as the river itself.

through Muscoda. Shorter trips use the same routing, with Lone Rock as the take-out or put-in.

Gradient is 2.4 feet per mile.

For **water levels**, see Wisconsin River 5.

Put in at Peck's Landing, upstream-right from the Highway 23 bridge. You can also start 2 miles upstream at Highway 14 (upstream-left). Islands follow Highway 23, and a sheer rock face lies at the base of the bluff on the left. Then the banks are rather low and densely vegetated for a while as beautiful cliffs continue on the left. When the river heads to the left, Bob's Riverside appears on the right shore (campground, restaurant, and landing). Power lines cross at one of the large, wooded islands that follow.

After a fairly straight, islandless stretch, the river curves left along wooded bluffs. Huge Long Island begins where the river heads back to the right, and soon a couple of small buildings and Highway 130 can be seen on the left at the base of a bluff. Within sight of the highway bridge, Otter Creek enters on the left. A public boat landing is located just a few feet up the creek, with

adjacent parking; this is an excellent **take-out** or **put-in** for a shorter trip. Lone Rock, a small community a mile to the north, was named after a huge sandstone formation in the river near here (cut away long ago for use in house construction).

Beautiful, continuous bluffs are now found on the left for a while, including many rocky cliffs. Before long, a low railroad bridge comes into view, running across the river at an oblique angle and resting on 12 concrete piers. Be careful of crosscurrents as you paddle between the piers, and stay away from the narrowly spaced metal supports on the left. The river is now wide and isolated, gently bending left past many sandbars and sandy shorelines.

When the river turns abruptly to the right alongside a large island, the setting becomes rather open, with sparse tree cover and huge, attractive beaches. For several miles downstream, the Avoca State Wildlife Area lies on the left, containing the largest tallgrass prairie east of the Mississippi. The lovely setting is enhanced by surrounding bluffs. Soon the river heads left again in another tight turn, passing sheer, 15-foot cut banks and a few houses. Just downstream from the cut banks and upstream-right from the mouth of the Pine River is a gravel boat landing with good parking. Situated south of Gotham, on the site of the once-important village of Richland City, this access is also known as the Buena Vista Landing and is another alternative for varying the length of the trip. (To get to the landing, drive from Gotham on Fulton Street, then Oak, and finally a road signed "Dead End.")

After the landing the river bends right, then pulls alongside Bogus Bluff and Highway 60 on the right. The bluff, which displays some beautiful limestone outcroppings, is said to have gotten its name from yellow rock that a settler mistook for gold. (Incidentally, many of the bluffs along the Lower Wisconsin have figured in legends about buried treasure and counterfeiters' caves.) A few houses can be seen on the right hillside in this long, wide, straight stretch. A series of cabins follow farther downstream.

Later, when the highway is farther from the river, a long, undercut cliff lines the right shoreline for a couple hundred yards, with some houses on top. When the buildings thin out, the excellent Orion boat ramp appears on the right (along Ginger Lane, off Highway 60). Several large wooded islands follow, and soon you see the Highway 80 bridge at Muscoda. **Take out** 200 yards upstream-left at the boat ramp of Victora Riverside Park, a very pleasant city park with campground, toilets, parking, and picnic facilities. Another excellent **take-out** lies just downstream from the bridge on the left (a gravel landing with adjacent parking).

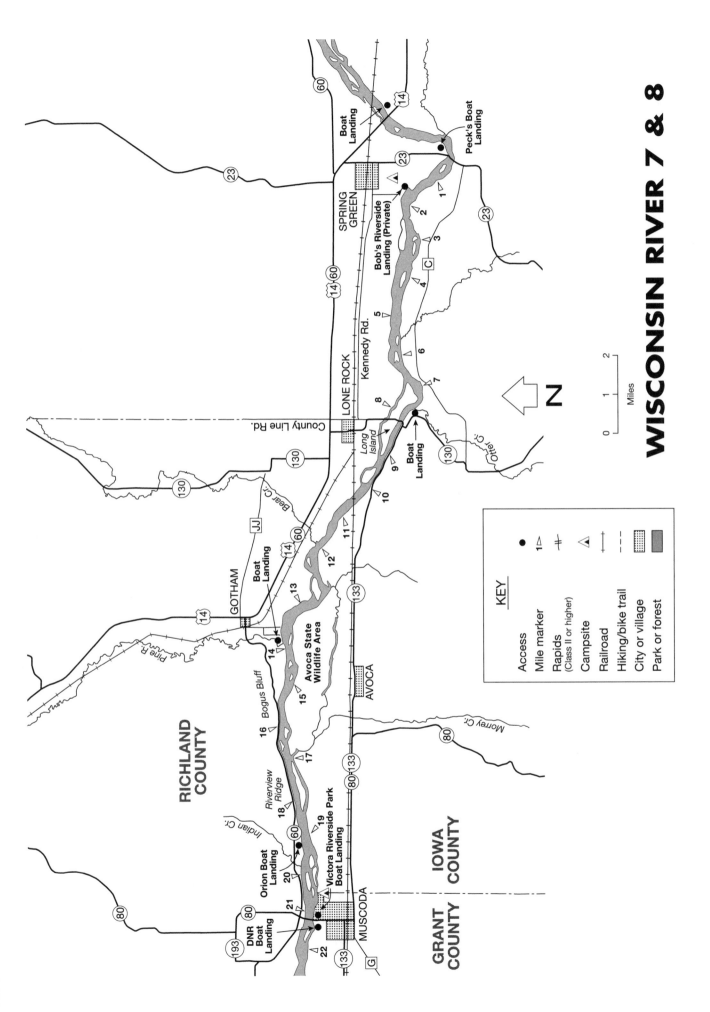

WISCONSIN RIVER 7 & 8

N

Miles
0 1 2

KEY

- Access •
- Mile marker ¹△
- Rapids (Class II or higher) ‡
- Campsite ◁
- Railroad ┼
- Hiking/bike trail ┄
- City or village ▦
- Park or forest ▨

RICHLAND COUNTY

IOWA COUNTY

GRANT COUNTY

SPRING GREEN

LONE ROCK

GOTHAM

AVOCA

MUSCODA

Boat Landing

Peck's Boat Landing

Bob's Riverside Landing (Private)

Kennedy Rd.

County Line Rd.

Long Island

Boat Landing

Bear Cr.

Pine R.

Avoca State Wildlife Area

Bogus Bluff

Riverview Ridge

Indian Cr.

Orion Boat Landing

Victora Riverside Park Boat Landing

DNR Boat Landing

Otter Cr.

Morrey Cr.

WISCONSIN RIVER 9
Muscoda to Boscobel (16 Miles)

Canal Fever

Before the advent of railroads in the mid-1800s, waterways were America's primary method of transporting goods and people. After 1825, when the immensely successful Erie Canal linked the Hudson River and Lake Erie, revolutionizing travel between the eastern and the Great Lakes states, would-be canal builders sprang into action everywhere. In Illinois, for example, the Illinois and Michigan Canal opened in 1848 (connecting Lake Michigan and the Mississippi) and was a big factor in Chicago's rapid growth.

Wisconsin wasn't immune to the canal-building fever. In 1838, for example, Governor Dodge signed a bill authorizing a canal from the Rock River at Watertown through the Madison area to the Wisconsin River near Arena. Milwaukee supporters hoped that the canal would ultimately run all the way to Lake Michigan at Milwaukee. In 1870 (and several times later, until as recently as 1952), it was suggested that the Bois Brule and St. Croix Rivers be "improved" to provide a canal linkage between Lake Superior and the Mississippi. Like many other canal schemes, both came to nothing.

Wisconsin's one serious attempt to build a canal—the Fox–Wisconsin Improvement Project—did produce a series of locks and dams, together with the short Portage Canal. But competition from railroads and the unrelenting need to dredge both the Fox and Wisconsin doomed the project, except for light commercial and recreational use.

An extremely quiet part of the river, this section features a series of huge, wooded islands. DNR wildlife areas run along the left shore all the way, and beautiful, rounded bluffs hover over the water much of the time. Boat ramps at the put-in, take-out, and intermediate accesses are convenient and well-maintained. For canoe-campers, stopping places continue to be plentiful. Charming, historic cities are found at the beginning and end of the trip.

Muscoda (from a Native American phrase meaning "meadow" or "prairie") was once a fur-trading post, then an important supply center after the railroad came through. Boscobel (from a French expression meaning "beautiful wood") began as a logging town, but also owed its growth to the coming of the railroad. Fortunately, in the 1960s a proposed dam in the Muscoda area was determined to be unfeasible.

Camping. In addition to sandbar, island, and shoreline camping, there is a pleasant campground at Victora Riverside Park in Muscoda (608-739-3786).

Canoe rental and shuttles on this part of the river are available from Rent-a-Canoe in Boscobel (608-375-5130), Bob's Riverside near Spring Green (608-588-2826), Blackhawk River Runs north of Mazomanie (608-643-6724), and Bender's Bluffview Canoe Rentals in Sauk City (608-643-8247).

The **shuttle route** (approximately 16 miles) goes south on Highway 80, west on Highway 133, and north on Highway 61.

Gradient is 2.2 feet per mile.

For **water levels**, see Wisconsin River 5.

Put in (1) upstream-left from the Highway 80 bridge at the Victora Riverside Park boat ramp or (2) downstream-left at the sandy DNR landing. After the first large island, houses appear on the right shoreline down to McClary Island. The river now narrows a little and passes a couple of houses and an old, seldom-used landing on the right (at the end of Newburn Road, off Highway 60). Another large island quickly follows on the left side of the river, then some modest rock outcroppings on the right and many small islands. The river has been mostly straight since Muscoda.

It takes more than rain to dampen the enthusiasm of Wisconsin River paddlers.

As you approach Steamboat Island in a left bend, the County T bridge can be seen in the distance. The biggest island of the trip, 2-mile-long Coumbe Island (named after the county's first permanent settler) begins upstream from the bridge. The larger right channel takes you to the Port Andrew landing alongside Highway 60, several hundred yards upstream-right. In the left channel is the Blue Island Landing, immediately upstream-right from the County T bridge. Both are first-rate boat ramps, and make splendid intermediate accesses.

In the right channel, Highway 60 follows the shore for half a mile before the river arcs away from it to the left, and a slough (Garner Lake) runs off to the right. Soon beautiful bluffs draw near on the left, then divert the river to the right.

The right bend continues to Big Island, which is followed by a steady succession of large islands. Misnamed Little Island follows Big Island. At Trumbull and Patterson Islands the river heads straight toward another beautiful set of wooded ridges, and Highway 60 draws near again on the right. A high sandy cut bank can be seen on the left as the river veers left alongside towering bluffs on the right. In this beautiful stretch, the left bend continues beside the bluffs and highway until, eventually, power lines cross and the bridge at Boscobel can be seen, immediately preceded by Feather Island. The city is attractively framed by the bluffs that surround it.

Take out just downstream-left from the bridge, where an inlet leads to the Floyd Von Haden Boat Landing, with nearby parking and picnic tables. Be careful how you approach the inlet to the landing: The current is usually fairly swift here, and entry can be a little tricky.

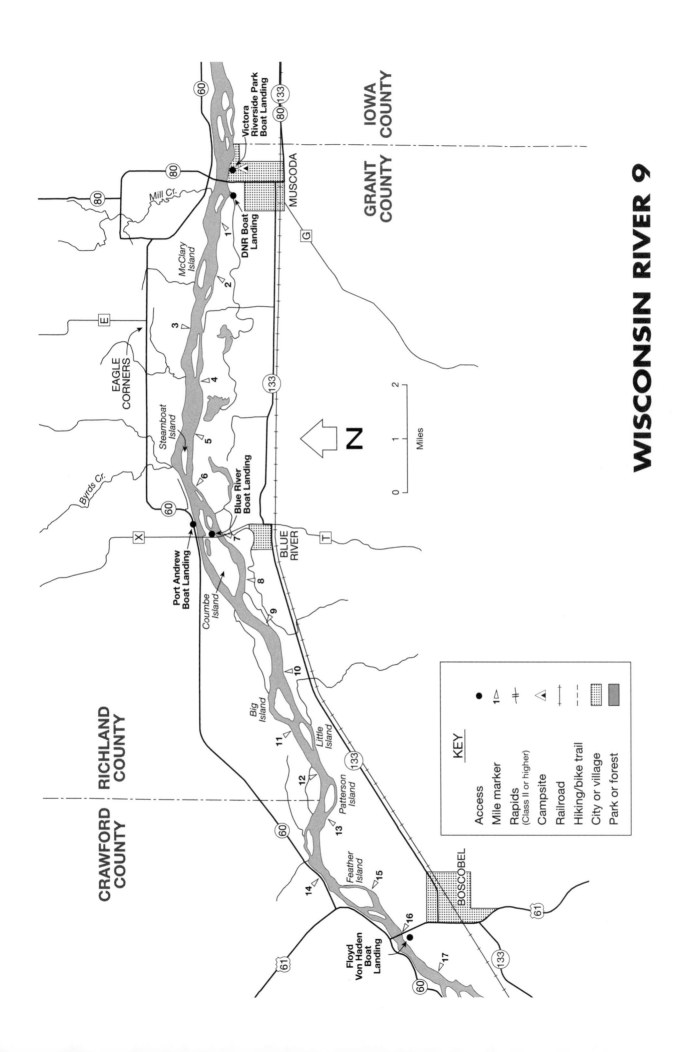

WISCONSIN RIVER 9

IOWA COUNTY

GRANT COUNTY

CRAWFORD COUNTY

RICHLAND COUNTY

Victora Riverside Park Boat Landing

DNR Boat Landing

MUSCODA

Mill Cr.

McClary Island

EAGLE CORNERS

Steamboat Island

Byrds Cr.

Blue River Boat Landing

BLUE RIVER

Port Andrew Boat Landing

Coumbe Island

Big Island

Little Island

Patterson Island

Feather Island

BOSCOBEL

Floyd Von Haden Boat Landing

N

Miles
0   1   2

KEY

●	Access
1△	Mile marker
╪	Rapids (Class II or higher)
◁	Campsite
┼	Railroad
┊	Hiking/bike trail
▦	City or village
▨	Park or forest

163

WISCONSIN RIVER 10 & 11

Boscobel to Woodman (9 Miles)
Woodman to Bridgeport (12.8 Miles)

Now begins the most secluded part of the Lower Wisconsin State Riverway. In fact, the 28 miles from Boscobel to the Mississippi typically are used by less than 20 percent of boaters on the riverway. Remoteness from population centers, not aesthetics, is doubtlessly the main reason, because this part of the river is the scenic equal of any other section.

In at least one respect it's even more beautiful. When glacial torrents broke through the terminal moraine at Prairie du Sac, they initially cut through soft sandstone in creating the broad valley of the Lower Wisconsin (4 miles wide at Prairie du Sac). Later in its westward course toward the Mississippi, however, the glacial meltwater began to encounter resistant limestone, resulting in a much narrower valley (2 miles at Muscoda and only half a mile at Bridgeport). Thus, even when the river's trademark bluffs aren't immediately alongside the banks, their 300- to 400-foot height can generally be seen in the distance.

Big islands continue in this section, often with enjoyably narrow channels. There are many sandbars, although they begin to decline in frequency in the approach to Bridgeport. As elsewhere, the accesses are exemplary, including landings near Woodman and Millville that facilitate shorter trips. Boscobel-to-Woodman is a particularly pleasant two- to four-hour trip.

Not exactly roughing it, but having a good time.

Camping on sandbars, beaches, and islands is popular. Excellent campgrounds are found upstream at Muscoda (Victora Riverside Park) and downstream (Wyalusing State Park).

Canoe rentals. In addition to the firms listed for Wisconsin River 9, canoe rental and shuttle service are available at Captain's Cove near Bridgeport (608-994-2860), and Marshview Canoe Rental near Wauzeka (608-875-6203).

The **shuttle route** (23 miles) for the entire 21.8-mile trip goes south on Highway 61, southwest on Highway 133, southwest on County C, and north on Highway 18/35. Short trips involving the Woodman landing as an access can use the same routing. The winding shuttle route is quite attractive: bluffs are never far away.

Gradient is 2.5 feet per mile.

For **water levels**, see Wisconsin River 5.

Put in at the Boscobel bridge, downstream-left. As soon as you paddle away from the Floyd Von Haden Boat Landing, Easter Rock can be seen on the opposite side, with a big cross on a rocky shelf. Settlers once celebrated sunrise services on this bluff. The scenery is quite lovely at the outset of the trip, with a series of wooded bluffs rising along the right bank.

A mile into the trip, as huge Allen Island draws near, the bluffs move away from the river. A straight, mostly islandless stretch follows. After Highway 60 pulls alongside on the right, the river heads left, passing under two sets of power lines. Soon a long, low railroad bridge crosses the river at Gillis Island, followed by a series of smaller islands.

After you clear the last of the islands, the Woodman landing appears on the left where the river begins turning sharply to the right. The landing is on the Green River, about 100 yards upstream from its mouth, tucked between a couple of beautiful, high bluffs—the first riverside bluffs in a while. If you're planning to take out here, be alert because the landing is easy to miss.

Several hundred yards downstream from the landing a house is somewhat visible through the foliage on the left. After huge Newton Island, the river passes equally big Harris Island, where the Kickapoo River joins the Wisconsin in the island's right channel. Some buildings can be seen on the right after the mouth.

Downstream from Harris Island the river swings to the right alongside gorgeous bluffs on the left. In the big left bend that follows, the river is wide and without islands. Then, after a straightaway, County C runs next to the river on the left. If you wish to take out at the Millville access, stay to the left when County C and some river-left bluffs come into view. The landing is at the mouth of Dutch Hollow Creek (downstream) alongside a big island, and has toilets, picnic facilities, and plenty of parking. Soon thereafter is a string of houses, near a cluster of small islands. A long line of wooded bluffs (Campbell Ridge) continues on the left.

After Highway 60 makes a distant appearance on the right, railroad tracks parallel the right shore, passing over small bridges where creeks enter the river. The only exposed cliff face—a very modest one—appears on the right at some power lines. In the last couple of miles before Bridgeport, the river passes through a maze of large islands. Eventually, emerging from the long island-cluster, you see the graceful, modern bridge at Bridgeport. **Take out** upstream-left at the splendid landing. Bridgeport was once a crossing for the first major road in Wisconsin. Built in the 1830s, the Military Road stretched from Prairie du Chien (Fort Crawford), past Portage (Fort Winnebago), to Green Bay (Fort Howard).

Other trips. (1) For an enjoyable two-river trip, you can put in on the Kickapoo at Plum Creek Landing or at Wauzeka, float out to the Wisconsin, and take out at Millville or Bridgeport (see Kickapoo River 5). (2) For a longer three-river trip, continue to the Mississippi, and take out at Wyalusing (see Wisconsin River 12).

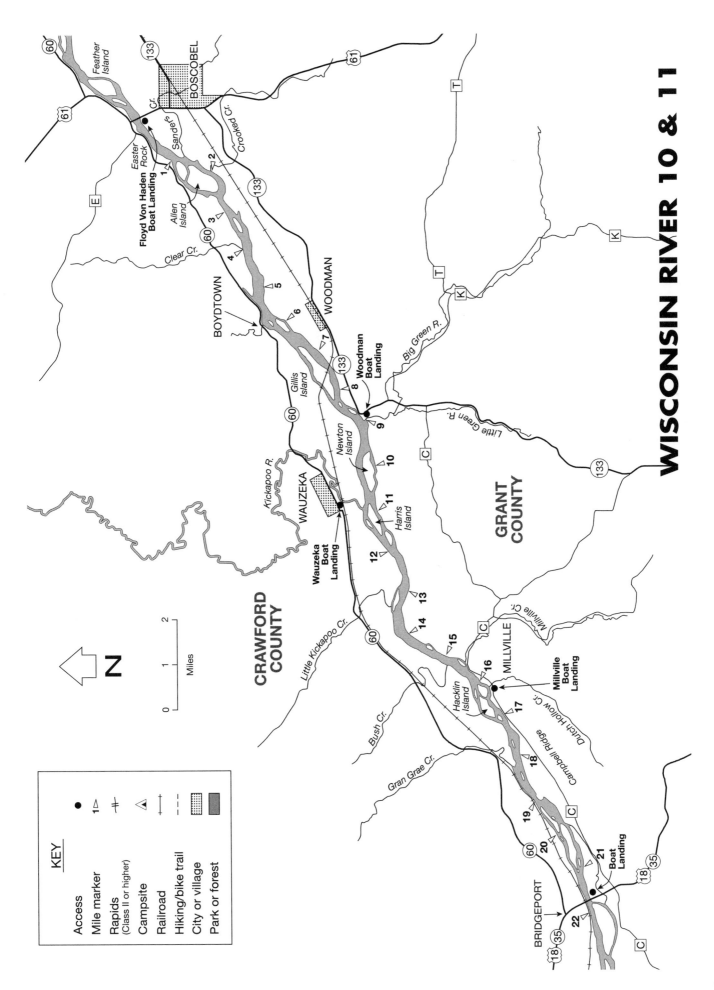

WISCONSIN RIVER 10 & 11

KEY

- • Access
- 1△ Mile marker
- ⊬ Rapids (Class II or higher)
- ◁ Campsite
- ┼ Railroad
- --- Hiking/bike trail
- ▦ City or village
- ▨ Park or forest

N

0 1 2 Miles

60
61
133
BOSCOBEL
Feather Island
Sandel's Cr.
Crooked Cr.
61
T
Easter Rock
Floyd Von Haden Boat Landing
1
2
E
Allen Island
3
60
4
Clear Cr.
5
BOYDTOWN
6
133
7
WOODMAN
K
T
K
8
Woodman Boat Landing
Big Green R.
9
Gillis Island
60
Newton Island
Kickapoo R.
10
Little Green R.
C
133
11
Harris Island
WAUZEKA
Wauzeka Boat Landing
12
GRANT COUNTY
13
CRAWFORD COUNTY
Little Kickapoo Cr.
14
C
15
60
16
MILLVILLE
Millville Cr.
Bush Cr.
Hacklin Island
17
Millville Boat Landing
Dutch Hollow Cr.
Campbell Ridge
18
C
Gran Grae Cr.
19
20
60
21
Boat Landing
18
35
BRIDGEPORT
22
18
35
C

WISCONSIN RIVER 12
Bridgeport to Wyalusing Recreation Area (9 Miles)

The Wisconsin River near the Mississippi, as seen from Wyalusing State Park.

River confluences are always interesting places for paddlers, but the experience is especially memorable when two fabled rivers like the Wisconsin and Mississippi are involved. Unlike the multichanneled deltas of many other rivers (e.g., the Black), the Wisconsin flows in a single, distinct channel all the way to the end. The Mississippi River portion of this trip is brief and interesting, highlighted by imposing bluffs on both sides.

In order to lend perspective to your trip, it is highly recommended that you visit Wyalusing State Park beforehand. Point Look Out provides a stunning overview of the confluence of the two rivers and the surrounding area. The aura of history that pervades the juncture of the rivers makes this trip all the more enjoyable: After Joliet and Marquette's exploratory journey of 1673, thousands of traders, missionaries, loggers, and settlers covered the same route that recreational boaters now paddle.

Camping on this part of the river is infrequent due to sparse sandbars, but Wyalusing State Park offers spectacular views and a very pleasant campground (608-996-2261). To the north, near Prairie du Chien, are Big River Campground (608-326-2712) and Sports Unlimited Campground (608-326-2141).

For **canoe rentals**, see Wisconsin River 9-11.

The **shuttle route** (6.8 miles) goes south on Highway 18/35, west on County C past Wyalusing State Park, and southwest on County X to the Wyalusing Recreation Area. The shuttle route is hilly, winding, and beautiful.

Gradient is only 0.6 foot per mile.

For **water levels**, see Wisconsin River 5.

Put in upstream-left at the impressive Highway 18/35 bridge near Bridgeport, a once-prosperous village where a covered bridge crossed the river. A catastrophic fire in 1936 destroyed most of what remained of Bridgeport.

The stretch begins straight, island-less, and very wide, with wooded bluffs in the distance. A mile into the trip, huge Weniger Island runs left-of-center, and the river gently bends right alongside river-left bluffs. After the river weaves its way through a string of islands, the line of bluffs swings away from the river to the south, and a railroad bridge comes into view. Just before the bluffs end on the left, you can see the high, exposed rock formations at Point Look Out in Wyalusing State Park. At this point, you are in the marshy delta of the Wisconsin River, although the surroundings don't look markedly different from river-level.

Immediately after the railroad bridge, the river swings left, and tall wooded bluffs (with houses on top) can be seen across the Mississippi. A large, wedge-shaped island lies at the mouth. Once you have entered the Mississippi (which isn't as wide here as you might expect), the riverside grain elevators of McGregor, Iowa, can be seen upstream. Not much farther upstream are Prairie du Chien (on the Wisconsin side) and the Highway 18 bridges.

The river-left shoreline along the Mississippi is low, wooded, and sandy; campers often pitch their tents here. When the huge bluffs on the right shore begin to recede, a slough on the left (marked with a small canoe sign) is the entrance to the Wyalusing State Park canoe trail. Some paddlers follow this trail and take out at the park's boat ramp. The Mississippi now widens, with green buoys marking the navigation channel for big boats, and bluffs begin to appear on the left.

As you approach the Wyalusing Recreation Area landing, there are several hundred yards of open rock faces on the river-left bluffs. Located just upstream from several small islands, the landing is easy to spot. **Take out** at the concrete boat ramp near a big, sandy beach. The popular swimming beach, with nearby toilets, picnic tables, and parking, is a great place for a dip at the end of your trip.

Other trips. If you'd like to see what the backwaters of the Mississippi are like, the 6-mile canoe route originating at Wyalusing State Park is recommended. Starting at the park's boat landing on Glenn Lake, the route follows Wood Yard Slough to the Mississippi, then reenters another slough farther south and returns to the boat landing; be careful of swirly current at the mouth of the reentry slough. Signs along the way keep you from getting lost. Maps of the route are available in the park.

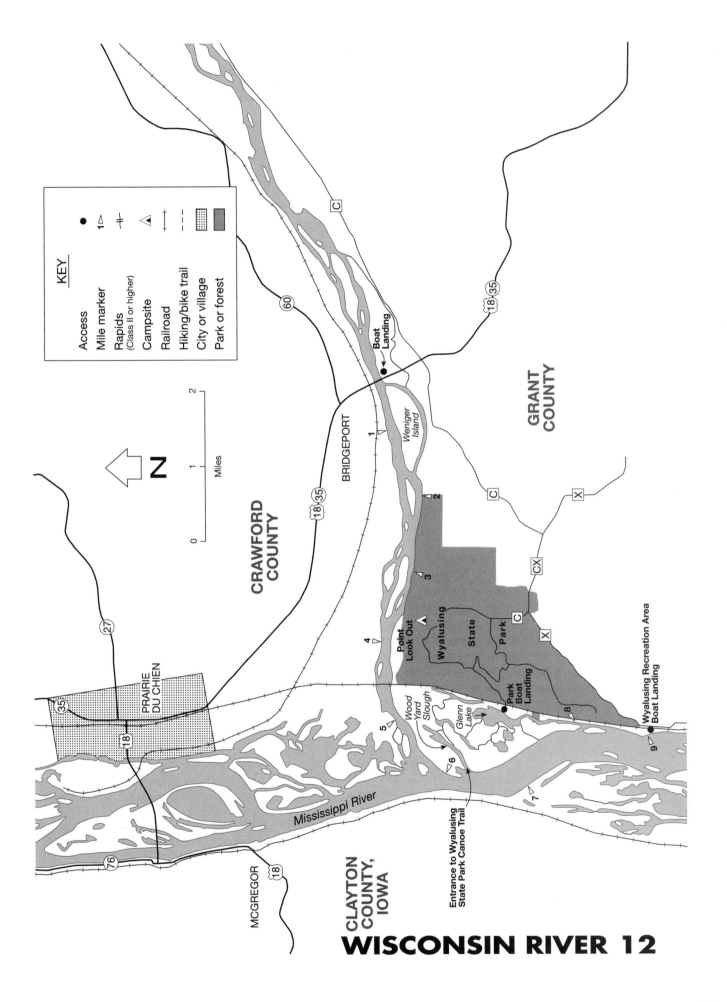

KEY

- **Access** ●
- **Mile marker** 1△
- **Rapids** (Class II or higher)
- **Campsite** ◁
- **Railroad**
- **Hiking/bike trail**
- **City or village**
- **Park or forest**

N

Miles
0 1 2

CRAWFORD COUNTY

GRANT COUNTY

CLAYTON COUNTY, IOWA

BRIDGEPORT

PRAIRIE DU CHIEN

MCGREGOR

Boat Landing

Weniger Island

Point Look Out

Wyalusing State Park

Wood Yard Slough

Glenn Lake

Park Boat Landing

Wyalusing Recreation Area Boat Landing

Entrance to Wyalusing State Park Canoe Trail

Mississippi River

60

18/35

18/35

27

35

18

76

C

C

C

CX

X

X

WISCONSIN RIVER 12

YAHARA RIVER
Stebbinsville to the Rock River (9 Miles)

Something for Everyone in Wisconsin's State Parks

Wisconsin's system of state parks is a blessing for lovers of natural places. The year 2000 marked the 100th anniversary of the system, which began with the creation of Interstate State Park at the St. Croix Dells in 1900. Together, Wisconsin's 43 state parks, 4 recreation areas, and 22 state forests offer almost 600,000 acres for use by campers, hikers, bicyclists, fishermen, boaters, and other outdoor enthusiasts. Twenty-two state trails—linear parks, if you will—add even more opportunities for recreation. Figuring prominently in canoe trips in this book are Aztalan State Park (Crawfish River), Black River State Forest (Black River 3, 4, 5), Hartman Creek State Park (Crystal River), Tower Hill State Park (Wisconsin River 6 and 7), Wildcat Mountain State Park (Kickapoo River 1), and Wyalusing State Park (Wisconsin River 12).

A relatively short river named after the Ho-Chunk word for "catfish," the Yahara flows through the state capital, forming Lakes Mendota, Monona, Waubesa, and Kegonsa. Originating several miles north of Madison, the river is dammed half a dozen times as it heads south to its confluence with the Rock. Paddlers frequently enjoy leisurely outings on the lakes and brief stretches of river in the Madison area, but the longest and most popular section of moving water is the part that begins at the final dam. The removal of a downstream dam at Fulton in 1993 has transformed this section into 9 miles of pleasant, free-flowing water.

Mostly wooded, isolated, and winding, the river here is generally rather narrow and sometimes riffly, with a few wide spots. Occasional limbs require maneuvering, but obstructions are seldom a problem. There are no designated boat landings, but accesses are easy, including an intermediate location that makes shorter trips possible.

Camping is available at Lake Kegonsa State Park 4 miles north of Stoughton (608-873-9695), Viking Village Campground and Resort near Stoughton (608-873-6601), and Kamp Kegonsa between Stoughton and Madison (608-873-5800). There are also several campgrounds to the east in the Edgerton/Newville area, near the western end of Lake Koshkonong.

Canoe rentals are available in Madison at Rutabaga (608-223-9300) and Carl's Paddlin' (608-284-0300).

The **shuttle route** (6 miles) goes east on Stebbinsville Road, south on Hartzell Road, south on Highway 59, and south on County H through Fulton to a turn-off along the Rock River (just past the point where Gibbs Lake Road meets County H).

Gradient is 3.8 feet per mile.

For **water levels,** check the gauge at Fulton (#05430175) on the USGS Web site. See "Water Levels" in the introduction.

Put in about 150 feet downstream-left from the Stebbinsville dam where the river flows alongside Stebbinsville Road. A short path leads down to a gravelly, undeveloped landing popular with bank fishermen. Accessing the river at the base of the dam puts paddlers directly into fast water, with an eddy that can carry boats back into the turbulence. In need of repair, the old dam no longer generates electricity, and one gate is open.

Fifty feet wide at the outset, the river winds around

The old dam at Stebbinsville.

between low banks, broadening to as much as 90 feet and becoming more shallow over a sand-and-gravel bottom. Badfish Creek—a canoeable tributary—enters on the right.

After the Highway 59 bridge, the setting changes markedly. A large bay immediately follows the bridge on the right, and the surroundings become marshy; trees are now some distance from the river. Eventually the wide, lake-like area below Highway 59 ends, and the river narrows to 45 feet, winding through dense woods. A guardrail, riprap, and the mouth of Gibbs Creek appear where Caledonia Road pulls alongside the right bank. Downstream, the first houses of the trip are seen at the Caledonia Road bridge.

A long pool after the bridge is followed by a small drop of a few inches, then a pleasant riffle. At one point the water splits around a couple of small islands. Later, within sight of a home in the distance, there's a long and pleasant riffle. The river narrows a little and quickens before the County H bridge, where Murwin Park is located on the left, both upstream and downstream from the bridge. The low, grassy banks of this Rock County park (with toilets, picnic tables, and parking) are easy to access. A dam was once located in the bend just upstream from County H.

After the park the river is narrow, winding, and often tree-canopied, with some limbs to dodge. Gravel bars appear occasionally, and there's a tall sand-and-clay bluff on the left where swallows nest. As you approach County M, several houses can be seen on the right.

Nearing the Rock, the Yahara widens somewhat, trees become thinner, and the low-banked environs become rather swampy. At the mouth, the Rock looks huge by comparison, with homes and docks on the opposite shore. Turn right and **take out** at a clearing on the right shoreline alongside County H. There's room on the shoulder to park several cars.

Other trips. It's a 7-mile paddle from Stoughton (where there's a dam) to Stebbinsville, but a weedy portage is necessary around the Dunkirk dam.

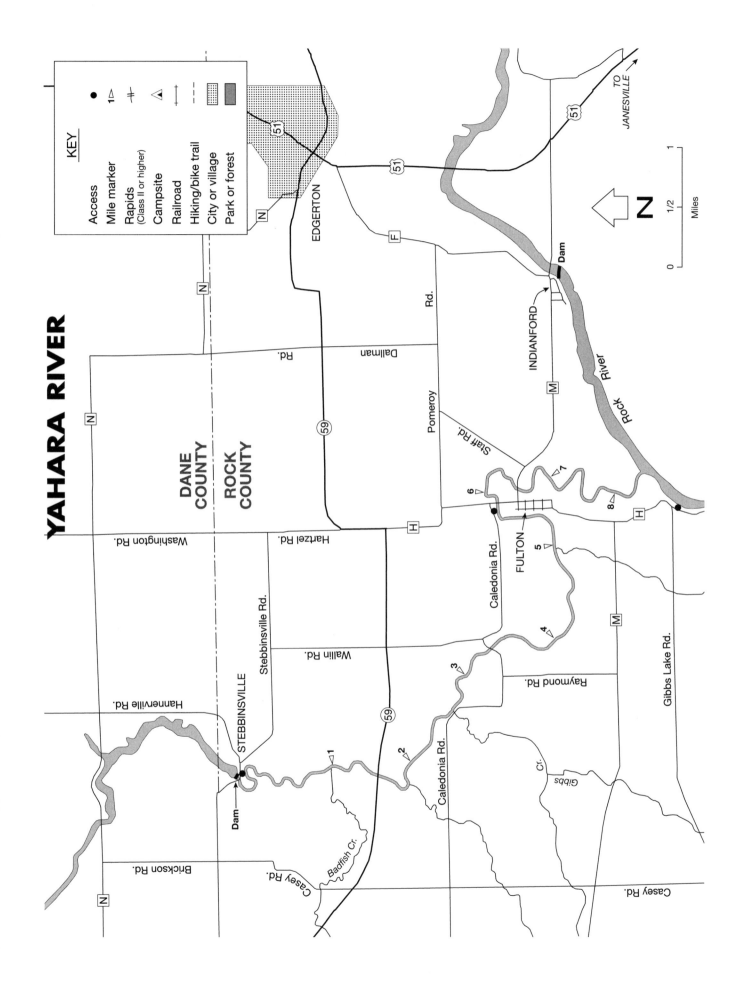

YAHARA RIVER

KEY

- **●** Access
- **1△** Mile marker
- **‡** Rapids (Class II or higher)
- **△** Campsite
- **╬** Railroad
- **┈** Hiking/bike trail
- ▦ City or village
- ▨ Park or forest

N
1/2 0
Miles

DANE COUNTY
ROCK COUNTY

EDGERTON

INDIANFORD

Dam

Rock River

TO JANESVILLE

FULTON

STEBBINSVILLE

Dam

Washington Rd.
Hanverville Rd.
Brickson Rd.
Casey Rd.
Casey Rd.
Stebbinsville Rd.
Hartzel Rd.
Wallin Rd.
Raymond Rd.
Gibbs Lake Rd.
Caledonia Rd.
Caledonia Rd.
Dallman Rd.
Pomeroy Rd.
Staff Rd.
Badfish Cr.
Gibbs Cr.

APPENDIX I

PADDLING SECTIONS GROUPED BY SKILL LEVEL

Under normal circumstances (i.e., low to medium water levels, and warm air and water temperatures), most of the sections described in this book are suitable for properly equipped and cautious beginning-level canoeists and kayakers accompanied by experienced paddlers. However, even beginning-level stretches can present situations that require maneuvering and good judgment (e.g., recently fallen trees, bridge repair work that has left broken concrete in the streambed, low-clearance bridges, rising water levels, etc.). WHEN THE WATER IS HIGH, NO RIVER IS APPROPRIATE FOR BEGINNERS. A number of sections could possibly be categorized either as Beginner or Experienced/Intermediate. In each of these ambivalent situations, I have conservatively placed the section in the latter group.

BEGINNER
Baraboo River 2
Bark River 1, 2
Black River 3, 4, 5, 6
Chippewa River 1, 2, 3, 4, 5, 6
Crawfish River
Crystal River
Des Plaines River
Eau Claire River 2
Fox River 1, 2
Galena River
Grant River 1, 2
Illinois Fox River 1, 2, 3
Kickapoo River 1, 2, 3, 4, 5
La Crosse River 2
Lemonweir River 2
Mecan River 1, 2
Milwaukee River 1, 2, 3, 4
Oconomowoc River
Pecatonica River
Platte River 1, 2
Plover River 1, 2
Red Cedar River
Rock River 1, 2, 3
Sheboygan River 1
Sugar River 1, 2
Tomorrow River
Trempealeau River 2
Waupaca River 2
Wisconsin River 1, 3–12
Yahara River

Rock formations line the Kickapoo from Ontario to La Farge.

EXPERIENCED/INTERMEDIATE
Baraboo River 1
Eau Claire River 1, 3
La Crosse River 1
Lemonweir River 1
Little Wolf River 1, 2
Manitowoc River 1, 2
Plover River 3
Sheboygan River 2
Trempealeau River 1
Waupaca River 1
Wisconsin River 2

ADVANCED/EXPERT
Black River 1, 2

APPENDIX 2

HIGHLY RECOMMENDED READING

The following is a selective listing of a few outstanding publications that are particularly recommended to serious canoeists and kayakers. Other works are mentioned elsewhere in the book.

Akerlund, Nels, and Ted Landphair. *Our Rock River.* Washington, D.C.: Chelsea Publishing, 1995. This stunningly illustrated book traces the Rock from its origin in the Horicon Marsh to its union with the Mississippi, with a wealth of interesting historical detail.

Akerlund, Nels, and Joe Glickman. *Our Wisconsin River: Border to Border.* Rockford, Ill.: Pamacheyon Publishing, 1997. A gorgeous commentary and photo collection on the river, from the source to Prairie du Chien.

Durbin, Richard D. *The Wisconsin River: An Odyssey Through Time and Space.* Cross Plains, Wis.: Spring Freshet Press, 1997. An exhaustively researched history of the river, with splendid photos and maps. Follows the river downstream from the source, pointing out fascinating features and anecdotes along the way. Less comprehensive but still quite worthwhile is *The Wisconsin: River of a Thousand Isles* (Madison, Wis.: University of Wisconsin Press, 1985), by August Derleth, one of Wisconsin's best-known writers.

Gard, Robert E., and L. G. Sorden. *The Romance of Wisconsin Place Names.* New York: October House, 1968. In a very engaging manner, the authors trace the origins of place names back to original sources. The classic book on the subject is Virgil Vogel's *Indian Names on Wisconsin's Map* (Madison, Wis.: University of Wisconsin Press, 1991)—much older, but still quite useful.

Gard, Robert E., and Elaine Reetz. *Trail of the Serpent: The Fox River Valley Lore and Legend.* Madison, Wis.: Wisconsin House, 1973. This entertaining and informative volume is filled with wonderful anecdotes, photos, and historical details, including the story of steamboating on the river.

Hattes, Anne. *Country Towns of Wisconsin: Charming Small Towns and Villages to Explore.* Chicago, Ill.: Country Roads Press, 1999. Has excellent chapters on many towns included in *Paddling Southern Wisconsin*: Spring Green, Kohler, Pepin, Alma, etc.

Martin, Lawrence. *The Physical Geography of Wisconsin.* Madison, Wis.: University of Wisconsin Press, 1965. First published in 1916, this classic work is dated in terms of some of its statistics, but it is still an extraordinarily informative and authoritative account of the processes that determined the topography of the state. There's a wealth of fascinating information on the rivers covered in *Paddling Southern Wisconsin*.

Metcoff, Jill. *Along the Wisconsin Riverway.* Madison, Wis.: University of Wisconsin Press, 1997. A beautiful collection of 104 photos of the Lower Wisconsin River, with text.

Svob, Mike. *Paddling Northern Wisconsin.* Madison, Wis.: Trails Books, 1998. A complement to *Paddling Southern Wisconsin,* this book describes 82 day trips on 26 different rivers—all north of Highway 29. Several rivers in northern Wisconsin continue past Highway 29, including the Black, Red Cedar, Chippewa, and Wisconsin, and are included in both books.

Svob, Mike. *Paddling Illinois.* Madison, Wis.: Trails Books, 2000. Describing 64 day trips on 33 rivers and streams, this book includes a number of rivers that begin in southern Wisconsin (the Apple, Galena, Pecatonica, Sugar, and Des Plaines), and many others that are just across the border.

Wisconsin Cartographer's Guild. *Wisconsin's Past and Present: A Historical Atlas.* Madison, Wis.: University of Wisconsin Press, 1998. Excellent maps and text dealing with many aspects of state history. Many sections are of interest to paddlers.

Wisconsin Department of Natural Resources. *County Surface Water Resources.* Madison, 1961–1985. Each booklet describes in detail the geology, topography, and other characteristics of a Wisconsin county, including the physical dimensions, wildlife, recreational uses, water quality, and other aspects of the lakes and streams in that county.

APPENDIX 3

INTERNET SITES RELATED TO PADDLING IN SOUTHERN WISCONSIN

The Internet is an increasingly rich source of information that is directly and indirectly valuable to paddlers. In addition to the information available at a given Web site, "links" often point to a multitude of other sites.

American Canoe Association: www.acanet.org

American Canoe Association Midwest Division: www.umsl.edu/~hsmith/MidwestACA/MidwestACA.html

American Rivers (organization): www.amrivers.org

American Whitewater Affiliation: www.awa.org

Badger State Boating Society: www.bsbs.org

Bear Paw Inn Outdoor Adventure Resort: www.bearpawinn.com

Campground Directory: www.campsites411.com

Canoe & Kayak Magazine: www.canoekayak.com

Canoe the Wisconsin River: www.iit.edu/~travel/wisriv.html

Canoeing and kayaking information: (a) www.paddling.net

                              (b) http://canoe.about.com/recreation/canoe

Capitol Water Trails: www.mailbag.com/users/paddler

Carl's Paddlin' (Madison): www.paddlin.com

Chicago Area Sea Kayaking Association: www.caska.org

Chicagoland Canoe Base: www.chicagolandcanoebase.com

Chicago Whitewater Association: www.nsn.org/eakhome/cwa

Club Chapparal (Baraboo canoe rental):www.chapparal.com

Driving directions: www.mapquest.com

Fred Flasher's Canoe Camping Trips (Wilton): www.wi.centuryinter.net/canoegrue

Glacier Valley Wilderness Adventures: www.glaciervalley.com

Great Outdoor Recreation Pages (GORP): www.gorp.com

Green Bay Paddlers United: www.gbpu.org

Hooker's Resort (at Dekorra on the Wisconsin River): www.hookersresort.com

Horicon Marsh: (a) www.horiconmarsh.com

                    (b) www.horiconchamber.com

Illinois Area Paddler: www.rivers-end.org/iap

Illinois Paddling Council: www.illinoispaddling.org

InfoHub: www.infohub.com/TRAVEL/ADVENTURE/RECREATION/kayaking.html

Kickapoo River Valley: http://windingrivers.com

Mad City Paddlers: www.geocities.com/yosemite/falls/1922

Mary's Paddling Page: www1.shore.net/~malmros/Paddling

Midwest Mountaineering (Minneapolis): www.midwestmtn.com

Midwest River Inventory: www.geocities.com/midwestrivers/index.html

National Weather Service: www.nws.noaa.gov

National Wild & Scenic Rivers: www.gorp.com/gorp/resource/us_river/main.htm

OnWater Sports: www.viewit.com/wtr/kayak.html

Paddler Magazine: www.paddlermagazine.com

Paddlers' Network: http://mindlink.net/summit/P.Net.html

Paddles and Pathways Through the Upper Midwest (Kirk Schutte): www.kscon.com/padlpath.htm

PaddleWise (sea kayaking): www.paddlewise.net

Prairie State Canoeists (Chicago area): www.psc.ctsserver.com

River Alliance of Wisconsin: www.wisconsinrivers.org

The River Pages Project: www.awa.org/awa/river_project/states.html

Riversport: www.riversport.com

Road construction and driving conditions (DOT): www.dot.state.wi.us/opa/roads.html

Rutabaga Paddlesport Shop (Madison, WI): www.paddlers.com

Sierra Club River Touring Section: www.sierraclub.org/chapters/wi/rts

Surf Your Watershed: State Environmental Profile: www.epa.gov/surf3/states/WI

Terraserver: http://terraserver.microsoft.com

Trempealeau Hotel (canoe rentals): www.greatriver.com/hotel.htm

University of Wisconsin Hoofers: <www.hoofers.org/outing

Water levels: (a) http://wi.water.usgs.gov

(b) http://iwin.nws.noaa.gov/iwin/wi/hydro.html

Weather Channel: www.weather.com

Wisconsin Association of Campground Owners: www.wisconsincampgrounds.com

Wisconsin Department of Natural Resources: www.dnr.state.wi.us

Wisconsin Department of Tourism: www.travelwisconsin.com

Wisconsin Department of Transportation: www.dot.state.wi.us

Wisconsin Events: www.wisconline.com

The Wisconsin Page: www.uwsp.edu/geo/wisconsin

Wisconsin Whitewater Rivers (Tom O'Keefe): www.paddleguides.com/Rivers

Wolf River Guides (canoe & kayak school): www.wolfriverguides.com

Maneuvering is required on the upper Lemonweir.

APPENDIX 4

CANOEING AND KAYAKING INSTRUCTION FOR SOUTHERN WISCONSIN PADDLERS

The best way to learn how to canoe or kayak is to enroll in a class or clinic offered by a college, paddling group, outdoor store, park district, or other qualified organization. Such instruction in conjunction with trips in the company of experienced paddlers will get you off to a good start. The following are some of the instructional resources available. Many of the organizations listed also offer guided trips.

American Youth Hostels/Wisconsin Council, Milwaukee, 414-961-2525 or www.hostellingwisconsin.org: basic canoe training class in the spring, together with an impressive schedule of canoe trips, May-October.

Badger State Boating Society www.bsbs.org: instructional pool sessions.

Bear Paw Inn Outdoor Adventure Resort, White Lake 715-882-3502 or www.bearpawinn.com: full range of canoeing and kayaking classes, including flatwater, whitewater, and lake paddling.

Carl's Paddlin', Madison, 608-284-0300 or www.paddlin.com: canoeing and sea kayaking classes.

Chicago Whitewater Association www.nsn.org/eakhome/cwa: beginning whitewater instruction in swimming pools throughout the Chicago area.

College of Du Page, Field and Experiential Learning Program, Glen Ellyn, IL, 630-942-2356: wide variety of paddling courses open to the public.

Hoofer Outing Club, University of Wisconsin Memorial Union, Madison, 608-262-1630 or www.hoofers.org/outing: beginning canoeing and kayaking instruction offered for Hoofer Outing Club members.

Hunt Hill Audubon Sanctuary, Sarona, 715-635-6543: basic "Canoe the Lakes" instruction.

Janesville Division of Leisure Services, Janesville, 608-755-3198 (Fax): introductory and intermediate canoeing and kayaking classes.

Minnesota Canoe Association, Minneapolis, MN, 612-985-1111 or www.canoe-kayak.org: whitewater kayak and open boat instruction.

Nicolet College Outdoor Adventure Series, Rhinelander, 715-356-6753 or 800-585-9304 or www.nicolet.tec.wi.us: extensive program of canoeing and kayaking classes and trips.

North Lakeland Discovery Center, Manitowish Waters, 715-543-2085 or www.discoverycenter.net: beginning and intermediate canoeing and kayaking classes for children and adults.

North Shore Adventurers, Chicago, 847-249-1007: trips on the Wisconsin and St. Croix Rivers include basic paddling instruction.

Oconomowoc Parks and Recreation Department, Oconomowoc, 262-569-6864: the summer outdoor education program for 7- to 10-year-olds includes a canoeing component.

Paddling in the Park, Palatine, IL www.umsl.edu/~hsmith/MidwestACA/PIP.html: annual canoe/kayak festival in July, including many instructional clinics on-water in canoeing, river and sea kayaking, and canoe sailing.

Rutabaga Outdoor Programs, Madison, 608-223-9300 or 800-472-3353 or www.paddlers.com: classes in solo and tandem canoeing and tour kayaking.

Sierra Club, River Touring Section www.sierraclub.org/chapters/wi/rts: variety of canoeing clinics offering flat water and whitewater instruction.

Team Leadership Center, 8 miles north of Sturgeon Bay, 920-746-9999 or www.teamleadership.com: kayaking and canoeing lessons and tours.

Trails North Naturalist Guide Service, Mercer, 715-476-2828: variety of trips on rivers and lakes, incorporating instruction in basic canoeing and sea kayaking.

University of Minnesota Outdoor Program, Duluth, MN, 218-726-6533: many whitewater and sea kayak classes, instructor training programs, and canoe/kayak tours.

Watertrail Adventures, Madison, Milwaukee, Chicago, IL, 608-255-2958 or www.watertrailadventures.com: canoe/kayak instruction and guided trips.

Wausau Kayak/Canoe Corporation, Wausau, 715-845-8200: July and August whitewater canoeing and kayaking training camps for beginners and early intermediates; March pool sessions.

Wolf River Guides (canoe & kayak school), White Lake, 715-882-3002 or www.wolfriverguides.com: classes and private instruction in whitewater canoeing and kayaking, and in river rescue.

Wolf River Youth Paddling Camp, White Lake (contact Wolf River Paddling Club, Madison, 608-233-6728): beginning, intermediate, and advanced whitewater training for 8- to 18-year-olds.

Zephyr Kayak Tours, Green Lake, 920-294-3949: variety of half-day and full-day kayak tours that incorporate basic instruction.

The portage trail around the dam at Jordan Pond on the Plover.

APPENDIX 5

BOOKS & VIDEOS TO IMPROVE PADDLING SKILLS

Books

American Canoe Association. *Introduction to Paddling: Canoeing Basics for Lakes and Rivers*. Birmingham, AL: Menasha Ridge Press, 1996.

Bechdel, Les, and Slim Ray. *River Rescue: A Manual for Whitewater Safety*. Boston, MA: Appalachian Mountain Club Books, 1997.

Foshee, John. *Solo Canoeing*. Harrisburg, PA: Stackpole Books, 1988.

Gordon, I. Herbert. *The Complete Book of Canoeing*. Old Saybrook, CT: Globe Pequot Press, 1997.

Grant, Gordon. *Canoeing: A Trailside Guide*. New York: W.W. Norton & Co., 1997.

Gullion, Laurie. *Canoeing*. Champaign, IL: Human Kinetics Publishers, 1994.

Harrison, Dave (ed.) *Canoe and Kayak Techniques: Whitewater Kayaking*. Mechanicsburg, PA, Stackpole Books, 1998.

Jackson, Eric. *Whitewater Paddling: Strokes and Concepts*. Mechanicsburg, PA: Stackpole Books, 1999.

Jacobson, Cliff. *Canoeing: Basic Essentials*. Old Saybrook, CT: Globe Pequot Press, 1999.

Krauzer, Steven M. *Kayaking: Whitewater and Touring Basics*. New York: W.W.Norton, 1995.

Kuhne, Cecil. *Canoe Camping: An Introductory Guide*. New York: Lyons & Burford, 1997.

Kuhne, Cecil. *Canoeing: An Illustrated Guide to Equipment, Technique, Navigation, and Safety*. Mechanicsburg, PA: Stackpole Books, 1998.

Kuhne, Cecil. *Kayak Touring and Camping*. Mechanicsburg, PA: Stackpole Books, 1999.

Kuhne, Cecil. *Paddling Basics: Canoeing*. Mechanicsburg, PA. Stackpole Books, 1998.

Landry, Paul, and Matty McNair. *The Outward Bound Canoeing Handbook*. New York: Lyons & Burford, 1992.

Lessels, Bruce. *Whitewater Handbook*. Boston: Appalachian Mountain Club Books, 1994.

Mason, Paul, and Mark Scriver. *Thrill of the Paddle: The Art of Whitewater Paddling*. Buffalo, NY: Firefly Books, 1999.

Ray, Slim. *The Canoe Handbook: Techniques for Mastering the Sport of Canoeing*. Harrisburg, PA: Stackpole Books, 1992.

Ray, Slim. *Swiftwater Rescue*. Asheville, NC: CFS Press, 1997.

Rowe, Ray. *Whitewater Kayaking*. Harrisburg, PA: Stackpole Books, 1992.

Solomon, Mark B. *The Kayak Express*. Boston: Aquatics Unlimited, 1997.

U'ren, Stephen B. *Performance Kayaking*. Harrisburg, PA: Stackpole Books, 1990.

Worthan Webre, Anne, and Janet Zeller. *Canoeing & Kayaking for Persons with Physical Disabilities*. Newington, VA: American Canoe Association, 1990.

Videos

Complete Guide to Canoe Trips and Camping. 45 min., 1991. Quality Video Inc., 7399 Bush Lake Road, Minneapolis, MN 55439.

Essential Boat Control. 48 min., 1996. Waterworks, P.O. Box 190, Topton, NC 28781.

Ford, Kent. *The Kayaker's Edge*. 22 min., 1992. Whitewater Instruction, Durango CO 81301.

Ford, Kent. *Solo Playboating*. 43 min., 1991. Whitewater Instruction, 160 Hideaway Road, Durango, CO 81301.

Foster, Tom. *Solo Canoeing*. Whitewater Bound. 120 min., n.d. Outdoor Centre of New England, 10 Pleasant St., Millers Falls, MA 01349.

Fox, Richard. *Kayak Handling: The Basic Strokes*. 43 min., 1989. Gravity Sports Films/Chrisfilm & Video Ltd., 100 Broadway, Jersey City, NJ 07306.

Heads Up! *River Rescue for River Runners*. 29 min., 1993. American Canoe Association, 7432 Alban Station Boulevard, Suite B226, Springfield, VA 22150.

Holt, Joe. *Kayaking 101*: Mastering the Basics. 45 min., 1995. Joe Holt Productions, P.O. Box 97, Almond, NC 28702.

L.L. Bean Guide to Canoeing. 105 min., 1985. L. L. Bean, Freeport, ME 04033.

River Rescue: The Video. 55 min., n.d. Gravity Sports Films, 100 Broadway, Jersey City, NY 07306.

Whitewater Self-Defense. 65 min., n.d. Performance Video & Instruction, 550 Riverbend, Durango CO 81301.

APPENDIX 6

PADDLING CLUBS AND ORGANIZATIONS IN AND NEAR SOUTHERN WISCONSIN

Paddling with other boating enthusiasts adds immeasurably to the enjoyment and safety of canoeing and kayaking. For beginners, clubs are a great introduction to the sport and an excellent way to meet other paddlers.

American Canoe Association Midwest Division: www.umsl.edu/~hsmith/MidwestACA/MidwestACA.html

American Youth Hostels/Wisconsin Council (a Milwaukee-based organization that annually sponsors an impressive schedule of canoe trips at minimal cost, mainly in Wisconsin): 414-961-2525 or info@hostellingwisconsin.org

Badger State Boating Society (a Milwaukee-based group with members throughout the state; primarily whitewater paddling): www.bsbs.org

Capitol Water Trails (a non-profit Madison-area organization dedicated to improvement of waterways, including the clearing of streams for paddling): www.mailbag.com/users/paddler

Chicago Whitewater Association (a Chicago-area group that conducts instructional programs and sponsors a number of whitewater outings, including trips to Wisconsin): www.nsn.org/eakhome/cwa

Green Bay Paddlers United (a group that paddles sea kayaks and whitewater kayaks, primarily in Northeastern Wisconsin): www.gbpu.org

Hoofer Outing Club, University of Wisconsin Memorial Union, Madison, WI (an outdoor recreation organization for UW-Madison students, faculty, staff, and Wisconsin Union members): www.hoofers.org/outing

Mad City Paddlers (a Madison-area club; all kinds of paddling, but mainly flatwater): www.geocities.com/Yosemite/Falls/1922

Prairie State Canoeists (a large, Chicago-area club with members throughout Illinois and Southern Wisconsin; over 100 trips annually; all kinds of paddling): www.psc.ctsserver.com

River Alliance of Wisconsin (a statewide, nonprofit citizen advocacy organization dedicated to protecting and preserving Wisconsin rivers): www.wisconsinrivers.org

Rock Dodgers Canoe Club (a relatively small group that paddles flatwater throughout Southern Wisconsin, taking special delight in intimate, little-known rivers and creeks)

Rock River Canoe Association (a South-Central Wisconsin club that generally paddles flatwater rivers and creeks)

Sierra Club, River Touring Section (annually sponsors a wide variety of trips on flatwater and whitewater rivers and streams throughout the state; offers instructional programs): www.sierraclub.org/chapters/wi/rts

Wausau Area Kayak/Canoe Corporation (a non-profit Wausau-based organization that promotes paddlesports in the Wausau area): http://home.dwave.net/~wkcc/index.htm

APPENDIX 7

SPORT FISH IN THE RIVERS OF *PADDLING SOUTHERN WISCONSIN*

Indicated below are the sport fish found in the rivers included in this book. The primary source of information is the Wisconsin DNR's *County Surface Water Resources* booklets—a series of publications that present detailed information on the geology, history, wildlife, physical dimensions, etc. of all lakes and streams in each county of Wisconsin. Some of the studies are several decades old, but the series still represents the best single source of such information. Please note that all fish listed for a river are not found *everywhere* in the river; trout tend to be concentrated in the upper reaches of a stream, for instance, and some fish are concentrated in the slow, deep water upstream from dams. The term *panfish* generally refers to such species as perch, crappie, bluegill, white bass, and pumpkinseed.

Baraboo River: Trout (upstream), smallmouth, channel catfish, northern pike, walleye, panfish.

Bark River: Channel catfish, panfish (especially crappie), northern pike.

Black River: Northern pike, walleye, muskie, largemouth, smallmouth, sauger, channel and flathead catfish, rock bass, bullhead, crappie, bluegill, pumpkinseed, perch.

Chippewa River: Walleye, northern pike, smallmouth, channel and flathead catfish, muskie, white bass, bullhead, sauger, bluegill, rock bass, crappie, paddlefish, sturgeon.

Crawfish River: Smallmouth, largemouth, walleye, northern pike, channel catfish, bullhead, white bass, crappies.

Crystal River: Trout (upstream from Waupaca), northern pike, smallmouth, largemouth, bluegill, rock bass, pumpkinseed, green sunfish.

Des Plaines River: Northern pike.

Eau Claire River: Smallmouth, largemouth, muskie, walleye, northern pike, sauger, channel catfish, bullhead, crappie, bluegill.

Fox River: Channel catfish, walleye, northern pike, largemouth, yellow bass, bullhead, panfish.

Galena River: Smallmouth, channel catfish, walleye.

Grant River: Trout (upstream), smallmouth, walleye, channel catfish, northern pike.

Illinois Fox River: Channel catfish, smallmouth, largemouth, northern pike, walleye, bullhead, white bass, crappie, panfish.

Kickapoo River: Trout (upstream), smallmouth, largemouth, walleye, sauger, northern pike, channel catfish, bullhead, pumpkinseed, bluegill, crappie.

La Crosse River: Channel and flathead catfish, walleye, northern pike, sauger, smallmouth, largemouth, trout (upstream from Angelo), white bass, bullhead, bluegill, perch, crappie.

Lemonweir River: Smallmouth, largemouth, northern pike, walleye, crappie, channel catfish, bullhead, crappie, perch, panfish.

Little Wolf River: Trout (above Big Falls), smallmouth, largemouth, northern pike, channel catfish, rock bass.

Manitowoc River: Smallmouth, northern pike, channel catfish, bullhead, trout (upstream from Lake Michigan during spawning runs).

Mecan River: Trout (upstream from Highway 22), northern pike, largemouth, panfish.

Milwaukee River: Smallmouth, northern pike, walleye, channel catfish, bullhead, rock bass, panfish.

Oconomowoc River: Northern pike, channel catfish, largemouth, walleye, panfish.

Pecatonica River: Channel and flathead catfish, walleye.

Platte River: Trout (upstream), smallmouth, channel catfish, northern pike.

Plover River: Trout (upstream from Highway 153), smallmouth, largemouth, northern pike, bullhead, crappie, pumpkinseed, perch.

Red Cedar River: Smallmouth.

Rock River: Channel catfish, northern pike, walleye, bullhead, largemouth, white bass, bluegill, crappie.

Sheboygan River: Northern pike, bullhead, walleye, largemouth, channel catfish, crappie, panfish.

Sugar River: Channel catfish, northern pike, smallmouth, bullhead, crappie, panfish.

Tomorrow River: Trout (upstream), northern pike, largemouth, bluegill, crappie, pumpkinseed.

Trempealeau River: Trout (upstream), northern pike, channel catfish, walleye, smallmouth, largemouth, white bass, rock bass.

Waupaca River: Trout (upstream from Highway 10), smallmouth, northern pike, channel catfish, panfish.

Wisconsin River: Smallmouth, largemouth, walleye, sauger, channel and flathead catfish, muskie, northern pike, crappie, bluegill, sturgeon.

Yahara River: Channel catfish, smallmouth, largemouth, walleye, white bass, panfish.

Well-behaved dogs are good paddling companions.

APPENDIX 8

ANNUAL PADDLING-RELATED EVENTS IN AND NEAR SOUTHERN WISCONSIN

MARCH

Canoecopia, Madison: canoe and kayak exposition with equipment, exhibits, and lectures; sponsored by Rutabaga Paddlesport Shop.

Paddlers' Rendezvous, Madison: demos and paddling lectures at Carl's Paddlin'.

APRIL

Burlington Pro C-1 Race.

Canoe/kayak race on the Pewaukee and Fox Rivers from Pewaukee to Waukesha; sponsored by the Kiwanis Club.

Downriver Canoe Run: 14-mile race on the Milwaukee River from Waubedonia Park to Grafton; sponsored by the Grafton Jaycees.

Midwest Mountaineering Exhibition, Minneapolis, Minnesota: outdoor equipment show, including lectures on paddling topics.

MAY

Arcadia Broiler Dairy Days Canoe Race on the Trempealeau River from Pietrek Park to Arcadia.

Paddlefest and Great Milwaukee River Run: a large on-water canoe/kayak demo and race sponsored by Laacke and Joys in Milwaukee.

JUNE

Seven-mile Canoe/Kayak Race on the Portage Canal and Fox River; sponsored by the Portage Canal Society, Inc., and the (Portage) Daily Register as part of Canal Days.

Darlington Canoe Festival: race from Calamine to Darlington on the Pecatonica River.

Badger State Summer Games: includes canoe and kayak competition.

JULY

Wisconsin River Race, Spring Green to Muscoda: 8-, 15-, and 21-mile races; sponsored by the Wisconsin Canoe Association and the River Alliance of Wisconsin.

Paddle and Portage canoe race, on Lakes Mendota and Monona.

Paddling in the Park, Palatine, Illinois: weekend canoe and kayak festival featuring clinics, displays, and canoe/kayak demos.

Great River Rumble: six-day, 168-mile canoe/kayak trip from Winona, Minnesota to Bellevue, Iowa.

Rock River Canoe Regatta at Mayville: C-2 pro race.

AUGUST

Lake Wingra Canoe Marathon: 2.6- and 5.2-mile races hosted by the Mad City Paddlers.

Class I rapids at Brainards Bridge Park on the lower Waupaca.

MORE GREAT TITLES FROM TRAILS BOOKS

Activity Guides

Paddling Northern Wisconsin: 82 Great Trips by Canoe and Kayak, *Mike Svob*

Paddling Illinois: 64 Great Trips by Canoe and Kayak, *Mike Svob*

Wisconsin Golf Getaways: A Guide to More Than 200 Great Courses and Fun Things to Do, *Jeff Mayers and Jerry Poling*

Wisconsin Underground: A Guide to Caves, Mines, and Tunnels in and around the Badger State, *Doris Green*

Great Wisconsin Walks: 45 Strolls, Rambles, Hikes, and Treks, *Wm. Chad McGrath*

Great Minnesota Walks: 49 Strolls, Rambles, Hikes, and Treks, *Wm. Chad McGrath*

Best Wisconsin Bike Trips, *Phil Van Valkenberg*

Travel Guides

Tastes of Minnesota: A Food Lover's Tour, *Donna Tabbert Long*

Great Minnesota Weekend Adventures, *Beth Gauper*

Great Indiana Weekend Adventures, *Sally McKinney*

Historical Wisconsin Getaways: Touring the Badger State's Past, *Sharyn Alden*

The Great Wisconsin Touring Book: 30 Spectacular Auto Tours, *Gary Knowles*

Wisconsin Family Weekends: 20 Fun Trips for You and the Kids, *Susan Lampert Smith*

County Parks of Wisconsin, Revised Edition, *Jeannette and Chet Bell*

Up North Wisconsin: A Region for All Seasons, *Sharyn Alden*

The Spirit of Door County: A Photographic Essay, *Darryl R. Beers*

Great Wisconsin Taverns: 101 Distinctive Badger Bars, *Dennis Boyer*

Great Wisconsin Restaurants, *Dennis Getto*

Great Weekend Adventures, *the Editors of Wisconsin Trails*

The Wisconsin Traveler's Companion: A Guide to Country Sights, *Jerry Apps and Julie Sutter-Blair*

Home and Garden

Creating a Perennial Garden in the Midwest, *Joan Severa*

Bountiful Wisconsin: 110 Favorite Recipes, *Terese Allen*

Foods That Made Wisconsin Famous, *Richard J. Baumann*

Historical Guides

Walking Tours of Wisconsin's Historic Towns, *Lucy Rhodes, Elizabeth McBride, and Anita Matcha*

Wisconsin: The Story of the Badger State, *Norman K. Risjord*

Barns of Wisconsin, *Jerry Apps*

Portrait of the Past: A Photographic Journey Through Wisconsin, 1865–1920, *Howard Mead, Jill Dean, and Susan Smith*

For Young People

Wisconsin Portraits: 55 People Who Made a Difference, *Martin Hintz*

ABCs of Wisconsin, *Dori Hillestad Butler and Alison Relyea*

W Is for Wisconsin, *Dori Hillestad Butler and Eileen Dawson*

Other Titles of Interest

Prairie Whistles: Tales of Midwest Railroading, *Dennis Boyer*

The I-Files: True Reports of Unexplained Phenomena in Illinois, *Jay Rath*

The W-Files: True Reports of Wisconsin's Unexplained Phenomena, *Jay Rath*

The M-Files: True Reports of Minnesota's Unexplained Phenomena, *Jay Rath*

For a free catalog, phone, write, or e-mail us.

Trails Books

P.O. Box 317, Black Earth, WI 53515

(800) 236-8088 • e-mail: info@wistrails.com

www.trailsbooks.com